"*The Vimy Trap* is a powerful exposé of the claim Canada was 'born' during a relatively inconsequential battle fought in a pointless and horrific war. There is no better book to understand World War I mythology and militarist Canadian nationalism."

— YVES ENGLER, author of *The Black Book of Canadian Foreign Policy*

"*The Vimy Trap* presents a careful, nuanced, and very readable examination of the many ways that the Battle of Vimy Ridge and the First World War as a whole have been understood in Canada over the last hundred years. In the face of the de-contextualized and hyper-nationalist mythology of Vimy that gets mobilized in support of war and empire in the twenty-first century, this book will be an important resource for those of us committed to struggles for peace and social justice."

— SCOTT NEIGH, author of *Resisting the State: Canadian History Through the Stories of Activists* and host of *Talking Radical Radio*

"*The Vimy Trap* is an essential antidote. The poison it seeks to counter is decades of English-Canadian nationalist history, both of the popular and academic variety, which constructs positive meaning out of a bloody, devastating, and pointless conflict. Domestically, the Great War revealed a Canada divided along class, ethnicity and race, gender, and geography. Ian McKay and Jamie Swift, in elegant and engaging fashion, portray how the dominant version of the war eventually became one of 'Vimyism' that included a Canada birth narrative."

— DR. STEVE HEWITT, Senior Lecturer, Department of History, University of Birmingham, UK

"*The Vimy Trap* offers compelling perspectives on current political and nationalistic projects that continue to glorify war. Using counter-narratives based on analysis of art, memorials, literature, and theatre, McKay and Swift have created a well-researched, notable read for the centennial of the Battle of Vimy Ridge."

> — JAN LERMITTE, specialist in Canadian literary studies and instructor at Trinity Western University and The University of British Columbia

"In *The Vimy Trap*, Ian McKay and Jamie Swift meticulously and artfully recount how tragedy was recast as triumph and 'Vimyism' became the lens through which Canadians were encouraged to view the Great War (and war in general). Rich in detail and precisely argued, *The Vimy Trap* debunks the official myth of Vimy Ridge as a battle that defined the spirit of an emerging, modern Canada—a myth conspicuously, gallingly out of step with Canadian soldiers' own experience of the war. Perhaps most importantly, *The Vimy Trap* warns that revisionist mythmaking can skew a nation's responses to challenging global events, even today, making it essential reading for anyone concerned with Canada's past, present, or future roles on the world stage."

> — STEPHEN DALE, author of *Noble Illusions: Young Canada Goes to War*

"Once again, McKay and Swift are as insightful as they are impassioned. *The Vimy Trap* is a must-read for those curious about the truths of Vimy Ridge, those who care about people who lived and died at Vimy Ridge, those seeking correctives to the current fallacies and fabrications about Vimy Ridge, and those convinced that what we think and say about Vimy Ridge matters."

> — REV. ELIZABETH MACDONALD, United Church of Canada

THE VIMY TRAP

Fred Varley, *For What?* The Group of Seven's Fred Varley was an eyewitness to war. The title of his grim warscape asked a question that would haunt many Canadians after the Great War.

THE VIMY TRAP

*Or, How We Learned to Stop Worrying
and Love the Great War*

IAN McKAY *and* **JAMIE SWIFT**

Between the Lines
Toronto

The Vimy trap or, how we learned to stop worrying and love the Great War

First published in 2016 by
Between the Lines
401 Richmond Street West
Studio 277
Toronto, Ontario M5V 3A8
Canada
1-800-718-7201
www.btlbooks.com

Library and Archives Canada Cataloguing in Publication

McKay, Ian, 1953–, author

The Vimy trap or, how we learned to stop worrying and
love the Great War / Ian McKay and Jamie Swift.
Includes bibliographical references and index.
Issued in print and electronic formats.

ISBN 978-1-77113-275-6 (paperback).—ISBN 978-1-77113-276-3 (epub).—
ISBN 978-1-77113-277-0 (pdf)

1. Vimy Ridge, Battle of, France, 1917.   2. World War, 1914-1918—Social aspects—Canada.
3. Collective memory—Canada.   I. Swift, Jamie, 1951–, author   II. Title.

D545.V5M35 2016   940.4'31   C2016-904720-2
C2016-904721-0

Cover Illustration: From a stamp advertising the "World Youth and Peace Congress," Geneva, September 1936, which carried the slogan "Help Send Canada's Delegation. Peace, Freedom, justice." Reprinted with permission from the Provincial Archives of Alberta, accession number PR 1968.0125.0477.
Cover and text design: Gordon Robertson
Printed in Canada
Second printing April 2017

We acknowledge for their financial support of our publishing activities the Government of Canada through the Canada Book Fund, the Canada Council for the Arts, which last year invested $153 million to bring the arts to Canadians throughout the country, and the Government of Ontario through the Ontario Arts Council, the Ontario Book Publishers Tax Credit program, and the Ontario Media Development Corporation.

This one is for Robert G. Clarke,
editor extraordinaire and fine friend

Contents

Acknowledgements

For invaluable research assistance, we thank Steffen Jowett, David Thompson, Katelynn Folkerts, Allison McMahon, Tena Vanderheyden, and Allison Ward. Robert Vanderheyden was indispensable as a guide and photographer in France and Flanders. Maarten Van Alstein of the Flemish Peace Institute was generous in sharing his insights into the political culture of commemoration in Flanders.

We also acknowledge with gratitude the help of the Canadian War Museum, Library and Archives Canada, McMaster University's Mills Memorial Library, and the Queen's University Archives. Thanks as well to Steve Wadhams of CBC-Radio and Paul Robertson of Cultural Services, City of Kingston.

Part of the material in this book was delivered by Ian McKay at the 2014 Joanne Goodman Lectures, established by Joanne's family and friends to perpetuate the memory of her blithe spirit, her quest for knowledge, and the rewarding years she spent at the University of Western Ontario. Jamie Swift's work on this book was supported in part by the Sisters of Providence of St. Vincent de Paul and the Queen's University Fund for Scholarly Research.

For hospitality and good company, we thank Jean Christie, Joe Gunn, Susan Gottheil, and Len Prepas. Both authors would like to single out the contribution of our editor, Robert Clarke.

PROLOGUE:

"THE DEAD ON THE FIELD"

IN THE FALL OF 1914 Tom Thomson was standing at the corner of Yonge and Bloor streets in Toronto. He was watching a parade of recruits march by, eight abreast—thousands of them. He saw young men, many recent immigrants from Britain, caught up in war fever. What would become the Great War had just begun, and the newly minted soldiers would soon be off to their homeland, taking part in the defence of its empire. The war would, according to the word on the street, be over by Christmas.

"Six months! Hell, three or four years it must be," muttered Thomson to his companions, Maud and Fred Varley, themselves immigrants who had arrived not long before from the Mother Country. "Gun fodder for a day."

Their friends and fellow artists Lawren Harris and A.Y. Jackson would head off to the recruiting office and join up, but Varley passed on the opportunity for glory. He even claimed, years later, that it was pressure to enlist during the conscription crisis of 1917 that prompted Thomson, perhaps the most famous landscape painter of them all, to take his own life that year, under mysterious circumstances.[1]

Like other artists in his circle, Varley had been amply exposed to glorious, hero-ridden depictions of the South African War of 1899–1902 in English publications such as *The Illustrated London News* and *The Sphere*; and in the end he did get to the Western Front, though not as a combatant. He became an officer assigned to paint the war on behalf of Lord Beaverbrook's Canadian War Memorials Fund. Arriving in England in 1918, he renewed his acquaintance with Jackson, who was in London after being wounded at Maple Copse near Ypres in 1916. Jackson had traded his rifle for a sketch pad. The two Canadians spent evenings together at 3 Earl's Court Road, where Varley studied the pencil sketches that Jackson had made under fire.

Varley quickly noticed that his friend had changed. By this time Jackson looked far older than his years. "I'm sure if he had to go through the fight any more, he would be broken," Varley wrote home in a letter. After one long discussion with Jackson, Varley said he suspected that the ordinary soldier was trapped in a "game of life and death [which was] nothing but a huge bluff conceived by some wise guys with business interests."[2]

Jackson's sombre Great War canvas *A Copse, Evening* is stark, its mutilated tree trunks and harsh landscape foreshadowing his postwar Canadian landscapes—*First Snow, Algoma* and *Algoma Rocks, Autumn*. The desolate battlefield scenes would find their echoes in Jackson's vision of the northern landscape of Ontario's boreal wilderness. This in turn would influence other members of what became the Group of Seven.[3]

Jackson's view of the war was coloured by both the artist's aesthetic sensibility and the ordinary soldier's experience. In a 1916 letter from the Somme to future Group member J.E.H. MacDonald, he observed: "You feel at times so very insignificant. A private is nothing, unless he disobeys an order, then there is a big fuss made over him, and he probably gets shot."[4]

What Varley saw when he finally got to the trenches only confirmed this insight. A letter to his wife, Maud, provides a remarkable eyewitness account by a painter who also saw himself as a writer:

> You in Canada . . . cannot realize at all what war is like. You must see it and live it. You must see the barren deserts war has made of once fertile country . . . see the turned up graves, see the dead on the field, freakishly mutilated—headless, legless, stomachless, a perfect body and a passive face and a broken, empty skull—see your own countrymen, unidentified, thrown into a cart, their coats over them, boys digging a grave in a land of yellow green slimy mud and green pools of water under a weeping sky.[5]

The letter predicted a canvas that, less than three months later, would garner Varley a kind of critical praise that he could hardly have imagined when he set out for Europe. Working from memory and a sketch he had made of Canadian Scottish Regiment gravediggers at work in a barren landscape, Varley painted the scene in London upon his return from the Front. The canvas depicts the gruesome scene that Varley described to Maud. The sky is crying over a flat vista. The field is muddy, with the pools of water all around. The two soldier-gravediggers are taking a break from their awful task of burying what was left of their comrades, the bodies that lie, covered with a cloth and jumbled together, in a tip cart. The scene, noted the London *Daily Telegraph*, conveyed a "sense of all-pervading tragedy."[6] The brooding sky is divided against itself. The muddy ground is saturated with blood, the cart laden with the dead, the corpses indistinct and collectivized in death.

Here is an awful new version of pastoral landscape. It recalled the first lines of the last stanza of Wilfred Owen's famous war poem, a "gas poem." "Dulce et Decorum Est" describes two beautiful youths now in hell:

If in some smothering dreams, you too could pace
Behind the wagon that we flung him in,
And watch the white eyes writhing in his face,
His hanging face, like a devil's sick of sin . . .[7]

Varley's "horror picture" was first exhibited in early 1919 as part of the massive new Canadian War Memorials Fund Exhibition at Burlington House, Piccadilly—home of the Royal Academy. The occasion came just as the Paris Peace Conference was set to start, and Canada's Conservative prime minister attended the opening. We do not know what Robert Borden thought of the painting, or of its title. Varley summed up his work with a question that would bedevil millions in the decades to follow.[8]

He named his warscape *For What?*

The romantic illusion of old-fashioned cavalry warfare, with its swords and lances, persisted even after the Great War. This commemorative window in Kingston's 1921 Memorial Hall finds its opposite in the tragic irony of much postwar remembrance. Forty-five thousand were killed or wounded during the three-day Battle of Amiens, 1918.

1

MYTHS, MEMORIES, AND A CREATION STORY

The reason the world pays heed to Canada is because
we fought like lions in the trenches of World War I,
on the beaches of World War II, and in theatres
and conflicts scattered around the globe.

— JUSTIN TRUDEAU, 10 June 2016

I T WOULD BE DIFFICULT to imagine a Great War that looks less like Fred Varley's blood-soaked field in *For What?*

The 2011 edition of *Discover Canada*—the late Conservative Harper government's citizenship guide for future Canadians—manages to paint a picture of the war that is so remarkably different that it seems to portray a world of warfare that once existed in some far-off fantasy land.[1]

The guide shows a valiant member of the Fort Garry Horse, mounted upon his steed and leading his troops into battle. A ruddy-faced General Currie, "Canada's greatest soldier," resplendent in his uniform and medals, meets our eyes as he gazes confidently into the horizon. A soldier astride his horse leads his troops into battle. In the foreground of the Vimy Memorial in France, one member of a party of uniformed soldiers bows down, seemingly in reverence, before the monument's twin towers. The "First World War," the text announces, proved that Canadians were "tough, innovative soldiers," whose valour earned Canadians a reputation as the "shock troops of the British Empire," in a war that "strengthened both national and imperial pride." At the bottom, in a section called "Women Get the Vote," a nursing sister, one of three thousand nurses in the Royal Canadian Army Medical Corps, or "Bluebirds," is the very picture of blue-and-white-clad femininity as she looks demurely down, the visual antithesis of the hyper-masculine, dynamic Currie.

In this short account, there is not a wounded body, bombed city, or mangled corpse to be seen, let alone a blood-soaked field. There is not even a trench. Welcome to twenty-first-century Canada. The Great War has become truly *great* again.

*   *   *

At five-thirty in the morning, snow and sleet were driving down. Towering ahead of the soldiers loomed a mighty fortress, the decisive key to a vast front stretching from the North Sea to the Alps.

For years they had said nobody could take this fortress. Many times the French and British forces had tried to do so. Yet as many times as they attempted it, they failed. The word was that it could not be done.

Least of all by the Canadians. The Europeans disparaged this ragtag army of colonial frontiersmen. They called them undisciplined because the Canucks did not obey all their rules. They thought them a rough, tough bunch of individuals.

And they were: men of valour who knew how to get a job done; straight shooters who talked rough and played rough. They had braved the frontier. Now they were braving the Western Front. The big question was: could they take the ridge?

For five months the Canadians had been preparing to answer that question. They had consulted with scientists. For five months the army brass had worked on finding new ways of firing the heavy guns and assaulting an enemy line. For five months they had broken with military conventions and told every soldier about the plan. For five months the battalions of Canadians had been learning to fight as a team.

Now, in the third year of a war of attrition, on 9 April 1917, at Eastertime, that Christian festival so symbolic of sacrifice, four divisions of Canadians—100,000 men—gathered together for the first time. Inspired by the man said to be Canada's greatest soldier, Arthur Currie, they had a plan to gain some important ground.

At 5:30 a.m. the earth shook. The sky itself seemed to tremble. With the loudest sound imaginable, the Canadians moved forward up the slope, and soon enough the world finally learned what the Canadians could do. By the following day their forces had taken the hill and consolidated their hold on what had been an important German position.

The advance started four days that changed the course of the First World War. The four days at Vimy Ridge not only showed the world what Canadians could do, but showed Canadians themselves what they could accomplish if they all worked together. Soon they would be marching into Germany—an army of freedom-fighters standing up to a bloody dictatorship foreign to our values.

They used to laugh at the Canadians. They said Vimy Ridge could not be taken.

But after the great Battle of Vimy Ridge, they stopped laughing. The Canadians had arrived. Canada rejoiced. And every year on 11 November, every true Canadian honours the memory of Vimy and our veterans.

There it was, on the record: 5:30 a.m., 9 April 1917. Vimy 1917. Turning point in the war. Birth of a nation.

*   *   *

Or so goes the oft-repeated story. Unfortunately for generations of Canadians eager to learn about the "turning points" in their nation's history, most of it is more than a little off course. This standard version of Vimy is a highly dubious, mythologized narrative. It is akin to a fairy tale for overaged boys who want their history to be as heart-thumping and simplistic as a video game. Parts of it are (roughly) true. About 97,184 Canadians in four divisions of the Canadian Corps, often also called the Canadian Expeditionary Force or CEF,[2] which was in turn a part of the British Expeditionary Force (BEF), did indeed unleash a formidable synchronized barrage of artillery upon three German divisions holding Vimy Ridge, a high spot of land offering a vantage-point over the western edge of the Douai Plain. Although the defenders put up a fierce fight, the Canadians ascended the ridge; and four days later, at a cost of 3,598 dead and 7,004 wounded, they held it. The Germans retreated to the east.

Especially since the 1980s Canadians have been told again and again that Vimy represents the "birth of the nation." Sometimes they have been told that the Great War as a whole, lasting from 1914 to 1918, proved to be Canada's "War of Independence." For Canada's most popular historian and myth-maker, Pierre Berton, writing in 1986, "The victory at Vimy would confirm the growing realization that Canada had, at last, come of age."[3] The popular hockey commentator Don Cherry, in his florid style, hammered that point home in an April 2014 "Coach's Corner" segment of *Hockey Night in Canada*:

April 9th—boy—this is when Canada . . . became a nation—birth
of a nation . . . the French and the British tried to take it for a whole
year . . . and General Currie said, "*No* British, *No* French involved.
I'm a Canadian general, we will take it in *two days*. . ." We are the
best. Afghanistan, Vimy, Second World War, Korea. We are the
best.[4]

Starting with its original publication in 2008, the federal government's
glossy *Citizenship Guide*—a less dynamic but more official source, and
perhaps just as far-reaching—began to deliver much the same message.
In addition to informing new citizens that Sir Arthur Currie—the gen-
eral applauded by Cherry and the supposed co-architect of the victory
at Vimy—was "Canada's greatest soldier," the guide stated of those days
of glory: "It was Canada from the Atlantic to the Pacific on parade."
Those unidentified words can be tracked down to a statement from
Brig.-Gen. Alex Ross, C.M.G., D.S.O., of the Dominion Council of the
Canadian Legion, in his introduction to a 1967 book by D.E. (Eberts)
Macintyre, a veteran instrumental in organizing a pilgrimage to the new
Vimy Memorial in 1936. "In those few minutes I witnessed the birth of
a nation."[5]

The Ross statement, ruthlessly decontextualized and made to appear
as though it were an eyewitness account and not the sort of thing normally said at commemorative services, is now repeated on countless official websites. It has received explicit approval from Governor General
David Johnston, who in 2012 remarked: "In many ways it was the birth of
a nation. It was the first time Canadians fought shoulder to shoulder. . . .
Not as a subordinate unit in the British army, but on our own."[6]

All immigrants hoping to become Canadian citizens had to attend
closely to Ross's words and similar statements because the newcomers
would later be tested on the *Guide*'s contents. The right answer to "When
and where was Canada born?" was coming to be, as a matter of official
policy, "Vimy Ridge, 1917."

Yet the answer to that question is not at all straightforward. Indeed,
the subject of Vimy Ridge, including the country's birth and the glories of
the war itself, falls onto a highly contested terrain. Perhaps the question
of the birth of this particular nation can never be readily answered; and
certainly no serious war historian actually sees Vimy as a decisive battle in
the Great War. The truth, evasive as always, is more complex.

What we call "Vimyism" was born on a battlefield a long time ago. Since then it has waxed and waned over the years and been constantly questioned, but still it persists. It is exemplified at its core by the achievements and sacrifices of the Battle of Vimy in April 1917, but it has become more than that, too. By Vimyism we mean a network of ideas and symbols that centre on how Canada's Great War experience somehow represents the country's supreme triumph—a scaling of a grand height of honour and bravery and maturity, a glorious achievement—and affirm that the war itself and anyone who fought and died in it should be unconditionally revered and commemorated—and not least because it marked the country's birth. An irreplaceable element of Vimyism—in Don Cherry's account and many other popular renditions—is Canadian exceptionalism: *we* succeeded where they failed. Unencumbered by useless old traditions and unafraid of hardship and death, Canadians carried the day, and it is strongly implied if not always said—even won the entire war.

It has become a Vimyist article of faith that the vast majority of Canadians believed that death on the Western Front was noble. Some soldiers and malcontents and cranks might have thought otherwise—but, it is said, most Canadians revered this war so much that they placed it at the core of their sense of nationhood. It became a kind of founding myth that the nation's rights and freedoms were established by our Great War soldiers. According to this "big bang" theory of Canadian history—that has Canada fighting its war of independence in 1914–18, after which Canadians understood what it meant to be Canadian—the citizens of the Dominion realized that, beneath divisions of language, religion, region, race, and ideology, they shared—after that magic moment on Vimy Ridge—deep-seated commonalities. They shared a great and unifying "myth of Canada," whose founding heroes were gallant male soldiers and whose founding moments were victorious battles.

Many writers have contributed to this point of view, piling example upon example to build the myth into an almost insurmountable edifice (we will meet a good number of them in the following pages). Among the notable historians is Jonathan Vance, who in a series of books and articles—from his *Death So Noble: Memory, Meaning, and the First World War* (1997) to "Remembrance" (2014)—argues that the Great War brought Canada a new sense of nationhood as its citizen-army carried Canada's colours, resisted an atrocity-perpetrating enemy, and thus inspired the people. The men willing to fight to defend "Canada, Western civilization, and Christianity" in the Canadian Expeditionary Force became "in a very real sense .. the nation in arms, the life-force of Canada transported overseas." At Vimy Ridge, Vance states, the Canadian Corps' "stunning success, a triumph of organization, preparation, training, and raw courage," represented nothing less than "the birth of a nation." The Great War constituted "the crucible of Canadian nationhood."[7]

Vimyism, then, encapsulates a form of martial nationalism that exalts the nation-building and moral excellence of soldiers. Its rampant militarism contends that war is fundamental to human flourishing, specifically because it toughens men and develops their characters. War from this point of view offers transcendent moments of beauty and release from humdrum realities and affords individuals an opportunity to reach their potential. A corollary of the rise of Vimyism, too, is that the Canadian perspective on the war has become progressively more and more provincial, far less conscious of the bigger picture, less sensitive to the people and conditions in other faraway places.

Even General Currie, the hero of the *Citizenship Guide* and Don Cherry, thought that Vimy Ridge was vastly overrated.[8] Yet, even if you do not fully believe that Vimy was the decisive battle in the Great War, it is still possible to be a "Vimyist" as long as you think the Great War was a truly *great war* for Canada—great in giving the country a proud place in the world and great for the values that Canadians ostensibly fought for, such as liberty, democracy, Christianity, and freedom, against an enemy standing for autocracy and lawlessness. What complicates this stream of thought is that during the war itself, and through the following decades, a quite common response to what turned out to be a human quagmire of previously unknown proportions was the very opposite of reverence. Moreover, many elements of Vimyism consist of outright errors, easily refuted; many others are dire simplifications. Other exclamations make untestable metaphysical claims (such as the one that nations, rather like people, are born) promoting questionable ideas that are far beyond any and all validation. After all, the construction of nationhood, as art historian Sue Malvern theorizes, is an evolving process that "is informed by telling stories, manufacturing fictions, and inventing traditions in a ceaseless and selective process of inclusion and exclusion, remembering and forgetting."[9]

The keys in that explanation are the combinations of "inclusion and exclusion" and "remembering and forgetting." We call the project of

Vimyism the "Vimy trap" because we, like many others, see the dangers of its deep pit: its strict rationale of narrow nationalism and its wilful refusal of the realities of twentieth-century warfare and its even more complicated asymmetric twenty-first-century cousin.[10] The Vimyist understanding that modern wars are designed by generals, fought by soldiers, and driven by such high ideals as democracy, freedom, equality, liberty, and justice confines us to perpetual confusion. The challenge, after a century has passed, is to imagine the Great War[11] (which is what, in deference to tradition, we are calling the First World War or World War I or the War of 1914–18) not as any metaphorical birth but as a moment of warning about the unprecedented possibilities of mass death under conditions of industrial modernity. Getting Vimy's history right brings home the complex horrors and suffering of modern warfare, nullifying the baseless celebration of engaging in war.

Vimy is a trap because, as it has come to be mythologized by militarists, historians, and nationalists, it tempts us to think that chivalric war somehow survived the coming of the epoch of mechanized warfare. There is a childishness to Vimyism. In its essence, it wants us to return to a day of glorious battle—as signalled by the *Citizenship Guide*'s visual homage to the charges of the mounted cavalry, which were, in one soldier's words, "exceedingly gallant, but futile" in an age of heavy artillery.[12] So many official and popular representations of war today avoid something that the returned soldiers of the Great War kept insisting upon: that under conditions of modernity, war had changed—changed quite completely.

Yet Vimyism persists. In November 2015, days after terrorists murdered civilians in Paris (while others had just, with far less publicity, murdered civilians in Beirut and bombed a Russian airplane over the Sinai), Saskatchewan premier Brad Wall responded by urging Ottawa to put a hold on refugee resettlement but not do the same for aerial bombing in Iraq and Syria. "As a citizen, I would rather they continue the air strikes. I would rather Canada continue the fight. That's Canada's history, that's our tradition. When tyranny threatens freedom-loving people anywhere, Canada has responded, yes, with a humane response. But Canada also fights."[13]

A different view of history urges us instead to remember other traditions, such as diplomacy and resistance to war; urges us not to fight but to discover other ways of facing the serious issues that can and do lead to war. That perspective has been shared by a vast number of Canadians from

1918 to our own time—people for whom the appropriate slogan for the Great War was not "birth of a nation" but "Please God—never again."[14]

Yet slogans only go so far. The politics of peace and war, of memory and commemoration, in Canada—then and now—is always complicated. Contrary to those who say there was one big, valorous war to which all right-thinking Canadians subscribed, there have been many competing and conflicting ways of understanding the Great War, and war in general.

*   *   *

Kingston, a small city tucked into the northeast corner of Lake Ontario, has a long military history. In a 1976 essay on the "character of Kingston," Great War veteran and eminent Queen's historian Arthur Lower explained that no Canadian town "has benefited more directly, positively, proudly and righteously [from war] than has Kingston."[15] Indeed, Kingston remains in part a martial town, with its old Fort Henry, its Royal Military College (RMC), and the sprawling army base (Canadian Forces Base Kingston), which is the city's largest employer. As the long-time home and political base of Sir John A. Macdonald, it trades on its colonial heritage in pitching itself as a tourist destination. Signs along the busy 401 highway advertise the Macdonald connection, offering up an official local slogan that attempts, rather awkwardly, to link past and present: "Where History and Innovation Thrive."

The waterfront City Hall building dates from 1843, with prominent colonial architect George Brown's neoclassical domed structure taking up an entire city block. The sprawling limestone building stares out across the Cataraqui River at the Royal Military College. Its Memorial Hall features a dozen stained-glass windows, each with its own Great War image, each scene signifying a different battle. Most show the work of war: marching; loading an artillery piece; nursing; tending horses; marching. The windows offer a romanticized view of the carnage, as does the language of the plaques that complement them. The men killed "gave their lives for liberty." They are "the fallen." This is the old rhetoric that attempts to describe war in terms of sacrifice, valour, and honour.

In any enterprise, the words used are always important—a message underlined by writer Paul Fussell, an analyst of the Great War's cultural legacy. In an introduction to Fussell's landmark work *The Great War and Modern Memory*, historian Jay Winter wrote about his friend's insight into how "language frames memory, especially memories of war."

War, he knew, is simply too frightful, too chaotic, too arbitrary, too
bizarre, too uncanny a set of events and images to grasp directly.
We need blinkers, spectacles, shades to glimpse war even indirectly.
Without filters, we are blinded by its searing light.[16]

Those blinkers and filters often lead to stark distortions of the light that
does get through. In the late winter of 2015, Susanne Cliff-Jungling,
a Queen's University staffer and long-time peace activist, attended an
evening meeting of Kingston city council and came away stunned by the
"imperial spirit" and militarist sensibility she witnessed there. She was particularly taken aback by a motion passed unanimously at the tail end of a
long meeting. The language, reflecting the sentiments down the corridor
in the Memorial Hall, seemed commonsensical enough in a military town.
None of the yawning politicians appeared to give it a second thought.

> Whereas brave members of this community stepped forward in
>   World War I and World War II to fight for King and country, and
> Whereas many made the ultimate sacrifice in battle, and
> Whereas interested supporters of the military community have
>   requested an area be designated to commemorate the departure
>   of the 21st Battalion and members of Queen's Stationary Hospi-
>   tal from Kingston 100 years ago in May 1915,
> Therefore Be It Resolved That staff be directed to bring a report to
>   Council in April 2015, after having completed consultation, to
>   consider designating an area spanning from the Kingston Armou-
>   ries to Fort Frontenac as "Valour District" to commemorate the
>   valiant military service of past Kingstonians.

The same imperial spirit expressed in that motion had already given rise to
the nineteenth-century street names that dot the environs of the proposed
downtown "Valour District"—immediately dubbed the "VD" by local
residents opposing the plan.[17] Balaclava Street, Alma Street, Redan Street,
Raglan Road: the names evoke the Crimean War, best remembered for its
notorious Charge of the Light Brigade—a historical testament to sheer
incompetence in the conduct of war. In the middle of the designated
Valour District are a limestone armory and a former parade ground now
called Artillery Park. Most bizarre of all is a road actually named after
ammunition—Ordnance Street. After that meeting Cliff-Jungling quickly
brought the plan to the attention of her neighbours living in and around

the proposed Valour District. A political fuss ensued—a clash between conventional martial commemoration and an ethic that emphasizes remembrance for peace.

Kingston's mayor, Bryan Paterson, a junior academic teaching at the Royal Military College and a man fond of promoting his jurisdiction as a "smart" city, adopted the time-tested "war-is-certainly-bad-but . . ." line favoured by those fond of emphasizing noble sacrifice when commemorating past carnage. He supported the Valour District idea because it recognized soldiers who had made "the ultimate sacrifice for the peace and prosperity we enjoy today." While acknowledging that wars "are terrible events in world history," Paterson argued that commemorating war "is in no way to romanticize or glorify" it. Instead, a Valour District would "honour the memory of young men and women who were willing to sacrifice their lives in order to serve their country, like those in the 21st Battalion."[18]

Valour District boosters had linked their efforts to the centenary of the 1915 departure of a unit for the war. It was a big event at the time, attracting throngs of patriots and empire boosters to watch the recruits march down the street. Given Kingston's military-inspired history, it was hardly surprising that an ambitious young politician employed by the Royal Military College would come out, rhetorical guns ablaze, for the proposed Valour District.

Despite the mayor's enthusiasm, things have changed in Kingston since Lower's sardonic assessment of the city's character. Just as the controversy over the proposed Valour District erupted, city staff members issued a draft Commemorations Strategy that they had prepared after extensive public consultation. It identified four new "priority thematic areas" on which Kingston's appreciation of its past should focus: First Peoples, ethno-cultural communities, francophones, and women. "British-Canadian history and military history are also important, but feedback we received noted that these are currently well-represented in comparison and therefore, not priority themes or subjects." The Strategy emphasized "Kingston's many stories," suggesting that a fresh strategy would provide "opportunities for celebration, reflection, discovery, dialogue and critique."[19] The public comment that gave rise to the new plan suggested that many citizens had experienced quite enough sacralization of war.

Another sign of changing times reflected the rethinking of traditional historical memorialization and commemoration. As the city was completing its new historical commemoration strategy, an official patriotic spasm accompanying John A. Macdonald's 200th birthday was itself accompanied by a "Talking Back to Johnny Mac" effort by citizens offering a critique of conventional Great Man understandings of the past. Kingston has innumerable plaques, statues, and a Parks Canada site honouring the country's first prime minister. A place called Sir John's Public House, occupying one of his former law offices, offers a Braveheart sharing platter and Sir John's chicken curry. But at Macdonald's 200th birthday, Métis artist David Garneau visited from Regina and—assuming the character of Louis Riel—donned a hood and a noose to ascend Macdonald's prominent City Park statue to engage the Scottish-born politician in a "conversation with the past." Some two years previously, persons unknown had daubed that same statue with slogans: "Colonizer," "Murderer," "This is Stolen Land."

Another indication that militarist-patriotic sentiment was no longer dominating public discourse in Kingston emerged later in 2015 when the city published comments from the local citizenry on the proposed Valour District. Over the course of ten days, 121 people submitted their opinions of the designation. Staff calculated that supporters and opponents were more or less equally divided, but failed to highlight what was clearly the most common reason for opposition to the Valour District proposal: over 20 per cent of all respondents pointed out that Kingston already had a sufficient abundance of war memorials. It was time for a shift in focus. The argument underpinned the thinking of the city's own commemoration strategy.

The Kingston commemoration dust-up, unfolding at the Great War centenary, reflected both conventional and oppositional understandings of history, war, peace, and public memory.[20] Many come to their knowledge of such big questions by looking back to their own experiences and those of their families. Several men who supported the Valour District spoke on behalf of their partners. One Legion member wrote, "My wife and I are proud of [Kingston's] military history and support." Another said, "My wife and I are in agreement." Others invoked family history. "Many Kingstonians including my wife's great uncle signed up and paid the ultimate price."[21]

Valour District opponents did not shy away from employing their own family stories to buttress their positions. One recalled her Uncle Jack, who paid a price when he helped to liberate the Netherlands in the Second World War.

What I saw on my childhood visits to Toronto was a very alcoholic ex-soldier only able to be marginally employed while he drank himself into oblivion for many decades, preparing his supper sandwich before the drinking began daily so that he would have something to eat. I now know that he who had seen so many battles, had done much killing, who had received such love and gratitude from the Dutch people he'd liberated, was a man torn apart by PTSD.

This respondent concluded with a suggestion more nuanced and difficult than the notion of putting up new street signs. "Let's remember war and its soldiers like my Uncle Jack with breadth and care. Doing that ought to mean more than using terms like 'valour' and 'hero.'"[22]

Another respondent opposed the renaming for personal reasons: "My grandfather was sacrificed to imperialism in the Great War. (He did not make a sacrifice.) He was gassed and wounded on the Western Front and committed suicide in 1931, a late casualty of the war. My father served in Holland in 1944–45 and taught me that 'valour' is a lie, used to justify sacrifice of young men for wealthier, more powerful men's interests."[23]

The most extensive comment acknowledged that "valour" can be a behaviour exhibited by soldiers in battle. But valour "by no means captures everything that happens in battles. It is a word that expresses the glorification of war. If—as I do—we want our community to help our nation and the world move beyond the tragedy that war represents, we need to make sure that we remember the ugliness and destructiveness of war, as well as its 'valour.'"[24]

Several supporters of the Valour District proposal used a familiar—if historically inaccurate—claim that Canada's wars have always been fought for virtuous and noble goals. "The story of this city," one respondent argued, "is grounded on its military history . . . and above all on the sacrifice by so many for our country and our freedom." Another also linked the idea of sacrifice to that of liberty. "I support the Valour District. This is about remembering those who gave their lives for freedom, not those who use their sacrifice to deny the very same." While ambivalent, the last part of this comment suggests impatience with the plan's opponents.

More direct was a militant supporter of the plan who weighed in with a particularly pungent observation: "Just when one thinks that the looney [sic] left have [sic] disappeared they waft by again like a bad smell." This analyst was perturbed by the idea that the Valour District signage would apparently feature a white poppy. Near the end of the consultation process numerous Valour District supporters denounced the white poppy, a peace symbol dating from 1926. The issue appears to have boosted the numbers for the pro side of the controversy. Yet the idea of a white poppy appearing on Valour District signage had not previously been a part of the discussion. It had received no mention in any Valour District background material provided by the city. A number of objectors to the purported use of the white poppy took up the usual argument that the Royal Canadian Legion holds a poppy copyright and the red poppy is the one and only remembrance symbol. "The white poppy," said one commentator, "is a meaningless bit of propaganda that was thrown out by the self-serving peace movement to obscure the real meaning of remembrance."[25]

The real meaning of remembrance is far from certain, as the sharp differences of understanding of this particular proposal clearly show. It has certainly changed over time. Although an outpouring of jubilation occurred at the conclusion of the war in 1918, the predominant tone of commemoration in the years immediately following the conflict was one of grief. Then, as the burdens of bereavement eased, a powerful current of critical remembrance arose—as Canadians en masse, veterans foremost among them, came to question both the purposes and the conduct of the war. Only in the last quarter of the twentieth century did martial values and virtues, the lionization of warriors, assume their present-day dimensions. Perhaps those who initiated the Valour District scheme were unaware of different historical traditions of remembrance. Perhaps, given the white poppy canard, these "interested supporters of the military community" were only able to understand remembrance for peace as an offensive push in the wrong direction or as a naïve, unrealistic way of making sense of the past.

In recent decades Canadians have witnessed a sustained effort to make one view of past wars hold sway over all others. The view is that Canadian wars are exercises in selfless sacrifice, struggles for freedom.

When one such view takes a firm hold it assumes a position of hegemony, which means that it comes to dominate discussion and policy in ways that are seemingly so commonsensical, so ever-present, that it becomes more or less invisible. This is the stuff and the strength of myth. As one person who weighed in against Kingston's Valour District proposal pointed out, "Myth-building has many parts. It happens in many places. It works best when we don't even know it's happening."[26]

Yet in 2015 it was quite clear to many in Kingston what was happening. The city had just erected a handsome new Memorial Wall at a new Veterans Memorial Garden. Unlike some of the more traditional monuments featuring heroic scenes, the Memorial Wall effort reflected a more contemporary mode of commemoration, most famously expressed in Washington's Vietnam Veterans Memorial. The names of Kingston people killed in war were etched onto a low wall, where they could be quite easily read. The polished stone offers visitors reflections of their own images as they look at the names of the dead, linking past and present in a human-scale setting.

Kingston's showcase City Park has long featured three war memorials, complemented nearby with the 1925 Imperial Order Daughters of the Empire monument. The green space, dotted with artillery pieces, is also home to Macdonald's larger-than-life statue. One of the City Park monuments is explicitly dedicated to the 21st Battalion that marched off in 1915, listing the Great War battles in which it fought. It is a typically triumphalist piece topped by a uniformed man with a rifle and fixed bayonet, looking to the heavens, his arm held high. "The bravery of our soldiers throughout these battles can never be underestimated," wrote one Vimyist blogger, who toured Ontario taking photos of such memorials. "The price was high, but victory was ours."[27]

Yet despite innumerable Great War memorials, plaques, and windows, the city was being asked to sponsor yet another homage to the glory of war. For some, it seems, there is no such thing as enough.

*   *   *

Fiercely debated while it was being fought, highly controversial in the two decades that followed its conclusion, and transformed once again in struggles over memory since 1945, the Great War has prompted an ever-shifting set of myths and symbols. The complicated, undulating terrains of war and peace—and the public memory of war—simply cannot be captured by rehashing old dualistic stereotypes of slavering warmongers with waxed mustaches and romantic, bright-eyed peaceniks when often—as the following chapters will show—some of the most romantic and idealistic Canadians have revered the Great War and some of the most businesslike and down-to-earth types have questioned it. This tendency has been the case from 1914 on. All the while generations of Canadians have strenuously challenged the limitations of Vimyism and continue to look for other means of commemorating past wars and avoiding new ones.

Among those who are familiar with an approach to commemoration that succeeds in going far beyond Vimyism are many Canadians who have visited the former battlefields of France and Flanders.

Over seven hundred years ago the small Flemish city Ypres was a vibrant commercial centre, its prosperity based on the Flanders wool trade. Twenty-first-century visitors come upon a fine square, the Grote Markt, hard by the cathedral and the former centre of the cloth trade, the impressively long Lakenhalle, or cloth hall. The town's narrow, cobbled streets and gabled buildings give the impression of a medieval city restored from its fourteenth-century heyday when it rivalled Bruges and Ghent. Except that Ypres has been entirely rebuilt, not restored. Reduced completely to rubble by German artillery fire during the Great War, it now stands again. Ypres's citizens meticulously reconstructed the ancient town, a remarkable testimony to their resolve to remain true to their history.

Not everyone agreed that this was the best approach. In 1919 Winston Churchill proclaimed that the devastated town represented something quite different than the locals might have imagined. "A more sacred place for the British race does not exist in the world," he said, reflecting an all-too-common passion that sacralizes war. Churchill had no qualms about suggesting that the British simply continue to occupy the place for their own commemorative purposes. "I should like us to acquire the whole of the ruins of Ypres." It was not to be. One historian observed wryly that Churchill's prescription for the future of the city "not surprisingly, found little favour with its long-suffering and displaced citizens."[28]

The town and its environs (the "Ypres Salient" in the military histories) symbolize for many the essence of the Great War. The battlefields became the graveyard for a quarter of a million British soldiers. In total, some 550,000 people were killed in Flanders, with places like Passchendaele, Hill 60, Messines, Hooge, Mount Kemmel, and Sanctuary Wood taking on indelible associations with fruitless carnage. Canadians had their lungs scorched in the war's first major gas attack near Ypres. Adolf Hitler served as a messenger in West Flanders. Peter Kollwitz, son of the eminent German artist Käthe Kollwitz, was killed north of Ypres early in the war. Canada's Talbot Papineau featured prominently in a 2007 CBC docudrama, *The Great War*, in which Justin Trudeau played Papineau, scion of Quebec nationalists on his father's side and affluent Philadelphians on his mother's. Papineau was reduced to a cloud of bloody fragments in the mud at Passchendaele in 1917. The story has it that his last words were, "You know, Hughie, this is suicide."[29] The prediction was telling. The war has been called the collective suicide of Europe. Yet, as Canadian literary theorist Sherrill Grace remarks, in the CBC's *Great War* it came to be seen as "patriotic and uplifting" in what amounted to a "*feel-good movie.*" Puzzling as it may seem to make such a film about such an unalloyed disaster, the CBC's twenty-first-century Vimyist tale was timed to coincide with the 2007 rededication of the Vimy Memorial. As Grace puts it: "It is films like this that produce the myths by repeating, reproducing and performing a story . . . and it is the peacetime creations of artists working on the home front that transform the stories into a national narrative."[30]

Talbot Papineau's name can be found etched on the walls of the Menin Gate. As the prominent British war memorial, opened in 1927 in Ypres, the Gate is most often the first stop for battlefield tourists on what promoters call the "Route of Remembrance" in Flanders. The names of tens of thousands of the "missing" (a euphemism for those who shared Papineau's fate) are etched on the grand arch emblazoned with the words *Pro Patria* and *Pro Rege*—for king and country. The imperial sentiment is reflected in the names of Sikhs and other men from Britain's colonies chiselled onto the walls. A hundred years after the Great War, a daily Menin Gate ceremony routinely attracts busloads of spectators as volunteer fire brigade buglers play the "Last Post." Just down Menenstraat from the Gate on the Route of Remembrance is the British Grenadier shop, a Canadian-owned enterprise offering war books and battlefield tours. Its window features poppies and a heavy machine gun. Shell casings and other bits of ordnance are displayed inside for the perusal of tourists waiting for the departure of their Salient Tours minibus.

In contrast to Belgian and French museums and sites of commemoration, where there are few if any remnants of patriotic perspectives on the war, the Salient Tours guide routinely deploys the first-person plural in describing the battlefield scenes in the historical present. "We're now behind the British lines and we're being hit from all sides," he intones. "We need to remove the Germans from Hill 60."

Even in the off-season, tour groups need to await their turn in the sanctuary of the Church of St. Nicholas at Messines, south of Ypres, before heading downstairs to the crypt that once housed a German dressing station. Visitors show considerable interest in a plaque that reads "Corporal

Adolf Hitler was treated here." The macabre and the sensational have their fascination.[31] The Salient Tours guide makes no mention of another part of the church, featured on a different sort of visit. The town of Messines Tourist Information Point highlights the story of Otto Meyer, a German veteran of the Battle of Messines who fashioned a huge, two-meter-wide copper chandelier for the church when it was rebuilt after the war. Such symbols abound in Messines. The Peace Carillon of St. Nicholas has fifty-nine bells. Every fifteen minutes the carillon plays hymns for the nations that took part in the Great War, including former enemies Germany and Austria-Hungary.

Just south of Messines the Island of Ireland Peace Park is dominated by a tall, cut-stone Round Tower fashioned from material found in an Irish workhouse and a British army barracks in Tipperary. The Peace Park, opened in 1998, attempts to do two things: commemorate Irish soldiers killed in the war, and serve as a symbol of reconciliation. The *island* of Ireland, not Eire and Northern Ireland, not Unionists and Nationalists. The monument makes an explicit effort to depart from framing armed conflict as it has so often been fatally portrayed in Ireland, as an our side/their side story. The humble Peace Pledge in the centre circle reads in part:

As Protestants and Catholics, we apologise for the terrible deeds we have done to each other and ask forgiveness. From this sacred shrine of remembrance, where soldiers of all nationalities, creeds and political allegiances were united in death, we appeal to all people in Ireland to help build a peaceful and tolerant society.

The Island of Ireland Peace Park is a place of quiet serenity, lacking any mention of glory or patriotic heroism. Along the main pathway nine inscribed stones are angled for visitors to read as they make their way to the Tower. The words are those of men who experienced the 1917 battle at Messines. As with many contemporary commemorative efforts, the curators have allowed the soldiers of a hundred years ago to speak for themselves. The Journey of Reconciliation Trust includes the words of David Starret, 9th Royal Irish Rifles:

So the curtain fell over that tortured country of unmarked graves and unburied fragments of men: murder and massacre; the innocent slaughtered for the guilty; the poor man for the sake of the greed of the already rich; the man of no authority made the victim of the man who had gathered importance and wished to keep it.

When it comes to war commemoration, there are choices to be made.

*   *   *

A common anecdote in popular storytelling about the Great War is especially prevalent around former Western Front battlefields: Vimy, Ypres, the Somme. We hear about shells and rusted helmets and the shattered remains of the heads they tried to protect. Gruesome artifacts thrown up by the soil and the winter frost persist in making their way to the surface a century later. Farmers maimed by Great War ordnance testify to the truth of the tale: the legacy of the slaughter, it is said, is still with us. The phenomenon provides ready metaphors. The war is indeed still with us, literally and figuratively.

Contending war stories also linger. Nowhere are these decidedly different narratives more evident than in Flanders. Nowhere was the impact of the war felt more profoundly than in this Flemish-speaking area of Belgium, with its strong linguistic and cultural identity, a feeling of a "distinct society" firmly rooted in historical consciousness. Despite the attractions of the Channel beaches and the nearby splendours of medieval Bruges (it escaped the fate of Ypres), by 2007 some 368,000 Great War tourists were flocking every year to West Flanders, bringing in nearly a third of the province's tourist revenue.[32]

As the sixtieth anniversary of the end of the Great War approached in the mid-1970s—and before the full flowering of Vimyism in Canada—a group of young people in Flanders began to look for alternative ways of commemorating the war. They expressed the need to go beyond parades and martial music and interviewed dozens of elderly people to record their Great War stories. The resulting book, *Van den Grooten Oorlog* ("On the Great War"), made an effort to parallel official historiography and state publications. In an edgier gambit, this Eleven November Group also developed a play, *Nooit brengt een oorlog vrede* ("War Never Brings Peace"), which had its debut on the anniversary of the armistice, November 11, 1978. The first scene features a representative of the Krupp company. Having sold weapons to both sides during the war, the company later proceeded into a promising new market—artificial limbs and machines to remove scrap metal from former battlefields.

"When you hear all those stories, you begin to reflect and wonder," explained the play's principal author, Marieke Demeester. Echoing Fred Varley's *For What?* she asked: "It is terrible what happened to those people during the war, and what has it gotten us?"[33]

The Eleven November Group's work on the culture of commemoration was crucial in helping to shift how people in West Flanders remember the Great War. The cultural activists sought to dispense with old, rigid certainties about the war—and the war experience—in one of the regions where the conflict had its most direct and dramatic impact. They wanted to develop a more nuanced understanding of the war's legacy. As Flemish historian Maarten Van Alstein explains, in the aftermath of the "wholesale slaughter," states found themselves necessarily attempting "to give some *meaning*" to the experience. "This was done by representing the deaths of frontline soldiers as a sacrifice for the nation, a patriotic martyrdom that the soldiers took upon themselves to save the fatherland from the existential threat of the enemy."[34]

This search for meaning can come from on high as part of the Official Story of the war's purpose. Or it can spring from the soil of culture, in this case that of a people whose territory was shattered by the war. Van Alstein describes a Flemish "commemoration landscape" that has changed, and been changed, with the passage of time. Sherrill Grace, exploring similar terrain, argues:

> The landscape of memory metaphor is an image of the broken ground of our history as we recall and rework it. This metaphor effectively captures the sense that history is like a field hiding stones/ stories that continue to surface and, as they surface, *change* the story, alter the landscape, make room for new, for more, stories and allow us to see/hear the repressed, forgotten memories excised from the official story of Canada and its wars.[35]

In the decades after the Great War some Flemish commemoration practices developed in ways, according to Van Alstein, that "linked the commemoration of the war with the message 'No More War.' The experience of the horror of war was transformed into a call to avoid and banish war forever." His reasoning was that "if the war of 1914–1918 could signify the end of all wars, then at least some meaning could be found for the boundless slaughter of the war, and the sacrifice of the frontline soldiers would not have been in vain."[36]

Van Alstein explains two distinct modes, or logics, of remembrance. The first way of looking at the landscape of commemoration, he says, considers "the past from the perspective of a contemporary objective, thus using it as a means to serve present-day ends, for instance by drawing lessons from history that can be applied in a present context." Canadian efforts to weld a support-our-troops message to the remembrance of past wars—inevitably recalled as glorious struggles for freedom in which our side was in the right—mesh with this logic. This is part of an imperial, or British, mode of commemoration. A respondent to a Flemish Peace Institute survey of differing approaches to commemoration put it delicately: "The British remembrance tradition is bathed in an atmosphere of heroics, of service to the current deployment of the British army in interventions which are often motivated by interests other than ideals."[37]

A different, second mode of remembrance

> starts out from the complex past itself and, by opening up various stories about that past, remembers it in such a manner that it gives audiences and participants an impetus to reflect critically upon war (and peace) and motivates them to work for peace in the present. It is evident that the former logic of remembrance more easily runs the risk of using the past in a one-sided and manipulative fashion than the latter.[38]

This second way of understanding and commemorating war tells no patriotic story. Exploring different war stories not only opens up the past "as a source of historical knowledge," but also helps to build a basic sensitivity to the complicated issues of contemporary conflicts and wars—and can lead "to a motivation to work actively on the present-day practice of peace."[39] In the Canadian context, this approach would mean turning on its head the dominant logic of an obligatory duty to remember in a certain way, and especially the politically charged instruction not to forget the heroic sacrifices of *our* soldiers. It means remembering for peace, avoiding "the sterile tyranny of the cult of remembrance."[40]

*   *   *

The First Battle of Ypres was part of the German "race to the sea," a standard phrase in many accounts of the Great War's opening months.

It was here that the initial German advance was stalled; and it was here, north of Ypres in 1914, that the German army suffered a disastrous defeat. The battle soon came to be known in Germany simply as the "Youth of Langemarck" or "The Volunteers." The latter refers to the enthusiasm with which Germans greeted the outbreak of war in August, with a zeal repeated in many countries, including Canada, where the rush to the colours was said, in many a telling, to be universal.

On 11 November 1914—a date, as it would turn out, freighted with irony—a German army bulletin sought to use Langemarck for some patriotic myth-making. "West of Langemarck youthful regiments stormed the first lines of the enemy trenches and took them singing 'Deutschland, Deutschland, über alles.'" Even the enemy bought the story, describing a "schoolboy corps" that tried to take their positions.[41]

That is what the myth of Langemarck would become, a much embroidered tale of youthful bravery. The battle was fought closer to a place called Bixchote, but that would not fit with the symbolism of patriotic zeal as the more Germanic-sounding Langemarck. Only 18 per cent of the regiments that fought were composed of students and teachers. The other story retailed for the home front was that Langemarck was a victory. But it was a total failure.

Warrior mythmakers on both sides would not hesitate to let facts stand in the way of a good story, both for morale-building during the war and for political reasons in later years. German-American historian George Mosse's *Fallen Soldiers: Reshaping the Memory of the World Wars* suggests that the Langemarck story would just as well fit into the noble narrative on the other side—"manly youth sacrificing themselves joyously for the fatherland." The theme, writes Mosse, is "that of war as an education in manliness . . . symbolizing youth grown to maturity without losing its attributes of youthfulness."[42] For German nationalism, the bloody defeat would serve as usable history. Hitler tells of the battle in *Mein Kampf*, painting a picture of youth becoming men in the crucible of battle, linking maturity to war.[43] This coming-of-age-through-war notion is familiar to young nations as well as to adolescent boys, echoed as it is in the Vimyist retelling of the story of Canada's Great War.

During the 1930s remembrance was much in evidence in many countries. But in Germany, the ripples of the Great War contributed to rather more sinister uses of commemoration. Depression-era Germany saw a flourishing of patriotic poems and plays about Langemarck. The "fallen" were to inspire a new, stronger country. In 1932 the right-wing writer Josef Magnus Wehner concocted a memorial speech that typified the cult of Langemarck. Summarizing the revisionist Great War history so successfully used by the Nazis, the speech was read in German universities: "Before the Reich covered its face in shame and defeat, those at Langemarck sang . . . and through the song with which they died, they are resurrected."[44]

Sacrifice and resurrection, familiar Christian themes, carry considerable cultural heft. They are particularly important for instrumental modes of remembrance. What is more frequently invoked in patriotic traditions of war commemoration than the notion of "sacrifice," which brings to mind virtue and selflessness? This tradition uses sacrifice in a manner suggesting an active deed, not as something to which soldiers were subjected. In his famous letter *Finished with the War: A Soldier's Declaration*, Lt. Siegfried Sassoon of the Welsh Fusiliers made it clear that he was protesting the "political errors and insincerities for which the fighting men *are being sacrificed.*"[45]

Sassoon, not one to mince words, was an early visitor to the Menin Gate. The monument prompted the poem "On Passing the New Menin Gate"—"Well might the Dead who struggled in the slime, Rise and deride this sepulchre of crime." In the 21st century visitors are not reminded of the dissident veteran's words until they stroll down the street from the Gate, past shops selling helmet-shaped chocolates and "In Flanders Fields" pâté. In the rebuilt Lakenhalle they find the In Flanders Fields Museum (IFFM), an exhibit space that promotes a post-patriotic understanding of the Great War. There is no apparent irony in a museum striving to create a sombre atmosphere being named after an onward-to-the-struggle Canadian poem.

The museum's creators and curators acknowledge contending traditions of commemoration. At the same time they recognize the need to go beyond artifacts to offer the personal stories of those most affected. This reflects the Eleven November Group's emphasis on people's everyday witness to war. IFFM co-ordinator and co-founder Piet Chielens describes it as being "different as a museum in comparison to others because it no longer took just the objects of the war as the main driver." Instead, "it took the human experience as the centre" and fashioned that understanding into the museum's first permanent exhibit.[46]

While the IFFM showcases the Great War's terrible consequences, often in lurid and compelling ways, it does not neglect the war's causes.[47] The *Museum Guide*'s frontispiece is the famous John McCrae poem "In

Flanders Fields" superimposed on an aerial photograph of the blasted landscape at Essex Farm, Boezinge. The guide explains that "competition between European states to extend territorial control overseas created international tension" in the years before the war. "Wealth was also acquired through the exploitation of large parts of the population at home and in the colonies." This Belgian analysis contains no reference to British propaganda's "plucky little Belgium," ravished by the Kaiser's armies. It does, however, explain a main cause of the war as the folly of "nationalist, capitalist and expansionist Europe."[48]

Like France's Historial de la Grande Guerre museum in Péronne on the Somme, the IFFM maintains no national framework. Its logo is a poppy with an important difference. Its stem is made of barbed wire, as emblematic of the Western Front as the famous flower. The museum is a dark place, literally and figuratively, with tall, vaulted ceilings. A foreboding soundtrack, low register, plays in the background. The gloom is broken by sharp spotlights highlighting exhibits and artifacts. In the relatively small farmland area around Ypres, dubbed "The Devastated Region" after 1918, the war killed over half a million people. The cataclysm unfolded in an area less than a tenth the size of the Greater Toronto Area. Jay Winter, who helped design the Historial, has suggested that a post-national approach is the only way of reaching a true understanding of the Great War. "The staggering character and implications of the Battle of the Somme, so significant in the overall history of the twentieth century, cannot be understood if only national units or national cultural forms are addressed."[49] The IFFM confronts this directly by emphasizing the role of colonial troops, stressing the war's intensely imperial character: some two thousand Chinese labourers dead on the British side; seven thousand "Anglo-Indian" soldiers killed; a thousand from the Caribbean died of illness, 185 killed in action, four executed by the British; thirty thousand Africans from French colonies killed.[50]

Given the low quality and scarcity of Great War film footage, the IFFM developed as a highlight a large curved screen and seating for several dozen visitors. Among the sequences shown is the dramatized testimony of three U.S. hospital staffers, two nurses and a doctor. The museum developed a script for actors who appear and then fade away, their black and white images intended to create a vaguely ghostly appearance. One nurse, her story taken from a book by American volunteer nurse Ellen La Motte, provides the kind of Great War snapshot unlikely to be found in Canada's eighty-three military museums.[51]

There were wounded men from whom no laughter came, nor any sound. One had his jaw clean blown away, men with chunks of steel in their lungs and bowels, men with arms and legs torn from their trunks, men without noses, men without faces. There was one that could stand it no longer, he fired a revolver up through the roof of his mouth, but he made a mess of it. So they bundled him into an ambulance and carried him, cursing and screaming . . . he must be nursed back to health, until he is well enough to be stood up against a wall and shot.[52]

The various scenes in this dramatization are separated by a recurring scene, a filmed dramatization depicting crowds stumbling towards the viewers through a field of mud and mist, below a sullen gray sky. The clouds above move quickly. These allegorical figures represent the soldiers and civilians of the Great War. In keeping with the museum's post-national theme, the soldiers do not wear recognizable uniforms, simply drab burlap outfits.

The Great War museum in the Lakenhalle takes an implicit but unmistakable anti-war stance. Yet it is neither one-sided nor manipulative, seeking as it does to stimulate a social memory of long-ago events by using the experiences of people who participated in or witnessed them. At the same time, it recognizes a diversity of commemorative traditions and does not seek to criticize martial-patriotic modes of remembrance.

"In order to talk about peace we have to talk about war. And then the idea of peace will come spontaneously," explains Chielens. "If people think about peace when they leave, then you can be pleased. Without mentioning the word even once."[53]

The museum portrays the horrors of war in a no-holds-barred manner. Ghostly, back-lit photos of the dead abound. Separate little teepee-like enclosures invite visitors to watch as ghastly images appear and recede, including men with mangled faces and bodies; one dead soldier lies in a field, his trousers nowhere in sight, his genitals fully exposed; other dead men lie in contorted positions in fields, shell holes, and trenches. These cringe-making images have, as with any museum exhibit, been carefully selected in a manner reflecting curatorial intentions.

The IFFM devotes significant space near the end of its permanent exhibit to pose fundamental questions about war. A blunt text accompanies *The Broken Bayonet*, a sketch by Frans Masereel: "Many found the official justification of the many war dead absurd and obscene. Instead, they placed their trust in radical international co-operation." Masereel was a prominent Flemish woodcut artist and pacifist who spent the war with the Red Cross in Geneva.

Adjacent to this display the museum includes a panel of particular importance to Canadians. It examines "Remembrance and Identity" and includes a Canadian ten-dollar bill. This is the former banknote, replaced in 2013 by a bill featuring John A. Macdonald and a picture of a train. The old bill featured images that addressed Canada, war, peace, and identity. Fraught with ambivalence, it included the McCrae verse along with a female United Nations peacekeeper, an elderly veteran and his family, a war memorial, some doves of peace, and, of course, some poppies. The panel commentary accompanying the Canadian banknote reflects the Great War's complex legacies:

> For many people, remembering the First World War is an essential part of their national identity. . . . In Canada, Australia and New Zealand many see the battlefields of the First World War as the birthplace of their status as separate nations. However, the hopes of numerous minorities were frustrated after the war. It had not brought them the rights they had hoped for and had fuelled nationalist sentiment. All over the world nationalist myths are rooted in the First World War.

These myths differ from country to country: invoking the wondrous campaign at Vimy or glorious death at Langemarck, inspiring a step along the road to the demise of the British Empire in India, or buttressing Arab nationalism in the oil-rich lands carved up by the French and British. Unlike many war museums, the IFFM attempts to explain the connections between nationalism and war but does nothing to reinforce nationalist narratives. This is remarkable, given a strong Flemish nationalist movement in Belgium. The museum is supported and promoted by Flemish regional and municipal governments. In the immediate wake of the Great War, Flemish veterans of a nationalist bent, offended by official Belgian gravestones proclaiming "*Mort pour la Belgique*," deployed the slogan "Here our blood, when our rights?"[54] Yet the IFFM emphasis is on peace. As they leave, visitors pass beneath imposing vertical banners made of red and white cloth. Listing every war since 1918 ("Chinese Civil War, 1927–1950" "Invasion of Grenada, 1983," "Afghanistan, 2001– . . .," "Syria, 2011–. . ."), they also describe Ypres's efforts to fashion itself as a City of Peace whose Peace Fund awards an International Peace Prize every three years.

"I think it would be a big mistake to just stay with national commemoration," Chielens remarked on the eve of the Great War centenary. He said he had recently seen a comment in a newspaper about how "It's time to remember our victories." The statement shocked him—"because no matter what [the Great War] was, it was a catastrophe for the whole of mankind."[55]

2

A GREAT WAR OF ATTRITION AND FUTILITY: A CAPSULE HISTORY

The effete rituals and gaudy uniforms, the "ornamentalism"
of a world still largely organized around hereditary monarchy [have]
a distancing effect. . . . And yet what must strike any twenty-first
century reader who follows the course of the summer
crisis of 1914 is its raw modernity.

— CHRISTOPHER CLARK
The Sleepwalkers: How Europe Went to War in 1914

THE MAJOR international books about the Great War make little or no mention of Canada and Vimy. Outside Canada, claims that Canadians won a tremendous world-shaping victory at Vimy, somehow changing the course of the war, are treated with incredulity. What you will find in these dozens of books—tens of thousands if you go back over the past century—are unresolved debates about the causes and culprits of the Great War. Perhaps the only point of agreement in this vast literature is that the Great War was one of the most significant events in twentieth-century history, modernity on the march.

The war even lacked a clear beginning and end. For Canadians, the war is generally considered to have started with Britain's entry into the war on 4 August 1914 and to have ended on 11 November 1918, when Germany agreed to an armistice—hence, Canada's Remembrance Day. Yet by general agreement the trigger for the war was the assassination carried out in Sarajevo on 28 June 1914 by the Bosnian Serb Gavrilo Princip of Archduke Franz Ferdinand of Austria, heir to the throne of the Austro-Hungarian Empire. That event provoked a diplomatic crisis in which the Austro-Hungarian Empire threatened the Kingdom of Serbia—thought, with considerable evidence, to have been behind the assassination. When the Empire did not attain satisfaction, it invaded its small neighbor on 28 July. The Russian Empire, which had by far the largest army in Europe and was greatly feared by Germany, then mobilized its troops. In response, Germany invaded neutral Belgium and Luxembourg. The French, allied with Russia but also keen to avenge their territorial losses to the Germans in a war four decades earlier, declared war on Germany.

Britain entered the war relatively late, after the German invasion of Belgium on 4 August, with a sizable portion of its ruling Liberal Party cabinet initially opposed to a declaration of war. These doubting Liberal politicians failed to be persuaded by arguments that German violation of Belgian neutrality constituted an infamy warranting a military response. They argued that British interests would not be served by a land war in Europe and that Britain, a nation more accustomed to naval power, was not at all prepared for such a struggle. They also believed that war could not be reconciled with liberal ideas about the interconnectedness of the world and the rationality of peace.[1] Nevertheless, the final decision was in favour of marching off to war, and over the following months and years the contestants lined up: with the members of the "Entente" or Allied Powers—France, Russia, Britain, Japan, Italy (which entered in 1915), and the United States (entering the war in 1917)—on one side; and the Central Powers—Germany and Austria-Hungary, joined later by the Ottoman Empire and Bulgaria—on the other.

As for the timeline, even after the armistice the war was not exactly over. After 11 November 1918 the British Empire persisted in enforcing its economic blockade on Germany, which from 1915 to 1919 undoubtedly provoked widespread suffering and death. The British naval blockade, a team of Protestant ministers argued in 1926, destroyed "men and women and children alike" and filled "half a continent with the diseases of prolonged under-nourishment." Even with the war supposedly finished, some 71,000 civilians lost their lives in the first half of 1919.[2] For war veterans in particular, as Canada's acting prime minister George Perley put it on Armistice Day in 1930, "The war did not end in 1918; for some of them, indeed, the struggle back to health and happiness has been as hard and as heroic as the holding of the Ypres line or the assault on Vimy Ridge."[3]

In the end the underlying historical causes of the conflict, historian Christopher Clark points out, were "so complex and strange" that both combatants and civilians on all sides were "confident that theirs was a war of defence, that their countries had been attacked or provoked by a determined enemy, that their respective governments had made every effort to preserve the peace."[4] Throughout the war, both sides blamed the other for the conflict and claimed the moral high ground. Many Germans, including liberals and social democrats, were convinced that without taking the strongest measures available they risked invasion from the massed armies of Russia, to which they sometimes ironically applied the term "the Huns." German Jews, numerous in socialist and liberal parties, were particularly impressed by the Russian menace, given that Empire's nasty history of anti-Semitic pogroms. Many Jews enlisted enthusiastically in the army, and one of them was instrumental in designing Germany's chemical weapons program—seen, like atomic weapons in the 1940s, as the regrettable but necessary tool that could help bring the war to a rapid conclusion. Many Germans found it difficult to grasp how the world could ever see republican France and authoritarian Russia as sharing the same outlook. The consequence of the alliance of these states was such that the Germans saw themselves as being squeezed in the middle between two hostile powers. The desperate measure of striking at France through Belgium, violating the latter's neutrality, could be justified as staving off the Russian menace and offering a swift counter to a French invasion.

The Great War was, in historian J.L. Granatstein's wise words, "a battle of rival imperialisms."[5] From the British point of view, the German Empire was aggressively seeking to challenge its supremacy on both the waves and the land, particularly in Africa. Many British power brokers and opinion makers saw Germany as an illiberal state run by a mentally unstable Kaiser, although a cooler retrospective judgment might be that by modern standards neither Germany nor Britain would win any beauty contests for liberality and democracy. The two powers had been locked in an arms race since the 1890s.

As the war proceeded, each side accused the other of war crimes, with people at home subjected to an endless stream of atrocity stories. The British focused on the actions of Germans in occupied Belgium—actions that were undoubtedly murderous, even if they never rose to the atrocity level of British claims. Based on one British report, for instance, the Halifax *Herald* told its readers that a teenage Belgian girl "dressed in a chemise" was "stripped naked and violated" in an open field. That report proved to be founded on false testimony by refugees.[6] The Germans emphasized the contentious legality of the British declaration that they had the right to mine international waters and block ships from using vast parts of the ocean. The Germans responded with a submarine campaign that succeeded in sinking a considerable tonnage of British ships but contributed to the entry of the United States into the war in April 1917. If one of the undoubted casualties of the war was the borderline between civilian and warrior, another was the idea of successfully putting any war to the test of a centuries-old theory of the "Just War" or of the newer conventions of international law.

*   *   *

Was "our" side totally in the right? The answer to that question has tended to change over time.

"Of course," cried out a legion of patriots and publicists during the Great War itself—and in this particular war their persuasive efforts were necessary to an unprecedented degree. In North America, not surprisingly—given the strength of the cultural ties linking English-speaking peoples on either side of the ocean—the Germans decisively lost the propaganda war. In May 1915 the German sinking of the ocean liner *Lusitania*, on the (subsequently substantiated) grounds that the vessel was carrying arms, proved a publicity debacle, as did the German declaration of unrestricted submarine warfare.

"Of course not," was the answer of another school of thought that arose a little later on, and especially in the 1920s. In the United States in particular, scholars pored over the volumes of official state documents released in great abundance by the major powers after the war, disputing the reasoning that had led the Americans into the war. These "isolationists," as they came to be labelled, had an impact in the United States that surpassed their influence in Canada. In the 1940s and 1950s the isolationists were answered by another generation of historians who, by effectively running the two world wars together, argued for a basic continuity in both German perfidy and British liberality.[7] New discoveries in the German state archives apparently revealed that, for years, the Germans had been plotting to take over much of the world. Yet another generation's critics pointed out that such alarming declarations had never been acted upon and, in any case, were reflected in the fulminations of power wielders in many other European capitals. Moreover, as time passed some researchers concluded that the supposedly reliable evidence of the peculiarities of Germans smacked of the crudities of now-discredited racial theory.

By the twenty-first century only a very unusual historian would argue that 100 per cent of the responsibility for the war rested with the Central Powers—initially Germany and Austria-Hungary, later joined by the Ottoman Empire and Bulgaria. Yet this charge of total responsibility was precisely what the Treaty of Versailles in 1919 forced Germans to accept, with enduringly toxic effects.[8] Few historians would maintain that on one side we find liberty and light, and on the other side tyranny and darkness—the latter being always a tough case for "our" side to make, given the alliance with the undeniably unenlightened and authoritarian Russian Empire (destined, along with its Austro-Hungarian, German, and Ottoman counterparts, for the "trash-can of history" by the war).[9] If the Allies were waging a war for democracy, a key member, Czarist Russia—hungering for Constantinople and much of Eastern Europe—had clearly not received the news.

At the same time a number of historians suggest that a focus on the "step-by-step" process by which Europeans entered their crisis is misguided; they believe that it is more useful to look at the existing socio-economic structures of the time, without which the Great War would not have assumed its vast dimensions. To use a homely metaphor: if the assassination of Franz Ferdinand was the open flame that ignited a warehouse full of dangerous gases, of even greater importance are the processes, including an armaments race, by which the warehouse became volatile—an "accident" that was "waiting to happen."[10] Among those combustible materials were new technologies and vast numbers of armaments being peddled by businessmen in search of an honest dollar, or pound, or franc, or ruble, or mark. The war would not have looked quite the same had it been fought with swords or with bows and arrows. In the beginning the cavalries, complete with sturdy horses, took to the battlefield; as matters progressed they were replaced by hulking metal tanks. The application of new weapons of war—airplanes, poison gas, tanks—aroused incredulity. "What in hell was the meaning of waging war in such fashion?" was one German's response to the sight of tanks.[11]

The arms race was in turn stimulated by a competition among empires for world domination: in Africa, the Germans wanted more colonies; in Asia, the British continued to lord it over India, the source of over a million of their soldiers in the war; and in the Middle East, the various colonial empires were engaged in the pursuit of territorial power—with results that still echo in headlines a hundred years after the British and the French carved up Asia Minor along arbitrary lines.

The Great War, as its later name implies, was not just a European war. Canadians tend to imagine that "World War I" was fought on the Western Front—that zone of conflict in Northern Europe stretching from the North Sea to the Alps. But more lives were lost in other, deadlier theatres—in Southern and Eastern Europe, in the Middle East, in Asia, and in Africa. (Reliable estimates indicate that far more African porters than Canadian soldiers died in the Great War.)[12] The more global our perspective on the Great War, the less adequate it becomes to focus exclusively on the comings-and-goings at the top of Europe—as important as these undoubtedly were; and the more compelling becomes the case for looking at these years as a clash among vast global structures only partly under the control of any person or group of persons.

In our zeal to make the Great War a collective "selfie"—it was all about us, we sometimes seem to be saying—we Canadians tend to forget that it was a war that killed an estimated ten million soldiers and seven million civilians. Canada's estimated 60,392 military dead—or 61,697, if the numbers include soldiers from the then-independent Dominion of Newfoundland—loom very large to us, but not to the world in general.[13]

By evading the war's moral complexity, and by imagining that our side was entirely in the right, we are acting the role of a kid in a schoolyard fight attempting to put a certain spin on a dust-up for the teacher. We avoid moving towards a deeper understanding of the issues—in this case those raised by modern warfare. If our "foe" in 1914–18 (and 1939–45, for that matter) is now our "friend," doesn't that mean that we must make an effort to revisit with scepticism all the things that were regularly said about the Germans' incurable penchant for militarism? At the same time, by narrowly focusing on "our" war and "our" sacrifices, we blind ourselves to another difficult understanding of contemporary war—which is that, over time, it comes to be extremely difficult to separate perpetrator from victim, noble sacrifice from gratuitous violence. As global modernity transforms the planet into one community (conflicted, divided, and threatened), it is anachronistic, at best, to insulate Canada by vaingloriously parading our victories and mourning our victims—and forgetting the vastly larger tragedy in which the Canadians of 1914 found themselves.

*　　*　　*

In 1914 Canada was a colony of Great Britain, and thus for many historians the Canadian entry into the war was a foregone conclusion. Constitutionally, when Britain was at war, Canada was at war. That statement is true enough, but, as always, the devil lies in the details. Canadians were certainly constitutionally obliged to support Britain. Such support, however, might conceivably have taken the form it took the last time Britain was engaged in a major war—in South Africa from 1899 to 1901, when Canada facilitated the dispatch of a small contingent of volunteers to that far-off territory. The early years of the Great War reflected this "voluntarist" atmosphere. In the beginning no Canadians were forced to go to war. Indeed, the vast majority of eligible, Canadian-born men chose *not* to do so. The majority of enlistees were British immigrants—some of them quite recent arrivals in Canada—not long-settled Canadians. Many of those who enlisted were unemployed men struggling to survive in the boom and bust economy of the time.

In the early years of the war, few people suspected that it would demand much more of Canadians than had the South African War—the cliché, once again, was that many thought it would be over by Christmas, a notion that informed military men surely regarded as curious.[14] Haphazard volunteerism, not state planning, was the order of the day. Historians R. Craig Brown and Ramsay Cook nicely evoke the atmosphere by remarking that the first training efforts displayed the combined attributes of a Scout Jamboree and a citizens' crusade. Col. Sam Hughes, minister of militia and defence, called for 25,000 volunteers to come to train at a new camp at Valcartier, near Quebec City. Some 33,000 appeared. The facilities at Valcartier were thrown up in no time, with Hughes surveying the chaos from a wooden castle erected on the site. (The camp's Quebec location was certainly ironic, for Hughes had referred to Catholics as "neither more or less than a disloyal murder-planning society.")[15]

By the end of 1914 the target number for Canadian Expeditionary Force enlistment was 50,000; by summer 1915 it was 150,000. By early 1916 the volunteer pool had virtually dried up. Significant differences were emerging in the response of various regions to the recruiting drive. Maritimers were underrepresented, and Ontarians overrepresented. Prime Minister Sir Robert Borden's New Year's message for 1916 raised the personnel commitment to half a million men, and he attempted to keep the voluntary spirit alive through a scheme of national registration. But both increased labour demands for war production and unsettling news from the front had eroded the enthusiasm for volunteer service.

Gradually voluntarism—which had been a nice fit with a philosophy that made a virtue of a small state, with its white inhabitants not infringed upon unless necessary—ceded place to something more coercive, even though Borden's Conservative government insisted it would never budge from its voluntarist position. As one New Brunswicker put it:

> From the beginning of this war, the highest and most sustained recruiting call . . . has been a call to stand behind the Empire because of the high moral principles she upholds. Thousands have rallied to that one clear call. Many of them have gone onward in response to an even higher call. The most emphasized of these moral principles was Freedom, for which our fathers died.[16]

From this liberal perspective, to impose "conscription"—that is, compelling fit men of the appropriate age to serve in the military—violated the fundamental values in whose name the war was being fought. The controversial step-by-step implementation of conscription aroused passionate resistance in Quebec and an outpouring of anti-French sentiment outside it.

In this phase of the war the principle of laissez-faire went so far that even the organizing of essential munitions business was left in private hands. A so-called "Shell Committee," not an arm of the state but an organization of four Canadian steel manufacturers, secured all the British shell orders. These firms then sublet the orders to other Canadian manufacturers and to themselves. The contracts were rich plums. Many of these business arrangements were made through the good offices of Col. Sam Hughes. Competitive tendering was as rare as windfall profits were common.

The drawbacks of doing business in this way emerged forcibly when Canadian troops began to complain about the infamous Ross Rifle, enthusiastically championed by Hughes. The Ross had been designed at the time of the South African War and adopted by the Canadian armed forces in 1911. Because it weighed over nine pounds and suffered from continual jamming problems, the rifle soon became unpopular with the troops, who discarded it at the earliest opportunity in favour of the dependable British Lee-Enfields. The Ross Rifle was but one of a number of growing scandals as the militia and defence minister became an embarrassment to the government. Charges of gross corruption in Sir Sam's Shell Committee were laid in Parliament. Hughes was finally forced out of active leadership

John McCrae. Famous for "In Flanders Fields," soldier-physician McCrae was a patriotic imperialist who "ached for war." During the 1917 conscription election, McCrae wrote, "I hope I stabbed a Fr. Canadian with my vote."

of the war effort in November 1916. The scandals involved everything from boots to potatoes.

Many had predicted "Business as Usual" when the war began. The struggle, it was hoped, would be financed voluntarily. Yet by 1915 military spending equalled the entire government expenditure of 1913. The federal government asked Canadians to lend it money, and in 1915 a bond campaign goal of $50 million generated $100 million.

Given that Canada had no public opinion polls until the 1940s, confident statements that "all Canadians believed this" or "no Canadians believed that" must be taken with several grains of salt and weighed carefully against evidence found in such sources as newspapers, magazines, private letters, and political statements. Yet the consensus among historians is that in 1914 and 1915 the war had widespread support—and not just the war, but militarism, the belief that war worked to strengthen Canada. As Ernest J. Chambers, Canada's chief censor during the war, and scourge of socialists, pacifists, and Quebec nationalists, whose *Le Devoir* newspaper he threatened to ban, proclaimed:

> The country realizes that its whole life has been stimulated, the standard of its manhood built up, the national character strengthened by the achievements of its sons in the Fenian Raids, the Red River Expedition, the Nile Campaign, the North-West Rebellion, and the South African War. True, the laurels have been moistened with the tears of Canadian mothers, but a price has to be paid for everything that is worth having. The mother of a coward does not often weep.[17]

Across a Canada long accustomed to expressions of imperial pride—orchestrated by such groups as the Imperial Order Daughters of the Empire and Boy Scouts, and confirmed by cadet troops in schools and celebrations of the British Empire in textbooks—such an opinion was not at all out of place in 1915.

It was a time of great enthusiasm, of celebrations, fireworks, parades: as in the first grand snowstorm of the year, people came together, feeling that great pull of common purpose. Children were not overlooked. In Nova Scotia they were told that the Germans were poised to destroy the Empire and seize their parents' farms, a lesson many "Young Bluenoses" dutifully noted in an essay contest sponsored by the Halifax *Herald*. Dorothy Curtis of Halifax won $15 in the "Class A" Division for children under the age of thirteen for an essay that hailed the never-say-die spirit of the "unconquerable" English people and concluded: "How proud we ought to be of these brave defenders of our life and liberty, and how thankful. For without a thought for their own safety, indeed we might say, offering themselves as targets for the enemy, they heroically go forward, so that we may be saved." In the same division, young Leslie Howard of Guysborough argued that England and Canada were "fighting for their existence," as they deterred potential German invaders.[18]

Further up the educational ladder, the president of Dalhousie University proudly announced at the end of 1915 that one out of every three male students at the university had enlisted—a splendid result that he credited in part to the oratory of their patriotic history professors.[19]

Pockets of dissent did exist. The country's small but active socialist parties did not sign up for the war. The more radical labour unions were against it. But these leftists were forced to admit that even some of their staunchest supporters—coal miners—showed mass enthusiasm for the war. The coal towns proudly claimed to be among the most prodigious producers of soldiers in the country.

On 9 May 1915, people crowded around a Halifax harbour bristling with mines and shimmering beautifully under the searchlights on a distant shore, and there they watched the first Nova Scotian regiment depart for France. "Left Halifax about 5 p.m. on board the [steamship] Saxonia," soldier Frank Byron Ferguson confided to his diary when he journeyed out of Halifax. "On the greatest adventure of my life."[20]

*   *   *

Then things changed. This turned out to be a war that did not resemble any previous war. The soldiers were among the first to receive the bad news about the war when they experienced first-hand the extreme hardships of training camps both in Canada and Britain. Eberts Macintyre, who as a survivor of Vimy would go on to become one of the foremost celebrators of that battle in the 1960s, discovered in 1914 the human costs of a haphazard war effort when he arrived from Moose Jaw for training in Winnipeg. The volunteers were quartered in a "Horse Show Building" consisting of an open amphitheatre ringed by wooden seats; the floor consisted of a "loose bed of sawdust and powdered manure." As men marched in the building, they stirred up clouds of dust. Macintyre, an insurance man, thought the resulting respiratory diseases had probably "cost Canada millions of dollars in veterans' pensions."[21] The recruits were ill-clad for a Manitoba winter; some perished of pneumonia. Others might have wished they had been sent quickly to England, but over there conditions at the training camp were even worse. Mud and meningitis on Salisbury Plain (near Stonehenge) brought home the downside of military improvisation. Back at home, journalists attempting to bring attention to such problems were threatened with public shame and the state's newly enhanced powers of censorship superintended by the hyperzealous Ernest Chambers. Information control became so extreme that a mass publication such as *Maclean's* magazine was forced, under threat of its complete suppression, to pull a story that had already been published in the British press. It concerned the Allied defeat at Cambrai in late 1917.[22]

In Western Europe the war was rather like a three-act play. In the first act the German armies moved swiftly through Belgium and Luxembourg in the vast wheeling motion planned and then refined years before by Field Marshal Alfred von Schlieffen (a militarist to the extent that he would read his children detailed battle descriptions as bedtime stories). The plan depended upon speed, precision timetabling, and on-the-ground initiative by generals—so much so that von Schlieffen himself doubted, before his demise in 1913, that it could be pulled off successfully.[23] He was proven correct. In the early Battle of the Marne in September 1914 the Germans were forced to retreat. For almost four years they remained in the position of holding on to the French and Belgian lands they had invaded, without making significant further inroads into France. Only in April 1918—the third act of the play—did they break out and make a last, desperate bid for victory. But there again, despite apparent successes, they were stopped short.

It is the second act of the drama—from December 1914 to August 1918—for which the Great War became most notorious, at least in Canada. Armies dug a long line of trenches—extending some 700 miles from Belgium's North Sea coast to the mountainous border of Switzerland. The trenches of various sorts were intended to offer soldiers protection from artillery and gunfire and, if laid end to end, might have stretched as far as 25,000 miles. The soldiers in trenches at the front were serviced by many more behind them. Here was an artificial, strange, temporary "city" with hundreds of thousands of inhabitants, people who rotated in and out of their duties on the line. The rats, mud, rotting bodies, and diseases became legendary—although hard-nosed military historians like to point out that, overall, it was safer to fight in the trenches than to engage in the open warfare characteristic of the opening and closing acts of the war.[24]

Some Canadians were engaged elsewhere. Future prime minister Lester Pearson found himself in the "Southern Theatre" at Salonika in Greece (a country the British invaded just as Germany invaded Belgium). But it is the Western Front that is most actively commemorated. One semi-official list enumerates some eighty-three "Canadian" battles.[25] Yet the nature of much of the Great War often made it difficult to tell one battle from another. That is why, for example, what Canadians think of as the Battle of Vimy Ridge (9–12 April 1917) is elsewhere considered merely a part of the inconclusive Battle of Arras (9 April–29 June 1917).

Moreover, determining "victory" or "defeat" in such a setting was (and remains) difficult. Many so-called victories resulted in the acquisition, after heavy losses on both sides, of small bits of land, whereas some defeats entailed giving up positions in order to consolidate forces in stronger defensive positions. Vimy Ridge is a prime example. What Canadians saw as their victory to end all victories was, for some Germans, perhaps just a draw. The Germans argued that the battle allowed them to effectively consolidate their front lines further east. Similarly, the battle of Passchendaele in October–November 1917 is sometimes encompassed in the "Third Battle of Ypres." That Canadian "victory" ended with winning control of a town that no longer existed after what British historian A.J.P. Taylor called "the blindest slaughter of a blind war."[26] It was a victory in a sea of mud that, for many, seemed a lot like a defeat.

The most important feature of this war of attrition was that, over long years and after astronomical losses of life, the Western Front changed shape only minimally. Accustomed to long distances in their native land, Canadians who today visit the battlefields of Northern France and Belgium return amazed at the relatively tiny size of the territory in which so many lives were lost.

Just as the Great War bore no resemblance to the adventures with which imperially minded Canadian children had grown up, so too did it no longer seem, after 1916, an enterprise that the Canadian state could undertake according to the conventional rules that had prevailed in Canada since before Confederation. The old Shell Committee was displaced after November 1915 by the Imperial Munitions Board, which organized production to meet the Empire's enormous requirements.

The Borden government introduced an income tax, long a bogeyman for laissez-faire individualists distrustful of government meddling in the economy. It was, people were told, only a provisional measure. The old official ideology called for a frugal state supplying minimal services to equally frugal citizens, though not-so-frugal railway contractors, coal and steel barons, and monopolists enjoyed wide loopholes. The new reality was a state that assumed a massive national debt, much of it war-generated. The debt became so large that in interwar Canada about a third of the monies brought in by taxation went to meet annual interest charges on it. Even more dramatic was the Canadian state's drive to control the public sphere, as it exerted itself to ban supposedly subversive organizations, arrest "enemy aliens" and detain them in concentration camps, and aggressively censor publications.

In the wake of Vimy, and in part inspired by it, Robert Borden made the fateful decision to implement conscription and orchestrated an election marred by unprecedented levels of prejudice and hatred. The Grand Master of the Orange Lodge, a force of no mean political potency, envisaged the enlistment of a quarter-million-strong army to repress Quebec. Toronto newspapers depicted Quebec as a blot upon the nation. It was not fanciful to imagine Canada, like Ireland, being on the verge of civil war in 1917 and 1918. In the war's final year soldiers from outside Quebec killed four civilians, one a teenage boy, who were demonstrating in the streets of Quebec City.

Many English Canadians voted against the Unionist government and its policy of conscription in the controversial election of December 1917, some of them aghast at the attacks against French Canadians and Catholic institutions.[27] After the vote, farmers, promised that their sons would not be conscripted, were appalled when the Borden government reneged. Some Canadians were attracted by the now greatly strengthened left, which argued that if the state was going to ask parents to give up their sons, it should also come up with a "conscription of wealth" to ensure that the burdens of the war were shared equitably. Some had been shocked by wartime inflation and sickened by wartime corruption and profiteering.

Already by 1917 the war's patriotic gloss had become badly tarnished. On a single day, 1 July 1916, as Canada celebrated Dominion Day, the British side suffered 19,240 men killed as the catastrophic Battle of the Somme began. Newfoundland, which lost a generation of men (or "boys") in the slaughter at Beaumont-Hamel that same day, would be scarred forever. It would be called "the day of the dead," and the Dominion of Newfoundland would henceforth commemorate the first of July as Memorial Day.

Although the nation was by no means "born" in 1914–18—and the country was but a small player in the war as a whole—the cataclysmic experience of the Great War had particular and long-lasting consequences for Canada. For one thing, the relations between Quebec and the rest of Canada were wounded, and would only continue to fester. Most lists of other effects—aside from the mass slaughter—include votes for women and the establishment of an income tax system. Not so often included is the end of the traditional two-party system in which political formations committed to free enterprise had dominated the electoral scene. After 1918 every election featured a third party and often a fourth and fifth: Progressives, United Farmers, Social Credit, Cooperative Commonwealth Federation, New Democrats, Canadian Alliance, Bloc Québécois. Each formation claimed to offer an alternative to the old-line Liberal and Conservative parties. That at the very least is one "democratic legacy" of the Great War in Canada.[28]

The Great War put liberal assumptions about reality under enormous pressure. Concentration camps for select ethnic minorities, the conversion of the "private sphere" of the churches into the "public sphere" of war recruitment, the killing of the protestors in Quebec City who disagreed with the government about conscription, the novel organization of government agencies to create public opinion and the reconstitution of others to enhance their surveillance capacity: none of these measures were easily described as being "classically liberal."[29]

That the "British and Dominion armies," as military historian Tim Cook points out, "went through the meat grinder of fighting without succumbing to massive breakdown in the form of mutiny is telling." Cook suggests that this peculiar staying power came about perhaps because the "military's draconian discipline" had to be adjusted to a war in which troops "were encouraged to think and act independently on the battlefield to achieve their missions." Yet he also documents impressive instances of soldiers' rebellions, some entailing the direct resistance to marching orders. When ordered to advance towards the Rhine River, the Canadian troops refused to do so until they were fed. The brass blamed some of the soldiers who had acquired "strong socialistic tendencies," but a mass refusal to obey direct orders was also a sign "that the rank and file were now more willing to kick against a system that was increasingly failing them." Another such sign was the full-scale uprising of 17,000 soldiers impatient at the pace of demobilization at Kinmel Park in Wales.[30]

The country left behind by the war would be equally messy—and it is a country about which, even today, opinions are fiercely divided, depending on your place of birth, the language you speak, how long you've been here (are you "old stock" or are you new and finding your way?), how you feel about equality and social justice, and the extent to which you identify with (or oppose) the imperial values that suffused Canada's war effort. After the war, the jingoistic claims that war was the engine of human moral progress were quite soon opposed by people who had experienced and observed the trauma and difficulty of war. But long-lasting militarist trends—gung-ho attitudes, reverence for strong men wielding awe-inspiring authority, a love of the adventure and cosmic splendour offered by war—did not swiftly vanish. Both in the last century and in this, the landscape of Great War memory has been as unsettled and as unsettling as the actual field painted by Fred Varley on that fall day in 1918.

3

IN THE WAKE OF WAR: EXPERIENCING AND REMEMBERING

Calm fell. From Heaven distilled a clemency;
There was peace on earth, and silence in the sky;
Some could, some could not, shake off misery:
The Sinister Spirit sneered: "It had to be!"
And again the Spirit of Pity whispered, "Why?"

— THOMAS HARDY, "And There Was a Great Calm"
(On the Signing of the Armistice, 11 Nov. 1918)

SAMUEL CHOWN was groomed for this moment. As a twelve-year-old lad in Kingston he had been swept off his feet by the "glamour of military parades, the glitter of soldierly uniforms . . . the thrill of martial music."[1] He adored soldiering so much that he paid a soldier's son to train him in the rudiments of military drill. Then he immersed himself in military school and became qualified as an officer. Even though he decided to go into the Methodist ministry rather than the military, his language, his values, his bearing—head held high, ramrod straight—smacked of soldiering. Nonetheless, he had rocketed into prominence as a preacher and church leader.

He was sitting on his verandah at 1710 Dunbar Road in Vancouver one sunny August day in 1914 when his neighbour called out that war had been declared. Chown was now sixty-two years old. The next day he volunteered his services in any capacity to the militia and defence minister, Sir Sam Hughes, in Ottawa. He then proceeded to hurl himself into a

Samuel Chown. The Great War was a Holy War for Samuel Chown, one of Canada's most prominent religious leaders and an architect of the United Church of Canada. But, like many others, he had a change of heart after 1918 and began preaching for the abolition of war.

rigorous training program in the B.C. mountains, readying himself for the challenge.

His son Eric, a student at the University of Toronto, was no less keen. All his classmates were desperate to get to Europe. Indeed, there were more students anxious to go than the War Department would allow. The officers decided that the fairest way to decide who would win the opportunity to fight was to draw lots. In his memoirs Samuel Chown wrote about his son's experience: "They put a number of little square pieces of paste board in a hat with a cross marked upon them equal to the number to be permitted to go to the Front. Then they added a sufficient number of blank pasteboards so that the total was equal to the number who desired to go. Eric had the first draw, and he drew a cross." An exhilarating, wonderful moment. He told his father about the method that had been used. "Father, I never prayed so hard for anything in all my life as that I might draw a cross." As Chown later recalled, "Such was the spirit of our home."[2]

Rev. Samuel Chown, as one of the foremost leaders of Canada's Methodists, needed to ready his church for battle, and he did. Churches resounded with cries for war. Rev. J.S. Woodsworth, who had been publicly resisting militarism since 1912, was amazed by what he saw at one Winnipeg church: war hymns, scriptural readings, all from the Old Testament, hailing the God of Battles; the organ belting out the national anthems of the Entente nations. "The climax was not reached when the pastor in an impassioned appeal stated that if any young man could go and did not go he was neither a Christian nor a patriot," Woodsworth wrote to his mother. "No! The climax was the announcement that recruiting sergeants were stationed at the doors of the church and that any man of spirit—any lover of his country—any follower of Jesus—should make his decision then and there!"[3]

Chown would have found nothing troubling in such a scene. The Great War was a holy war that called out for the support of every true Briton and every true Christian. "All Methodists should rally to the Standard and stand foursquare to the blast."[4] So fervently did they do so that soon Methodist parsonages had hundreds of vacant chairs as ministers signed up as chaplains or, failing that, ordinary combatants.

At age sixty-four Samuel Chown accompanied Eric to Europe in May 1917 as senior chaplain on a vessel carrying six hundred soldiers from Canada and Newfoundland. He remembered later how he had worked to buck up the spirits of the men. Canadians, he told them, were "the best fighters in Europe to-day because they have the most comprehensive understanding of the basic principles of the British Empire." Few people believed more firmly than did Chown in the efficacy of classical warfare, and, at least initially, he was convinced he had found a noble war. He was deeply moved by his visit to a casualty clearing station, where 2,600 wounded men were brought in during the course of just one day, with one hundred graves dug just in case. "Glorious to say," he said with reference to gravely wounded soldiers, "if a padre asked them 'What shall I tell your Mother?' they generally would answer: 'Tell her I'm slightly wounded, Sir. Tell her I got a scratch.'" Such men were "consecrated to the death" for "what appeared to them to be a worthy cause" and "were not willing to have any unnecessary suffering endured by their friends."[5]

Yet Chown's narrative of this time also suggests another side to the war. He visited Vimy Ridge, its shell holes still full of bloody water after its capture by Canadian troops. He was escorted closer to the Front and saw "small squads of British soldiers returning from the trenches. Their eyes seemed filled with a meaningless luminosity as though they were trying to forget the terrible ordeals through which they had passed."[6] He would never forget the sight of them.

Finally he had found the real war of which he had dreamt for more than half a century. Yet, did it really look like and feel like that sort of war? In the conflict's early years Chown often invoked God's providence. But now he often expressed doubts about whether he would ever really understand His plan.

*   *   *

Samuel Chown was typical of the many Anglo-Canadian men who gloried in the poems of Rudyard Kipling and were transported by the novels of H. Rider Haggard. They thrilled to stories of a Greater Britain that was bringing civilization and liberty to the world. The Canadian John McCrae, later to be renowned as the author of "In Flanders Fields," simply "ached for war." For McCrae's fellow Montrealer and close friend Andrew Macphail, a prominent Canadian physician and essayist, "The guns of August 1914 had lifted the gloom. War was to be the cleanser. It was to purge the collective soul and clarify the politics of Canada."[7] Macphail was eventually knighted for literary acumen and his service to king and country.

Towards the end of 1916, after he had gone off to the war, Macphail wrote about having just spent "the happiest" time of his life. For him, war would "counteract the enfeebling effects of modern society." Indeed, the days of peace were "dreadful," with "the whole world sunk in sensuality and sloth, where only the feebler vices and the meaner virtues could thrive in the stagnant and fetid atmosphere." War was the only cure for this sad state of affairs.[8]

The religious—and most Canadians of the time were religious to some degree—sometimes found themselves thinking of the war as God's punishment for shallow materialism. For Chown, the noble self-sacrifices of the soldiers generated a realization that the "real use and enjoyment of life" consisted "not in an abundance of things . . . but in a broad sacrificial service to humanity." God was correcting "our national sins, and personal and social transgressions." In the "imperfect moral condition of the human race," God uses the "experience of war" to accomplish a higher purpose: that is, "to call men back to the primitive and basic virtues of courage, loyalty and sacrifice, and to set men in a large place in respect to the vision of life."[9]

Liberal imperialism was to many of this generation a living, breathing faith, almost as powerful as Methodism itself. Hundreds of Protestant missionaries left Canadian shores to carry the Gospel to Asia and Africa. Some even ventured to convert the Catholics of Quebec. Christianity and Empire were fused in a dynamic synthesis. Chown's fellow believers had approved of every British war since the 1850s—including the Opium War in China.

The Great War was linked with a long succession of British struggles in which oppressive enemies had been routed and British liberty guaranteed. The *Christian Guardian*, published by the Methodist Church, often carried articles and letters summoning up the spirit of Elizabeth I and the defeat of the Armada and the British triumph at Waterloo (not bothering to consider Wellington's reliance upon Prussians at that battle). Chown would often give such British campaigns a Biblical gloss by likening them to the struggles of the Israelites against the Philistines.

In "A Call to Prayer" in April 1918, Chown, as the church's general superintendent, summoned the faithful to passion week: "I now desire to press upon your hearts the duty of praying without ceasing for the success of the arms of the allies in this decisive battle in the greatest struggle known to history." Methodist churches resounded to the heart-stirring hymns of the faith: "The Son of God goes forth to war; A kingly crown to gain; His blood-red banner streams afar; Who follows in his train?" Even Methodist youngsters were urged by the *Guardian* "to badger young men on the street in the hope of shaming them into enlisting," perhaps by bestowing upon them the dreaded white feather of cowardice. Methodists were warned off voting for Liberal leader Wilfrid Laurier and his anti-conscriptionist party in 1917. Chown even imagined that Catholic Quebec might be plotting "political or military aggression" at a time when so many English-Canadian Protestants had gone nobly forth to "slaughter and decimation."[10]

For some English Canadians, French-speaking Quebec was a "blot" upon Canada, as one Toronto newspaper put it.[11] Others resisted such divisive rhetoric. Yet, like Chown, they did not waver in their conviction that the British side was carrying the torch of civilization itself. A victory for Germany would be a victory for thuggishness and a defeat for evolution—a return to medieval despotism and slavery. It would be a victory for the "German God," who was a "mere figment of the mind," and not to be confused with the "God of Christ" who was cheering for our soldiers as they died nobly for the "redemption of generations as yet unborn."[12] It would also spell the end to the world's greatest political achievement, a British Empire within which a "new soul" was animating the Dominion of Canada.

Even when wounded Canadian soldiers were receiving the sting of antiseptic on their wounds, Chown exclaimed, they found it within themselves to sing "The Maple Leaf Forever," that proud hymn to the hero of the Battle of the Plains of Abraham, General James Wolfe. In 1917 Chown told the British Wesleyan Conference that he was "proud to be a Canadian." He immediately added: "I am thankful to God that my Father was . . . English and my mother of pure English stock. . . . I speak to you as a Britisher."[13]

Here was a spiritual adventure for the times, however painful. One of Chown's two sons fighting in Europe told his father that thirteen of his fifteen college chums had been killed, and added: "But you needn't worry about me, Father, I am game for anything, and it does not seem like death over here, only like going up to something better." Chown found these words inspirational, and in a letter to a grieving father he wrote: "Of course death is a great adventure, but we Canadians are a venturous people; and so believing that the cause for which we are fighting is worth the sacrifice, we carry on."[14]

Throughout these turbulent years, what Paul Fussell calls the "High Diction" of the war was pervasive. Not only was death a "great adventure," but Canadian soldiers were "gallant," "virtuous," and "sportsmanlike," making sacrifices for the good of all. Yet, as Fussell points out, much of the "modern irony" that saturated many Great War writings arose from the contrast between such chivalric notions and the war's gruesome realities.[15]

*   *   *

As Varley asked in 1918: *For What?* To which Samuel Chown's answer would be: *To cleanse the world.* Or, perhaps: *Stand up for righteousness. To defend a Godly Empire and defeat an ungodly one. To be strong men who stood up when duty called.*

High Diction was not only for militarists. On 1 March 1916 the *Christian Guardian* published "An Open Letter to Pacifists" from Alice Chown of Clarkson, Ont. She was Samuel's cousin, and had breathed the same air and absorbed many of the same ideals. She too was a product of soldierly Kingston and Sydenham Street Wesleyan Methodist Church.

Alice Amelia Chown was thirteen years younger than Samuel. After high school and an unfinished stint at university, she stayed home to care for her ailing mother—a hard fate for a convention-defying feminist rebel who had once scandalized the congregation by removing her gloves as she sat in her pew. The opening lines of her novel *The Stairway* (1921) remain somewhat shocking: "Today I am free. My first day of freedom! It is my new birth!"[16] Alice was writing of the death of her mother.

That novel, a thinly disguised memoir, also tells of Alice's search for new ideas about relations between men and women. She was inspired especially by Edward Carpenter, who preached a gospel of sincerity, freedom, and spontaneity, spurning "all conventions which men deem necessary, and which in return choke their souls." Without ever herself adopting the name, in her middle age Alice became a sort of anarchist, unyielding in her fierce independence. As one commentator wrote about her in 1935, "She has crossed conventional barriers, jumped intellectual obstacles and torn her gown not infrequently on the bristling hedge of opposition."[17]

During the Great War, Alice joined a small but prominent group of women pacifists across North America, a number of them in Canada. Alice was directly involved in the Women's Peace Crusade, a movement that wanted "compulsory arbitration, universal disarmament, and the establishment of a league of democratic nations."[18] The socialist feminists focused intently on war's ravages upon the human body. "Mangled, torn, blinded, maddened, slain, are the victims of this inhuman strife," cried one 1917 manifesto. "Europe is a vast charnel house, yet still the Molochs of War cry out: 'More men; more of the flower of earth's manhood,' and still the monster is insatiate."[19]

When readers of the *Christian Guardian* opened their papers in early March 1916 and read the latest emission from a Chown, they were indeed receiving yet more High Diction—but put to a markedly different purpose. Alice based her sermon-in-a-letter upon a series of resonant statements attributed to Christ: "My kingdom is not of this world," "The kingdom of God is within you," "They that worship God must worship him in spirit and in truth," "God is love," and "Love your enemy." Every individual, she wrote, "does create his own environment, his own circumstances, from the desires of his own heart." Those who (like her cousin Samuel) thought "that force in some form is necessary to put down evil" were guilty of a profound error. They believed "that you must overcome evil by creating some institution, some military or police power, to restrain or overcome it. It is because people lack faith in the injunction, overcome evil with good, that they resort to force."

Foremost for believers was the "principle for which Christ was willing to die—the brotherhood of man." A soldier went off to war "often at great sacrifice to himself, and always with the prospect of giving up his life because of his belief," even if his belief was the mistaken one that force could overcome evil. Canadians who believed in peace had to show a similar courage. Alone among all the warring nations, Canada, she said, had no "groups of people who are standing up for the principle of loving their enemies," trying to inculcate "a faith in love instead of hate." Canadians should be willing to consider "both sides of all disputes" and try to achieve justice "irrespective of their sympathies." If, as Alice maintained, the war had come about because of an idea—"a belief in militarism"— then it would only end because this idea had been renounced.[20]

Alice's pacifism aligned her with some of the historic peace churches— Quakers, Mennonites, Doukhobors—and their total opposition to war in all its forms. The profoundly Methodist and more generally Protestant idealism at work in her letter would also have aligned her with a more diffuse disquiet with war in general and this war in particular. The visible cruelty, squalor, and suffering of the war seemed a reflection of a breakdown of Christian moral order, and Alice was hardly alone in this feeling. William Lyon Mackenzie King—who had been minister of labour in the Laurier government—wrote in December 1916 that he felt acutely the "ruthlessness" of the war. He said it was contradictory to denounce "efforts for peace" and profess Christianity: "Ye cannot serve God & Mammon,—and Christ's message & gospel is peace."[21]

Immediately under Alice's letter the *Christian Guardian* offered a response, confining itself to a terse paragraph that concluded: "There are those of us who hold that slavery is worse than death."[22]

Alice persisted. "We will not rid the world of militarism through force," she told the readers of the sensationalist and disreputable *Toronto World* on 4 November 1916. This time she struck a less otherworldly tone. Alice tied the war to the arms buildup of the past decade, which had been accelerated by the capitalists interested in making money. War arose out of greed—and ignorance. Echoing British playwright George Bernard Shaw, Alice urged any person who encouraged war because he or she believed in force to "at least be honest with yourself . . . and acknowledge yourself a pagan." In the eyes of the *World*'s editor, the international pacifist women's movement was little more than a conspiracy of pro-German traitors who had swallowed the Kaiser's line. How dare Alice Chown claim that there were spiritual truths bigger than nationalities? Didn't she know that "Nations stand for principles and ideals? The German nation stands for militarism and force. . . . The Kaiser appeals to God to enable him to slaughter all his enemies and annex their territories."[23]

Alice tried again six days later. Even people who did not believe in force had "allowed the militarism of the Germans to frighten us into espousing it." She refused to see the Germans as an intrinsically benighted people. "There is only one way for women to put an end to war," she concluded, "that is, to refuse to countenance it." Once more the editor responded. Over a quarter of a century, Germany had refused to respond to such "love messages." As for Alice's reference to Jesus' call to "Love your enemies," the editor reminded her that the "Man of Galilee" had said he had come to bring, not peace, but the sword. He likened Alice to Judas Iscariot.[24]

Both Alice and Samuel stayed true to their faith, as they construed it, through the war. Alice moved to New York, where she frequented left-liberal circles. Just a month after the armistice, Samuel sent her a friendly Christmas card—perhaps as a peace offering after their trying wartime conflicts. The response he received was vintage Alice, ruthless in its honesty and forthright in its criticism. For her, it was not a matter of "Merry Christmas." She said she was not willing to let Samuel think they were following the same path. He had put too much of his faith into armed force. Samuel, in her opinion, had betrayed his church and his duty. He had been complicit in wartime censorship, and as a leader of the Methodist Church, he should have known better, checked his facts, and protested—instead of becoming, along with the others, "the dupe of the militarist press." Now he should ready himself for the revelation of more and more facts about "the lies and the traitorous acts of the allies." The only question was whether people would awaken to the truth quickly enough to prevent the perpetuation of the iniquitous terms of the armistice in the Paris peace agreements. "If they are embodied in the peace treaty then the conditions which will make impossible the avoidance of the next war will be created," she hoped. For that next war, "the real guilt will be with the people who were too indifferent to know their facts."[25]

*   *   *

If the Chowns conducted their debate in the highest of High Diction— absolutes contending with each other in the pure, thin air of abstraction— for those who made it to the Western Front the contrasts between High Diction and Low Reality were bayonet sharp.

Canadian soldiers on the Front often sent home letters infused with another sensibility altogether—irony.[26] Indeed, the ordinary fighting Canadian was often among the war's most gifted ironic observers. Correspondence from soldiers at the Front reveals a thoroughly unromantic sense of the war, an attitude that they were quite willing to share with the folks back home. Many wrote of a war far different than the conflicts imagined in their old history books. "If the people at home could see the real horrors of the battle-field[,] they would be worried to death," wrote one soldier.[27] One lieutenant called the use of gas "murder, not war," and another said, quite similarly, "This is not war, it is simply murder." German soldiers shared the sentiment: "You can no longer call it war, it is mere murder," or "This butchery is madness." As one desperate Canadian private put it, "I should not call this war—it is slaughter."[28]

"They say the first seven years are the worst and after that we won't mind it very much, so 'cheer up,'" was one soldier's attempt at black humour about the war. Jokes about the skulls and bones found in trenches, and about mistaking the dead for the living, were commonplace. Some soldiers pondered the ironies of medical services on the Front: "We were maintained by science," said one, "to be killed by shells."[29]

Soldiers sometimes even waxed ironical about the stirring propaganda calculated to rouse their patriotism. Near Lens in 1917, as Tim Cook describes the scene, the sun fell upon a battlefield littered with bloated corpses, "forcing out odoriferous gasses day and night that jerked soldiers to attention. Mounds of bodies were reduced to mounds of body parts as dead flesh was dismembered and churned up by the cascading shells." One Canadian captain wrote, "If only some of those famous orators, who shout fight to the finish, could only see this sight, they would pause, and would wonder whether they were in hell, instead of living in this supposedly enlightened twentieth century."[30]

The most conspicuous moment of ironic distance from the official line came in 1918, when General Arthur Currie issued what he hoped would be an inspiring message to his soldiers to stand fast: "You will advance or fall where you stand facing the enemy. To those who will fall I say, 'Your names will be revered forever and ever by your grateful country and God will take you unto Himself.'" It was a grand rhetorical gesture that fell flat with the troops, who satirized it: "Did you stand where you fell?" As one of Currie's friends said afterwards, "Appeals to the higher ideals only made them ill."[31] Clearly, among the ranks High Diction only went so far.

Chown himself was well aware of some of these issues. He knew that in their sexual and drinking habits overseas, many of the supposedly heroic, self-sacrificing Methodist soldiers drifted far from the teachings of the church. Many of the soldiers, as it turned out, contracted venereal disease in Europe. In a report to the church, Chown struggled to explain the Canadian soldiers' promiscuity by stressing the shock of war and loneliness for home.[32] The army had not only allowed soldiers to drink off-duty but supplied them with rum. "We thought we had sent you soldiers, and they have turned into sots," he complained.[33] Were we really so much better than the Germans, if we allowed drunkenness to prevail among the troops?

High Diction necessarily became even more muted when other front-line issues came to the fore: prisoner-killing, trench-raiding, summary executions, and procurement scandals, for instance. The fighting was so fierce that Canadian soldiers, whether out of a sense of revenge or "blood frenzy," or under orders, sometimes killed surrendering Germans rather than taking them prisoner. Canadian soldiers developed a widespread and enduring reputation for killing prisoners, one that would haunt them into the next world war. As Pierre Berton recounts in his *Vimy*, Maritimers "with no time for niceties" sealed Germans forever into a dugout, without—it seems—making a strenuous effort to take them prisoner, which was all the consequence of the soldiers following a "strict timetable" that "made them ruthless." Trench-raiding became known as something of a Canadian specialty—it was warmly esteemed because it brought soldiers into close quarters with their enemies and bayoneting them would stir up their blood lust. As Lieut. Eberts Macintyre put it, the practice was a "mad enterprise." Berton has a story about one such raid: a Yuletide truce was disrupted when Canadian raiders launched a surprise attack, destroying dugouts and a supply dump and seizing fifty-eight prisoners, "some of them lugging Christmas parcels."[34]

The documents of the 5th Battalion at Vimy give a glimpse of the experience: "The tactics of the enemy, as usual, consisted in the use of his machine guns to the very last, and our most effective weapon against them was undoubtedly the rifle grenade. At one or two places, there were smart bayonet fights, in which our men proved much superior. Several cases of treachery on the part of the enemy were summarily dealt with." In short, when German machine-gunners raised their hands to surrender, they stood a considerable risk of being shot.[35]

As for executions, it was odd, said another soldier about the shooting of a fellow soldier for presumed cowardice, that some soldiers were executed for not killing during wartime, whereas in peacetime, "the penalty for killing is death." Here was a world gone mad—in the words of soldier Herbert Burrell, an "insane combat."[36]

Fine words about noble service to the Empire also contrasted vividly with sordid procurement scandals involving everything from rotten potatoes to broken-down horses to defective rifles. The "profiteer"—a capitalist who took advantage of the business opportunities provided by the war to reap a fortune—became the maligned antithesis of the "patriot." In 1919 the Vancouver Unit of the Army and Navy Veterans' Association in Canada demanded that anyone whose profiteering caused "hardships . . . to the people and the bitter and dangerous feelings towards classes" should be brought to justice and punished. The Vancouver Trades and Labor Council more puckishly suggested that the government pair each labour activist deported from Canada with one of the "big profiteers," and it suggested that Sir Joseph Flavelle, whose meat-packing profits won him the sobriquet "His Lardship," should head the list.[37]

When the issue of conscription loomed after 1916, Samuel Chown was caught in an awkward dilemma. His co-religionists dwelt upon the jarring disjunction between exalting an army of volunteers who wanted to sacrifice themselves and creating an army of conscripts who did not. Chown's idealization of war included the principle of a free individual making a choice to sacrifice his well-being, and perhaps his very life, for a higher cause. "We have sent no conscripts to the front, and never shall. The sense of duty will be all sufficient for the utmost strain of war," he stated in 1916. True Canadians, as spiritually mature Protestants, and somehow quite unlike the enemy, were drawn to fight by reason, not sophistry, "without the hatred which consumes manhood," and without "murderous feelings."[38]

As one New Brunswick Methodist pointedly asked Chown, "What is Conscription but Militarism in action, militarism applied?" Later Chown reversed his previous stand and supported conscription, and found himself forced to adopt another argument. "Does it not appear to you a most horrible thing," he asked a correspondent, "that our boys should become voluntary murderers? Would it not be much better for their character if they should kill only at the stern compulsion of the State?"[39] Had they been "voluntary murderers" before? Had they not been noble crusaders? The fundamental categories that explained war as a religious experience were shifting. The stars that guided Chown suddenly seemed disturbingly in motion.

*   *   *

After a while even true believers like Chown found it increasingly hard to fend off their doubts. Before the war Chown had once served as the vice-president of a society promoting peace with Germany. During the war he always distanced himself from the hate-filled propaganda that deemed Germans "Huns," and in some of his wartime prayers he even appealed for their souls. After the war, his doubts accumulated.

He was in good company. Across postwar North America many scholars became sceptical of their governments' official line about the war. In Canada, nationalists in the 1920s began to assert a distance from Empire. Even during the war, the 1918 Easter Riots in Quebec City, the shooting of anti-conscription activist Albert "Ginger" Goodwin in British Columbia in July of the same year, and a mounting wave of labour unrest were all difficult to square with the image of a united patriotic Canada led by the Unionist government.

In both Britain and the United States, thinkers started to treat the notion of exclusive German war guilt as a belief suitable only for children, and the Treaty of Versailles as a monumental mistake. In Vienna, Sigmund Freud amended his model of the human psyche to include a "death-drive."[40] The Great War and the Russian Revolution of 1917 prompted others to look to the social relations of capitalism for the origins of war. A commonality of these and other approaches was to set at a distance any reading of the Great War in black-and-white terms pitting a spotless "we" against a pernicious "them."

Closer to home, many former enthusiasts of the war were, like Chown, turning into sceptics. By 1917 Andrew Macphail, for example, was saying, "I have seen all of war I desire to see." As his biographer notes, a chasm loomed between "what he had expected of the war . . . and what the reality was." His initial enthusiasm turned into "a mixture of resignation and dis-illusionment." He was particularly upset by how his fellow officers treated their men in "punctilious, even cruel ways." He was upset, quite under-standably, by the executions of Canadian soldiers. He was not especially surprised by the divisive results of the 1917 federal election: "The French Canadians hate us; they always did." When he came to write the official history of the Canadian medical service, his account constituted a wither-ing critique of the war's conduct.[41]

During the war novelist John Buchan—who later, as Lord Tweedsmuir, served as governor general of Canada—proved to be one of the British Empire's most talented, if also factually challenged, propagandists. In his *Nelson's History of the War*, brought out in multiple volumes as the conflict was still underway, Buchan had transformed many a bloody but incon-clusive battle into an inspiring Allied victory. Sometime later he privately came to view the war as a "folly." He was no longer able to stomach High Diction: "I acquired a bitter detestation of war," he later remembered, "less for its horrors than for its boredom and futility, and a contempt for its *panache*." He became convinced that "every sane man must be a devo-tee of peace, for most of us, except the very young, have had some per-sonal knowledge of the terrible consequences of war. Heaven forbid that I should minimize these terrors; the best guarantee of peace is that the world should remember them."[42]

Samuel Chown's transition would be no less complete. He had been moving in that direction since the end of the war. As early as 1919 he remarked that "the competitions of commerce" had "let loose a menagerie of wild animals upon mankind," implying that the war had been caused by forces other than the supposed innate German wickedness. Later he asked, was not the "capitalistic spirit," if not capitalism itself, responsible for some of the division in the world?[43]

In a major sermon in 1924, titled "The Abolition of War," the same man who had loved soldiering so wholeheartedly as a boy announced his change of heart. It no longer seemed clear that the British Empire had been entirely right and the German Empire entirely wrong. Militarism, he noted, was hardly a problem confined to Germany. By the mid-1920s, rather than stressing German "barbarism" and British "civility," Chown was citing the words of a British admiral: "Moderation in war is imbecility. Hit first, hit hard and hit anywhere." As he reminded a U.S. audience, "You Americans were prepared to drop mustard gas upon the enemy of such strength as to destroy all life over several acres, leaving not even a rat behind."[44]

Yet even as he spoke, Chown had the sense that another war—with even deadlier weapons—was in the making, just as cousin Alice had warned him in her letter of 1918. He was aghast at what he had learned about the Somme, horrified by the images of wartime destruction, and shaken by the sight of the mutilated veterans he had encountered in military hospitals. He was alarmed at the prospect of a recurrence of war that resembled not at all his childhood fantasies. He thought it imperative to rouse the public to the imminent danger of another, even more catastrophic war. Echoing his cousin's letter, Samuel urged his audience to go out and "get the real facts about war and its aftermath" and spread the word about war's "savagery and futility." The church's most important duty now was "to work for the displacement of the war spirit by the spirit of peace and goodwill." He spoke of "disillusionment," and how peace would come through the League of Nations, United States, and British Empire acting together in the same cause. War was always to be considered a "very last resort and should never take place unless absolutely necessary for pure defense."[45]

Chown was joined in both his enthusiasm for the war and his subsequent recoil from it by his fellow Methodist W.B. Creighton, who joined with him to help create the United Church of Canada in 1925.[46] The new church, frequently roiled by the politics of peace and war in the 1920s and 1930s, became one of English Canada's principal religious organizations.

*   *   *

Chown was not the only thinker in the postwar period who changed his mind about the war. Books from the Front that told the story of a different reality had begun to appear even as the war was proceeding—supplementing, in effect, the critical letters sent home by participants—and by the late 1920s a world-wide culture of "disillusionment" had set in, with corrosively ironic treatments of the Great War produced by such writers as Robert

Graves, Siegfried Sassoon, Erich Maria Remarque, Ernest Hemingway, and Canada's own Charles Yale Harrison. In this regard they joined a broad swathe of Canadians in the 1920s and the 1930s who articulated a powerful sense of disillusionment with the Great War, a tendency based not upon disloyalty to the country but on a stubborn adherence to their still-vivid memories of the events. The different takes on the war experience only added to the dramatic impact of works of art such as Emanuel Hahn's sculpture *War, The Destroyer* in 1915 and Varley's *For What?* in 1918.

Later on some writers, such as Jonathan Vance in *Death So Noble* and Pierre Berton in *Vimy*, would argue that Canadians, both grief-stricken and patriotic, were relatively unmoved by this wave of disaffection because it threatened to undermine the almost holy reverence with which they had come to regard the Great War. Many believed so deeply in the sanctity of "the fallen" that any questioning of their crusade called their honour into question and carried the risk of "spiritual desolation." For others, swept up in "Vimy Fever," any questioning of the conflict was tantamount to disloyalty.[47]

Yet this interpretation of how most interwar Canadians remembered the war—as a noble crusade—does not jibe with the historical record: the letters home, the works of art, the various pieces of writing both from the war years and after, and phenomena such as the mass movement against conscription, centred on but not confined to francophone Quebec. Adding to the mix, and even more critical of the war, were many discontented veterans, as evidenced not only in their protest movements but in their numerous memoirs and novels about the war.

One of the better-known books to come out of the Front was written by a British-born poet who had become legendary in Canada: Robert Service, renowned for "The Cremation of Sam McGee" and other hugely popular poems from the Klondike Gold Rush. After attempting to enlist at the age of forty-one, Service covered the early years of the war for the *Toronto Star* and then worked as a stretcher-bearer and ambulance driver for the American Red Cross. He was convalescing in Paris when he wrote *Rhymes of a Red Cross Man* (1916), dedicated to the memory of his brother, killed in France while serving in the Canadian infantry. The collection of poems dealt with such touchy subjects as prisoner-killing and the shared Christianity of German and British soldiers.

"Only a Boche" tells the story of a German prisoner who has been brought back to a dugout, where he slowly dies while the soldiers nearby are playing a game of bridge: "And his face is white in the shabby light, and

I stand at his feet and stare. Stand for a while, and quietly stare: for strange though it seems to be, The dying Boche on the stretcher there has a queer resemblance to me." This startling similarity between captor and captive provokes the thought: "Oh, it isn't cheerful to see a man, the marvelous work of God, Crushed in the mutilation mill, crushed to a smeary clod." While the Great War certainly generated, not surprisingly, a vast amount of Canadian patriotic commemorative poetry as it was being fought, here, even while the war was proceeding, this poet—a cultural celebrity of his time—was sounding sharply critical notes about the conflict.[48]

Those notes were discernible even in works that can be described as propaganda tools. Jack Munroe's *Mopping Up! A Dog Story of the Princess 'Pats'* (1918)—thought to be the first book-length account of a Canadian soldier's war experience—is seemingly the pro-war antithesis to Service's poems. Like Service, Munroe was a man's man, a "famed football star, amateur boxing champion of the American West Coast, and challenger for the World Heavyweight Title in 1904." In Northern Ontario he had won fame as the hero who saved his community from a forest fire in 1911. His Collie, "Bobbie Burns," became the mascot of the Princess Patricia's Canadian Light Infantry. Smuggled into England and then France, Bobbie was among the many pet dogs kept by soldiers on the Western Front.[49]

Bobbie, as the canine narrator of *Mopping Up!*, rails against the maniacal Hun, a menace to humanity and dog dom, and even adds his approval to the killing of German prisoners. When they cried "Merci, Kamerad" (We surrender), they were merely emitting the "Hun squeal of fear that Allied raiding parties have come to know so well; the hypocritical yelp of baby-bombers, murderers of women, Red Cross destroyers, when faced with the steel-points of justice." Did the Canadians take prisoners? Well, says Bobbie, "*Some* prisoners were taken back to my boys' lines."[50]

The real Bobbie escaped both German and British bullets and returned with his wounded master to Canada, where both were feted by the Toronto Humane Society and a host of other patriotic bodies. Munroe and his dog became famous, and the soldier was put to work drumming up enthusiasm for the war in both Canada and the United States. Yet the former boxer had grown to detest the war. "I hate the very thought of war," he told the *Daily Nugget* of Timmins.[51] Even *Mopping Up!*—whose very title is a salute to the bayonet-wielding Canadian trench raider who gives no quarter to the Germans—contains passages in which the Collie narrator reveals unsuspected levels of canine complexity. "It seemed to me that all the world was turning into an uncompromising morass," Bobbie muses, "a thing discordant, irreconcilable with what I believed. I suffered the supreme hurt . . . the cynical hurt of utter disillusion."[52]

Harold Reginald Peat, a private in the 3rd Battalion of the First Canadian Contingent, and even more famous than Munroe as a war-booster, went through a similar and more public transition. His *Private Peat* (1917), written with his future wife while he was hospitalized, presented a tub-thumping call to arms, in which (it was said) Canadians put the "Vim" into "Vimy Ridge," and in which God Himself "is with those who fight for the Right and on the square," that is, not with the "German hordes . . . the unspeakable Hun—the barbarian, the crusher of hope and love and ideals," who richly merited everything the valiant Canadians meted out: "When we reached the enemy trench and presented the bright ends of our bayonets, Mr. Fritz went down on his knees and cried, 'Kamerad! Kamerad!' What did we do? We did exactly what you would have done under like circumstances. '*Kamerad!*'—Bah!" After all, the Hun had crucified three Canadian sergeants—Peat swore he himself had seen one of the bodies and knew of photographic evidence of the crucifixion. Yet for all his swagger and frightfulness, the Hun was also just a coward—reduced to a whimpering wreck when he caught sight of a Canadian bayonet. Even to speak of peace with such contemptible specimens was disloyal: "Every man, woman or child who talks peace before the complete defeat of Germany is a Kaiser agent, spreading German poison gas to the injury and possible destruction of his own countrymen," proclaimed Peat—with one eye on a still-vacillating U.S. public. The book reached the bestseller lists, and Peat went on to play himself, as a "red-blooded American," in *Private Peat*, a popular film.[53]

Then in 1923 Peat brought out *The Inexcusable Lie*. Since 1918 he had been reading and reflecting, and one of the writers who influenced him was Philip Gibbs, whose nuanced *Now It Can Be Told* (1920), with its searing portraits of "the Armageddon of our civilization," excused neither side for their excesses in the Great War. Gibbs pointedly included the brutal economic blockade of Germany after November 1918 and wondered about the sanity of the states that had accelerated the war: "What a mad villainy there had been among rival dynasties and powers and politicians and peoples to lead to this massacre! What had any one gained out of it all? Nothing except ruin."[54] For Peat it was now as plain as day. War was a "disease germ cultured in human mentality," one nurtured in the immature brains of children:

We have prepared the ground by vainglorious histories, propagated the seed with misleading bigotries, fertilized the virgin soil of youths' thoughts with the filth of national hatreds, saturated it with national contempts. We have stimulated the evil growth with scarce headlines, a bought Press, hysterical outbursts of effervescent patriotism. No wonder we have War, the canker, the cancerous growth of a foul devil force.[55]

In his fervent polemic against war, Peat singled out the Canadian history textbooks that had filled the heads of children with the romance of war and the war memorials that lied about its nature. He imagined what a realistic war memorial might look like, with the features of its figure

distorted with rage, the mouth twisted in curses; his enemy prone at his feet . . . his features caked with mud, spattered with blood and dead men's brains; contorted bodies of dead comrades heaped on shattered bodies of dead enemies . . . a head here, a limb there. Can any artist—dare any sculptor design and execute in stone, in bronze, the ghastly truth of the soldiers' fate in War? Will any town decorate its parkway, the city hall square, with that thing which truly visualizes War, truly commemorates with eternal greenness what War means?[56]

Private Peat—once the poster boy for the Great War—had by 1923 become the public face of its critics. He even had some dismissive, if disguised, things to say about Vimy.[57]

Another ex-soldier, James H. Pedley, struck a different critical note with his book *Only This: A War Retrospect* (1927). Pedley, a militia officer before the war, enlisted with the 216th Battalion, known as the "Bantams" because it was made up of men shorter than the official army height requirements. Serving as an officer in the 4th Battalion of the 1st Canadian Division, Pedley penned many a fond description of cozy officers' messes, one with "walls tastefully finished . . . windows with real curtains, and in the background a piano"—places full of fellowship and lusty, merry rounds of drinking. It was "not a bad war after all," Pedley says, after describing a fine breakfast of bully-beef croquettes, bacon, and coffee. Of a later time, when he remembered having almost no tasks to carry out, he writes: "My hardest job each day was getting out of bed." His memoir is steeped in cynicism, especially with respect to his fellow officers, one of whom is ruthlessly skewered as a petty tyrant; if that man had not been killed by the Germans, he would have been enthusiastically terminated by his fellow Canadians. Pedley describes a world of officers addicted to the spit-and-polish rituals of inspection and of the arrogant General Currie, old "Guts-and-Gaiters," with his supposedly inspirational words to the troops in 1918:

> And one day I paraded my scouts in the rain and read them (it was orders) that ludicrous, bombastic sham-Napoleonic message of Currie's done in the most approved opera-bouffe style in which he told the troops that they were the saviours of civilization and pre-pared their minds for slaughter: " . . . you will not die but will pass into immortality, and your mothers will be proud to have borne such sons . . ." Lord, how the boys laughed, and sneered.
> "He won't die, not likely!"
> "Bloody old bomb-proofer, trust him for a safe billet!"
> "We'll fool him, eh?"[58]

Pedley's critique of irrational militarism sometimes comes uncomfort-ably close to a personal vendetta against specific people whom he intensely disliked. But at other times he takes a step back, analysing the irrational structure within which they worked—one in which survival depended upon explicitly disobeying dangerous, even suicidal orders. The death of his dear friend John teaches him that war is not pageantry, but "terrible, too terrible." It seems even more terrible and irrational when the Cana-dians kill German stretcher-bearer Michel Wolfsteiner, who made the mistake of wandering into a Canadian shell-hole post. He attempted to surrender but was shot so that a "crazed B company officer" might atone for a botched trench raid. Wolfsteiner, who dies with a postcard from his wife in his pocket, inspires Pedley to reflect on his predicament:

> He had been wandering for hours in No Man's Land, had been taken prisoner, fired on by machine-guns, and bombed. As I write his photograph is before me, taken with a group of his comrades under a tree. The grass is long under his feet. Behind him a hedge, and pleasant woods in the distance. He is smiling, his cap is askew and he holds a cigarette.

"Is there a God?" Pedley wonders. "Must this kind of rough-and-ready justice be ascribed to all-seeing Deity, or to sportive chance? Who will dare to say?"[59]

Wilfred Kerr's *Shrieks and Crashes* (1929) struck yet another tone. Kerr, a signaller with the 11th Battery, Canadian Field Artillery, was a trained historian, a professor at the University of Buffalo, and later renowned as a scholar of responsible government. He was fond of quoting Herodotus and sought to project himself into the past, "to recover as accurately as possible the thoughts, the mental attitudes, the reactions, the experiences of my comrades and myself of twelve years ago." Not for him, then, the emotional polemics of other authors. He spurned sensationalistic attempts to depict the horrors of war and consistently reminded his readers that as an artillery-man he had experienced far less hardship than had the average front-line soldier. Unlike Peat and Pedley, Kerr was not out to rock the boat. On the vexing question of Canadian cold-blooded prisoner-killing, he reported the story but, in the absence of direct evidence, declined to confirm it. Nor did he question the importance of following orders in the army, because without them the "war could not be won."[60] He might be considered the safe mainstream Canadian writer on the war, questioning neither its underlying purpose nor, for the most part, how it actually transpired.

Yet what might even now be seen to be a temperate, rather dry account of the war was very differently regarded by official Ottawa. As Tim Cook reveals, A.F. Duguid, the official historian of the newly formed Army Historical Section, worked energetically to shape the history of the Great War. He was specifically anxious to protect the reputation of the CEF's upper leadership. After reading *Shrieks and Crashes*, he decided to deny Kerr access to war records.[61] Duguid perceived a critical edge in *Shrieks and Crashes*—a persistent questioning, all the more challenging because it came from such a moderate perspective, of the leadership of the war.

Kerr called into question what would later become a staple of Vimy-ism—the notion that Canadians were united as never before in their fight in France and Flanders. "There was a gulf between the officers and the other ranks," Kerr writes. "We could tell pretty well what was in their minds, but they, I am sure, were ill-informed of the currents of opinion among us. Accordingly, this book is an attempt to reflect the viewpoint of the common soldier, the 'plain buck private.'" He repeatedly notes the irrationality of the orders that ordinary soldiers were expected to carry out. English officers, especially, "imbued with their ideas of feudal class superiority," were apt to be a problem, especially those who, out of a feeling of inferiority, "felt impelled to a constant assertion" of legal authority. A sensible leader attuned to Canadians realized that "parades, polishes, smart-stepping and standing at attention, the frills so dear to the heart of the regular officer," would be accepted by them only to a certain degree. Ordinary soldiers came to regard orders as coming in two classes: those directly related to winning the war, and those that were mere matters of routine. If, on the line, orders were generally swiftly and enthusiastically obeyed, in the rest camps behind the lines one found "a fair amount of slackness, passive resistance, evasion, excuse making, with consequent tension between officers and other ranks."[62]

The chasm between officers and men was most grievously experienced in 1916 and 1917, when a series of appalling decisions undermined the credibility of the military leadership. When he discusses Passchendaele, a normally measured Kerr becomes openly indignant:

> The losses of the Corps at Passchendaele were in the neighbourhood of 16,500 men; all these in exchange for a few wretched heaps of bricks on a small rise in water-soaked Flanders! For some time the Corps was too stupefied to think; but gradually, in the months that followed, as the Corps regained its strength and reviewed in detail the action and the price, questions arose, doubts were implied which grew stronger with every passing week and were confirmed, the men thought, by the occurrences of the spring. Had we not been doing precisely the same as the Germans had done at Verdun, sending our best and bravest against a well-prepared enemy, who knew for weeks in advance where we were going to attack and could almost guess the date? Was this not mass slaughter, as theirs, even if ours were in less degree? And was this the best plans our Generals could devise, to sacrifice us in Battalions in a useless attack, under conditions where we could not possibly make any gain at all commensurate with the loss? Could our Generals not see how hopeless it was? Had they no originality, no ideas, no inventiveness? Did not the whole Flanders battle, from beginning to end, reflect serious doubt on their competence?[63]

Kerr was reminded of the "bitter jest" about the British troops: "An army of lions led by asses!" Here was a "vast and useless sacrifice of men in the war," and one that justified "growing distrust of the Generalship." For in 1916 and 1917, "our Generals failed lamentably. . . . Initiative and imagination were at a heavy discount in all the General Staffs." Nor was Vimy Ridge exempt from this critique. Had only the generals arranged for fresh columns to push on after the capture of the ridge, the British might well have captured a vast territory. But "the chance was missed; no use was made of our victory."[64]

All five of these writers—Service, Munroe, Peat, Pedley, and Kerr—had been direct participants in the war, and three of them were well-received public performers. All five subscribed to the rightness of the British Empire's war with the Central Powers, and both Munroe and Peat served as propagandists for the cause. Yet all five also shifted to more critical positions—Munroe privately, the others conspicuously. Service, Pedley, and Kerr all described Germans as human beings whose sufferings should be regretted, and Pedley and Kerr critiqued the very management of the war. But the key point is that none of them was remotely "Vimyist," in the sense of seeing one battle as Canada's birthdate or a turning point in the war, or the Great War itself as a seminal Canadian moment. Indeed, when Kerr mentions Vimy, it is as an example of the obtuseness of an unimaginative high command that threw away the victory and rendered it redundant. In the 1920s and 1930s, Vimyism in our present sense is seldom to be seen.

In the mid-1920s a legion of Protestant ministers, boosters of the war from 1914 to 1918, joined the early critics. In a widely read and much discussed book, *The Christian and War* (1926), six distinguished Protestant ministers in Montreal, two of whom had served with the CEF, fiercely argued that the use of force in general could only be defended "where it does not obscure the moral ends in view, where it can be controlled with reference to those ends, where the spirit of its use is consonant with the ends sought." Twentieth-century war, failing to satisfy those conditions, could never serve Christian ends. In modern war it made no difference whether you were innocent or guilty—you were punished either way—and the question of "right" could be determined by any means—"submarines, poison gas, burning oil, disease germs."[65] Contrary to the culture of memorialization, war did not ennoble soldiers; it degraded them. The issue of Canadian soldiers killing German prisoners came in for special attention, including an account, based on first-hand experience, of how the ironies had been discussed in the field:

> If it was permissible to blow a man's body to pieces with a five-nine [explosive shell], why was it reprehensible to kill him with mustard-gas? If it was permissible to kill him when he was un-wounded, why

was it not permissible to kill him after he was wounded? If he were not killed by us we had to employ stretcher-bearers and doctors and nurses and attendants to take care of him and thus deprive our own men of a certain amount of care. Moreover, we had to feed him! . . . Similarly with the prisoners. . . . What was the sense of taking prisoners when they could be more conveniently dealt with by getting them all into a corner and turning a Lewis gun on them? There would be less food for our own side if we had to feed prisoners![66]

The ministers, explicitly conceding that the Canadian side had committed this war crime, dwelt upon the "foul circumstances" that had impelled "decent men in peace, decent men in war" to kill their captives. The soldiers had justified themselves with a pragmatic cost-benefit analysis wholly out of keeping with the High Diction of the war. For a soldier, the idea of preserving the life of an enemy soldier he had just been trying to kill carried its own peculiar irony.[67] Romantic expectations *for* the war were utterly confounded by on-the-ground experiences *of* the war.

War bred such an intensity of hate that it became more and more unlikely that a righteous settlement could ever be reached. Although wars might begin with the powers committing themselves to "execute judgment and justice in the earth," they tended to end, the ministers said, with punitive treaties that sowed the seeds of yet more wars, and so—in conjunction with economic imperialism—war itself became "the most fruitful cause of more war."[68]

*   *   *

In the late 1920s the writers of what came to be called the "Literature of Disillusionment" sometimes answered Varley's question "For What?" with "For Nothing."[69] One of the most prominent authors of the time was Erich Maria Remarque, whose *All Quiet on the Western Front* (1929), the publishing sensation of its time, drew extensive Canadian interest.

Born in 1898 into a working-class family, Remarque was conscripted into the German Army at age eighteen; he served on the Western Front from June 1917 to the end of July, when he was injured and repatriated to a hospital in Germany for the rest of the war. The protagonist of *All Quiet* is Paul Bäumer, who tells of his time on the Western Front, in the company of his friends and schoolmates and an older soldier. Written in a spare modernist style, the novel focuses upon Paul's struggle to survive amid the dismal conditions of trench warfare. Some readers find in it a depressing, self-absorbed text that reflects its author's own suicidal tendencies, while others find in it a refreshingly candid view of the hardships of war, one that epitomizes the unchivalrous ironies of war.

Still in print in the 2010s, with sales of roughly forty million since 1929—and twenty-four printings in its first year of publication—the book became a much-contested site of memory. It was banned as pro-German in Poland, burned as anti-German and defeatist by the Nazis, and condemned by conservative militarists as an inaccurate and uninformed account of the war.[70] Canadians were also polarized. *All Quiet* was serialized in the *Winnipeg Tribune* and *Toronto Star Weekly*, and reviewed, generally favourably, in publications across the country; the Academy Award–winning film based on the book was a smash hit when it played at Toronto's Royal Alexandra Theatre. But the novel, which strayed into descriptions of defecation and unmarried sex, was also condemned; it was excluded, amid controversy, from the Ontario school system. At a time when Canadians read many more U.S. periodicals and consumed far more films from Britain and the United States than their own homegrown fare, *All Quiet*, both the book and the film, was undoubtedly a more significant force in shaping their outlook on the Great War than most made-in-Canada efforts.[71]

Charles Yale Harrison's *Generals Die in Bed* (1928) is widely regarded as the Canadian *All Quiet on the Western Front*. Philadelphia born Harrison was raised in Montreal, worked at the *Montreal Star*, and fought on the Western Front as a member of the Royal Montreal Regiment. He was injured in the Battle of Amiens in August 1918 and dedicated his book to "The bewildered youths—British, Australian, Canadian and German— who were killed in that wood a few miles beyond Amiens on August 8th, 1918." Like Remarque, Harrison became a lightning rod for emotional critics and conservative historians.[72] He also confronted attempts to suppress his novel altogether, although these were unsuccessful, and his book remains a widely read classic of the Great War—the one Canadian book in the genre that often receives attention in the international critical literature.

The novel was, according to Jonathan Scotland, "modernist in style, political in argument, and contentious in content." Many readers sent the author letters of appreciation; one veteran remarked that finally someone "who knows what he is talking about" had written a war story.[73] Although Harrison's book rarely ventures into outright anti-war editorializing, it undeniably presents the Western Front as a series of grotesque incidents.

In one scene a group of soldiers take a bit of time off to go swimming in a river back of the Front. They see "something dark in the water near the bank."

> It is a dead body. It is wearing the field blue French uniform. We see the thin red stripe wriggling up the trouser-leg. An underwater growth has caught a bit of the uniform and the body sways to and fro, moved by the current. In the water it looks bloated and enormous. . . .
>
> He is different, this Frenchman, from the hundreds of corpses we have seen in the line. We thought we were safe. We thought we could forget the horrors of the line for a brief few weeks—and here this swollen reminder drifts from the battlefield to spoil a sunny afternoon for us.[74]

Still, the soldiers "must carry on, carry on . . ." They had their roles and their duties drilled into their heads "in a thousand ways": "The salute, the shining of our brass buttons, the correct way to twist a puttee, and so on. A thousand thundering orders! A thousand trivial rules, each with a penalty for an infraction, has made will-less robots of us all. All, without exception."[75]

Generals Die in Bed demolished a central theme of war commemoration: the equality of sacrifice in death. In the postwar decades many rank-and-file veterans seemed on the brink of insurgency, and the Great War itself had become a subject of intense debate. At such a time it was unendurable, especially for generals and their friends, to be reminded of the stark hierarchies that had prevailed in the Great War. And some readers since 1928 have been unsettled to the point of violence about Harrison's fiercely humanistic scepticism about the Great War, with Arthur Currie in particular describing the novel as "a mass of filth, lies . . ."[76]

Harrison not only pointed out the different fates awaiting generals and enlisted men, but also attacked another central conceit of Canadian martial nationalism—that Canadian soldiers exercised far more individual initiatives than did their robotic European counterparts. His passage on the Canadian looting of Arras also shook images of a well-disciplined army helping out French civilians.[77]

At one point his narrator imagines the capturing of a sniper and how the German will "crawl out of his hiding-place." The Canadians "will fall upon him and bayonet him like a hapless trench rat."

He will hold his trembling hands on high and stammer the international word for compassion and mercy. He will say that beautiful
word *comrade*, a word born in suffering and sorrow, but we will stab
him down shouting to one another, "Hey, look, we found a sniper!"
And our faces will harden, our inflamed eyes will become slits and
men will stab futilely at his prostrate body.[78]

In another incident a "wounded sniper" crawls on his knees towards
a group of soldiers who have their rifles trained on him. The German
"is middle-aged and has a gray walrus mustache—fatherly-looking. His
hands are folded in the gesture which pleads for pity." He tells the Canadians he has "three children"—"*Drei Kinder*"—but they close in on him
nevertheless and show no mercy.

> We are on top of him.
>   Broadbent runs his bayonet into the kneeling one's throat. The
> body collapses.
>   Some of us kick at the prostrate body as we pass it. It quivers a
> little with each kick.[79]

Harrison's graphic depiction of prisoner-killing by Canadians was perhaps the most controversial, and disbelieved, element of his book. Yet,
although his scenes were attacked for their supposed sensationalism, a
passage based on documented fact in Cook's non-fiction *At the Sharp End*
outdoes the novelist in intensity:

> One German tried to escape the slaughter by jumping out of the
> trench, dodging in and out amongst us to avoid being shot, crying
> out 'Nein! Nein!' He pulled out from his breast pocket a handful
> of photographs and tried to show them to us in an effort to gain our
> sympathy. . . . As the bullets smacked into him he fell to the ground
> motionless, the pathetic little photographs fluttering down to the
> earth around him.[80]

Harrison's fictional version of the battlefield, as it turns out, was not all
that far-fetched. Indeed, at the centenary of the Great War's beginning,
Annick Press, a leading Canadian children's and young adult fiction publisher, reissued *Generals Die in Bed*—describing it as a "landmark novel" of
historic importance: "With veterans of WW I no longer here to tell their

stories, this book stands as a lasting monument to the horrors of war."[81]

Perhaps the most interesting Canadian example of the "literature of disillusionment" came from Will R. Bird. The Nova Scotia–born Bird fought in France, was decorated for bravery at Mons, and in the 1920s became a one-man "remembrance program," a folksy, much-favoured after-dinner speaker at service clubs.[82] He was incensed that many of the officers' books purporting to remember the war fundamentally distorted it by leaving out the ordinary soldier. The everyday Canuck, he argued, was being written out of the histories of the war. He demanded that the enlisted men be given access to the records and allowed to gain their moment in the sun.

Of the various war books he brought out, *And We Go On: A Story of the War by a Private in the Canadian Black Watch; a Story Without Filth or Favor* (1930) was the most ambitious. Bird, a Methodist, teetotaler, and small-town conservative, took direct aim at Remarque for producing a negative portrayal of "the soldier as a coarse-minded, profane creature, seeking only the solace of loose women or the courage of strong liquor." Remarque and by implication Harrison had insulted the veterans, Bird cried, by claiming that the war had reduced them to animals and by focusing on their drinking and sexuality. His memoir—more appropriately considered a novel based upon actual experiences—would set them straight.[83]

But then Bird undertook incensed denunciations of sadistic and unbalanced officers on the Canadian side. His descriptions of the killing fields are more shocking in a way than those in Harrison because they were presented without any sense of an underlying political agenda. Bird's readers were repeatedly assaulted with memories of the horrible *smells* of the war. At Ypres, an "awful, death-ridden ground where shaky duckboards still survived among obscene slimy places more horrible than words could paint," what most bothered Bird was the "fearful stench of death . . . hovering, clinging. . . . Standing there in the twilight one could *feel* the damp odors, and with them a mysterious eddying clamminess." On his first day on the Front, at Vimy, he was sent to collect body parts from a field, the "most-tortured scene that man has trod."[84]

Some reviewers were displeased by Bird's acid criticisms of officers, thinking them overdone; but his loyal following among ordinary soldiers would have disagreed. Reviewers also commented on scenes in which the author pondered the irony of Christian Germans and Christian Canadians praying to one and the same God before slaughtering each other.

Bird offers no intimations of existential despair—or scandalous depictions of soldiers defecating, drinking to excess, or consorting with prostitutes, of the sort to be found in both *All Quiet on the Western Front* and *Generals Die in Bed*. But what there *is* in Bird is a sustained critique of the Great War, coming from someone sharing the middle-class values of mainstream Canada. The existence or non-existence of God, the possibility of a world without war—none of these big questions interested Bird in the slightest (although he did share with many contemporaries a belief that the spirits of the dead might guide the living). What did interest him was a grossly mismanaged war, injustices meted out to ordinary soldiers, and the sheer awfulness of the experience.

Veterans thronged to his lectures, lauded his books, and some even wrote to Prime Minister R.B. Bennett to nominate Bird as the CEF's official historian. Bird criss-crossed the country with his illustrated lectures, often whipping up outrage as he went on about the sanitized military past that was being written to the specifications of the Top Brass. He even thought that many of the medals handed out in the war reflected a recognition of the social status, not the courage, of the recipient—an inflammatory opinion indeed among military men who cherished such honours.

One time when he was on leave, Bird—or the man depicted as Bird in *And We Go On*—was talking about Passchendaele with an admiring Briton. The Brit told Bird that as a soldier in the famous battle, he had "lived in a great day." "I don't think so," Bird replied. And then he added, in a most striking departure from twenty-first-century Vimyism, "This war is wrong."[85]

In 1931 Will Bird returned to tour the lands where he had fought as a private in the Black Watch Regiment of Canada, and the mass circulation *Maclean's* magazine went on to publish an account of his trip in installments. Most readers apparently found the story to be quite enjoyable.[86] One critical reader thought it a pity that Bird was still on the warpath against the officers—denouncing his "sneering witticisms at the expense of the commissioned ranks." But another correspondent, a child when the Great War was underway, said Bird had accomplished the impossible and brought faraway places to life.[87]

After thirteen years—and for the rest of his life—Bird retained vividly critical memories of the war. "War—I hated it, despised it, loathed it," he had written the previous year in *And We Go On*—"and yet felt I was part of it." Now, surveying the landscapes of war in Europe, he was shouting out: "Ruins, ruins, ruins! . . . Desolation, wreckage, disaster—war!" The years had done little to dull his sense of the jagged edges of war. After visiting Ypres, he said: "Only the sky above you seems fit and clean. It is a place of horror, tortured with sinister gullies and gulches, upheaved, blasted, disemboweled, an unsightliness few tourists ever see."[88]

Bird's book *Thirteen Years After*, based on the *Maclean's* articles, provides both a traveller's impression of the old Great War battlegrounds and a close inspection of how people and places had coped with the conflict. A few war-damaged villages had overcome the past, Bird thought, but many delinquent towns had simply not shaped up. Such places were populated with dour, primitive folk, faint-hearted French and Belgians glumly trapped in the past.

Everywhere in the Salient in 1931 Bird came across dispirited people. At Messines, with its "enormous graveyard of countless dead," he found "a dreadful, solemn depression." The gloom was readily apparent in the faces of the inhabitants. "All year long they see people coming to visit the dead; all year they work their ground with careful touch, never knowing when they will uncover a corpse or a live shell. It has made them the dour, dead-eyed race they are." In the vicinity of Cherisy, "a dirty town" with a "vile" street, the barn doors, duck puddles, crows, magpies, pigeons, and peasants were all blended into the mire of failure and defeat.[89]

> Even the people seem different in this war region. They are a duller lot, almost stupid, it seems, from the effects of their struggle with war debris. One old man told me of losing a fine colt down an old dugout shaft, of his son being killed by the exploding of a shell in the garden, and how another of his family died from blood poisoning, a scratch from old barbed wire. They hate the war, loathe it; don't want to talk about it at all.[90]

How then should Europeans, and visiting Canadian tourists, engage with the history of the Great War? Clearly, not by brooding over the unsurprising feeling that, after thirteen years, the cataclysm was still slowly unfolding in the lives of individuals and communities. Rather, they should go to places where effective individuals were up and doing things. In Armentières, for instance, the buildings were "all very new and the shops were city-like. The main square was really impressive. We seemed, after the sameness of the Salient towns, to have entered another world. Every place had a flag flying, all the population seemed in holiday attire. . . . Everyone seemed cheerful happy, responsive."[91]

What a relief, then, for Bird—the small-town conservative, booster of small business and forward-looking communities, and generally a master of positive thinking—to arrive at Vimy Ridge itself, where he found tangible evidence of progress.[92] For here was a clear, forceful statement of a country with something to say and the capacity to say it. For Bird, the Vimy Memorial (not yet completed) promised to be so magnificent "that Europe, viewing the finished work, will change her impression of Canadians as a people." The tourist would want to experience the "wonderful, marvellous" concrete trenches of Vimy. If the tourist happened to be a male Vimy veteran like Bird, he would be "thrilled beyond words" by the exactitude of the restoration. Bird recalled the response of a "great French artist" who spent three days at the ridge: "He was shown a picture of the model of the memorial. Tears ran down his face and he said with deep emotion: 'I am glad. It is the finest of them all beyond words—and it is in France.'"[93]

*   *   *

The key actors in shaping the ironic distancing from the High Diction so prevalent in interwar Canada were the returned soldiers—or veterans, to use a term that only came into vogue after the 1930s. If the very people who had fought the war no longer believed in it, or in the social and political order in whose name it had supposedly been fought—then any notion of it as the inspiring myth of the nation was in trouble.

Over half a million returned military men and women, out of a Canadian population of roughly eight million, had a huge impact on their return to Canadian society.[94] As a result, with the creation in 1918 of the Department of Soldiers' Civil Re-establishment (DSCR), the state took on new or greatly expanded activities, including the administration of pensions and the provision of training and employment programs. Yet an irony of such welfare measures was that they were predicated upon a philosophy of individual self-sufficiency. A Soldier Settlement Act (1917) introduced back-to-the-land schemes whereby each successful applicant got a 320-acre farm and a loan for stock and equipment; as many as 25,000 settlers may have been involved in the program by 1921. That project, though, proved largely unsuccessful, with a failure rate in the neighbourhood of 80 per cent or higher; in some cases veterans were directed to substandard land in remote infertile locations.[95]

In an October 1921 "Declaration of Principles," the Great War Veterans' Association (GWVA) presented a strange mixture of High Diction and down-to-earth criticisms of the ways things stood, combined with demands for the making of a better world. While nobly renouncing any "claim to special or peculiar favours," the veterans pledged their "unswerving loyalty to King and Country" and reminded the country that its soldiers had "fought . . . and died to establish forever among us the ideals of sacrifice, unselfishness and brotherhood." They urged fellow Canadians to pay more attention to "the great history and literature of our country and empire" and to teach the young to revere the flag. They disdained Bolshevists and other troublemakers. Yet they also wanted to receive "such pensions and allowances, as will enable them to live according to the accepted standard of our people." They strongly disapproved of the "increasing love of luxury which permeates all classes of our community and the riotous extravagance everywhere shown in gratifying this mania, thus courting as a nation, final disaster." The remedy for this cultural decay lay in "a return to Spartan simplicity." The veterans wanted more planning, unemployment insurance, and the abolition of commercial employment agencies.[96]

Spending about $60 million per year on veteran relief over the first postwar decade, in a country whose debt load had jumped from about $220 million in 1914 to roughly $3 billion in 1920, was strong medicine for traditional liberals raised on maxims of laissez-faire and balanced budgets. For many high-ranking Canadians, yesterday's inspiring heroes swiftly became today's onerous liabilities as the damages that war had wrought came fully into view. At first there was only limited understanding, fiercely contested, about the psychological effects of war. War veteran and journalist Gregory Clark remembered that even the phrase "shell shock" aroused the soldiers' hostility. The treatment required for venereal diseases entailed both stigma and financial cost. Those who evaded detection brought such ailments back with them to Canada, where their partners also became casualties of the Great War. "I must say I surely have done my share of suffering with sickness," said a wife who was suffering from such a "blood infection," adding that it "seems it is growing worse, as I am nearly a wreck now."[97]

Clark recalled in the 1960s, "with a great sense of tragedy," how swiftly the authorities' attitude towards the veterans changed within a few months of the war. Now they came to be viewed as "lead swingers" and "bums." Many of them had not reported health problems during the war, not really seeing the point of it—Clark himself emerged from Vimy Ridge without hearing in his left ear. If they required support they now faced authorities demanding stringent documentation from any claimant. In such a world, "the war never ends for the wounded." Even General Currie, disinclined to sympathize with the veterans' campaign for better state support, was provoked by the rough justice meted out to those who could not establish beyond any doubt that their ailments were war-related. He knew of one man, a veteran of four years in the trenches, who had suffered TB for eight years. Yet the man's medical history did not record that he had suffered from lung trouble during the war, and so he was denied support: "That," Currie wrote in 1929, "to my mind, is simply a damnable thing."[98]

The veterans' struggle now was often waged against a formidable bureaucracy and even against a consolidating veteran elite as well as against a general public that had other things to worry about. What happened in Canada was a worldwide phenomenon: after briefly making heroes of the veterans, many host societies quickly lost all patience with them.[99] Some veterans contrasted the "true fellowship" they had experienced in Europe with the stone-cold treatment they were accorded at home.

The most glaring contradiction, in Britain as in Canada, was that in the "Land Fit for Heroes," a large percentage of veterans found themselves jobless and poor. In 1920 the government had a pension budget of $25 million, with over 177,035 recipients.[100] In the veterans' "second battle" for economic survival they often found themselves disparaged and ignored, with pensions that were less than adequate.

By 1923 roughly 20 per cent of the veterans across the country were unemployed.[101] The Secretary-Treasurer of the GWVA reported in 1922 that 1,100 veterans were without work in Halifax, and he warned of dire consequences if the government did not do something to address their condition, an "evil" that had reached a stage where it seriously impairs the national vitality." When the ranks of the unemployed in general began to organize protests, Lt.-Gen. G.E. Burns, a District Intelligence Officer in the Montreal District, conveyed some of officialdom's exasperation with the unruly veterans. He thought about 20 per cent of the recent demonstrations had been made up of veterans, who were undeserving of public sympathy. They consisted of "sun fish" and "wharf rats"—that is, layabouts.[102]

Postwar pensions mirrored wartime divisions between officers and men: privates received a maximum of $480 per year; officers might receive twice as much. One veteran denounced the situation as "unfair, unjust, unsound, undemocratic, unreasonable, unBritish, unacceptable, outrageous, and rotten." When Gen. R.O. Alexander asked whether most veterans thought the government had stood by the men who fought in 1914–18, he conceded that most would say, emphatically, that it had not. His own mid-1930s statistics showed that most of Canada's 77,000 pensioners were receiving annual pensions that were insufficient to sustain life.[103]

The veterans responded to these issues, especially in 1918–20, by channeling a sometimes inchoate populist rage, sometimes against national and racial minorities and sometimes against authority in general. In Halifax, on 25 May 1918, a crowd of thousands broke windows, threw stones at the police, overturned vehicles, and finally attempted to burn down the city hall by lighting piles of straw stacked up against the building. Another serious episode of veterans' rioting took place in the same city the following February, with dozens hospitalized and property damages over $20,000, prompting the ultra-conservative *Halifax Herald* to cry, at the sight of rioters wearing the unmistakable trench caps and overcoats from the Front, "No! No! No! Not the Work of Huns in France and Belgium but the Work of Hoodlums in Halifax."[104] Veterans' rebellions punctuated the 1920s and, in the shape of a more general movement of the unemployed, would persist into the 1930s.

Although the Canadian Legion, founded in 1925, would become known as the primary voice of the veteran, in the 1920s and 1930s veterans organized a plethora of movements that often gave voice to their underlying rage at both the system and the way in which the war was being remembered. One veteran, surveying the dismal conditions of the jobless in Calgary, exclaimed, "My God! Is that what we went overseas for? It would have been better had we been defeated."[105]

The GWVA, formed in April 1917, had boasted as many as 200,000 members in 1919, but by 1924 it had become both an organization associated with the ordinary soldier (as opposed to the officer) and embroiled in a complicated controversy over the handling of monies from wartime canteens. As historian David Thompson demonstrates, a host of more radical groups flourished in the 1920s, including the Committee of Unemployed Veterans of Canada (which organized an on-to-Ottawa march in 1922), the explicitly revolutionary National Union of Ex-Servicemen (CNUX) in Western Canada, and the Montreal Ex-Service Men's Unemployment Association (MEMUA). Established as a result of a mid-1920s visit by Lord Douglas Haig, the British army's field marshal in the Great War, the Canadian Legion represented a more conservative approach to veterans' issues. As Sir Percy Lake, its first president, explained in 1926, it aimed to rein in the veterans' demands upon the public purse and discourage "unworthy or undeserving claims," but, even so, it was neither fully united behind a conservative program nor reluctant to remind the federal government of the explosive consequences of ignoring veterans' issues. Lake went on to warn the government that "hard cases" among the veterans threatened to create a "Red feeling in cities like Winnipeg and Vancouver."[106] In the 1930s the Communist-linked Workers' Ex-Servicemen's League was popular in both cities.

Yet, benefiting from government recognition, the Legion slowly supplanted its rivals. It was consciously designed as a body that would soothe the veterans' temper and moderate their demands. If the government wanted to combat the Reds, it could look to Lake's organization—but Ottawa would have to demonstrate it had grasped the seriousness of the veterans' complaints and understood the kind of challenge they could mount against the system.[107]

*   *   *

In the 1920s Alice Chown hitched her star to the League of Nations, even though, as she told Samuel in 1919, she was well aware of how much the organization had been wounded by the defective Treaty of Versailles and U.S. non-participation. In Toronto she became a staunch supporter of the Women's International League for Peace and Freedom, a group founded in the United States during the Great War and which had struggled to find a peaceable end to the conflict. It now launched campaigns against cadet training in schools. As she entered her sixties she was still indomitably radical, pushing for the outlawing of all aggressive weapons, specially "air bombing and poison gas." Yet she also believed in the importance of crafting a "propaganda for ordinary people."[108]

Alice and Samuel, the two cousins so divided during the war, were united after it. They shared a sense that peace must be placed at the centre of the politics of all decent people. And the movements striving for it must be things of this world, not anticipations of the next.

Samuel Chown found it difficult to give up on war. Andrew Macphail had a tough time seeing his martial dreams collide with the realities of executions and mismanagement. The Montreal ministers who had delivered the 1926 anti-war statement, men of substance and two of them veterans of the Front, had trouble with the idea of reversing their religion's teachings on war. For Bird it could not have been easy to begin his time at Vimy collecting the fragments of body parts. Many readers ever since 1928 have been uneasy with Harrison's radical and humanistic scepticism about the war.

In the more comfortable world of High Diction, all the sacrifices of the blood-stained twentieth century can somehow be redeemed in a radiant future. Confronting modernity can sometimes seem to be an exercise in spiritual desolation, as a harsh unforgiving light is shed upon things we would prefer to surround in the aura of patriotism. For a martial generation, the answer to Varley's *For What?* was *For God, King, and Empire*—all of them words designating certainties. But for legions of those who had been through this experience, and those who had pondered it from afar, the better answer to Varley's question was: *So that, in witnessing and understanding this abomination, we might do whatever is necessary so that nothing like it should ever happen again.* For decades after, a mass movement of Canadians sought to put that answer to the test of practice—and prominent among them were a great many Great War veterans themselves.

4

THE WOUNDS OF MEMORY, THE PUSH FOR PEACE

And he would speak with real bitterness, bitterness I've never seen
in another man about the stupidity of the whole performance which
he had embarked on himself! . . . by God he had come to some
pretty violent conclusions about it . . . about the idea of war.

— GEORGE FERGUSON, speaking of his friend and
fellow Great War veteran, economist Harold Innis

EARLY in 1934 the war records department in Ottawa released a series
of pictures to the Canadian Press wire service—items from its collection of roughly 6,000 photographs. The department appealed
to people who recognized themselves or the depicted locations to supply
Ottawa with details. The Canadian Press made the photos available to
newspapers across the country, and each of these gatekeepers had to make
their own decisions: how many pictures to display, how to present them,
and what to say about them.[1]

In the early months of the year two major Canadian newspapers, the
Toronto Star and the *Winnipeg Free Press*, ran the photographs, combining them with other Great War images drawn from American Laurence
Stallings's *The First World War: A Photographic History* (1933) and other
sources.[2] While Canadian writers such as Harrison, Peat, and Bird, and
others such as Hemingway and Remarque, had already drawn in thousands of Canadian readers, the photos would reach hundreds of thousands. Several hundred Canadians took the time to write letters to the
editor, revealing an overwhelmingly dominant theme—in essence, the
endorsement of a sceptical critique of war—but also some fascinating differences of opinion.

In Toronto the *Star* claimed to be breaking new journalistic ground with the 370 graphic war images it printed. "This is the first war that was ever photographed," said the *Star*, dramatically if inaccurately. If in the past, contemporaries in search of insight into war had been restricted to the work of painters and writers, now they could encounter a rather more "objective" reality itself, preserved by the camera's eye.[3]

The Star was clearly aware that it was taking a risk in publishing such candid photographs of the war—that it was in danger of reopening "the wounds of memory," especially those of the broken-hearted and bereaved. To reassure its readers, it ran endorsements from a number of eminent Ontarians. Sir William Mulock, Ontario's former lieutenant governor, commended the "marvellous reproductions of the dread details of war." He believed the series would introduce the public to "the horror, the waste, the shame, the sin of war," and, though the images might hurt, there was an overpowering need to warn Canadians against any glamorizing of military conflict.[4]

Rather more surprising endorsements came in an article outlining the response of veteran patients at the Christie Street Military Hospital. Many of the men there had been disfigured by the war. "No picture is too gruesome to be published," said one hospitalized veteran. "Our children should be made to look at them until they hate them, until they have the most utter contempt for war and all it stands for." The chaplain at the hospital, Rev.-Capt. Sidney Lambert, declared: "People have no conception of the horrors of war, or the filthy conditions under which men lived and died." Lambert, wounded in the war, thought it "foolish for persons to say that the soldier is being made to remember the horrors he is trying so hard to forget. It is not the soldiers who are being retaught war horrors, but the youth of to-day who are being taught them for the first time."[5] If any group had a natural investment in a myth that sanctified the Great War as the birth of the nation, in which they played the role of heroic martyrs, it would surely have been this one. Yet none of the wounded veterans invoked this myth.

The series was hard-hitting. The images of dead and disfigured soldiers and civilians might well be censored in a twenty-first-century publication, certainly in a North America squeamish about depicting the bodily consequences of battles. Often the photographs were framed by headlines that forcefully underlined the gruesome nature of the scenes depicted. "Roast Men, Boiled Men, Tortured Men—War!" proclaimed one. "Man Demonstrated That He Was Still a Cave Man," said another. "What is the Net Result Save Death and Ruin?" asked a third.

Still, in the series the *Star* was careful to avoid images of mutilated or killed—and identifiable—Canadians. The paper's Gregory Clark, who wrote most of the captions, identified with suffering soldiers on both sides. Clark had spent three years on the Western Front, and as a major with the Canadian Mounted Rifles he had won the Military Cross for conspicuous gallantry at Vimy Ridge. Ernest Hemingway, for a time his colleague on the *Star*, considered him one of the best journalists at the paper, as did a growing legion of readers and listeners entranced by his sports stories and radio broadcasts tinged with gentle humour.[6]

Yet Clark's captions in 1934 were hardly gentle. They were both funny and biting. Clark's humour had the cobalt hue of someone for whom the war was suffused with the bitterest irony—as, again and again, we behold people unaware of the fate about to befall them. Of a picture of a recruiting meeting on the steps of Toronto City Hall in 1915—titled "Your King and Country Need You"—Clark asked, with quiet sarcasm, "What is missing in this picture? Why the Cenotaph, which entirely changes the appearance of the city hall square!" Commenting on a shot of an excited crowd outside Buckingham Palace on the night of the declaration of war, Clark wrote: "Whatever our honest and noble intentions this night, if any eye in this throng could have foreseen four years ahead, and a roll of 1,000,000 British men dead, could we have cheered as we did? Now we know that a declaration of war is the occasion of national mourning." An image of an Austrian firing squad executing Czechs prompted Clark's scathing denunciation of how the Great War had been sold to the young: "In war, you have to be strong, because if you don't nip anti-war sentiment in the bud, goodness knows how it might spread. Bullets or white feathers, it matters not how you stampede the lads in. The main thing is, get them in. Then let them try any sentiment!"[7]

The *Star* repeatedly underlined the theme that the line between civilians and warriors had been erased in an age of mechanized warfare. A caption under a shot of a torpedoed British merchant ship sinking beneath the waves stated, with a prescient foreboding:

> Hundreds of pictures like this were published in Germany and sent to the front to prove that if the boys would just do their job in the trenches, it would not be long before France and Britain would be starving, their munitions exhausted, and both of them ready to surrender. In the next war, the scheme will be to bomb enemy cities from the air until even the babies will be begging for peace.[8]

Fig. 1. "After a Night Raid by the 78th Battalion—The idea of raids was to discover for the high command what troops were opposite. But the best of raids hardly expected to get a surprise like this. He bears little resemblance to the cartoons we used to see of the hated Hun." *Toronto Daily Star*, 23 Feb. 1934.

A representation of the sinking of the German cruiser *Blücher* in 1915—an event that took 750 German sailors to their deaths in the North Sea—prompted Clark to put the image to work as a reminder that "war plays around with us all, making us blood brothers one day and the most desperate of enemies another day. And it is the common sailor, the common soldier, Tom, Dick and Harry, who starve and freeze and suffer and die."[9]

Clark stressed the shared humanity of soldiers on either side of the Western Front. He worked especially hard to debunk the "Myth of the Hun," according to which the German people were predisposed by nature or history to cruelty and aggression. Sometimes this led him to deflate German pretensions to military prowess. Clark pointed out how fear-inspiring German soldiers had been transformed into "sad gray hosts bearing their wounded to Canadian dressing stations in September 1918." He said of one diminutive German prisoner, caught in a May 1919 trench raid: "He bears little resemblance to the cartoons we used to see of the hated Hun."[10] [Fig. 1.] A picture of a dead German with a Canadian soldier handling a Mauser rifle standing over him carried the caption: "What Price Glory?" [Fig. 2.]

Fig. 2. "What Price Glory?—This German, like his comrades, had dug himself a little rifle pit, as he retreated beyond Valenciennes, in October, 1918, but it wasn't good enough to hold back the Canadian cavalry that came streaming over the autumn fields. There he lies. A Canadian is examining the Mauser rifle that wasn't good enough. Or was it the man, perhaps?" *Toronto Daily Star*, 25 Feb. 1934.

An image of the Canadian and German wounded helping one another across the mud of Passchendaele prompted Clark to write. "All Brothers.— And a good thing it was, too, because if you fell wounded in this Passchendaele mud, you ran the chance of never rising again." [Fig. 3.] A caption for a similar shot from Hill 70, showing two Canadian soldiers helping a German soldier, pointed out that the soldiers "almost seem as though they were hugging one another. Such is the tender power of imminent death over men."[11]

Clark used an image of a crowd of "damaged Canadians . . . waiting outside a dressing station in Ypres" in November 1917, after Passchendaele, to describe their attitude towards the one German to be seen standing amongst them:

> There seems to be little hate here. But of course these are just common front line soldiers. Every mile you went back of the line, the hate grew stronger, until at last, when you got right back to civilization,

Fig. 3. "All Brothers.—And a good thing it was, too, because if you fell wounded in this Passchendaele mud, you ran the change of never rising again." *Toronto Daily Star*, 26 Jan. 1934.

> there you found hate in its pure, unadulterated essence. These boys called him Jerry. Back home, they called him the Hun.

Here Clark was directly echoing (and just slightly altering) an insight from *Generals Die in Bed*.[12]

Even when Clark did not frame photographs in a humanistic manner, readers might well have been brought to do so on their own. For example, the paper featured one photograph depicting "two schoolboy Germans" offering a "very awkward lift to a Canadian wounded in the foot" as evidence of an anti-romantic vision of the war: the clumsily carried Canadian was "Hardly the Subject for a Painting." [Fig. 4.] Yet with his emphasis on "schoolboy Germans" who were helping a Canadian, Clark was effectively suggesting that the soldiers were simply young human beings caught up in a situation far beyond their control.[13]

Images of the acute sufferings of Germans during and after the war brought together Clark's two great themes—anti-militarism and humanism. Under the headline "War Is No Longer a Sport for Glittering Heroes,"

Fig. 4. "Hardly the Subject for a Painting.—Two schoolboy Germans giving a very awkward lift to a Canadian, wounded in the foot in the September advance, 1918. When artists paint pictures of heroes carrying out wounded comrades, they get more grace into it. But grace is most unusual in war." *Toronto Daily Star*, 16 Feb. 1934.

an image of baby-bearing German refugees fleeing from East Prussia was placed in a religious context: "Between Herod and the Twentieth Century Lies a Long Time for Learning.—But still the little babies flee the wrath of power and pride." The *Star* did not spare its readers sights from the Eastern Front, where Canada's Czarist allies carried out atrocities. A photograph of an execution of German civilians by Russians carried the caustic caption: "If they aren't in uniform, they would be as soon as possible, said the Russians, who stood these civilians up and shot them down. It looks as if certain people can't be trusted with a war, doesn't it?"[14]

An image of a dead German soldier sprawled on the ground was headlined: "Now I Lay Me Down to Die." That he was a German was incidental: millions of soldiers died "with their faces to the earth, as little children lie down to weep. . . . There are war debts, of course, but here is cash." Of the body of another dead German soldier, Clark speculated: "Maybe He Was a Lady's Man!—At any rate, this German was only a boy. The French took this picture at Verdun. Like thousands upon thousands of his

Fig. 5. "Shambles for Man and Beast.—Carrying out their wounded comrades, these men would have a twinge of conscience as they looked at the poor horse and wondered to themselves what horses had ever done that they should be drawn into men's wars. And after a battle, horses were strewn along all the roads." *Toronto Daily Star*, 29 Jan. 1934.

comrades, at that desperate objective of his imperial highness, the Crown Prince, this lad will sing no more of Schubert's songs." Considering a photograph depicting a crowd of German-Americans leaving to fight for their "fatherland," Clark launched into his own haunting memory of a German captured in a trench at Vimy Ridge. Clark had clearly heard the German saying, "I suppose you boys know Buffalo?" Then the soldier died, "with a queer twist on his lips. We buried him tenderly."[15]

A consistent theme of the *Star* photo-spread was the ordinariness of the beings caught up in the war. The photo "Bringing His Bread with Him" depicted two Germans helping a wounded Canadian at Arleux in 1917; one of them, under the impression that the British were short of bread, carried a loaf with him. "Shambles for Man and Beast" [Fig. 5] showed tired stretcher-bearers carrying a wounded comrade, with a caption pondering whether the men "would have a twinge of conscience as they looked at the poor horse and wondered to themselves what horses had ever done that they should be drawn into men's wars"—a question that haunted one

Fig. 6. "Canadian and German Boys at War.—In 1918, down the tree-lined roads out from Cambrai came the hordes of youth of Germany to look with wonder at the youthful faces of their conquerors. This remarkable photograph is surely one of the bitterest arguments against war ever advanced." *Toronto Daily Star*, 30 Jan. 1934.

of the key figures in *All Quiet on the Western Front*. For some readers, the single most arresting photograph was captioned "Canadian and German Boys at War." [Fig. 6.] It showed captured German teenagers, one of them shooting a worried glance towards his captors, being led down the "roads out from Cambrai" by equally youthful Canadians. Clark remarked, "This remarkable photograph is surely one of the bitterest arguments against war ever advanced."[16]

The *Star* editors' heavy-handed didacticism says something about the emotions they hoped to elicit from the paper's mass audience. They wanted readers to question—and then reject—war. But what did Canadians make of this message? Not all of the letter writers who responded to the *Star* series liked it. Some outraged patriots took the trouble to write to the paper. Yet if we place in the "thumbs down" category all those who expressed serious qualms about the series, those entries comprise less than 10 per cent of the total number of people whose letters appeared in the paper.

For its part, the conservative Toronto *Telegram* published a letter from one "Major Mc" on its front page. The major denounced the *Star's* experiment for awakening "unpleasant memories in the minds of those who lost relatives or whose health has been sadly affected by war time service." The *Mail and Empire*, the *Star's* other local right-wing adversary, sniffed disapprovingly that its rival was printing images that nobody would ever want to place in a scrapbook.

*　　*　　*

Other newspapers also started printing war photographs. The pictures clearly had a market. Indeed, so heavy was the demand for scrapbook-friendly photographs that the *Star* offered to print images on one side of the page only. Then too, on 15 February 1934, the crusading newspaper was pleased to announce that the Toronto School Board had decided to make the war series available in all schools.[17]

The *Star* rightly concluded from the available evidence that the photos, and their message, were resonating with a wide audience. Most of the eighty-nine letters about the series that it printed were signed, either by individuals acting on their own or by writers who said they were responding on behalf of groups of people. The veterans' organizations that wrote in to officially endorse the series included the Oshawa, Mount Dennis, and Toronto branches of the Canadian Legion, as well as the Legion's Zone 4, covering a wide swathe of Southwestern Ontario.[18]

Other veterans took care to indicate both their ranks and their institutional affiliations. One letter listed Lt.-Col. J. Keiller MacKay, ex-president of the Ontario command of the Canadian Legion, plus four other officers.[19] Many individual veterans complained that people had forgotten the war, praising the *Star* for breaking the silence around it. Some remarked that only now could they get people to believe their war stories. One soldier wrote that the pictures revealed "the full fallacy of war" and spoke "to those who have forgotten the truth which the men themselves have never spoken of."[20]

By choosing to publish forty-five letters from men claiming veteran status, the *Star* was emphasizing their voices above others. The paper also included nine women correspondents. Some of them argued that as mothers or potential mothers they had special insights into the harm that violence could do. Writing from the "woman's view," "A.B.C." reported that she had boys of her own who were duly instructed about "the horrors of war," and she pointed out how little had been said about the nursing sisters in the series. Another writer, "A War Sufferer," expressed great gratitude for the series. She had lost sixty-two relatives to the war, including her own son; a younger brother had been crippled for life. "As the daughter, wife and sister of a soldier," said "Ex-Land Army Girl," "I sincerely hope that your campaign will have the utmost success and that never again will our men-folk have to face death daily on the battlefields."[21]

A constant theme of the series, and of the letters responding to it, was the need to understand that war was no longer chivalrous or romantic. Again and again the *Star*'s correspondents used a particular word: "futility." The sights of "desolation, carnage and suffering" brought tears to the eyes of one reader, who exclaimed on "the utter madness and hellishness of modern war." Syd Smith, the president of the Toronto and District 18th Battalion, hoped that the series would "create a desire in the hearts of all patriotic and peace-loving citizens to fight with a new determination for the prevention of any repetition of this holocaust of human sacrifice and death."[22]

Ethel Iris Wax said of the *Star*'s photographs that they revealed "the ugly, brutal side of war. They tear away the veil of romance and paint war as it really is—a futile, cruel and meaningless business." Another writer, who signed himself "A Casualty"—he had been "gassed and wounded" in the war—said the series managed to "warn our youth of the 'camouflaged glory' that lies before them in the event of another war." A Peterborough letter writer who signed himself "Canadian" echoed Varley's painting. "No pen can do more than intimate the mental agony, the torture, and physical wretchedness endured," he cried. "For what?"[23]

Contributors also dwelt upon the anti-Christian essence of the war. One of them was Rev. (Lt.-Col.) G.O. Fallis, C.B.E., E.D., D.D., who was mounting his own peace crusade and would in 1936 be a keynote speaker at the unveiling of the Vimy monument in France. He declared, "The only hope lies in making the world hate war—as I hate it—as every man who went through the awful ordeal hates it."[24]

For many of the letter writers the coming generation was at particular risk, because people were already starting to romanticize the war and rediscover the magic of militarism. It was imperative to educate children about the horrors of war and to thwart the militarization of the school system. Cadet training in schools, the observance of holidays recalling wars, the exaltation of war in school curricula: all of these were hot issues throughout the 1930s, and in many places war resisters carried the day. In the responses to the *Star* series this emphasis clearly came through in an analysis from School Trustee E.J. Bell, who had served as a dispatch rider at Ypres. It was hardly "patriotism," in his books, to fill children's minds with martial imagery. He drew attention to the persistence of chivalric images that played up war's "alleged pomp and circumstance and adventure."[25]

The veterans who wrote in were particularly adamant about the need to shield young people from militarism. The spirit of war must not be passed on to a younger generation. As Joseph Morris "of the 10th Battalion, 417223," remarked, "I do hope that if another war should come our youths will say, 'No war for us. Our fathers suffered quite enough in the last war.'" Even Brig.-Gen. G.S. Cartwright, an RMC graduate and director of military studies at the University of Toronto, perhaps an unlikely critic, issued a warning for the "young generation": "Their blood must learn to chill when they think of the whining shells, of the rat-a-tat of machine guns, of the boom of bombs dropped from overhead. These things they must learn if there is to be peace."[26]

Those who dreamed of world peace found grounds for hope in the *Star*'s series. Many readers responded empathetically to the *Star*'s images of soldiers crossing the lines of nationality to help fellow soldiers. A Christie Street hospital patient wrote, "One of the pictures which made the deepest impression on me . . . was that of a Hun and a Tommy, both of them wounded, half-carrying each other from the battlefield."[27] Another writer, "Artillery" from Winnipeg, was particularly moved by the expression of the young German captive being escorted by equally young soldiers [Fig. 6]:

> He displays his mental uncertainty as to what manner of enemy lines he has found himself in and the intense, suspicious glance he casts at his captors is enough to soften the heart of the most hard boiled. Why should this young fellow be put through the mental anguish of suspecting good Canadian boys, his own age, of being "enemies"?[28]

A few readers went further, pushing past humanistic appreciations of the soldiers' shared lives to an angrier and more radical assessment of a system that had driven decent people into such indecent situations. R.M. Garrioch studied the face of one German captive and said he saw "a man of rather gentle manner, thoughtful, introspective, probably taken from some business or profession, totally antagonistic to physical combat."[29]

A number of writers feared a resurgence of martial nationalism and the arms buildup accompanying it. Militarism had found a home in Germany, but it was by no means restricted to it, some pointed out. The "narrow spirit of nationalism" they encountered in Canada alarmed them. Frederick Noyes, the official historian of the Fifth Canadian Field Ambulance, lamented that "our very vocal super-patriots" knew nothing of "the terror that gripped our hearts when high-explosive shells were shrieking and detonating around; when aerial bombs were crashing, blasting and maiming all that was made by God or man."[30]

Contributors could build on wartime denunciations of profiteering to mount a critique of militarism in the 1930s. When Private William Wisner's children cut out the pictures, he took it as an opportunity to explain to them "what war really means—what my comrades went through to make fortunes for bacon barons and munition manufacturers." Col. W.N. Scarth was blunt in his denunciation of those who sought profits from war: "It's about time our government did something to prevent private firms from manufacturing munitions of war, and anything that will hasten that stand is all for the public good . . . you know we ex-soldiers aren't peace-at-any-price advocates, but we do feel that it was about time the nations all did something really serious about peace." W. Livingston, president of the Canadian Legion in Leaside, thought that only "the munition manufacturer and the international banker" benefited from the "insanity of war."[31]

From time to time the series also kindled warm feelings among veterans. Some of them were touched to be included in such a representation of recent history. They felt nostalgic for the days of their youth, even if those days had been filled with war. One woman in Mount Hamilton was delighted to see her father in a picture of five men looking out from a double wall of sandbags. "Old Contemptible" from Stratford waxed nostalgic about the "the old tank" shown in one picture, saying that it "brought back memories" for him. "How real it looked. If I had a cent for every time I passed within 10 yards of the old tank, I would not be depending on relief."[32]

Others were glad that with the images now being widely disseminated, their own war stories might finally be believed. P.W. Price said, "How it all comes back again, the drumming of the guns, able-bodied men going forward in single file and remnants of battalions coming out, the long line of wounded, the field of devastation." The newspaper's series revealed that "the returned man wasn't just spreading it on a bit thick." A similar note was struck by Robert J. Clarke, D.C.M., of Trenton, who reported:

"A good many people thought we exaggerated things when we came back, but the pictures speak for themselves. I served with the 4th C.M.R. [Canadian Mounted Rifles] and have seen all the war I ever want to."[33]

Some correspondents hoped that the graphic proof of their wartime suffering would soften the hearts of Canadians regarding veterans' grievances. Some called for pity for the veterans, and some of the veterans, describing themselves as "broken" men, hoped that "the publication of these pictures gives some idea of the horror, filth and abuse that is the daily lot of an active service soldier." But more characteristic of the letters was the demand for justice, not pity. Ex.-Sgt. R.D. Morin, 3rd Echelon G.H.Q., said, "People have forgotten, and the war pictures will do much to refresh their memories." Frederick Gibson of Scarborough was blunter: "I am a returned man and in sore need of a job and if some employer will be good enough to offer me a job I would be ever so grateful."[34]

Many saw an ironic contrast between the symbolic soldier, the darling of the militarists, and the actual soldier, forgotten and impoverished. Just as heroic as the battles fought as part of the war in Europe, insisted W.P. Ellis of Holstein, were the struggles fought in Canada by the "survivors of that titanic conflict." As one resident of Belleville who signed himself "War Disabled" wrote, "You are doing a real service in publishing these war photographs, more especially because many returned men are unable to get any recompense for their wounds." "One Who Went" agreed. War-induced illnesses had made it nearly impossible for him to do physical work, while Ottawa continued to deny him a pension.[35]

Some ex-soldiers wanted to go beyond veterans' issues to a more comprehensive critique of the established order. "Ex-Service," from Oshawa, was aghast that Canada still contained people who thought another war would offer a cure for the Depression of the 1930s. He urged his fellow citizens to reflect upon "the real value of war promises, war results, and the product of a system which is both antiquated and un-Christian." He hoped the old comradeship of the trenches might take a new form in a revived peace movement, "thereby ushering in that glad new day we have prated about while doing nothing toward its advent."[36]

Letter writers even contested the establishment of war memorials. One veteran from Scotland, Ont., referred to Vimy Ridge when he remarked that the photos were but a mild reminder of the actual fighting, and that even as Canada was erecting "a memorial going up on Vimy Ridge costing two million dollars," many veterans were left "with a wife and family and no work, no pension and 'burned-out.'" The letters made almost no mention of Vimy.[37]

*   *   *

In Winnipeg the influential *Free Press* carried roughly the same number of photographs as the *Star*, stirring many of the same reactions. But the grim images generated a much more heated debate over the rights and wrongs of the war.

Although sharing the *Star*'s liberalism, the *Free Press* of the legendary editor John W. Dafoe was much more an establishment paper, far less likely than its Toronto contemporary to mount crusades on behalf of the disadvantaged. In a city that had undergone an epochal General Strike in 1919, polarized class-based politics still prevailed. No less than the *Star*, the *Free Press* introduced the photographs dramatically, announcing "Canada's Epic Story Told in Official War Photographs . . . the whole chronicle of Canada's heroic deeds and sacrifice," presented in "images that neither soften nor exaggerate."[38]

The *Free Press*, unlike its Ontario counterpart (which secured only a handful of commendations), printed no fewer than ninety-two solicited endorsements.[39] They were drawn "from every field of human enterprise in Manitoba, from men prominent in government, from prelates and churchmen of many denominations, from the judicial bench, from educationists and men and women engaged in social service of every kind, from business and from the professions." From this collection of notable citizens, the newspaper claimed, not entirely accurately, that it had received "a unanimous tide of approbation."[40]

Based on the approving letters, it appears that ideals critical of war and militarism were upheld by a vast proportion of respectable opinion in Manitoba, predominantly made up of people bearing good English or Scottish names. The *Free Press's* solicitation of favourable reviews was a way of spreading the word, a marketing strategy. It was also a political strategy, serving to shield the paper from any suggestion that it had, somehow, caved in to leftists.[41]

The *Free Press* presented the shocking photos with none of the *Star*'s crowd-pleasing humanism. The captions had little of Clark's biting humour. They also had a markedly different orientation—one that still listed heavily towards a pro-British interpretation of the war. The *Free Press* emphasized Canadians going over the top, braving "the inferno of shellfire with hearts pounding and heads down . . . enemy machine guns mowing and enemy barbed wire in huge tangled hedges ahead of them." The Somme was not criticized as a senseless sacrifice, despite being described as the "longest and bitterest battle of the war." One photograph of a devastated hospital had as its headline, "The Bodies of Nursing Sisters Fell Here," and the caption explained that German night fliers had bombed the hospital, "enabling them to chalk up on their score sheets three nurses and two doctors."[42] As one reader perceptively noticed, the *Free Press* borrowed selectively from Stallings, whose photographic history had depicted crowds in Serbia, Britain, Germany, and France deliriously welcoming the war. But the *Free Press*, for its part, focused exclusively on German war enthusiasts. "They are citizens, fat and prosperous, watching a parade." The accompanying text indirectly allowed that other countries had also lost their perspective and their "generals" had done much damage. But the visual emphasis was emphatically on Germans, whose "complacency" would be shattered by the war.[43]

Still, the newspaper did not stray anywhere near the Vimy trap. It did not depict the Great War as the birthplace of Canada, and did not feature Vimy as a heroic battle. One photograph shows two Canadians holding the skull of one of the thirty thousand French soldiers who had already fallen on the ridge when the Canadians took it; another depicted the damaged walls of a cellar in which unseen Canadians were huddling. Another photograph, "The Crest of Vimy," showed the German communication trenches and its dead German defenders.[44] The capture of Vimy Ridge was treated with an irony unthinkable a century later, as in the caption to a photograph depicting a "German of 1915" in a scene that was little more than rags, bones, and water bottles:

> High ground fascinates soldiers, because look you at Alexander the Great, King of Macedon and king of kings. Then look you at Hill 60, Hill 70, Hill 304, Vimy Ridge, and all the rest of the high spots. The next war will probably have developed a hill-builder so that the troops will not run short of heights to die for.[45]

The *Free Press*, like the *Star*, highlighted photographs showing Canadians and Germans sharing a common predicament—as in a picture that both papers published of German prisoners carrying a wounded Canadian. Its caption dwelt upon the irony of the situation: "An hour ago, killing each other. Now just a little group of God's children, holding onto one another and wondering what it is all about."[46]

As with the *Star*, the overwhelming tone of the *Free Press* series was anti-militarist, and so too were the printed responses. The Great War had taught, or should have taught, humanity that the abolition of war was an urgent priority. Of the respondents, a third wrote of the urgency of warning the coming generation of the perils of war. For Professor Watson Kirkconnell of Winnipeg's Wesley College, already making a name for himself as an authority on cultural questions and eventually to figure as a pivotal influence on the philosophy and practice of multiculturalism, the younger generation was growing up knowing nothing of war. The publication of the pictures, he said, might help to dispel the "false romanticism that literature so often casts about war." Indeed, anything that might help the young grasp that war was no "blood-stirring challenge to young manhood" but a "horrible reality" was welcome.[47] Historian Arthur Lower, who had served in the Great War as a sailor and was now at Wesley College—and was later to become renowned as the man who taught Canadians about their long pilgrimage from "colony to nation"—also wrote to the paper. He expressed the opinion that photographs informing the "youth of today" about the "horrors of war" were long overdue, at a time when the "whole experience has more or less gone over our heads." The secretary of the Lesia Ukrainka Branch of the Ukrainian Women's Association, whose son was in public school, hoped that all public-school teachers would use the photographs "as a lesson on the mean and debasing nature of war." O.B. Cosette, the principal of a school in Morris, agreed, suggesting that everything possible should be done to "show our boys and girls the awfulness of war, to educate them to be peace-minded, to abhor the butchery of human beings and the wanton destruction of material wealth."[48]

Dr. G.B. Shortreed, the ex-mayor of Grandview, believed that although the photographs were "splendidly realistic and productive of anti-war sentiment," they were inappropriate for the "child mind, which always needs an interpreter." The images might have a brutalizing and cheapening effect on youngsters. War veteran J.H. Cameron, now the principal of Grandview High School, begged to differ. For him the more hard-hitting the presentation of the war, the better: "Tell the facts. Tell them graphically, forcibly, personally. You have got to hit some people with a brick to give them a hint."[49]

For John Queen, MLA (soon to become Winnipeg's mayor), the *Free Press* was quite right to attempt to overthrow notions of war as a "glamorous, glorious adventure," in the interest of creating an "anti-war psychology." He thought it urgent to dispose of the sham of "swaggering uniforms and martial airs." For Maj. E.B.C. Wilcox, M.C., of the Manitoba Regiment, now in Treherne, the passage of time had blurred the memories of "the blood and the mud." As an old soldier, he was now brought back into touch with his ardent hope, in November 1918, "for civilian clothes and other trappings of peace." It was good that the younger generation would be brought to realize "that war is a thing of suffering, death and bestiality," not of "military bands and smart uniforms."[50]

Wilcox was in good company: of the Great War veterans whose opinions the *Free Press* solicited, the vast majority endorsed the series without reservation. As Capt. W.H.G. Gibbs, M.O. (Medical Officer), a former mayor of Selkirk, remarked, the series might be a good thing to reveal war "to the rising generation, stripped of its false glamour, and in all the stark hideousness as it was actually experienced by those of us who were there." It might stimulate people to "spare no effort to ensure that their like should never be allowed to occur again."[51]

For "An Ex-Veteran," again capturing something of the spirit of *Generals Die in Bed*, the problem with the photographs favoured by the newspapers was that they were not hard-hitting enough. He wanted images of soldiers "who had been destroyed by liquid fire and gas," of the "horror and suffering of torn and battered soldiers," juxtaposed with others depicting "the ease and luxury of officers and higher-ups." Another letter writer, "18th Battalion," commended the series as something that might shock his own children and stop them from being sent "to the slaughter at the instance of the big boys in the armaments racket and on the orders of high military officials."[52]

In contrast to Toronto, a high-profile crusade was also mounted *against* the series. Here the pivotal figure was Mayor Ralph Humphreys Webb, long a stalwart of the Citizens' Committee, which ever since the city's General Strike of 1919 had fought to keep Winnipeg safe for business and secure from radicals. Like most of the city's elite, Webb was of British origin. He had served in the war, winning the Distinguished Service Order medal, Military Cross, and Croix de Guerre. He had also lost a leg, which made his very body a graphic reminder of the war.[53]

Webb was a Conservative writing to a staunchly Liberal *Free Press*. Yet his initial response to the series was positive. He congratulated the *Free Press* for the series, declaring: "One of the greatest ways of preventing war is to show the horrors which follow in its wake. No man who went through the Great War, seeing service in the front line, wants to pass through a similar experience."[54]

Shortly after issuing this commendation Webb was quite possibly called to account by Winnipeg's more conservative veterans, because he soon reversed his stand. In an address to social welfare workers just three days after his letter was published, the mayor denounced the *Free Press* series as a "circulation stunt to sell newspapers." He reported that the "returned soldiers are up in arms" because their experience was being exploited "to make profits for newspaper owners." Moreover, he argued that only those who had not gone to war were apt to "paint the horrors of it." As someone who had been to war, he would like to "show the funny things and the really interesting parts." Like so many other things about the Great War in Winnipeg, veterans' issues were sharply polarized. The veterans were divided among many organizations, one of which, the Manitoba Command of the Canadian Legion, would later come out with a ringing denunciation of those who would seek to overthrow law and order.[55] From the perspective of this increasingly vocal and powerful minority, the *real* veterans were those who still idealized the war; the *false* veterans were those who complained about it.

Webb's stand was subsequently affirmed by the Winnipeg Branch of the Canadian Legion B.E.S.L. (British Empire Service League), taking a position in sharp contrast to equally well-established veterans' associations in Ontario. "We see no useful purpose being served by the publication in the daily press of war pictures which are being produced as an inducement toward the sentiment of world peace," the Legionnaires proclaimed.[56]

Some *Free Press* readers were amazed at the mayor's about-face. One remarked that he did not know any "old sweats" who were in the least upset by the photographs. Claiming the authority of "thousands of Canadian mothers," Bellun Lethale of Brandon took Mayor Webb to task for his suggestion that only those who had never been to war would depict it in horrific colours. That, to her, seemed like the "ravings of a war-god." Walter King, another of the mayor's critics, noted his recent battles with social gospel clergymen. He described the mayor as typical of the "fire-eating die-hard Conservatives who insist war is inevitable."[57]

Other readers were more sympathetic to the mayor. The most sceptical of such responses came from one J.B. Ryan, who believed most veterans, of whom he was one, resented the "pettifog method" of the photographers, who had evidently stayed well out of no man's land: "Many of

Fig. 7. "They Have a Rendezvous with Death!—Canadians at the Somme, leaving their trenches in one of the innumerable daylight attacks of that ill-omened battle, reckless, fed-up, exhausted with the mud, bludgeoned by incessant shell-fire and counter-attack." *Winnipeg Free Press*, 7 Feb. 1934.

us still have in our memories the heroism of our valiant buddies who fell and the horrification of it all. It belongs to us."[58]

The *Free Press* generally presented the photographs with little consideration of their possible emotional impact on survivors. "They Have a Rendezvous with Death!" said the caption for a photograph of Canadians at the Somme who were about to embark upon a daylight (and "ill-omened") attack. [Fig. 7.] It would not have been difficult for survivors to make out—or believe they made out—their loved ones. "Temporary Dressings" depicted a bayonet and an entrenching tool being used as splints on a Canadian's smashed arm. Unlike the *Toronto Star*, the *Free Press* had little compunction about displaying wounded Canadians. In "First Aid," a shot of physicians in a medical station near the front line, the faces of wounded Canadians were clearly visible. [Fig. 8.] A few readers did recognize themselves, including one who said he did so while chatting with members of the "Amputations Association." Mrs. J.R. Newell saw her brother in another shot; he had died from his wounds in 1922.[59]

Fig. 8. "First Aid—The medical officers put their front line dressing stations as handy to the battle as they could but it was still a long walk to many a man." *Winnipeg Free Press*, 14 Feb. 1934.

Some of the most thoughtful responses, from women, queried not the intentions of the *Free Press* but the overall strategy of shocking people into resisting war. Miss Gertrude Clark of First Presbyterian Church in Winnipeg believed the photographs revealed the "futility and indescribable horrors of war," but she worried that the peace movement was not sounding a "more positive note for peace." Military symbols retained a power to "get men's blood to tingle and their pulse to quicken" that no peace propaganda had yet equalled. Mrs. W.F. Osborne, president of the Women's International League for Peace and Freedom in Winnipeg, warned that printing photographs that were "merely scenes of carnage" would do little good. Mrs. A.M. Campbell, the president of the Women's Canadian Club, thought the photographs might generate two reactions: one an "utter despair of civilization," the other a greatly strengthened resolve on the part of the "common people" that no such thing would ever happen again.[60]

As the series unfolded it became obvious that many contemporaries, including some of Mayor Webb's long-time left-wing adversaries, saw in the photographs confirmation of their own politics of peace. From their perspective, the *Free Press* needed, in addition to publishing such photographs, to push itself harder to analyse the social and economic relations that made such horrors possible. S.J. Farmer was glad the *Free Press* was running the series, for war was caused by capitalism. Hopes that Canada might avoid being "dragooned into taking part in another such orgy of wholesale butchery" could only be realistic if they proceeded from recognition of this basic reality. When war came again, wouldn't young men respond as they had done in 1914 to the "same heady music of drum and fife," and—he asked pointedly—wouldn't this very same *Free Press* mount a martial crusade comparable to the one it had supported in 1914–18? MLA John Queen believed that war arose from a "competitive individualistic system," and urged the readers of the *Free Press* to realize that the pictures they were seeing were the "result of competition, each country striving against the other." The Workers' Ex-Servicemen's League, one of the Legion's left-wing rivals, also announced its sympathy with the "exposure of the horrors of war, so long as such exposure is directed along anti-militaristic lines and with the object of preventing the youth of all countries from being catapulted into another world war, through false ideas as to the glories and glamour of war."[61]

In the Depression years in both Toronto and Winnipeg—and presumably in many other cities in which these same photos appeared—the terrain of Great War memory was highly contested. In Winnipeg a conservative push-back against the sceptical consensus was emerging, and such sentiments would ultimately contribute to Vimyism. What is most surprising, though, is that in both Winnipeg and Toronto the photographs were only occasionally denounced by martial nationalists keen to defend the valour of Canada's soldiers and the honour of battles like Vimy. The vast majority of the responses revealed a mindset in which the Great War could no longer be a suitable focus of patriotic celebration. It might be mourned; it could not be sanctified. Sentiments that smacked of Vimyism were almost totally absent.[62] In 205 letters from the Prairie provinces, mainly Manitoba, scarcely anyone argued that the Great War had been a crusade for freedom against barbarism, or that it had constituted a Canadian coming of age. Themes that would rise to the forefront later in the twentieth century were basically missing in action in 1934—especially among the men who had actually fought in the war.

5

THE CONTESTED POLITICS
OF PEACE AND WAR

*We live in a period in which memory of all kinds, including the
sort of larger memory we call history, is being called into question.
For history as for the individual, forgetting can be just as convenient
as remembering, and remembering what was once forgotten can be
distinctly uncomfortable. As a rule, we tend to remember the awful
things done to us, and to forget the awful things we did.*

— MARGARET ATWOOD, *In Search of* Alias Grace:
On Writing Canadian Historical Fiction

"DEAD AIR." It is a term that radio broadcasters dread: those seconds in
which the constant flow of words is suspended and the audience is
left without stimulation. Yet in certain moments the silence of dead
air can provide an eloquent testimony to unfolding events.

On 3 September 1939, Ernest Lapointe, Quebec's giant in the cabinet, was before a microphone in an Ottawa studio. In theory, Lapointe was
the justice minister. In actuality he was the co-prime minister, a "French
lieutenant." Without him Mackenzie King would not have become prime
minister and would never have been able to hold Quebec. Lapointe had
fought for two decades to wean Canada from Britain. On a host of issues
related to the country's foreign policy, Lapointe's voice mattered. From
Lapointe's perspective, King and he had concluded a two-sided pact:
there would be no further call for Canada to remain neutral, but there
would also be no conscription—and underlying both terms of the pact
was the decisive place of Canada's Parliament in deciding whether or not
the country would go to war.

A year earlier, in autumn 1938, hopes had been aroused that the
world would see "Peace in Our Time" after British prime minister Neville

Chamberlain's optimistic assessment of an agreement reached with Adolf Hitler at Munich. But through the early months of 1939 it had become ever clearer that the Great War of 1914–18 was to be followed by a Second World War. The issue of conscription would once again come to the fore—back in 1917, as a backbench Liberal MP, Lapointe had denounced it as the "very opposite of democracy"[1]—along with the question of Canada as an independent country that could chart its own course in world affairs.

For a long time, too, Lapointe and King had drawn the same lesson from the Great War: that of the incalculable dangers of unbridled militarism. They were fully backed in that regard by King's undersecretary of state for external affairs, O.D. Skelton, the behind-the-scenes architect of much Canadian foreign policy in the 1930s and the man who wrote many of King's better speeches. All three men supported the League of Nations—on condition that it not impose commitments on Canada to enter future armed conflicts. Yet the League lacked the participation of powerful states: the United States, which in March 1920 rejected the Treaty of Versailles; the Soviet Union, which the capitalist countries were keen to isolate; and defeated and disgraced Germany, whose colonies were parcelled out and whose population was expected to pay reparations as punishment for allegedly causing the war.

Early in 1939 the Canadian consensus, never as complete or as full as it might have seemed in retrospect, began visibly to fray. When Parliament opened on 16 January 1939, Mackenzie King repeated an old saying of Wilfrid Laurier from the days of the Great War: "When Britain is at war, Canada is at war." Lapointe was aghast. What had happened to Canada's independence, supposedly achieved by the Statute of Westminster in 1931? Surely an independent country had the right to decide on its own when it was at war?

When King rose in the House of Commons on 30 March, the clarity of 16 January had given way to a cloud of obfuscation—the fog of peace—that left listeners scratching their heads. If Britain went to war, *was* Canada at war? J.S. Woodsworth, the ardently pacifist leader of the socialist Co-operative Commonwealth Federation (CCF), wryly noted: "I really do not know, in the event of war, what action the government would take. . . . The Canadian nationalist, the imperialist, the League of Nations collectivist, the pacifist, the North American, the belligerent militarist—each will find some crumb of comfort in the Prime Minister's speech."[2] For his part, Lapointe was clearer, declaring that it was not possible for Canada to remain neutral in the event of a war involving Britain. But English Canadians had to realize how deep the wounds of 1917 still were. Many French Canadians believed they had been promised there would be no involvement in a British war. Many English Canadians believed such involvement was simply a matter of course. French Canadians would never agree to conscription for overseas service. Canadians should put Canada first in any decisions about peace and war. In this case, it might well be possible to limit the country's liabilities. It was imperative, in Lapointe's view, that King underplay the extent to which Canada was coming to Britain's aid. It was far more attractive, from the Quebec perspective, to say that it was fighting for freedom against a tyrannical enemy.[3]

On the afternoon of 3 September, then, King took to the airwaves to talk to Canadians. That very morning Britain and France had declared war on Germany. Yet, with his faltering French, King could not speak to French Canadians in their own language. Thus he turned to his co-prime minister, Lapointe, who—incredible as it might seem, given the gravity of the occasion—had not been given the text of the French translation before he sat down before the microphone to read it.

At first the address went smoothly enough: the French text corresponded to the terms of the King-Lapointe pact. Lapointe, mirroring King's English text, stressed the attempt by Hitler and the Nazis "to extend their control over other peoples and countries . . . and peaceful methods of adjusting international disputes. . . . It is this reliance upon force, this lust for conquest, this determination to dominate throughout the world, which is the real cause of the war that to-day threatens the freedom of mankind." But then things got a bit trickier. In English, the text reads: "This morning, the King, speaking to his peoples at home and across the seas, appealed to all, to make their own, the cause of freedom, which Britain again has taken up. Canada has already answered that call. On Friday last, the government, speaking on behalf of the Canadian people, announced that in the event of the United Kingdom becoming engaged in war . . ."—or, in French, "*a annoncé que dans le cas où le Royaume uni serait engagé dans un guerre.*"[4]

The period of dead air followed that statement. It is unlikely that Lapointe simply lost his way in the text. He was a phenomenal speaker. His own speech in the House of Commons was to hold it completely spellbound—unlike that of the prime minister, who failed to hold the attention of the House even when explaining why the country was yet again embarking upon a world war. What Lapointe did during those seconds was frantically read ahead to verify the details of what he was about to say to his French-language audience. Would King make any statements along the lines of "When Britain is at war, Canada is at war?"—with all the colonial subservience that implied? Or would he honour the explicit and implicit terms of the solemn pact?

The eight seconds were what it took for Lapointe to find out that King had, indeed, said that it would be up to Parliament to decide how best to render efficacious assistance to Britain. King had not pulled a fast one. But still it always paid to keep a close eye on him.[5]

From 1929 to 1939, many Canadians were immersed in the complicated politics of peace and war, powerfully shaped by conflicting memories of the Great War. They were no less implicated in the shift in their country's geo-historical position, which could be construed as one of growing independence—or as one of a return to an imperial protector, whether British or American. The debates shaped those eight seconds of dead air.

In that period Canadians had largely reached a consensus—even if expressed in a myriad of different ways—that the Great War had been an abomination that should never be repeated. The Great War had deeply shaped Canadian perceptions of peace and war. When a massive war did come about once again, there was, in historian Ian Miller's words, "little of the naked enthusiasm for war of August 1914. . . . The citizens of 1939 drew upon experience unavailable 25 years earlier. They understood that a continental European war would not be a brief and glorious meeting of honourable armies."[6] The various truths about the war disseminated by writers, ex-soldiers, family members, artists, filmmakers, and a host of others, including politicians, had registered.

*   *   *

As the 1934 newspaper debates about peace and war so vividly suggest, many returned soldiers now viewed the Great War as a cautionary tale, not Canada's coming-of-age saga. A vast number of the critics of war, after all, were veterans.

Irony was not just for poets: when veterans came to describe their penury and suffering, they reverted time and again to the stark contrast between their wartime hopes and their postwar despair. During the 1930s veterans sometimes made up the majority of those on relief in major cities. In the Depression this was really saying something. As the Canadian Legion explained in January 1935, the unemployment crisis weighed heavily upon veterans, whose average age was estimated to be about forty-seven, because they were competing with a "great army of Youth," none of whom had given up years of their lives to fight a war in Europe. "These men ... feel their country has let them down, that they are neglected and forgotten." Many such veterans were in the relief camps, where radicals were mobilizing a mass resistance movement.[7]

Their enemies mobilized to discredit them. Conservative factions in the Legion drew upon quasi-Darwinistic arguments to suggest that the "unfit" had been allowed to enlist in the early rush to war. In 1936 a Special Parliamentary Committee on Pensions and Returned Soldier Problems recommended that a board of psychiatrists and neurologists be convened to explore the issue of whether the Great War had undermined the mental health of soldiers. Guardians of the public purse painted the veterans as scroungers. Yet anyone could see that war meant huge expenses—both during the killing and long afterwards. If veterans succeeded in making claims upon the state, the upshot might be a state with a greatly enhanced social vision.[8] The idea of public provision for the public good might spread.

"Men are seeing red," wrote veteran H.A.E. Coo of Toronto to Opposition Leader Mackenzie King in 1931. "There are armies of men in Canada who have tasted blood during the war who will not be so easily controlled as some of our authorities seem to think. I am telling you frankly that Hell is going to break loose." Another veteran wrote to Prime Minister R.B. Bennett wishing him "a merry Xmas" and added, "whilst you dine in splendor a Canadian Soldier is Dying a Slow Starvation." How could Bennett accept the "murder" of such a disabled veteran, condemned to support himself, his wife, and his daughter on $8 a month? When King regained office in 1935, he got a warning from Toronto. Veterans were resisting evictions with violence. He was told, "The situation is bordering very close to the line of bloodshed." The fear was that "organized groups" of veterans were getting out of the control of their leaders.[9]

Many veterans were joining radical organizations. The authorities received regular reports about agitators and subversives. The Workers' Ex-Servicemen's League was growing. In Vancouver it went so far as to denounce the cult of the poppy associated with its more conservative rival because, it argued, the "Last Post Funds" and "Poppy Funds" were charities that stigmatized poor veterans. It even suggested that poppy-themed insignia should be removed from tombstones.[10]

Brig.-Gen. Alex Ross of the Canadian Legion pointed out that "many ex-servicemen" were ready to embark upon political projects "completely repugnant to British traditions . . . the British system of Government and the British tradition which we cherish." For Ross the Empire's military and moral rearmament went hand in hand.[11] He set himself the task of establishing law and order within a veterans' community seething with discontent and gravitating to radical alternatives.

Veterans, along with many others, were turning en masse to the peace movement. A petition submitted to Ottawa in January 1932 called for Canada to beef up its contribution to world disarmament; it included over 480,000 names—a huge number in a country with a population of just over ten million.[12] In the absence of public opinion polls, such an astonishing result, paralleled by a renewed movement against rearmament in 1937–38, suggests that a majority of Canadians embraced perspectives sceptical of war in the 1930s. Some of this mass movement was organized by the "usual suspects" on conservative scunner lists—social democrats and other leftists, feminists, Quakers, Quebeckers, and religiously oriented pacifists.[13] But much of it was organized by other, more "unusual" types—small-town service club members, businessmen, mainstream politicians, evangelical Christians. And veterans.

Leftists, gaining strength in the 1930s, added clarity and polemical punch to the movement. Communists now supported a peace movement that they had previously considered bourgeois and anti-Soviet. It helped that the Soviet Union was admitted to the League of Nations in 1934 and the political line of the Communist movement went from self-isolating orthodoxy to almost indiscriminate alliance-building in 1935.[14] By the late 1930s the Communists discovered audiences they had never before reached. French-Canadian Catholics were responsive to messages about peace and Canadian neutrality.[15] The left rhetoric that some Canadians found off-putting inspired numerous veterans longing for someone to call out loudly for their rights. The more loosely organized and heterogeneous forces of the Co-operative Commonwealth Federation contained many peace activists—hardly surprising coming from the party of J.S. Woodsworth and Agnes Macphail.[16]

The ranks of *unusual* suspects were, however, crooning from the same songbook. They included men who had been Conservative prime ministers. In 1931 former Conservative prime minister Arthur Meighen told readers of *Maclean's* that "civilization has to end war, or war will end civilization." To an imagined critic who sneered that such views were merely utopian, Meighen, the man (as the Unionist government's interior minister) mainly responsible for implementing mandatory military service in 1917 and strongly associated in Quebec with conscription, replied: "I put against him the plea of necessity: the sovereign right of a single people must yield to the sovereign right of all to live." Robert Borden described the League of Nations as the "most wonderful venture ever attempted in human co-operation" and predicted that "this century will witness no greater thing." R.B. Bennett condemned governments that, having signed the Kellogg-Briand Pact of 1928 renouncing war, then proceeded to rearm themselves: "To what end does the maintenance of enormous armaments still continue?" He declared: "The development of democracy depends upon the maintenance of peace. War is destructive of all democratic forms of government."[17]

Perhaps the most surprising peace advocate was Ontario's future Conservative premier George Drew, who had gained a well-deserved reputation as a prominent red-baiter, imperialist, and conscription booster. He was *Lieutenant-Colonel* George Drew—wounded in 1916, commander of the 64th Battery in Guelph, author of *Canada's Fighting Airmen* (1930), and president of the Canadian Military Institute—all in all, an unlikely resumé for a peace protester. But in the 1930s Drew was an apostle of disarmament who urged Canadians to rise up and demand the nationalization of the armaments industry. This industry, a "Frankenstein monster," had to "be smashed or it will smash civilization." He even charged humanity with the task of focusing its resistance against the "propagandists of hate," who endlessly repeated arguments for armaments based on the "grounds of national security."[18]

Strangely enough, the conservative, populist Drew was opening up new critical vistas—suggesting the need for an examination of the business interests that were active in war preparation, not to mention the patriots who were whipping up war frenzy. Drew asked Canadians to ponder the underlying structural patterns of twentieth-century wars. The burden of his analysis—that Canadians had to get involved in putting an end to the global arms race—implicitly undercut assigning exclusive blame to Germany. From his prominent pulpit, Drew could bring his message to broad audiences. Readers of *Maclean's* and members of the Imperial Officers Association of Canada, Canadian Legion, Navy League of Canada, and Imperial Order Daughters of the Empire—all of these enlisted in Drew's anti-armaments crusade. Rotary Clubs in Kitchener and Waterloo, Ont., Red Deer, Alta., and Campbellton, N.B., became enthusiastic supporters of his core argument: unless arms manufacturers were reined in, the world was heading for Armageddon.[19]

While Drew had attended the upper-crust Upper Canada College, another unlikely suspect, Brooke Claxton, was a Lower Canada College boy. The Montrealer and future defence minister was, like Drew, a Great War veteran. In 1934 he was teaching commercial law at McGill University when, intent on encouraging business interests to join up with the League of Nations Society (LNS) and its peace campaign, he introduced a long article in *Canadian Business* with four points drawn from worthy voices of the day:

> (1) If you prepare for war thoroughly and efficiently you will get war, and (2) another war in Europe would be the end of the civilization we know. (3) The only way to escape another war is to prevent it. (4) Through the League, the states of the world have groped forward to something better than the old way of composing their differences.

Maybe, Claxton told his business readers, they might be tempted to dismiss these four theses as the thoughts of an eccentric crank. In fact, they came from a British general, a future British prime minister (Stanley Baldwin), Canada's own Ernest Lapointe, and U.S. president Franklin D. Roosevelt. Unless the traditional notion that countries attained security through armaments was discredited, unless the machinery of the League of Nations was put to good use, unless Sir Robert Borden's hope that "war's curse . . . be banned and banished by human purpose and endeavour" was realized, their world was headed for ruin. Claxton argued that if business interests were worried about the costs of Canadian participation in the League of Nations—$331,822.43 for the fiscal year 1932–33—this was less than the price tag for two days' participation in the Great War.[20]

Fairly crawling with Royal Society of Canada types, the League of Nations Society listed Bennett, King, Borden, and Lapointe on its masthead. Yet its Toronto roster also included Alice Chown, working tirelessly to turn the local LNS into a grassroots movement warmed by the fire of feminism, dauntless in its pursuit of peace. Again and again Chown would complain about the stuffiness of *Interdependence*, the LNS house organ. It was typical of the organization's tendency, she believed, to overlook engaging a broad Canadian base in the struggle. "Colonel Drew wants to enlist influential citizens," she remarked in September 1933. "We are

Like her cousin Samuel, Alice Chown came from a devout Methodist background. During the Great War she was involved in the Women's Peace Crusade, and later she went on to become a leading peace and disarmament campaigner.

more interested in the masses of people."[21] Yet she kept at it, believing that the League's imperfect internationalism represented the world's only hope to avert its next Armageddon. In Canada, in Geneva, and in London, Chown became an intrepid campaigner against militarism. In the eyes of one prominent conservative correspondent, the outspoken activist was a "Belligerent Female" who refused to shut up about peace.[22]

Many shared Chown's opinions, if not her stalwart capacity to express them. Kiwanis and Rotary clubs were hotbeds of peace supporters. The Vancouver and Island Life Underwriters Association condemned the "terrible burden of armaments." The Canadian Business and Professional Women's Club of Kitchener and Waterloo called for "very radical reductions" in their number. The national executive of the Imperial Order Daughters of the Empire and Children of the Empire was not quite so forthright. But it did note that "so long as the manufacture, sale and distribution of armaments are operated under private control and administered for private profit, effective progress cannot be made towards the reduction or ultimate elimination of such methods of warfare." In 1935 a group of Canada's leading psychologists and psychiatrists signed a petition circulated by some 350 of their colleagues worldwide. It stated: "War means that all destructive forces are set loose by mankind against itself. War means the annihilation of mankind by technical science." They found attempts—fashionable then as now—to justify war in terms of Darwinian theory to be reprehensible and, like Claxton, were keenly aware that many of those who said they wanted to achieve peace by preparing for war were merely trying to disguise their war psychoses. Militarists, they suggested, were both mentally ill and morally impoverished.[23]

Many Canadians put their arguments against war in religious terms. United Church members increasingly placed "Peace" at the centre of their spirituality and were vital to driving up the numbers on the Disarmament Petition.[24] Other more unusual suspects also joined in the cause. The YWCA's National Council issued an "Appeal of Women" that called for the abolition of war. At an annual dinner the YMCA's veteran members declared their "entire and unanimous abhorrence of war." The Catholic Knights of Columbus of Winnipeg stated that since "the early days of the Great War, the devastating evils of the war have wrought untold sufferings upon humanity, wrecking whole civilizations, and threatening Christianity itself." The Baptists of Owen Sound, Ont., declared: "No one can regard war, especially modern methods of waging it by indiscriminate slaughter of whole populations by incendiary bombs and poisonous gases, as a good way of settling disputes."[25]

For many people—and especially women—combating militarism meant changing the school system. Peace petitions from teachers' associations flooded Ottawa. The B.C. Teachers' Federation echoed Drew in targeting the private manufacture of armaments.[26] At a meeting of the Women's International League for Peace and Freedom on 31 May 1931 at Bloor Street United Church in Toronto, addressed by the U.S. social reformer Jane Addams, renowned feminist Rose Henderson decried capitalist influences on schools, and she later went on to make the abolition of cadet training a central plank in her successful campaign to win a seat on the Board of Education. Rather than teaching children to "prepare for war," schools should be instructing them on the interdependence of all human beings.[27] A number of women argued that mothers had a biologically based interest in preserving peace. In Hamilton, Agnes Sharpe, elected to the Board of Education in 1929, won notoriety by refusing to sing "God Save the King" at an Empire Day ceremony. She joined the National Council of the left-wing Canadian League Against War and Fascism to help it launch a "conscious and militant mass movement organized from below to . . . halt the warmakers." Many Hamiltonians condemned Sharpe for her resistance to Empire and militarism alike—but she was nonetheless re-elected. In 1939 she took the extreme step of refusing to take part in the city's ceremony of greeting for King George VI and Queen Elizabeth, because doing so would mean publicly taking an oath that implied "willingness to bear arms in defence of the crown . . . contrary to her pacifist convictions."[28]

Over the course of the 1930s and 1940s, the peace movement could claim substantial victories in discrediting cadet training in schools. The struggle against this martial tradition went back at least three decades; historian Thomas Socknat notes that peace groups thought it an integral part of the trend towards a militaristic society.[29] Every year Macphail and Woodsworth spoke out against the annual federal grant for the training of cadets. (One year Macphail ingeniously sought to undermine the intent of the Parliamentary grant by reducing it to $1.) In 1934 government-sponsored cadet training ended. While some schools continued the tradition without funding, women school trustees especially were pushing back vigorously. To an unprecedented extent, inculcating children in warlike ways was being questioned in the 1930s. "Should My Boy Play War?" asked one Saint John letter writer to *Maclean's* in 1931. He remembered the famous Christmas Truce of the Great War, when British and German soldiers had come together to play football and consume plum puddings. If only their spirit had influenced all the troops, the war would have stopped. Perhaps then the "few so-called leaders" who had brought war into the world might have been "branded as criminals" and given their just desserts—the electric chair. His was an unusually vehement expression of a common mindset in the Canada of the 1930s. In Hamilton in 1933, the veterans in the Workers' Ex-Servicemen's League in Canada not only stated their opposition to "war or anything appertaining to war" but also announced that, should war come again, "they would refuse to take any active part."[30] In anticipation of the next war, they were already declaring themselves mutineers.

* * *

Much of early twenty-first-century writing on peace and war assumes that people can be roughly categorized into one of two camps: pacifists and militarists. Pacifists, according to this line of thought, view all war as impermissible and preach non-resistance to evil. Pacifists can be found in many peace churches, such as the Quakers. Militarists rejoice in war as a necessary and valuable part of the human condition, often because it toughens character and turns boys into men. If in a nuclear age out-and-out proponents of war as character-building are far less numerous than they were in the era of the Great War, the militarist position nonetheless continues to be a point of departure in video-game culture, Hollywood movies, or governmental strategies to fight terrorism with massive bombardments.

Still, those absolute positions are not the only measure of responses to issues of peace and war.[31] Martin Ceadel, a British scholar who has studied the politics of war prevention, introduces five "ideal types" that appear along a spectrum of people who take stances on these questions. *Militarists* believe that war is a good thing in and of itself—a wonderful way of developing character, especially in young men. *Crusaders* believe that war—even an aggressive war—can be justified if it aims to overcome a glaring evil or attain a worthwhile objective in the name of higher values (liberty, free enterprise, "our way of life," or even peace). *Defencists* believe that aggressive wars are wrong, but wars of self-defence are always right—indeed, the building up of a strong, capable defence makes war less likely ("If you want peace, prepare for war" is their slogan). *Pacificists* hold that the exercise of military force should always be a last resort—and then only if undertaken under the auspices of legitimate international institutions (such as the United Nations). They believe that, in a modern age, the abolition of war is not only possible but also imperative—especially in an era in which the next world war would almost certainly be our civilization's last. Finally, *pacifists* believe that war is wrong in all circumstances; some of them believe it can be readily abolished in our own time, and others more pessimistically conclude that the best they can do is "bear witness."[32]

From the pacificist standpoint, war is rarely a good option; when it is, tragically, the only option, then the lesson to be learned is not that the prior attempts to create peace-building and peace-enforcing institutions were wrong, but that they were insufficiently wholehearted and realistic. Often, they did not address the underlying social and economic reasons as to why, for powerful constituencies and corporations, war always seemed to be an attractive political and business option.

Like other sensible authors of bold typologies, Ceadel freely acknowledges that his "ideal types" are just that—idealized, tidied-up categories that in historical reality often take more complicated forms. Indeed, many people who (directly or indirectly) experienced the Great War cannot readily be slotted into one or another of the main camps. As the record shows, many people might have not only celebrated the nobility and purity of heart of chivalric soldiers who became better and stronger people because they went to war (militarism) but also took time to critique the logic of the senseless and futile war in which those soldiers were killed, and to hope that such a thing never again be repeated (pacificism). Others might also have believed that the achievement of peace should be at the absolute centre of social and political existence while also championing an institution threatening aggressive, invading states with sanctions.

Pacificist thinking was pervasive among soldiers fighting the Great War itself, and after 1930 it was predominant within the many novels and memoirs turned out by combatants.[33] From the mid-1930s on, too, pacificists could detest the thought of an impending war with Germany and firmly believe that many if not most wars were accelerated by imperialists bent on enlarging the scope of their countries' possibilities and benefiting business interests. It was possible to hope against hope that Canada and other Western countries and international institutions would come to their senses and avoid war, possibly by uniting with the Soviet Union against fascism—and yet also reluctantly concede the necessity of Canada's war against Hitler. Such pacificists, after the Second World War was done, might have looked back on the world's history since 1914 as an example that inspired them to redouble their efforts to find alternatives to war because, following their line of analysis, far from constituting a noble crusade and the birth of the nation, the First World War's major contribution to humanity, besides offering a sobering indication of how murderous industrial warfare could be, was to lay the basis for a second, even more catastrophic war.

Yet the pacificist position has always been challenged—even today, by people (and an entire culture of infotainment) who still implicitly or explicitly see war as intrinsic and beneficial to human nature; by others who, when confronted with human wrongs abroad, imagine many of them can be ameliorated by bombs from the sky or boots on the ground; and by yet others who will mobilize acute feelings of insecurity to bolster our own sense of being under permanent threat and hence in need of an ever-expanding defence capacity. A recurrent Canadian pattern is for there to be high levels of support for military engagements when they begin—as Canadians respond to militarist, defencist, and crusading arguments, in Ceadel's terminology—and less and less enthusiasm as they proceed, as the human costs and disappointing practical outcomes of military engagements become ever more plain.

*   *   *

In retrospect it seems readily apparent that the League of Nations was an unworthy institution in which to invest great hopes for peace. Despite the establishment of that body, distant diplomats driven by the traditional imperatives of power politics ultimately made all the big decisions. Considerable hope had been invested in the World Disarmament Conference, held in Geneva (1932–34); yet some of the principal participants came to believe that the campaign had largely been a farce. O.D. Skelton's appearance in Geneva in March 1933, as Norman Hillmer puts it, was part of Prime Minister R.B. Bennett's "well meaning but haphazard" foreign policy and could be dismissed as "a political show," or, in Skelton's own words, "Eyewash . . . designed to make the Canadian public realize Canada is on the disarmament job, even if as a matter of fact we will & can do nothing." Much time and effort were spent in campaigns to beef up Canada's delegation, but Skelton's fellow traveller in 1933 was the hard-drinking former Ontario premier Howard Ferguson, whose knowledge of foreign affairs was slight.[34]

The League of Nations was, as one writer puts it, a bit like Shakespeare's Richard III—"deformed, unfinished, sent before my time, Into this breathing world, scarce half made up."[35] Although it came into the world with a charter suffused with the most high-flown liberal and pacificistic idealism, with its frayed membership it became, as historian Susan Pedersen aptly remarks, more of a "League of Empires"—the French and British first and foremost, but with input from Italy, the Netherlands, Belgium, and Portugal—whose members shared an agenda aimed at preserving much of their old power and privilege. When King repeatedly remarks in his diary that the League was the plaything of imperialists, he was not simply being paranoid. The League's neo-imperialism was no more graphically in evidence than in its "Permanent Mandates Commission," which (in the words of the League's charter) was supposed to watch over "peoples not yet able to stand by themselves under the strenuous conditions of the modern world," which in plainer English meant that the

League's established empires had a chance to divvy up the territories of defeated powers, notably Germany and the Ottomans.[36]

The atmosphere of aloof privilege that permeated Geneva was another piece of this unflattering picture. As one League critic remembered, when a Spanish delegate heard the loud pop of a champagne cork at a festive lunch, he exclaimed: *"Voilà l'artillerie de la Société des Nations!"*—there is the sound of the League of Nations artillery.[37] For Skelton, European diplomacy entailed a taxing round of five-star hotels and exhaustingly exquisite dinners. The assumptions of the key players in the League bespoke an older world—one in which long-established French and British officials fully believed themselves entitled to rule their colonial inferiors. People like Bennett and Borden might well comfortably sing the praises of the League, since it put so few of their Anglo assumptions at risk.

Still, for Alice Chown and many others—rather like contemporary observers who deplore the ineffectiveness and bureaucracy of the United Nations yet would not wish it to disappear—the compromised League was the only game in town. If the League could only be given teeth—the capacity to administer effective sanctions, as envisaged in its Charter—then it might become a force capable of instituting disarmament and, perhaps, even abolishing war. Chown thought that a massive transnational crusade for peace, a movement combining a global vision with local activism, might force the League to transform itself into something much nobler and finer than it was.

Yet making the League effective—which meant turning it, in some sense, into a world government capable of reining in aggressor states and regulating the international economy—was a project with which King and Lapointe, buttressed by Skelton, had no interest. They did not want the League to become anything like a world government. They opposed every step that might give the League powers to coerce an aggressor.

The one great departure from this Canadian tradition came in 1935, when the federal government was in transition from the Conservative Bennett government (which had been less risk-averse when it came to the League) to a new Liberal King administration (which feared anything that smacked of League coercion). Canadian diplomat Walter Riddell, taking a step that placed him beyond an unclearly stated Canadian position, helped shape a stance that would have blocked Italy's access to resources necessary for war, just as it was busy invading Abyssinia (a.k.a. Ethiopia). The Canadian people were "immensely more interested in Alberta than Abyssinia" had been Skelton's reflection on Mussolini's brutal invasion of the African nation—and he spared no effort to demonstrate to the world that Riddell had not proceeded with the approval of the Canadian government. After the Ethiopian debacle it had become obvious that the League was no longer a plausible instrument for world peace. By 1936 King felt that the organization had become an entity made out of papier mâché.[38] The once formidable League of Nations Society of Canada rapidly declined.

At the Imperial Conference of 1937, Britain's dominions secretary strove heartily to introduce a common imperial foreign policy—to forge new bonds of unity joining together the dominions with the motherland—so that in the event of war the dominions would automatically be involved. King was willing to assent; Lapointe, shaped profoundly by the memory of the Great War and the conscription crisis, could not. Averse to anything that looked like compliance with imperial centralization, King also had his eye on the still-powerful pacificists who dreaded the coming of another war: when in early 1937 the House of Commons approved a hike in the defence budget (from $13 million in 1935–36 to $35 million in 1937–38), his government was inundated with petitions from city councils, as well as an enormous array of other groups—representing veterans, taxpayers, workers, religious denominations—against the increase. King outraged pacificists by allowing the manufacture in Canada of Bren light machine guns—a decision that opened him up to a furious campaign led by Drew that suggested embarrassing parallels with Great War profiteering. In August 1938, King felt obliged to call a judicial inquiry into the contracts related to the gun.[39]

The wave of petitions suggested just how pervasively and deeply the values of pacificism had influenced interwar Canadians. As senator and constitutional authority Eugene Forsey remarked in a letter to Mackenzie King, "The proposed armaments expenditures seem to a large section of public opinion nothing less than a scandal, an outrage and a racket."[40] The 1937 campaign against rearmament was a high-water mark of the peace movement in interwar Canada.

*   *   *

In the mid- to late 1930s, with world war once again looming, did Canadian minds searching for inspiration turn back to Vimy—and the Great "War of Independence"? Especially after 1936, with the unveiling of the soaring Vimy monument in France, it would have been surprising had no one in 1939 brought up Vimy. What is startling is how seldom anyone did.

At the time a few vaguely Vimyist references did turn up.[41] The *Halifax Herald* proclaimed that "the Prussianism that met and broke before the Canadian forces in the great war knows the quality of the Canadian citizen-soldier," citing the Vimy Memorial as proof of the country's continuing promise to support France and Britain. The *Calgary Herald* spoke of how Canada had "achieved her nationhood in the first World War" and that it would "justify it in the second." In the *Ottawa Journal* a writer evoked the memory of the "tragic generation" that had perished in 1914–18, thanks to which "another cycle of free life" was vouchsafed. Canada had "emerged into a nationhood that was given status in blood on Vimy Ridge and Passchendaele and at the breaking of the Hindenburg Line." The same paper carried French newspaper reports referring to Vimy and British propaganda praising Canada's role in the previous war. The *Winnipeg Tribune* published photos of Great War trenches, including one of "Canadian soldiers snatching a few minutes rest," and wondered, "Will This be Repeated?" Jean Giraudoux, a spokesperson for the French government, alluded to "the tremendous feats of gallantry of Dominion soldiers at Vimy, at Thiepval, and on many other famous battlefields," as they sought to rid the world from "intolerable tyranny."[42]

Yet writers tended to place far more emphasis on the Great War as a cautionary tale. For the *Halifax Herald*, the moral of 1914–18 was that war fever was to be avoided. Halifax in 1939 was pervaded by an "extraordinary calm. . . . There were no demonstrations, no crowds, nothing to indicate that it was any different from any other day. . . . This is as it should be. Nothing is to be gained by hysteria or 'jitters.' Nor, for that matter, by demonstrations of 'super-patriotism.'" But, the *Herald* observed, "We didn't know very much about war 25 years ago. We are wiser today . . . and for that reason better equipped to meet it as it comes."[43]

Contemplating Canada's declaration of war on 10 September, the Regina *Leader-Post* noted that some people were surprised that Canadians seemed so unenthusiastic about the war:

> There are no bands playing, no cheering crowds, no hysteria, no flaunting of colors. Some people wonder if Canada is really serious about the job that lies ahead. They contrast the surroundings and the spirit today with what they remember of August, 1914. War broke on Canada in 1914 as an adventure. It was a new experience.

For many, the newspaper remembered, it was just a chance to go "home" to England, Wales, Scotland, or Ireland. But in 1939 Canadians had a more realistic grasp of the job at hand. "War was the last thing in the world they sought. And they would still avoid it if they could. But no one need mistake the quietness and grimness of today's Canada as rising from fear or uncertainty."[44]

For the *Toronto Star*, the Great War and the war that was just beginning were not at all morally equivalent. An editorial argued that the line between good and bad in 1939 was far easier to discern in the case of a Germany that "jeered at pacifism." Yet the paper did find a strong connection between the wars in the legacy of the Treaty of Versailles, in which "the victors made the defeated countries admit that they were solely responsible for the war." It argued that a "vicious system" after 1919 had made "every first class country guilty to a greater or lesser degree."[45]

At Toronto's Christie Street Military Hospital, whence had come so many comments on the *Star*'s 1934 photo-spreads, the same newspaper described the mood as one of "restraint": "Some veterans who had lain in hospital cots since the last war ended and many who had come to hospital in later years, expressed indignation, sorrow or patriotic determination, but there was neither excitement or hullabaloo. . . . There appeared to be neither anxiety nor fear but surprise and regret among the men."[46]

For the *Winnipeg Tribune*, what was most striking about the news of Britain's declaration of war with Germany was the "sharp contrast" with 4 August 1914: "Twenty-five years ago the city responded to the message that the Empire was at war against a great power with ebullitions of popular enthusiasm." But in 1939 the writer saw "impressive calm" and "sober silence." Indeed, "Nowhere was there any excitement at all. There could have been no sharper contrast to the flushed crowds on these same streets a quarter of a century ago when war was declared on the same enemy."[47]

In Regina the *Leader-Post* found "in every voice . . . a silent prayer that the news was not true." Young men, it said, were "silent and unsmiling." It seemed "that the long rows of white crosses and fields of blood-red poppies in Flanders today were vividly pictured in their minds." Among these men, the "most common comment" ran along the lines of, "I have no desire to kill anybody. I don't believe it ever did any good. I don't know yet what I'm going to do. . . . It's hard to think right now." One woman, on the verge of tears, cried on the phone: "Oh, no, it just can't happen, it can't." Another young man doubted he would make a good soldier. "I don't think it's very appetizing," he said. "I'm not much for blood-and-thunder myself."[48]

The *Edmonton Journal* contrasted the atmosphere of 1939 with that of 1914: "There were no parades here on Sunday, no bonfires, no patriotic curbstone speeches, no impassioned outdoor singsongs like the deeply emotional demonstrations seen in Edmonton when the previous world war broke out a quarter-century ago." Edmontonians "waved no banners, burned no effigies, thundered no challenges at the far-off foe as an earlier generation had done." Instead, people were saddened, not elated, by the coming of war. Of one woman, "lightly-built . . . in her middle fifties," kneeling in a church, the paper remarked, "She knelt there, visibly alone among strangers, her pale lips moving wanly, her eyes glistening with unshed tears."[49]

In Vancouver, editorialist Gus Siverts reasoned that the memory-work of the war generation had amounted to a kind of "scarring": "Mothers whose husbands made the supreme sacrifice a quarter of a century ago, now looked upon their sons with anxious eyes and sinking hearts. . . . Deeply Scarred. Too many men and women are too deeply scarred even to forget. That is why they were so quiet yesterday . . . so grim and determined."[50] Many of Vancouver's citizens reportedly stayed up through the night to hear Chamberlain's declaration of war:

Men who had tramped through the mud and witnessed horror 25 years ago listened grimly as Prime Minister Chamberlain . . . told a waiting empire that a state of war existed between Great Britain and Germany. Women whose husbands lay beneath white crosses in France looked at their sons with eyes cleared of all illusion. There was no jubilation—no singing—little laughter. . . . Children sensed the tension and in hundreds of homes, tiptoed down stairs to see why Mother and Dad sat so sombrely around the radio.[51]

The most famous of all the pacifist declarations against the Second World War came on 8 September 1939, when the CCF's Woodsworth stood in the House of Commons to expound views that he explained were his own, not those of most of his party. Woodsworth appealed to "expatriated Britishers" to realize that they were no longer in Britain but in Canada, rather like the people of Quebec had separated themselves from France. Canada included many nationalities, and they could hardly be unified if conscription were introduced.

> I suggest that the common people of the country gain nothing by slaughtering the common people of any other country. . . . I personally cannot give my consent to anything that will drag us into another war. I have boys of my own. I hope they are not cowards, but if any one of these boys, not from cowardice but really through belief, is willing to take his stand on this thing and, if necessary, to face a concentration camp or firing squad, I shall be more proud of that boy than if he enlisted to go to the front.

At that point Woodsworth's speech was interrupted by a cry of "Shame" from a Conservative, but he persevered: "The honorable member can say shame, but that is my belief, and it is the belief of a growing number of Canadians." Mackenzie King would later express his admiration for Woodsworth, even though he said the CCF leader seemed to have forgotten that throughout history "the forces of good and evil had contended with one another."[52] Most of Woodsworth's followers—who were anti-imperialist pacificists, not absolute pacifists—agreed.

In vivid contrast to the treatment of the *nationaliste* politician Henri Bourassa and other opponents of conscription in 1917, Woodsworth was not shouted down. In an editorial in the *Vancouver Sun*, he was even lauded as a man who had spoken his mind: "That is the democratic way for which we are fighting the war, without which the war would not be worth fighting. If ever the time comes when a man like Mr. Woodsworth cannot speak as he chooses, as his conscience directs, our democracy will be lost, the war will be lost, whatever the military verdict."[53]

Ultimately, the CCF did opt for pacificism over pacifism: it opposed conscription, but not the war itself, whose scope it nonetheless tried to limit. It blamed the Second World War on "the same struggle for trade supremacy and political domination which caused the last war, and was perpetuated in the Versailles Treaty." It hoped that Canada might limit itself to offering Britain and the Allies economic assistance, preferably through taxes on higher incomes; emphasize home defence; desist from sending soldiers overseas; and preserve democracy at home.[54] Each point was an implicit critique of the war of 1914–18.

Editorialists recalled the previous war's issue of profiteering. This time a few capitalists must not become rich off the backs of the soldiers who went off to fight and the civilians at home who bought the manufactured goods. The *Halifax Herald* proclaimed its opposition to "the attempts by the few to wring the last grain of material profit from conditions which war creates. . . . There must be no war-profiteering, no trafficking in the machinery and materials of war." The *Winnipeg Tribune* agreed, praising the government for setting up a board to prevent profiteering and arguing that the Canadian public was "in no mood to swallow a repetition of the profiteering scandals which emerged in the course of the last war." Other papers, such as the *Vancouver Sun* and *Winnipeg Tribune*, were concerned about the heavy long-term financial costs of war, including war-related pensions and the payments for the rehabilitation of ex-soldiers. A lesson the *Halifax Herald* drew from the Great War was that greater selectivity should be applied in the recruitment of soldiers, because signing up "the unfit" had proved so expensive. Among other issues, the *Calgary Herald* touched on the need for the government to be clear about what it was offering soldiers when the war ended.[55] The coming of the Second War was haunted by the experience of the veterans of the First.

The possibility of war was no less haunted by the troubling memories of conscription, imposed in 1917 with such ruthlessness upon Quebec. Lapointe had done his best to bring Quebec onside: when he delivered a masterful speech in the House of Commons on 7 September, at a decisive point he turned his back on the opposition benches across from him to speak, face to face, with his French-Canadian compatriots. On 9 September 1939 Maxime Raymond, the Liberal MP for Beauharnois-Laprairie—and later to be leader of the nationalist and anti-conscriptionist Bloc populaire canadien—presented a petition to the House of Commons signed by thousands of Quebeckers, who declared themselves "categorically opposed to any participation in a European war. . . . We do not want participation—not even voluntary participation—in a war in which we have no interest and regarding which the population of Canada was not consulted."[56]

When on Sunday 10 September 1939, shortly after 1 p.m., Canada officially declared war on Germany, as signified by a formal proclamation in the *Canada Gazette*, it did so with the "almost-unanimous" will of Parliament, with only four members—Woodsworth and three French-speakers—in opposition.[57] Yet everyone knew in 1939, as they did not in 1914, that seemingly overwhelming initial support did not signify more deep-seated, fundamental agreement with the war among major segments of the Canadian population—some of them opposed to it outright, many more extremely hesitant about entering yet another global conflict.

Had anyone forgotten about differing French-Canadian perceptions of peace and war, they were reminded of them at a large rally in Montreal on 4 September 1939. Paul Gouin, the leader of Action libérale nationale, told a milling crowd that French Canada adamantly opposed Canadian participation in a war abroad. The theory that if Britain went to war, Canada was also at war was "inept," he said. Let the politicians pushing war feel free to proceed into the trenches. Had not the governor general proclaimed that a Canadian owed his first allegiance to Canada, not the Empire? And could one really trust promises that there would be no conscription, given the record of the past war? Gouin wanted the rally to be read as an unequivocal warning to "the Ministers and the members of Parliament at Ottawa . . . that Quebec is against all military participation in wars of Empire. We don't want that tragic adventure of 1914–18 repeated insofar as Canada is concerned."[58]

When it contemplated the uproar in Quebec, the *Vancouver Sun* reflected that at least Gouin was more moderate in tone than Bourassa had been during the Great War. Montreal's *Gazette*, never reluctant to tutor French Canadians on their duty to the Empire, considered Gouin's rally an "outrage" that had been "profoundly disturbing to other elements." It recommended that the federal government consider the powers it enjoyed under the War Measures Act to nip such dissent in the bud. Conscription once again became a volatile issue that threatened to divide the country. Many onlookers in September 1939, including both Prime Minister King and Opposition Leader Robert James Manion, thought it likely that Canada would not be asked to send a "huge expeditionary force." As King explained, "The days of great expeditionary forces of infantry crossing the ocean are not likely to recur." Indeed, Manion added, the British would probably neither expect nor want such a vast Canadian army.[59]

In addition to worrying about splitting the country on French–English lines, editorialists also reflected on the chilling history of minorities in the Great War. The Regina *Leader-Post* took care to emphasize that the "local Germans" were "horrified" at the news and reminded the newspaper of the "long-standing friendships between German and English citizens." The *Calgary Herald* reminded readers that war entailed "infamies and degradations," and it urged Canadians to steer clear of "senseless intolerance toward innocent people." In particular, it wanted there to be no shaming of children who bore German names. The *Vancouver Sun* told its readers, "We are fighting, first, against the German system, not the German people, who are the chief victims of it." Likewise the *Calgary Herald* said that Canadians were not at war with "the Germany of Handel, Bach and Beethoven; we are not at war with the Germany of Thomas Mann and Paul Ehrlich and Gustav Stresemann."[60]

Newspapers that had been beside themselves with martial enthusiasm in 1914 were critical of war in general in 1939. On 1 September 1939 the *Halifax Herald* argued: "War and the menace of war disrupt things. The whole world today is living a disrupted life. It is an intolerable condition which will only be ended when the war-makers are dethroned." Accompanying the editorial was a cartoon by Robert Chambers depicting Hitler about to knife an angel of peace, as "Starvation," "Pestilence," and "Death" looked on. "Modern mechanized war," the newspaper warned, had become a "grim, implacable business." It would no longer entail "gestures or junketing trips or passing out white-feathers to young men."[61]

Apart from two muted references to Vimy, almost nobody in 1939—not King, not Lapointe, and scarcely an editorial writer—cited the Great War as a sacred struggle to which Canadians should refer when embarking on what would be the Second World War.[62] The overwhelming sensibility of the editorials was not a martial celebration of a Canada founded at Vimy—or the sense, pervasive in 1914, that now at last the nation's young men shall have a fitting, muscular and Christian focus for their lives. Rather there was a sense of grim resolution, as though a much-dreaded eventuality had finally come to pass, and dreams of peace had been undone by Hitler and Mussolini.

On 3 September 1939 King reluctantly stopped outside his office to have his picture taken by journalists curious about the impending war. He noticed some people who seemed remarkably cheerful. "How little," he wrote in his diary, "they realize what lies ahead."[63]

*   *   *

That comment—and a thousand more—suggested that the pacificist sentiments of the 1930s did not simply evaporate in 1939. Rather, the tendency was an integral part of how a great many Canadians now thought about themselves and their world. For these Canadians the choices appeared to have opened up. Neutrality or military alignment? Republic or empire? Rather like the "dead air" that seemingly appeared out of nowhere in Lapointe's 1939 broadcast, the "long week" separating Britain's declaration of war on 3 September from Canada's announcement on 10 September was rich in implications. Even very late in the day, Mackenzie King fretted about compromising the country's neutrality. Even after the declaration of war, he speculated about Hitler being yet brought to terms.

Many people enlisted in the Second World War in an entirely different spirit than that shown by the recruits of 1914. The contagious lack of enthusiasm, Ian Miller suggests, had a number of causes, many of them systemic. "The memory of the Great War and all its sacrifices was still fresh. No one could be enthusiastic about the prospects of renewed fighting in Europe."[64]

Modern war generates an immense fog—of propaganda, disinformation, fear. But this state of affairs also means that the boundaries of war and peace grow ever more permeable. It becomes difficult even to say if a country is at peace if war and rumours of war permeate its politics. One powerful lesson of the Great War, as revealed by the crippling consequences of the post-armistice blockade of Germany, was that seemingly un-military sanctions could wreak havoc as effectively as bombs and artillery. Those who opposed giving the League its teeth were not necessarily militarists—though some were—but often people who genuinely feared war. Among those who were less than impressed by the League as a force for a better world—as was much of the left, deeply embittered by its incapacity to stop the war that overthrew the Spanish Republic and its failure to rein in Fascists—were critics who saw League-promoting "peace propaganda" as "war propaganda." In response to the *Free Press* photospread, the Workers' Ex-Servicemen's League worried, "The horrors of war are paraded with the sole intent of creating in the populace a desire to give the league 'its teeth,' and the individual nations a carte blanche war-preparedness expenditure."[65]

For the likes of Alice Chown, any backing down meant that the aggressors could continue bullying weaker states with impunity. In response to the Munich Agreement of 1938, she scolded Canadian-born journalist (and British politician) Beverley Baxter, who was reporting on events from London, charging that Britain and its Empire would be doomed if they continued to follow such a short-sighted policy. Chown likened Baxter to a peddler of patent medicines, who seemed willing to stand by while the Nazis inflicted suffering on the Jews, and the Japanese upon the Chinese.[66] For Chown, who had fought so hard to make the League of Nations into something it perhaps could never have been, it was immoral to countenance dictators as they carved up the world, even though standing up to them might also lead to war. The world of 1938–39 provided no easy answers.

What was particularly impressive about the peace movement of the 1930s was its comprehensive vision of an all-embracing politics of peace. The efforts of its members entailed little things (not singing "God Save the King") and big things (pushing for world disarmament at Geneva) and many things in between, such as the protracted campaign against cadet training in schools. They dreamed of a peaceful and peacemaking state—one, the more insightful of them realized, at odds with the dominant political economy of the day. Theirs was a precocious, daring, complicated, and ultimately inspiring struggle to break free from the traps of martial romanticism—then British imperialism, today Vimyism—and to reflect upon the responsibilities for peace and war borne by all.

6

SCULPTING THE JAGGED EDGES OF WAR: MOMENTOUS QUESTIONS, MONUMENTAL DECISIONS

The membrane between remembrance and glorification is very thin.
— MICHAEL ENRIGHT, CBC Radio, "The Sunday Edition"

A SHROUDED FIGURE, head bowed, gazes down at a sarcophagus. The solitary statue suggests nothing else but a graveside mourner. The artist's intention is unmistakable. Walter Allward's brooding *Canada Bereft* portrays a woman—and a country—in mourning. Its place of prominence at the Canadian Battlefields Memorial at Vimy underlines the Toronto sculptor's intention in fashioning his masterpiece. The Memorial's Rodin-inspired sculptures, including the figure of a woman who has come to be known as "Mother Canada," adorn a massive monument that dominates the landscape of the Douai Plain in Northeastern France. The Vimy Memorial stands as a public recognition of private grief. It took Allward, an accomplished draughtsman and stickler for detailed perfection, fifteen years to complete. By 1933 he was explaining that the Vimy Memorial had to be understood as a "sermon against the futility of war."[1]

Some seventy years later, when the Canadian government decided to restore the weather-damaged limestone monument, architectural historian Jacqueline Hucker reflected: "Allward's design was unlike any previous Canadian war monument. It made no direct reference to war or victory, but alluded rather to the consequences of war and the suffering of those who were left to grieve. Through reference to the cyclical myth of sacrifice and spiritual rebirth, it also offered solace to the living."[2]

Allward's magisterial Vimy Memorial offers nothing of the romantic heroization and victory celebration common to many Canadian monuments commissioned in the aftermath of the Great War. Other more conventional sites tend to offer Christian symbols of resurrection and ascension. Lofty angels of victory look to the heavens; noble soldiers hold their rifles high; crosses of sacrifice stand solemnly. In the years after 1918 a distinct whiff of militarism wafted through a number of the commemorations. Under the newspaper headline "Splendour and Gaiety Characterize Annual Military Ball," Calgary readers learned in 1921 that a highlight of the local social calendar included a triumphal arch artfully fashioned from machine guns and bayonets.[3]

By the time the war ended, Walter Allward had emerged as the most sought-after designer and sculptor of monuments commemorating war. He already had a solid track record. His imposing *South African War Memorial* (1910) occupies a prominent place in the middle of Toronto's grand University Avenue. Its lower level features a young woman, one arm aloft, between two soldiers in period military garb. That woman was in essence a "Mother Canada" long before the commissioning of the Vimy Memorial: in 1919 a Canadian critic described the woman featured on the South African memorial as a "young mother, Canada, sending out her sons to battle for the Empire."[4]

Allward, born in 1876 in Toronto, was a prodigy. He was one of those people whose childhood interests eventually became a lifelong calling. As a boy he had fashioned models of family members and family pets, anything he could persuade to sit still. He skipped school to spend time in a taxidermist's shop, watching birds and fish take shape. In 1890, at the age of fourteen, he started work as an apprentice to his carpenter father, soon moving on to an architectural firm and a brick works—all the time maintaining his penchant for modelling. One story has it that when he completed a job for a Toronto company, his patrons refused to pay the entire invoice because they decided he was too young to receive such a sum all at once.[5] Allward's first major commission, at age nineteen, was for a statue called *Peace* to be placed atop the *Northwest Rebellion Monument* (1895) in Queen's Park, Toronto, at the upper end of University Avenue. Like the woman down the avenue sending her sons off to do battle with the Dutch settlers in South Africa, Allward's tribute to the 1885 Métis war of resistance is a woman with one arm held high. Bare-breasted, she appears to be holding laurel leaves and has one arm outstretched—early evidence of the artist's ability to portray gesture. A sword hangs prominently from her waistband.

Allward's War of 1812 memorial (1903) stands in dramatic contrast to the South African and 1885 memorials. The *Army and Navy Veterans Memorial* commemorating this war does not occupy pride of conspicuous place. It sits in the undistinguished Victoria Memorial Square west of Spadina Avenue, a short distance north of the railway tracks. Unlike Allward's other early war memorials, this work has no full, standing figures. Instead, a bust of a lonely old soldier of the early nineteenth century sits alone, a half-figure with prominent sideburns and epaulettes. The balding man wears a pensive, solemn expression. As in the later *Canada Bereft*, war seems to have taken a sad toll. The figure's left sleeve hangs empty.

The Great War would profoundly influence Allward. He was both a consummate perfectionist and a romantic whose feelings animated his work. He had already developed a reputation for missing deadlines; he was a stickler for detail who was only satisfied when convinced that his work was the absolute best he could do. But what was a sculptor to do in the face of the mounting evidence of the monstrous disaster that was the war? Allward would have to wait for a flurry of postwar commissions in Ontario—Stratford, Peterborough, and Brantford. In the meantime, in 1917, he wrote to the Ministry of Militia. He had perhaps heard of what wounded soldiers called "the tin noses shop," the Masks for Facial Disfigurement Department at a London hospital. Perhaps the work of fellow sculptor Anna Coleman Ladd and her Studio for Portrait Masks in Paris had caught his attention. With the widespread effects of shards of hot metal splinters or "shrapnel," industrialized war generated a huge demand for facial repair. Allward offered his sculpting services, suggesting that he could reconstruct the disfigured faces of maimed soldiers "by modeling missing parts." His offer was generous—it meant he would be setting his own professional work aside—and he received a pro forma response indicating that his offer would be passed along, but nothing came of it.[6]

If he could not assist those the French call *les mutilés de guerre*, Allward could work on the memorials that he hoped would in some way help Canadians struggling to cull any meaning from four years of mass death. His Stratford memorial *Might Versus Right* foreshadows the Vimy monument. Its two allegorical figures, one dragging a battered sword by its blade, are neither noble nor valiant. They seem downcast and are not the conventional "heroes, heroines and patriots" of the day. "By avoiding the stock stereotype emblems and attributes so typical of his contemporaries," writes Lane Borstad, a student of Allward's career, "Allward aligned himself closer to the French romantic tradition of Rodin than the academic sculpture tradition of Canada." One of the bronze figures in his Peterborough war memorial carries what Allward described in 1920 as an "idle shield" and an "idle sword" that signify that "there can be no further conflict." The other figure represents "strife or barbarism, beaten and retreating before the strength of civilization, the sword has fallen to the ground and the flambeau has been extinguished."[7]

The sculptor was not able to complete the Peterborough memorial. Instead, a splendid commission loomed in the form of a competition for a Canadian Battlefield Memorial in France. Work on the Vimy Memorial, Allward's masterpiece, took up much of the rest of his creative life. Its construction encompassed most of the interwar period—an ambitious, expensive, and controversial project that taxed the designer's considerable energies and perfectionism to the limit. Less than two years after Allward secured the job in 1921, the project was being attacked by ex–Great War officer Garnet Hughes, the son of the eccentric Sam Hughes, as a "waste of money as well as being a tribute to vanity."[8] When the Imperial War Graves Commission insisted on having the names of missing soldiers carved on the front walls of the monument, Allward objected, trying in vain for a compromise that would display the names on the floor. Carving some 11,000 names on the wall, argued Allward, carried "the danger of having it look like a huge sign board."[9] In 1925, four years into a project that would not be finished until 1936, Allward's supervisor at the Canadian Battlefield Memorials Commission was already sounding the alarm over concerns surrounding the selection of the best stone. Col. H.S. Osborne warned Allward that delays were costly and "will place the Commission (and the whole project) in a bad light before the public." Allward replied that he had been "eating and sleeping stone for so long that it has become an obsession with me, and incidentally a nightmare."[10] The architect was having trouble with quarry operators in Yugoslavia, English contractors, and the War Graves Commission, among others.

Several months after becoming prime minister in 1930, an obviously impatient R.B. Bennett visited Vimy. Project supervisor Capt. D.C. Simson reported to Allward, living at his London, England, studio in Maida Vale, that Bennett's "attitude was critical." Bennett had told Simson that other big memorials had been put up in twelve or eighteen months.

Allward soon got a stern warning from the prime minister himself. "This work must be completed in 1932. That does not mean 1933, but in June or July of that year [1932]." Not long after that, Allward received the chair of the Canadian Battlefields Memorial Commission at his Maida Vale studio. Gen. S.C. Mewburn, a Hamilton lawyer, was apparently under none of Bennett's illusions. He asked if the job could be wrapped up by 1934. Allward said, "I told him I sincerely believed it could be done then."[11]

The Vimy Memorial was finally completed in 1936. Though neither on time nor on budget, it was almost universally admired. One Toronto newspaper called it "a symphony in stone." Edwards Lutyens, the famous architect and designer of the *Memorial to the Missing of the Somme* at Thiepval and the Cenotaph in Whitehall, London, declared it a "great masterpiece" that would "make a great impression for all time."[12]

At the turn of the next century Jane Urquhart created a fictionalized Walter Allward in her novel *The Stone Carvers*. Urquhart had visited Vimy and was so moved by the monument that she made Allward and his creation central to the story of Klara Becker, a Canadian woodcarver desperate to work on the sculptures that would pay tribute to her lover, killed in combat. Donning men's clothes, Klara passes as a man and goes with her brother in an attempt to get hired on by Allward at Vimy. Her brother had lost a leg in the battle of Vimy Ridge. In Urquhart's story:

> Allward took all of this in, the two damaged people, the now distant pain of bereavement and lost youth, the warmth of the affection that surrounded the pair, a warmth that in some ways was engendered by the bloody, endless tragedy of the war and this huge white structure meant to be a monument to grief, on the one hand, and a prayer for peace, on the other.[13]

In 1936 the designer himself played little role in the ceremonies that accompanied the unveiling of the memorial. Before the crowds of Canadian pilgrims and other visitors descended on Vimy for the formalities, Allward told a London reporter that he had wanted to create "something beautiful" that was "worthy of the men who gave their lives and, as a protest in a quiet way against the futility of war, may make men regret that humanity has to go to war instead of being proud of it."[14]

*   *   *

Allward's sermon against war is often simply presented as a memorial meant to arouse admiration for "our side" in the Great War—for the "valour of those Canadians who, in the Great War, fought for the liberties of Canada, of the Empire, and of humanity," as one patriotic historian describes the events of the Second Battle of Ypres, in a neat formula eliding liberty, empire, and humanity.[15]

For decades writers have been intensely interested in how individuals and societies remember the past. The more that people discover about how some things come to be remembered and others forgotten, the less this seems to be a matter of straightforward factual retrieval from some vast collective filing cabinet full of well-marked, separate dossiers ready to be consulted by anyone considering a particular question. On both the individual and collective levels, manifestations of public memory—or, as historian Alan Gordon puts it, "conceptions of history enshrined in historic sites and public monuments"—raise questions about how "social traditions" connect "to the distant past by attempting to preserve an idealized memory that presents the established social order as natural." As Gordon argues, "Events and people chosen as subjects for commemoration reveal much about the sense of history of the men and women who select them."[16] War in particular accentuates this tendency to make one view of history—usually officially sanctioned—the proper view.[17]

Over many years the Canadian landscape has become crowded with monuments to wars, and many of those sites carry messages that no longer engage with a great number of people: Crimea (the Sebastopol Monument in Halifax) and South Africa (Allward's soaring monument on University Avenue) are prime examples. The Vimy monument, though, has survived to become the epicentre of a network of myths and symbols centred on the war—in 2012 even replacing an image of an elaborate sculpture by First Nations artist Bill Reid on the twenty-dollar banknote. Yet, in the case of Vimy, what people think they discern in the monument has changed remarkably over time. As solid as most monuments might seem to be, the messages that they convey are not necessarily "concrete."[18]

A prevailing pattern of commemoration in the early postwar years was to follow pre-existing traditions—to adhere, as Jay Winter puts it, to "notions developed before, and to a large degree independent of, the war."[19] The Great War in itself did not initiate a sudden cultural rupture into the artistic forms typical of what has become known as "modernism"—of works iconoclastically replacing cultural idioms popular in the nineteenth century with new modes associated with the twentieth century, such as free verse, non-representational art, and secular scepticism about life after death. But after the Great War the bereaved had to take solace in the cultural resources readily available to them; and the almost incomprehensible burdens of bereavement became all the more grievous because the bodies of the beloved were so far away, often in unknown places, left for good in Europe.[20] As Jonathan Vance points out, in Canada the Great War was conventionally commemorated in romantic novels, stained glass windows, sculptures representing heroic soldiers, and patriotic poems: funeral after funeral exhibited no break with long-standing Christian notions of noble crusades, rewards in the afterlife, and the valiant struggle of Canadians against a barbaric "other."[21] Saintly soldiers, eulogized in services, were commemorated as heroes in honour rolls, spotlessly depicted in stained-glass windows, and made to stand steadfastly in the squares of small-town and big-city Canada from St. John's, Nfld., to Victoria, B.C.: the thesis that such commemorations repeated age-old Christian motifs of redemptive suffering and ultimate salvation is persuasive.

Especially down to the mid-1920s most Canadian war memorials were in one sense public—they were meant to be viewed by anyone who came to see them or happened by—but only a few of them were the result of publicly managed projects by the state. Many were orchestrated by local community organizations, generally consisting of the notable and respectable portion of the citizenry.[22] Especially to the extent that commemoration aimed to provide condolence and support to the bereaved, it took the form of a public funeral—with the normal assurances that the departed had ascended to a better place and that his or her life represented an unblemished record of service to others.

Yet, especially after this initial funerary period was over, the Canadian experience gradually diverged from this pattern, at first subtly, and then with increasing clarity. As time passed and more and more people came to see the war in an ironic light—as they did massively after the early 1920s—they could find a measure of such healing in monuments that aimed not to commemorate the dead but to ensure that nothing like the Great War could ever happen again.

As the larger state—outside local communities and private individuals—came to involve itself in memorialization, it found itself wrestling with all the unresolved ambiguities and tensions of the Great War, including the experience of disgruntled veterans, critiques of officer-oriented history, and a lingering distaste for the whole experience in Quebec. After the early 1920s, as the commemoration of war became more and more state-focused and hence, inescapably, politicized, a sharp sense of the ironies of war had not only taken root, but by the mid-1930s had become pervasive.

*   *   *

To say that Canada's longest-serving prime minister cared about the memory of the Great War would be a considerable understatement.

Before 1914 he had declared himself a member of the "peace movement." When war came, William Lyon Mackenzie King hoped against hope that cooler heads would prevail in Britain's Liberal cabinet. He complained when people spoke of "our" Empire. He blamed the war enthusiasts he often called "the Jingoes" for much of the trouble. He likened a Europe gorged on "huge rival armaments" to a man who had ingested "substances that were foreign to natural living, and now like a disordered stomach was dislodging them all." He regarded militarists as "diabolical" for arguing for the destruction of German power. They risked plunging all of humanity into chaos: "It is devilish to my way of thinking and madness having regard to the welfare of mankind in the world. For the most highly civilized and cultured nations to destroy each other is scarcely believable."[23]

Throughout the buildup to war King maintained a sceptical stance about the "German scare." In 1913 he urged a Toronto audience to imagine a Canada *not* joining Britain, France, Germany, and other European states in acquiring the "paraphernalia of war"—but rather committing itself to more pacific ways of bolstering the Empire. "My mind," he told them, "does not run on the lines of war; my mind runs rather along the lines of peace. (Applause.)"[24] King considered Czarist Russia—keen to seize Constantinople and much of the Austro-Hungarian Empire—to be a major influence in contributing to the war in Europe.[25]

As his many opponents never allowed him to forget, King did not fight in the war. He instead took up a position advising the Rockefellers on how they might conduct labour relations without massacring workers and their families, as their Colorado Fuel and Iron Company had notoriously done in 1914. For King, such reforms in labour relations were themselves a form of "war work," and he considered the perplexingly metaphysical book in which he outlined them, *Industry and Humanity* (1918), as his greatest contribution to world peace. (The problems of "international & industrial war" were "closely allied," he remarked in his diary as the guns of August started to sound in 1914.)[26]

Ever famous for his capacity to see at least two sides to every question, King favoured conscription "as a principle" but opposed it as a coercion of Quebec because that would "help to destroy the fabric of Confederation" and thereby display "more weakness to the Central powers," while adding little to the strength of the Entente.[27] Despite his ambivalence, he ran on the anti-conscriptionist Liberal platform in 1917, and that campaign helped him win the Liberal leadership in 1919, which he did only with Quebec's support. For him, the "problem of being Canada in the aftermath of the Great War" entailed, through much of the 1920s and 1930s, addressing the issue of preserving a country propelled by the Great War into damaging conflicts between French-Canadian Catholics and Anglo-Canadian Protestants.

When King visited the European battle sites in 1919, he found the "scene of desolation" almost indescribable. If the war had one great impact upon him, it was to strengthen within him the conviction that war was the enemy of humanity: "It is impossible to put into words the feelings that come into one's breast amid a scene of desolation such as the one by which we are at the moment surrounded. I suppose the feeling of concentration is the one that lies deepest of all, the consecration of one's life to the cause of Peace and Truth and Justice. War is the antithesis of all these things."

Mackenzie King was a complicated man, both as spiritualist and political leader. He spoke of the "tragedy of the late war," "noble soldiers," and "the places of sacrifice." In 1926, speaking of Vimy Ridge, King paraphrased Lt.-Gen. Lord Julian Byng, 1st Viscount of Vimy, in his remark that nine provinces had ascended the hill "side by side, animated and united by a common ideal," which could only be a lesson to Canadian politicians inclined to fractiousness.[28] Yet he was no martial nationalist. Nor was he, as one scholar suggests, the prisoner of an "instinctive loathing of military men."[29] Rather, in reflecting on his dreams or in announcing war plans to the cabinet, he evoked not the martial glory of Canadians in arms, but the principles of the liberal tradition, which posited that in a world of interconnected markets wars were irrational holdovers from a distant age.[30] As a precondition of order, peace—even more than liberty—was liberalism's most indispensable principle. For him, the only consolation to be drawn from another such eruption in the twentieth-century world was in being able to claim that its participants had, themselves, yearned for peace. In King's mind, the "foe" to be always quarrelled with in "Flanders Fields" was war itself. He recoiled from the notion that Canada was born on Vimy Ridge, that the country had secured its independence and freedom through the exercise of its military might.

Nor, in his eyes, was the German Empire the sole locus of militarism. The authoritarianism that had surfaced within it could be found in many aspects of state and civil society in Canada and throughout the Empire. King believed himself to be an apostle of "Peace, international and industrial." Here was the "great work" he hoped to accomplish in this world.[31]

As a sympathizer of what he called the "peace movement" and an evolutionary thinker who placed peace at the indispensable core of his liberalism, Mackenzie King was Canada's ultimate liberal pacificist.[32] Indeed, King's tendencies in this direction would lead Pierre Berton (who fifty years later became the great celebrator of Vimy) to lament the long-serving prime minister as the emasculating underminer of Canada's virile image. It would be neither the first nor the last time that detractors impugned the Liberal leader's unsoldierly and even un-Canadian gender ambiguity.[33]

As early as 1919, at least according to his own perhaps self-aggrandizing memory, King was keen to acquire the site of Vimy; throughout the 1920s and 1930s, to an extent that almost strains credulity, he was seized by the mission to shape the interwar memory of the war in a way that suited his pacificist and idealistic world view. He came strongly to believe that the site of Vimy must be preserved—that if the battleground were to be "ceded to Canada, it should be maintained by the country in an appropriate manner. Really, to know our own country one has to see Courcelette and Vimy Ridge. Not until then can one appreciate the heroisms and sacrifices, as well as the achievements of which Canadians are capable."[34]

Even when he did not directly shape a monument—as in the case of Allward's Vimy—King provided the context in which the major Great War monuments of his time took shape. The federal cabinet devoted considerable energy to questions of war monuments. Great War elements were built right into the Parliament Buildings, with the Peace Tower,[35] the Book of Remembrance, and a central commemorative pillar all bearing witness to the conflict.

King had a direct and personal role in shaping *The Response*, Canada's National War Memorial in Ottawa commemorating Canadians' response to the call to arms in 1914. (Since 1945, over the objections of the Legion and other groups, it has come to be considered a monument to all of Canada's war dead, not just to those who served in 1914–18.) From its inception the national war memorial in Ottawa was directly planned by the federal cabinet. In May 1923 King told the House of Commons that his government planned to erect a monument "in commemoration of the nation's accomplishments and sacrifices during the Great War."[36] He was clear about what he wanted: a non-militaristic commemoration, one that under no circumstances would promote war, but rather emphasize the commitment and sacrifice of all Canadians, irrespective of their distinctive cultural identities. From his left, the prime minister was prodded by Woodsworth to make sure that Canada's national monument would on no account "glorify war or militarism"—King even urged Canada to create a memorial that placed special emphasis on the "futility of war." From his perspective, the Canadian state should express its sympathies with "the fallen" and their families—while conveying the principal message that "war is a 'miserable failure.'" King did declare his resolve to celebrate the "spirit . . . ready for sacrifice" that the Canadians had exhibited in 1914, "in a cause which was the greatest the world has known in the history of human freedom."[37]

The fine distinction—between glorifying the war itself and glorifying the self-sacrificing warriors who had fought in it—was enshrined in the application guidelines for the monument competition. The *Conditions of Open Competition* declared, "It is not the intention that this monument should glorify war or suggest the arrogance of a conqueror." Backtracking slightly, the guidelines then announced that an expression of "the spirit of victory" was essential to "immortalize Canada's defenders" and to "convey a feeling of gratitude that out of this great conflict a new hope has sprung for future prosperity under peaceful conditions."[38] Thus the Canadian soldiers who had lost their lives "in the service of humanity" were to be hailed, without in any way glorifying the war in which they had fought. The result was also to be a *Canadian* monument—with scarcely an acknowledgement of the war's imperial character—that saw soldiers working both as "Canada's defenders" and as servants of humanity: they were imagined to be both *very* local and *very* global, but never imperial.

As so often, King could thus, seemingly, square the circle: he could glorify the warriors, who had in his mind sacrificed themselves for freedom, without glorifying the war. As a man who saw his whole life as a struggle to uphold the claims of the spirit over those of mere matter, King was intent on seeing the war as one in which self-sacrificing Canadians gave of themselves so that war might be forever abolished. In his years, and at least partly under his influence, war commemoration became more and more ethereal and spiritual—with the apex of this development to be found at Vimy.

In the case of the National War Memorial, both the entries that failed and the one that succeeded illuminate the processes of cultural selection proceeding from these contradictory criteria. The failing entries included one that had a "pair of lions," signifying the "Courage, Fortitude, Strength, and Reliance of the Defenders." Another had a "mounted horseman of the Middle Ages" going forth to vanquish the justice-hating foe. A third featured "a lion stamping out evil represented by an eagle," which surely would have offended both King's anti-militarist sensibilities and his keen sense of needing to conciliate both the British and the Americans. The winning entry, from Vernon March of Farnborough, England, managed to fit the bill almost perfectly—in part because King "guided March when creating his entry" to meet the commemorative criteria he himself had established. "It is difficult," historian Malcolm Ferguson explains, "to overemphasize the role that the Prime Minister played in this phase of the monument's creation."[39] *The Response* captured Mackenzie King's lifelong quest to sideline all social divisions and to emphasize the interest of all people in a harmonious social order. The National War Memorial characterized a group of Canadians all pulling together as a united team, evincing in their very bodies a common purpose.

It took from 1926 to 1939 for the memorial to come to completion on Ottawa's Confederation Square—formerly known as Connaught Place. Entire buildings had to be demolished. The details on all twenty-two figures had to be checked and rechecked because they were intended to be accurate representations of various kinds of servicemen (and two servicewomen). The artists had to take great care to render the figures' faces to avoid any suggestion of belligerence; instead, the subjects were to "express movement and the eagerness and enthusiasm of the people" in responding to the call to war.[40] Without making any visible concessions to Canadians' various backgrounds, the designers provided discernible differences of age, gender, and rank in the various figures, blending the whole comfortably into a portrait of a group determinedly working together. The generational, hierarchical, or linguistic divisions of the actual CEF are by no means emphasized, and so, in Denise Thomson's words, the monument reveals the "equality of war dead."[41]

The "Spirit of Canada" was on display as it paraded through the memorial arch—just as, in the later official memory of the 1990s, the "Spirit of

Canada" manifested itself on 9 April 1917 on Vimy Ridge. Duly spiritual-ized, the past was insulated from rational critique in moves that countered in advance any critical objections—such as those made by soldier-writers such as Harrison, Bird, Pedley, and Kerr—affirming that officers and men had had markedly different wars; or those, coming from the likes of Abbé Lionel Groulx and Ernest Lapointe, affirming that francophone Quebec had experienced a markedly different war than had its Anglo counter-part. As designed, the memorial did have one possible complication. It is topped by two allegorical figures. In the original description of the design, the *two* figures alight upon the sculpture bearing the *three* "blessings of Victory, Peace and Liberty" in the footsteps of the hard-working heroes below. In King's mind, the allegorical figures represented *Peace* and *Free-dom*, terms that evaded the more (French and American) revolutionary resonance of "liberty" and avoided the martial overtones of "victory." For what King saw as a "national monument of the most significant epoch in our history," which "cannot be made too credible to the nation," no atten-tiveness to ideological overtones was excessive.[42]

The unveiling of the war memorial in May 1939 was performed by King George VI, whose speech—which claimed that "Canada's sons and daughters" had fought "for the cause of peace and freedom"—outlined Mackenzie King's distinctive take on liberal ideology, that is, that peace was a core value, and not a collateral consequence, of liberalism. This uncanny coincidence of King's political philosophy and the king's speech was wholly non-coincidental. the monarch was reading a text written for him by the prime minister.[43] King micro-managed the politics of Great War memory very carefully indeed.

*   *   *

One of the most important attributes of Canadian war commemoration was the early involvement of a federal state especially keen to see its war commemorated in stone. As early as 1915 Conservative prime minister Robert Borden was already eagerly anticipating the monuments that he hoped governments would erect in celebration of the achievements of Canadian soldiers.[44] In May 1919 Col. Sam Hughes was urging that war memorials should all be standardized (making some allowance for bigger communities to have bigger ones), and although the plan went nowhere, it was striking that across Canada the dead were often commemorated with mass-produced memorials purchased in the United States. Although bereavement was undoubtedly personal, the production of commemorative monuments could, under conditions of modern warfare, become almost as standardized as the production of corpses.

Elsewhere, memories of the war could not be so easily handled. In Quebec the issues of war memorialization remained particularly prickly. In Montreal one leading monument, unveiled in a contentious ceremony, cites in English the soldiers' sacrifice for "King and Country" and in French mentions only "La Patrie." Some of the wayside crosses that the Québécois continued to erect in large numbers in the 1910s and 1920s were appeals to God to protect their sons from army recruiters: "Young men hiding in the woods sometimes promised a cross if God would prevent their capture."[45]

From 1924 to 1928 multi-ethnic, often tempest-tossed Winnipeg became embroiled in a debate over war commemoration involving two Canadian artists, Emanuel Hahn and Elizabeth Wyn Wood, who were among the leading sculptors of the day.[46] Hahn, born in Reutlinger, Württemberg, Germany, on 30 May 1881, had immigrated to Toronto with his family in July 1888. His father was a lawyer, but the son early on took an abiding interest in art, and particularly in the ideas of William Morris and the Arts and Crafts movement. Hahn came to believe strongly in using public art to elevate and reform the community, and he found a nice match for his enthusiasms by working in Toronto from 1908 to 1912 as Walter Allward's studio assistant.

Hahn's divided sympathies on the coming of the Great War were expressed in his first independent sculpture, *War the Despoiler* (1915), which proved, according to art historian Victoria Baker, to be "one of the earliest formal statements by a Canadian artist about the war." Like Varley's *For What?* Hahn's sculpture depicts war as an unmitigated disaster, "a rapacious reptilian monster," a Moloch figure into whose "fiery, gaping maw human victims are helplessly carried in a rushing stream."[47] Hahn got away with this unqualified rejection of war, at a time when Torontonians were generally embracing it wholeheartedly, because his audience could imagine that the Moloch of his statue was Germany—although that was assuredly not the sculptor's intention.

After the war Hahn worked for the Thomson Monument Company, where he produced one design after another for monuments commemorating the Great War. The company's advertisements, carried in magazines such as *Saturday Night* and in trade journals, offered communities an upscale, made-in-Canada alternative to the purchase of ready-made statues from U.S. distributors. The work found favour with the Ontario Advisory Committee on War Memorials, formed in early 1919 "to counsel prospective community sponsors," and which "included among its recommended types of memorials: fountains, tablets, symbolic groups, and commemorative portrait statues." The idea, by implication, was to raise their sights above the conventional portrait statues of individuals that tended to prevail in many communities. When two reviewers looked upon Hahn's art in 1924, one contrasted it with the "miserable examples of statuary that have appeared in Toronto as a result of the Great War." The other observed that Ontario municipalities that had settled for "statues of American soldiers to commemorate our own dead boys" should feel bitterly ashamed.[48]

In Winnipeg Hahn's German background was to fuel a debate that demonstrated the war's unhealed wounds. In Canada's third-largest city, roughly half the population was born outside Canada, many of them drawn from Germany and the Austro-Hungarian and Russian empires. This demographic pattern bequeathed an air of permanent cultural crisis to Winnipeg civic politics. In the Winnipeg General Strike in 1919, some veterans had rampaged through the streets and demanded that those who did not appear to be British pay homage to the British flag.

Such polarization influenced the city's selection of a monument to commemorate its war dead—who numbered over 1,600.[49] A fund of $10,000 had been raised by Winnipeg women in 1916 as a tribute to the soldiers. By 1920 the idea that the money would be spent on a monument instead of bettering the lives of living veterans was fiercely opposed by such spokespeople as R. Crystal Irving, the Dominion Secretary of the Army and Navy Veterans, and P.G. Rumer of the Central Winnipeg Command of the Great War Veterans' Association. A temporary cenotaph, costing about $2,000 and unveiled at the corner of Portage and Main, was the focus of intensely personal acts of grieving the dead: at the time of the anniversary of Amiens, the cenotaph was covered with handwritten cards, plants, and cut flowers. "This time two years ago I did not know Jack was dead," said a card that accompanied a pot of daisies and wild flowers. "He was killed at Amiens." Another, with a wreath of brown-eyed Susans, simply said, "My Son." A bereaved family left another inscribed, "Our Dear Daddy."A card from Margaret mourned "My sweet-heart, Charlie." As Winter observes in a commentary on the surprising way in which Britons adopted London's unadorned cenotaph as a sacred space set apart from institutional religion, the monuments and moments in which the bereaved took leave of their beloved in the wake of the war had an intensely personal, local quality.[50]

Yet soon, in Winnipeg and elsewhere, things became rather less personal and far more contentious. By November 1923, the Winnipeg GWVA waited on city council to establish a permanent cenotaph. Some worried that a monument to victory, and not a memorial grieving the dead, was in the works. By 1924 the themes of patriotic commemoration and hostility to Winnipeg's non-Anglo population were coming together. At the city's left-wing May Day parade in 1924, 98 per cent of the marchers were said to be foreign-born; but at a meeting on that same day a spokesperson for the GWVA rather truculently proclaimed that, if he were in charge, such people would be forced to place a wreath on the cenotaph.[51]

On April 1925, after $26,000 was raised for a permanent cenotaph, the city launched a competition for its design, and on 23 December, from over fifty entries, the War Memorial Committee selected Hahn's submission. Soon rumours about the artist's nationality started to circulate. The Winnipeg Board of Trade, catching wind of Hahn's German heritage, pronounced the choice of his monument an "insult to the memory of our heroes." Similar resolutions were passed by the Amputations Association, Army and Navy Veterans, Imperial Veterans Association, and the GWVA.[52] Some letters to the editor took on a violently anti-German hue: one writer remembered accounts of German atrocities and recalled the saying, "The only good Hun is a dead 'un," and asked whether "any man of the Second Brigade" who remembered the gas attack on Ypres in 1915 could "accept a German-designed memorial." Would not the mothers, widows, and orphans of our veterans shrink from any thought of a "born German" designing a memorial to their dead? As A.E. Parker of the Board of Trade suggested, a German was a German—the naturalization of an individual did not make him a Canadian "in the true sense of the word. It didn't instil into him ideals of British justice." A spokesperson for the Commercial Travellers' Association stated that the very fact of Hahn's German ancestry would impel him to spit upon the monument in contempt. Here was a man "whose ancestors helped to kill our boys. It would be an insult to every soldier in this country."[53]

Some Winnipeggers remembered the Great War as a noble crusade against a devilish enemy and saw accursed Germans as a people carrying the taint of militarism. But others believed the Great War's meaning lay elsewhere. One letter writer remembered McCrae's "In Flanders Fields." What would "our dead soldiers" make of all this rancour?

> Would their message again be "Take up our quarrel with the foe?" The foe? What foe? During the war we all first blamed the Germans. . . . We were told this was a war to end war, and that we were fighting that we might enjoy peace, permanent peace. Who or what today then is the foe? The enemies of peace, honorably righteous peace, race prejudice—inhabited or restricted patriotism. . . . Are we to prove victors in war and vanquished in peace? Vanquished by petty and nationalistic prejudices? . . . Citizens of Winnipeg, you have an opportunity to do your bit in the cause of peace if you but rise to the occasion. Shake off your war time hates. . . . Erect your war memorial? No—your Peace Memorial.[54]

Even after Hahn withdrew his design in February 1926—his models were returned to him in 1927, along with a $500 honorarium—the storm over remembrance continued. One veteran from the Princess Pats, who pointed out that his motherless children were being ministered to by a helpful Swede, remarked that "the majority of real fighting veterans" opposed the outcry against naturalized subjects. The executive of the city's Canadian Club denounced the "Prussianism" that had victimized a blameless Hahn, "an individual who is guilty of no wrong," and it urged Winnipeggers to honour the "memory of those who have fallen" by realizing their ideals of freedom and justice by establishing peace and goodwill throughout the world." The Independent Labor Party supported the Canadian Club "in condemning the proposal to deny to Emanuel Hahn the award won by him in the cenotaph competition."[55] The Great War was clearly remembered in starkly different ways.

The competition was restarted, this time with the proviso that it was open only to "any Canadian citizen born in Canada, elsewhere in the British Empire, or in any of the late allied countries." Of the fourscore models submitted in this second competition, one stood out. It had been submitted by Elizabeth Wood, whose proposed statue had a bare-chested near-naked man holding a long downward-pointing sword, with the inscription, "We have Gained a Peace Forever." As Wood explained:

> He is not aggressive; he is protective. He holds behind him, clasped in his hand, a great branch of maple, symbol of the far-flung Dominion

he has been aroused to guard. I have felt the spirit of the Canadian soldier. He went out there not merely to die but to serve his country and to protect his homeland. He gave his strength and the best years of his youth.

One jury member exclaimed how delighted the judges, unanimous in their verdict, had been when they beheld such a "distinguished piece of statuary, arresting and dignified, with a certain romanticism." In her eyes, it was all the better that it was the work of a woman sculptor.[56]

But then the debate erupted afresh, for it turned out that Wood was married to Hahn. Wood's family had been in Canada a long time. She had not been married to Hahn through the earlier controversy. The two of them maintained separate professional identities. Yet, when aldermen learned of the link between the two of them—that Miss Wood was also Mrs. Hahn—they laughed nervously at the terrible jinx that had somehow come to afflict the cenotaph competition. The public controversy once again caught fire.

Some of the conflagration's ingredients persisted. People argued that, although it might appear that Wood was her own person, in fact she was under the control of her "German" husband. Others professed to find something "Teutonic" in her design. As the comments came in, Wood had little doubt that it was her husband's German background that had made her design controversial.[57] Other ingredients in this debate were different. Hahn's still-mournful design had constituted only a mild departure from the British funereal precedent, whereas Wood's strong, youthful, and courageous youth suggested the opening of a more cheerful chapter. Some critics found the figure unsettlingly pugnacious: he did not summon up the sacrifices of the battlefield; he did not look as though he were part of a "sacred shrine." It did not help that he was almost naked. Perhaps not entirely in tune with classical conventions calling for disrobed allegorical figures, some Winnipeggers were rather startled by a statue that brought to their minds "an artistic ad for some well-known brand of summer underwear, an attractive presentment of the virtues of an expensive toilet soap, or merely the cave-man hero of the latest high-voltage film."[58]

Wood's idealistic crusader, it seemed, was at once too classical and too much a figure of modernity—too much a part of the everyday world of advertising and commodities, and insufficiently evocative of a distant, more romantic era. In response to this renewed outcry, on 2 December

1927 the War Memorial Committee rejected Wood's design. Its members selected another: a drab conventional cenotaph that returned to the funereal conventions of the immediate postwar period.[59]

In October 1928, just before the completion of this memorial, vandals set the tarpaulin covering it on fire. In 1929 the bedraggled condition of its environs—a weed- and litter-infested quagmire, said some—provoked the Winnipeg Canadian Legion to pronounce the grounds "a disgrace to the city and a mockery of heroes whose memory it was built to commemorate." Yet when Winnipeggers successfully petitioned the city to spend $2,500 to clean up the site, William Kolisnyk, North America's first Communist alderman, wondered why the "gentlemen taking such an interest in the cenotaph" did not spend an equal amount of energy "in trying to stop future wars." How would more money on the cenotaph help the "widows and children of the fallen men"?[60]

The meaning of the site was further contested in 1930 when businessmen asked for permission to create a miniature golf course on the adjacent lot: "It opens the wound wider than ever and makes my heart bleed at the insult to injury." How could one ever understand those who, for a little money, would "stoop to stab a widow's or a soldier's mother's heart"?[61] When one war widow considered Armistice Day ceremonies at the cenotaph, she was moved to write:

> To me, as I am sure it is to many others, the week of Nov. 11 is a strain. We hear it on the radio, we hear it in the churches, we read it in the papers. During that week we are constantly reminded of our great loss. . . .
>
> It reminds me of the darkened streets, the food lines . . . the cripples who came back, and finally it reminds me of a letter, "Killed in action."
>
> I have never been to an Armistice service and if I can help it I never will go, because my brother, like the others, did not want to die, neither did he want to kill.
>
> Do I respect the cenotaph? I do, and as I pass it I pay silent tribute because I know what it means, and all that it stands for. After 14 years I respect it more than ever, because we no longer can fool ourselves. "They died in vain."
>
> . . . As we now find social conditions I cannot see how any particular nation could claim victory, so I see no need for any celebration on Nov. 11.[62]

Did the storm over commemoration in Winnipeg merely show, as Prairie historian James H. Gray had it, that the mere mention of a German name in the same breath as the cenotaph caused "our well organized babbitry to give vent to a war-whoop that echoed and re-echoed from coast to coast"? Writing in 1934, Gray joked that "all is quiet on the cenotaph front," and pondered the "type of mind" that had made the whole storm possible.[63] Yet the Winnipeg debate revealed just how fiercely contested memories of the Great War remained.

*   *   *

Given the challenging politics of commemoration, it is striking how little controversy was aroused by Allward's visionary work at Vimy.[64]

The process of marking out and commemorating battle sites in Northern Europe had begun as early as February 1919 with the formation of the British "Battle Exploits Memorials Committee"—the very name sounding a note of martial enthusiasm. Its mandate was to "identify and name the principal battles and to allocate the sites to their appropriate countries." The Canadian representative, Brig.-Gen. H.T. Hughes, after consultation with Canadian officers, among them Gen. Sir Arthur Currie, put forward eight battlefield candidates. By 1922 Vimy had triumphed over its rivals—and Allward's design had been selected in a competition from a field of over one hundred entries. On 5 December 1922 the French agreed to give the Canadians a site of some 248 acres at Vimy. King was delighted. Earlier that year he had complained to Peter Larkin, High Commissioner in London, that neither the former government nor the Battlefields Memorial Commission had moved on his suggestion to acquire the Vimy site, which fifty or a hundred years hence would appeal to Canadians as a "scene of the European war," consecrated ground where "Canadian genius and bravery" had prevailed.[65]

Although the Canadian state had considered erecting a war memorial somewhere in Northwest Europe, the selection of Vimy, which many soldiers did not regard as a decisive battle in the war, was not inevitable. Many enthusiasts preferred Hill 62 in the Ypres Salient, and it was only several years after the war that Vimy was singled out as the site for a major memorial. What one senior official called the "obvious superiority" of the Vimy site resided, not in its historical significance, but in the picturesque view.[66]

No less than the National War Memorial designer Vernon March, Walter Allward could be said to reflect King's highly idealized interpretation of the war. Allward explained his vision in mystical terms that could only have warmed King's heart. When "things were at their blackest in France"—most likely referring to 1918—Allward recalled:

> I dreamed that I was in a great battlefield. I saw our men going by in thousands and being mowed down by the sickles of death. . . . Suffering beyond endurance at the sight, I turned my eyes and found myself looking down on an avenue of poplars. Suddenly through the avenue I saw thousands marching to the aid of our armies. They were the dead. They rose in masses, filed silently by and entered the fight to aid the living. . . . Without the dead we were helpless.[67]

In 1921, while seated in a park, he pulled out an envelope and sketched two pylons—one for Canada and one for France—and imagined a line across their bases signifying "the spirit of sacrifice."[68] And so it was—at least this story says—that the Vimy monument was born.

By April 1926 the monument project had become bigger and more expensive, but even a parsimonious King, who penny-pinched programs for living veterans, would not turn off the cash faucet when it came to erecting a mammoth monument to their dead counterparts. King was fully onside with the construction of what he hoped would be the "finest monument I believe on the continent" and a commemoration of the "most significant epoch in our history." He particularly wanted to preserve the trenches and underground passages, which for him brought home as could few other war landscapes the mole-like or rat-like existence to which Canada's "fine brave men" had been reduced in 1917.[69]

Significantly, Allward's monument met with little resistance from critics of militarism. Through the 1920s, scepticism about monument-building had been periodically fanned by the left. In the controversies that shook Winnipeg, the stock left-wing response—expressed in the *One Big Union Bulletin*—had been to call for what was called a "living memorial"— perhaps a rehabilitative centre for disabled veterans afflicted with "some sort of mental trouble."[70] Through much of the 1920s, as David Thompson shows, a slew of leftists took potshots at war monuments as a way of dramatizing the social injustices of the post-1918 world. In 1921 the Halifax city council was urged to hire unemployed and disabled workers and veterans. The following year the local labour paper argued that "democracy" was the only suitable monument to the war dead, not the $50,000 monument the city had in mind. Socialist (and future Toronto mayor)

James Simpson drew a portrait in 1921 of the profiteers, sitting "over their wines and in their luxurious automobiles," talking of "the monuments they will erect to our gallant dead who fell in France," all the while plotting to force those who had returned from the war to live in oppression and misery. A member of the Vancouver Women Workers decried military memorials in 1922. If you sought the true legacy of the war, she cried, look to the "overfilled hospitals, cemeteries and the extended bread lines." The unveiling of the cenotaph in Vancouver in April 1924 was picketed by left-wing veterans who were themselves attacked. Another Vancouver veteran stated, "We do not want war shrines and war memorials," but work. In the House of Commons, such progressives as J.S. Woodsworth, William Irvine, and Agnes Macphail made a regular point of arguing against war memorials. In 1923 Woodsworth quoted from one woman's letter who argued that the men "who had the great misfortune to return to Canada with their lives" were entitled to the money that was otherwise going to be wasted on a memorial.[71] He pointed out that Canada's enormous accumulated war debt constituted "a very imposing war memorial, and one that is likely to prove very enduring indeed."[72]

Leftists found that official commemoration offered a convenient means of highlighting government hypocrisy. It was an argument that appealed more broadly. Some down-to-earth minds queried the wisdom of erecting a National War Memorial that served no practical purpose. Critical letter writers in the *Ottawa Citizen* thought that the Great War dead would be better commemorated with something more practical; one complained of spending money "on the dead who do not want it," while "the living may go to ___."[73]

The Vimy Memorial does not seem to have been a monument associated with any glorification of war. Had it been—in a country roiled with debates over cadets, rearmament, and neutrality—a peace movement growing ever-strong would surely have denounced it. Instead, peace promoters embraced Vimy with enthusiasm.

*   *   *

Some 7,565 "pilgrims" congregated at the site north of Arras on 26 July 1936 for the unveiling and dedication of Allward's Vimy Ridge monument. In a sense somewhat different than the Royal Canadian Legion meant it to be, this was "a history-making service," although the history it made was, as usual, fraught with complexity and contradiction.[74] Few if any of the 1936 pilgrims noticed that the alphabetical list of names chiselled onto the monument included over forty Taylors but only one lonely Tremblay. Tremblay is, of course, one of the most common Quebec surnames.

The 1936 pilgrimage to Europe's fabled battlefields had precedents: a much smaller Canadian outing in 1927; a 15,000-strong American expedition the same year; and a 1928 tribute at the Menin Gate Memorial involving 11,000 members of the British Legion.[75] Organizing more than 7,000 pilgrims strained the Legion's capacity to the limit. The Canadians left Montreal in five ships on 16 and 17 July, to the cheers of a crowd of thousands. Eberts Macintyre, appointed organizer by the Dominion Command of the Legion, believed it to be the "largest civilian undertaking of its kind ever carried out in Canada." The pilgrims paid $160 apiece, a price that included a return passage and land tour in France. That price tag meant that only certain better-heeled veterans—"the best type of ex-Service man and his relatives," explained Ben W. Allen of the Legion—were able to make the trip.[76] The government offered practical assistance through various departments. It smoothed out tangles related to expediting passports and searched out particular cemeteries, but according to the Legion it did not supply a direct subsidy.

Making the arrangements in Europe was taxing. On the night of 25 July, on the eve of the great ceremony, pandemonium reigned. Pilgrims poured in, sometimes arriving at hotels for which they lacked bookings, in other cases complaining of the accommodations offered, some were billeted on cots in schools. Some travellers got onto the wrong bus and found themselves miles away from the site; they needed to be transported to Vimy Ridge by taxi. At a time when no fewer than 250 buses were needed, France was in the midst of a great wave of strikes. Macintyre feared that acts of industrial sabotage might occur. Nonetheless, despite the odds, a vast crowd—some said 100,000, although Macintyre thought it was only half that size—arrived at Vimy Ridge.[77] Some came to pay their respects to the war dead. Others wanted to see the new King of England. A good number were eager to take in a site that had already achieved a certain renown as it was taking shape in Northeastern France. What, then, was the meaning of the lofty monument? What did it say about the monumental questions raised by peace and war?

*   *   *

Many people, especially in the Legion, wanted to celebrate Canada's martial traditions and salute those soldiers who had upheld them. This was, after all, a battle site, and these were returning soldiers and their families.

As Jacqueline Hucker remarks, the Vimy monument was intended to serve three martial purposes: to mark the site of one specific battle, to commemorate "the valour of all Canadians who fought in the First World War," and, through the inscription of the names of 11,285 missing Canadian soldiers who died in France, to "serve as testament to those Canadians who lost their lives in France and whose bodies were never identified." In 1936 a Legion writer declared that here was a "shrine of the glorious dead," which called out for reverential worship.[78]

Not surprisingly, then, martial themes were present and accounted for on that day in 1936. As Hucker notes, the veterans stood "in pride of place in the amphitheatre," with family members watching from the sloping sides.[79] The King of England inspected the Guards of Honour, "scanning them closely," including smartly dressed Canadian naval personnel and a cavalry contingent from Morocco. Although the veterans wore civilian clothes, many of them stood at attention as though they were soldiers. *The Epic of Vimy*, the Legion's copiously illustrated and immensely popular official book about the event, enthused: "Erect as ramrods, no longer civilians but transported again by some magic to the days when they too had served, the ex-Servicemen for a few brief moments were once more youthful soldiers, doing their cheerful spot of work proudly, loyally, and conscientiously." Just as the king and the president of France were about to take their seats on the monument, two squadrons of the Royal Air Force approached the site from the West.[80]

King Edward VIII's speech asked those gathered to remember that "the deeds of valour done on those battlefields long survive the quarrels which drove the opposing hosts to conflict." The address of Lt.-Col. Reverend C.C. Owen of the Anglican Church urged that children learn about the "finer aspects of courage and sacrifice which emerged during the war."[81] The martial themes were accompanied by celebrations of imperialism. At Vimy 1936 a basic faith in imperialism was everywhere—of a piece with the reassertion of the glories of the British Empire in the 1930s, typified by attempts to revive the Empire as an economic unit and to promulgate British culture through such agencies as the Rhodes scholarships. The "wildly loyal throng of Canadian war veterans" was enraptured by the king,[82] who was making his first ceremonial appearance (and virtually his only one, as it turned out) as monarch. So thought organizer Macintyre:

> The Pilgrims had travelled thousands of miles to attend a ceremony on Vimy Ridge, and to hundreds of them the deciding factor was the announcement that King Edward would preside. Patiently they had waited within that amphitheatre for His Majesty to arrive. Now he stood before them, smiling, waving his hat, and himself honouring the occasion by wearing the Vimy Pilgrimage Badge. He was King and also a Pilgrim.[83]

The king stopped and chatted, especially greeting those men adorned with medals suggesting they had done something memorable. For some it was thrilling that the king honoured the singing of "O Canada" by standing bare-headed as the patriotic song, not yet an anthem, was played at the event.

A more surprising imperial theme throughout Vimy 1936, and one more directly related to the historical legacy of the Great War, was the attempt to shore up and celebrate the Entente between Britain and France of 1914–18, which was visualized as a pact going far beyond that military conflict. In an early exercise of what is now called "cultural diplomacy," the French assiduously cultivated manifold contacts with leading figures in the British Empire, part of a scheme, even then, of ensuring sympathizers in present and anticipated conflicts with Germany.

The "national structure of Canada," *The Epic of Vimy* explained to the perhaps hesitant members of the Legion, entailed the perpetuation of "two great civilizations of Europe," and thus it made perfect sense for Ernest Lapointe to address the Vimy crowd in French. Rising to the occasion, Lapointe reminded his audience that Canada "unites within her bounds two races who preserve faithfully the ideals of social progress and democratic liberty transmitted by these mother countries." Indeed, when Canada rose in arms in defence of the *two* motherlands, it had had the "spontaneity of a crusade."[84] The "history-making service" managed to package the Great War as one of friendship between the two Canadian peoples who had actually been quite conflicted about the historic events. No one, it seems, wanted to bring up the issue of conscription.

What was especially odd was that the ceremony ignored Belgium, whose victimization had supposedly provided the British rationale for the war in the first place. The pilgrimage's French emphasis was so pronounced that Macintyre had to soothe the spirits of Belgian officials, who complained that their country was being systematically slighted.[85] For his part, French president Albert Lebrun imagined a day when French workers and farmers would pause to reflect on the Canadian soldiers, many of them "faithful to the call of blood," who had returned to "their ancient motherland" with their minds full of the memory of Champlain, Maisonneuve, and Montcalm.[86] Moreover, other supposedly grateful colonials—the Spahis, French Moroccan mounted troops—were also on hand to take part in the festivities, underlining the imperial theme. The Legion's *Epic of Vimy* described them as "tawny and bearded natives from North Africa . . . a picturesque contribution to a picturesque scene."[87]

The martial nationalism of the phenomenon of Vimy was clear enough in 1936. Depictions of no fewer than thirty-two maple leaves bedeck the single title page that leads off *The Epic of Vimy*, which sold out its first run of 3,000 copies and was into its second edition in 1937. The Legion also advertised *Salute to Valour*, a film hailing both wartime patriotism and pilgrimage-induced international goodwill. As the Canadian Battlefields Memorials Commission explained in 1929, this was not a memorial to an individual (or by inference to a particular battle) but "a memorial for a nation."[88]

Canada was a person—loyal to its king, loyal to its empire, loyal to its soldiers. This person can be seen on the Vimy monument—as *Canada Bereft*, also known as "Mother Canada"—mourning the losses of her children, that is, the people who flocked to the imperial banner and valiantly lost their lives. "Mother Canada" reveals Canada as an organic entity, not just akin to an individual person but unified by a collective mind. Mackenzie King was channelling this vision when he stated: "Canada asks that the nations of Europe strive to obliterate whatever makes for war or death. She appeals to them to unite in an effort to bring into being a world at peace."[89]

The nationalism of Vimy 1936 also shines through the monument itself—indeed, in its very size—especially in the eyes of Canadians who had internalized the "don't-rock-the-boat" mentality of junior partner to empire. Spending upwards of $1,125,000 (in 1930s dollars) on a single, huge monument in Europe constituted a significant statement, which some enthusiasts took to be a sure sign of Canada's coming of age. Rather like Will Bird, writer Sandra Gwyn in the 1980s was struck by the sense of Canadian nationalism implied by Vimy's "almost pharaonic" character.

The figures are of a "heroic scale," and even the surrounding landscape of the Douai Plain, "its level expanse studded with heaps of coal tailings," brought Ancient Egypt to her mind. The woman representing "the Spirit of Canada," along with her nine companions, conveyed a message not of elegy but of defiance: "The Spirit of Canada seems to be saying that somehow, what happened here was worth all the cost. Many sons may have fallen but they won the day and thus were reborn."[90]

For all that he had been instrumental in making it happen, when he laid eyes on the monument, King himself thought it over the top. Conservative politician and League of Nations supporter George Perley agreed with King that the memorial was "more ambitious than I would have chosen," although he also hoped that the crowds of Canadians who flocked to it would come to learn something about their country.[91] The towering site—arising out of a generally flat landscape, atypical of the area in which Canadians fought—was thought to be especially ideal for projecting a sense of national strength, investing those who held it with a sense of being "Masters of All They Surveyed."

The unveiling of the monument was, then, a moment of high nationalism for some—in which the exaltation of Vimy as the apex of Canadian achievement found its full expression.[92]

*　　*　　*

The Vimy monument embodies an almost unendurable contradiction. Do we celebrate, in the spirit of so many twenty-first-century militarists, the persistence and ingenuity that led Canadians to take the ridge in 1917? Or do we mourn, in the spirit of peace-lovers and war critics, the great suffering and loss of life entailed in the entire war, with Vimy one of its costliest and most terrible battles? Vimy is, paradoxically, both Victory Column and Garden of Gethsemane. This derives from the decision in the early 1920s to inscribe upon the monument the names of missing soldiers. The martial triumphalism inherent in so many Vimy memories and histories became conjoined with mourning. The inscription of the names of the missing meant that martial triumphalism was mitigated by the melancholy task of mourning the dead. When Randal Marlin, who studies the ethics of persuasion, considers the monument, he sees it as conveying "grief, pain, and suffering rather than false pride and triumphalism."[93]

The 1936 ceremony reverberated with denunciations of war. Rev. George Oliver Fallis of the United Church struck a very different note from his Anglican colleague. He reminded his audience of the men who had been "shot, bayonetted, gassed, slain with artillery shrapnel and machine guns, and bombed from the skies. They wandered about in gas masks, living in dugouts and ditches, being tormented with vermin. They were thirsty. They were hungry. They were cold and frost bitten. They were imprisoned." Recalling these horrors of war, and how these men had not "reached their glorious goals," Fallis called upon God to strengthen Canadians, "that we should finish their task and make real their vision of a world swayed by peace and brotherhood." At Vimy he appealed to the spirit of McCrae's "In Flanders Fields": "To us they throw the torch"— that is, "finish their task and make real their vision of a world swayed by peace and brotherhood." The "foe" with whom one should quarrel, in this 1936 vision, was war itself. For his part, A.E. Deschamps, the Auxiliary Bishop of Montreal, called on his Christian listeners not only to work for peace but also to "hate and curse war, this universal evil." He imagined that the honoured dead of Vimy Ridge, "who fell dreaming of a world freed from the war by the war," would agree with him.[94]

In Allward's sermon against war, accompanying the figure of *Canada Bereft* are figures of "Truth, Faith, Justice, Charity, Knowledge and Peace" singing "the Hymn of Peace."[95] These are the "Defenders," one of them engaged in the "Breaking of the Sword" and the others expressing the "Sympathy of Canadians for the Helpless." Conspicuous by their absence are figures of "Victory, Valour, Courage, Cunning, Strength and Sweet Retribution." One story has it that Allward had considered incorporating, in his sculpture of "The Defenders—The Breaking of the Sword," a German helmet being crushed under the foot of one figure, an idea he discarded because of its "militaristic imagery."[96] Had Allward wanted to incorporate any of these themes, he could have drawn upon a plethora of well-accepted sculptural motifs, such as the eagles and lions rejected early on in the contests for Ottawa's National War Memorial; or of St. George slaying the dragon—a popular theme with both Britons and Germans, who retained different respective conceptions of who was St. George and who was the dragon. But he did not do so.[97] He could also have gone back to his own 1910 *South African War Memorial*—the statue on Toronto's University Avenue celebrating the Empire's victory in the South African conflict—had he wanted to consult his own triumphalist repertoire. None of his Vimy figures seem to be having a great, triumphal time, and *Canada Bereft* especially does not seem to be advising us to embark on another martial adventure.

As historian Victor Huard argues, "The Vimy ceremony exemplified almost every facet of the interwar liberal internationalist dream of peace." Instead of military parades, medal presentations, and artillery salutes, the "Peace Hymn" was part of the official program, as were scriptural and poetry readings. The assembled audience heard a reading of Geoffrey O'Hara's poem "Guns," ever-popular at public peace rallies and plays. The final two stanzas are representative:

God of our prayers, speed on the years,
Until a world, vainglorious hears,
Sobs of a million mothers' tears,
Echo from the Guns!

Let Thy hand reach from shore to shore;
O God of love for evermore,
Crush out the hated curse of war,
The Guns! Guns! Guns![98]

The official program described Allward's allegorical figures as chanting the Hymn of Peace. Vimy was so associated with the demand for peace that the image of the monument was used in pamphlets and on stamps—including a stamp advertising the 1937 World Peace Congress.[99]

Given that the veterans at Vimy were not in uniform—not even the one-hundred-strong "Honour Guard of Canadian Great War Veterans"—the only visible concessions to military tradition, apart from proudly worn medals, were the "standard pilgrimage khaki beret with green maple leaf badge" and the round buttons indicating organization or company. The pilgrims stood in formation as though they were soldiers—but, by design, they looked like civilians: "Canada's Peacetime Army."[100] As the United Church magazine *New Outlook* pointed out after hearing the Vimy broadcast: "The note struck at the great gathering on the battlefield, and sounding through the ceremonies, was a note of peace. The absence of the martial mood and the spirit of vainglorious boasting was something for which all good citizens have felt profoundly thankful." Vimy 1936 received extensive coverage in Canada, and most newspapers picked up that peace vibe. Said the *Winnipeg Free Press*: "In the addresses and invocations there was no exaltation in victory. No word of triumph, no laudation of war. It was an occasion of proud thanksgiving by Canada for her fallen sons; but from their sacrifice nothing was drawn but a fervent hope for peace, unbroken and universal."[101] Is the Vimy Memorial, then, a *war* memorial at all? Allward himself thought his monumental sermon against war had little to do with celebrating Canadian martial valour.[102]

To deliver his own speech, Mackenzie King had dispatched Charles Gavan (Chubby) Power, a veteran of the Somme, staunch foe of conscription in 1917, and minister of pensions and health, to France. King stayed at home and nervously listened to the broadcast from his house in Quebec's Gatineau Hills—even standing up when "O Canada" and "The Maple Leaf Forever" were played. He was, according to his own diary notes, "terribly disappointed" in Power's all too fast-spoken delivery of his message.[103] King's speech was overwhelmingly focused on the need for peace. He recalled fallen soldiers but inserted them within an overarching narrative of disarmament and peace: "Canada asks that the nations of Europe strive to obliterate whatever makes for war or death. She appeals to them to unite in an effort to bring into being a world at peace." The "leading figures of [the] Great War" had been "outspoken in stressing destructiveness and cost of modern war," he said in his background notes for the speech, but as those figures passed away, it was important to remind a new generation of the "lessons learned from war."[104] King hoped that his call for peace might resonate throughout the world. All of the living held in trust the hopes of those who had suffered and died, he declared. In his most memorable line, he declared that a "world at peace" was the "only memorial worthy of the valour and sacrifice of all who gave their lives in the Great War."[105]

Ottawa radio station CKCO declared that King had "left a thought that will abide with everyone." Whenever people gazed upon a war memorial, even in a village square, the question should arise: have we built the real monument to the soldiers in the trenches, a world "truly living at peace"?[106] For King, one of the most significant contributions of the Vimy monument and unveiling was to re-enchant the world, not with the Great War per se, but with the high ideals he associated with it, above all the vanquishing of militarism and the achievement of peace in all aspects of life.

Although it would be a mistake to conflate King with Canada, it would be similarly erroneous to minimize his impact on the public history surrounding peace and war in the 1920s and 1930s. His contradictory impact was to commemorate war by extracting from it the enduring values of sacrifice and selflessness so that all such conflict would be abolished in the future.

But what of our soldiers in the Legion? Surely they resisted the peace-lovers? It seems not. Even the Legion's *The Epic of Vimy* is chock-a-block with pacificist sentiments. It begins with an opening from "G.R.L." in Ottawa. After bitterly recalling the demise of the ideal of the "war to end war" for which soldiers had died, he asks:

Shall there come a dawn to war's dark night?
A day when, narrowing boundaries over-passed,
As friends, as brothers, men shall strive at last,
Their God, the Truth; their only Law, the Right.[107]

From the Legion organizers' perspective, the ceremony was not just an "act of homage to the War Dead," but also "a demonstration and an appeal for a cessation to those quarrellings afflicting the human family."[108] Capt. W.W. Murray concludes his write-up of the ceremony by terming the monument an "enduring testament of Canadian ideals—Sacrifice, Peace." Even though Canada was small, it could use its "unique place in the affairs of great nations" to live up to its obligations to these dead men and "not falter in her work for Peace."

Eberts Macintyre noticed the unmistakable signs of awakened European militarism in 1936 and was dismayed to see young men in uniform marching past. "It was terrifying. Many thousands in this country seem to be in some sort of uniform," he wrote in his diary. "Everyone fears trouble soon, internal and external, but they are not sure when it will start. I wondered how many of those young men would be dead in the course of the next few years."[109] His son, Flying Officer John Macintyre, would be killed over Germany seven years later.

Legion leaders, revealing pacificistic sentiments, pursued contacts with German veterans with a view to fostering "international tolerance, fellowship and justice by means of ex-service men's organizations in every country." Like Gregory Clark in 1934, they refused to demonize their old enemies. Capt. Murray and several other pilgrims even went unofficially, and at their own expense, to Germany, finding "much in common with ex-service men especially as to the futility of war and kindred subjects." They encountered no evidence of German hostility against Canadian veterans. In May 1937 Brig.-Gen. Alex Ross of Saskatchewan, a pugnacious and effective leader in a strengthening Canadian Legion, headed up a delegation of twenty-five men in a visit to the German Union of Ex-Servicemen. They laid a wreath at the grave of the famous "Red Baron" and met with officers of the "New Army," which, the Canadians were assured, would never be used for the purposes of aggression. Ross hoped that such veterans' contact could be an "effective instrument" for promoting the understanding "necessary for the preservation of peace."[110]

At Vimy in 1936 the "birth of the nation" rhetoric was conspicuous by its absence.[111] Vimy '36 did resound with claims that Canada was a special country, but that specialness was exemplified by the monument's representations of the breaking of the sword and sympathy for the weak. Canadians stood nobly above and beyond the squalor of conflict, serving as a beacon of civility and order in the world. Canada's links with both the United States and Britain exemplified the peaceful, rational handling of relations among states. For the noble sacrifices of our soldiers to have been worthwhile, they needed to be redeemed in a Canada effectively pursuing peace in the world—at the League of Nations, for example. For King, Vimy was "Canada's altar on European soil," on which Canadians were sacrificed "for the cause of humanity."[112]

The "cause of humanity," in his conception, was that of defeating militarism forever and instituting a national and international regime of peace, without which there could be no lasting freedom. In July, welcoming U.S. president Franklin D. Roosevelt to Quebec City, King included a "Message of the New World to the Old." It declared:

> So long as nations strive to advance their separate aims by Force, rather than the common ends by Reason and Co-operation, so long will War be inevitable, and the fear of War continue to make of Science and Industry a vast machine, to further the destruction of Humanity. Science and Industry were meant to be the instruments of progress; they are God-given instruments for the relief of human suffering and human need.[113]

King did finally visit the Vimy Memorial three months after the unveiling. He liked the monument and appreciated the grounds, yet something bothered him. The monument was impressive—almost too much so. It had become the "most pretentious war memorial in the world," yet it was redeemed by being an expression of "Canada's idealism." Perhaps King's biggest regret was that it was a *Canadian* monument, suggestive of nationalism, and not a European and international monument, gesturing towards humanity's next evolutionary step—a world whose nations had all learned to live in peace.

In both the widely publicized speeches, and in his subsequent visit to Vimy in October 1936, King never once declared the site in which he had invested so much of his time and energy to be Canada's birthplace.

*   *   *

The monumental questions, and monumental decisions, of Depression-era Canadians wrestling with peace and war do not lend themselves to easy judgments. Supposedly war-oriented veterans travelled to Germany to meet their counterparts. Supposedly peace-oriented politicians micromanaged monuments exalting the Canadian war effort. In the end, war monuments were—and still are—among the many messages, and perhaps the most powerful, that subtly and overtly call for peace, in both Ottawa and in France.

The complications surrounding commemoration were not confined to Canada. Without the French involvement and contribution of the land, the famous battle might well have sunk into obscurity. When the textbooks of the 1920s saluted the Great War they tended to focus on Ypres, not Vimy. The tenth anniversary of Vimy Ridge raised almost no attention in either daily newspapers or national magazines. On Dominion Day 1927, only one newspaper remembered the battle as a symbol of "Canada's rising nationhood." Only one major newspaper offered detailed coverage of Vimy's fifteenth anniversary in 1932. When *Saturday Night* devoted sustained attention to Canada's new powers under the Treaty of Westminster, on the anniversary of Vimy Ridge in 1932, it did not focus on the battle or even on the Great War. As David Inglis suggests, it was the Vimy monument itself, the "main Canadian memorial for the entire war and for all her missing dead," that became a force that strengthened the Battle of Vimy Ridge as a cultural symbol. In 1936, indeed, some veterans were frank enough to say they had not realized that Vimy had been all that significant until it was pointed out to them nineteen years after they fought the actual battle.[114]

Vimy 1936 was thus a moment rich in ambiguity.[115] Did it celebrate a Canadian victory or mourn the Canadian dead? Did it broadcast that Canada had arrived as a big player, or did it merely reaffirm the country's subordinate status within the Empire, as King Edward VIII's star turn suggested? Was Vimy '36 about preparing for war—as might have been inferred from the aircraft flying overhead and the martial tenor of certain pieces of the event—or was it an appeal for world peace—which was the predominant tone of most speeches? The Vimy Memorial was itself a bundle of contradictions: a sepulcher for the missing, an ambitious tower proclaiming Canada's wealth and power, a symbol of the world peace movement. If peace was its main theme, it was a theme articulated on a site associated with a triumphant feat of arms. A large vault under the monument, large enough for broadcasting equipment, also showed that this was a monument designed for the modern age in which "Vimy" was meant to be much more than a place in Europe: its symbolism could be projected to the world.

Both the martial and peace-oriented versions of Vimy sought to invest the war with transcendental meanings. Allward's towering white pylons and the antiseptic trenches cleanse war of both its filth and its moral ambiguity. From the mid-1930s, martial nationalism would start to make claims for Vimy that were scarcely credible and would have been generally unrecognizable in 1917. Yet they would come to be repeated ever more frequently as those who had experienced the Great War passed from the scene. There is a sense that, after the opening of the monument in 1936, Vimy and the Great War attained a certain untouchability in Canada. What was lively and creative about the debates that rocked so many spheres in the 1920s and early 1930s—fundamental debates about peace, war, and Canada—was that their participants felt able to ask difficult questions about the war. But as a kind of historical orthodoxy tightened its hold, as the government exerted itself to impose one reading upon the Great War experience, Vimy entered the realm of "that which must not be questioned."

One person attending the 1936 ceremony *did* ask her own hard question about the Great War. Charlotte Susan Fullman, Canada's first National Memorial (Silver Cross) Mother, was working as a laundress in England when she married Frederick Wood near the turn of the twentieth century. Charlotte Wood and her family immigrated to Canada in 1905, by which time she had already had one stepson killed in the South African War. By 1916 eleven of her boys had enlisted. Son Percy had joined up at the age of fifteen and was killed at Vimy Ridge before he turned eighteen. Wood lost five sons to war.[116]

Her tragic story gave Wood a few fleeting moments of prominence in the 1930s. She received the George V Jubilee Medal in 1935. She travelled with the Vimy pilgrims the following year, placing a wreath on the tomb of the Unknown Soldier at Westminster Abbey. She was probably among the Vimy pilgrims in their smarts who went to Westminster Hall

Charlotte Susan Wood (far right), Canada's first Silver Cross Mother. The Great War killed five of her sons. In 1936 she said to King Edward VII, "I just can't figure out why our boys had to go through that."

to hear British prime minister Stanley Baldwin's speech on the Great War. "I am confident of this. If the dead could come back today, there would be no war," Baldwin said. "You all tasted that bitter cup of war. [The dead] drank it to the dregs. If Europe and the world can find no other way of settling disputes than war, even now when we are still finding and burying the bodies of those who fell twenty years ago, the world deserves to perish."[117]

Charlotte Wood died a few weeks after the start of another catastrophic war. Her obituary was headlined "World War Mother Succumbs as Big Guns Roar Once More." A working-class woman whose family was unable to afford a memorial, she was buried in a simple grave in Winnipeg's Brookside Cemetery, one of the city's oldest burial grounds and home to the graves of some 12,000 veterans and their families. Thanks to Ceris Schrader and the generosity of Larsen's Memorials sixty years after her death, her grave is now marked with a handsome memorial that sits among the towering elms. A quotation is chiseled onto the polished marble marker that sits on a granite base.

"'Please God, Mrs. Wood, it shall never happen again,' King Edward VIII."

That is what the king said to Charlotte Wood when she met him at the Vimy inaugural ceremony in 1936. Her gravestone does not tell the whole story. The king was responding to what Wood had just said as she looked out over the former killing fields. "Oh! Sir," she exclaimed. "I just can't figure out why our boys had to go through that."[118]

Wood was most likely not familiar with Fred Varley's sombre battlefield painting *For What?* Yet she and countless others, then and now, would certainly have joined the great artist in raising that anguished question.

7

THE LONG AND WINDING
ROAD TO VIMYISM

"Invented traditions" are highly relevant to that comparatively recent
historical innovation, the "nation," with its associated phenomena:
nationalism, the nation-state, national symbols, and the rest.

— ERIC HOBSBAWM, *The Invention of Tradition*

REMEMBRANCE DAY, 1950. It was five years after the end of another war that few Canadians in the 1930s could have imagined being as devastating as the Great War. But it had surpassed that tragedy's carnage. And the Great War had become "World War I." Many were still trying to come to terms with the Second World War—and the Holocaust and mass aerial attacks that had killed millions, culminating in Hiroshima and Nagasaki.

Still, on 11 November 1950, Jane Scott was looking back twenty-five years, recalling the scene in 1925. "Today as we pause before the grey granite Cenotaph, let us not forget to remember along with the 'glorious dead' the patient 'glorious living' who through the intervening years have become the living sacrifices laid on the altar of peace."

Scott, in a "Religious Thoughts" article for a Toronto newspaper, was reflecting on what had happened in the aftermath of that First World War. In 1925 she had seen veterans, widows, orphans, the maimed, and the blind bowing their heads as a hymn "wafted out over the sorrowing heads of bereaved citizens." It was a time when memories of the Great War were still fresh. But Scott now had more on her mind than that war's losses. She was also recalling the war that had only recently ended, and the psychic scars left, once again, on those who returned.

"The growing consciousness of the futility of war did not hinder the people from perpetrating the individual and national sins that make war inevitable." Scott pointed to greed and lust for power so pervasive that Canadians might someday find themselves "in the midst of a carnage so awful that the First World War seemed insignificant."[1]

By 1950 Remembrance Day commemorations had, however, become something more than reflections on the past, occasions to remind Canadians of war's tragedy. They were opportunities for making political points about the Cold War. Canada's defence minister was Brooke Claxton, Great War veteran and reform-minded Liberal, who had in the 1930s warned of excessive military spending. He now weighed in with a call for more of such expenditures, soon to be evidenced in his department's ballooning budgets. Having repented of his Depression-era revulsion against war, Claxton took the occasion of Remembrance Day 1950 to call for increased military enlistment. It was all about "the defence of freedom everywhere." Reserve soldiers, Claxton argued, made "better citizens because they are good soldiers." In an early example of a trope that would become ubiquitous sixty years later, Claxton was equating war and the military with the achievement and defence of liberty. The effort, at the time, was surely rooted in the idea of the Second World War being that rarest of all armed conflicts, a "good war."[2]

As Canadians gathered at cenotaphs and war memorials on Remembrance Day in 1950, their country had just signed up for another faraway war. Like the Great War in 1914, it was to be another of those home-by-Christmas efforts. Canadian troops, mobilized that summer, headed for Korea on a U.S. ship to engage in what was essentially a U.S. war. The geopolitical machinations and the imperative to dispense more of the national treasury on the military were clearly top of the mind issues for the men who weighed in at Remembrance Day in 1950. The messages were familiar. J.S. Keefler had been a divisional commander in the Second World War, going on to become chairman and president of Canadian General Electric, a leading arms producer. (CGE's parent company made a Korean War killing, its engines powering the F-86 "Sabre" jet fighter. "The war," exults General Electric, "created a boom environment.")[3] It was time, said Keefler, to bring in mandatory military training for young Canadians imperiled by peacetime softness. They were prey to the "easy-going, perhaps even self-satisfied attitude." Now was the time. Korea was the place. "If we are to join again in a fight for freedom, does anyone seriously believe that Canada should or would limit her effort to being the arsenal of democracy?"[4]

The warrior dreams—and careers—of men like Keefler became manifest in the North Atlantic Treaty Organization (NATO). They saw themselves as hard-headed realists. NATO, established in part at the urging of Lester Pearson, would dominate Canadian defence policy for two generations. Although Pearson hoped the Atlantic alliance would turn into more than "an instrument of unimaginative militarism," that particular dream was not to be.[5] Despite Canada's growing reputation—and self-image—as a country whose military was all about peacekeeping, its Cold War efforts concentrated overwhelmingly on NATO and readiness for a much ballyhooed Soviet attack on Western Europe. The argument used by retired officers and other proponents of military spending in the decades after 1950 was that NATO was surely the best peacekeeping force Canada ever had, and that it deterred the Red Army from moving in to occupy Paris. These were scarcely disinterested opinions. As Gwynne Dyer suggests, "Asking our soldiers if NATO was a good thing was like asking the barber if you needed a haircut."[6]

After Korea, the country's military was not engaged in war, though the officer class was getting to play with the big boys in the big leagues. War games designed to deter a Soviet invasion that never came kept the troops busy in Europe, but during the 1960s the armed forces were reduced by a third. Remembrance Day assemblies continued to honour the war dead. But the bellicose cries of the early 1950s no longer dominated. The times were changing.

A Remembrance Day editorial comment in Winnipeg's *Free Press* in 1960 noted that now, forty-two years after the armistice of 11 November 1918, "No one who is not far advanced in middle age can remember the occasion or the emotional reaction against war in the years that immediately followed." Not only that, but since the end of the Second World War a new generation had come of age: Canadians who knew "little or nothing" of the relief of 1945.[7] The prominent paper ran another editorial comment under the headline "Uncomfortable Thought."

> All remembrance of war's dead must, if it be authentic, have a dimension of judgement; judgement on the ways of men which make for war and judgement of what men make of the opportunities bought for them in their dying. But we are quite adept at evading the judgement which is in remembrance. We practice this comforting evasion by making Remembrance Day primarily an occasion for some patriotic emotionalism. . . . It is a mark of our insensitivity that in

much of what we do and say on Remembrance Day, the note of self-congratulation seems louder than the note of contrition.[8]

Here was an author, signed "J.A.D.," reflecting on the conflicting meanings of commemoration in a way that transcended the usual clichés.

*   *   *

The Remembrance of Canada's Great War was, of course, not confined to November 11 commemorations. By the 1960s English-Canadian artists, journalists, and other opinion makers were looking back at the war with fresh eyes. In 1961 Ralph Allen, a leading journalist, came out with a snappily written and exhaustively researched book about Canada from 1914 to 1945. He had been a distinguished *Globe and Mail* war correspondent during the Second World War before going on to edit *Maclean's* magazine from 1950 to 1960. His *Ordeal by Fire: Canada 1914–1945* (1961) trolled school texts and popular poetry, his considerable network of personal contacts, and Canada's growing body of historical research.

Like any good journalist, Allen was an iconoclast. He described General Arthur Currie's high-blown rhetoric issued to troops facing death in 1918 as "claptrap," and covered the financial machinations behind the use of the Ross Rifle, "the most loved, hated and debated military weapon of its time."[9] His fifty-three-chapter survey was far more interested in the controversy over that weapon than in the victory at Vimy Ridge. A brief chapter on Vimy acknowledged that the battle was "rightly counted as one of the great Canadian military successes" but "not a decisive victory." Future scholarship would bear him out, although a generation of historians who would probe the minutiae of Canada's war would never deign to describe the decision to attack the Vimy Ridge in quite the same words—as being, "like so many command decisions in the war of 1914–1918 . . . mainly decreed by lack of anything better to do."[10]

Allen's story of Canada's Great War shunned any lofty, nation-building conclusions. He concluded simply by listing the war's casualty totals and its main political effects at home. Not simply the *Canadian* casualties, but the 8,538,315 killed, 21,219,452 wounded, and 7,750,919 captured or missing as a whole. The totals certainly underestimated the number of dead, though Allen did not hesitate to focus, beyond the terrible human toll, on the damage that the war inflicted in Canada. "In the inner battle of Canada the triumph at Vimy Ridge settled very little," he observed.

"Canada had lost nearly as much ground in its struggle for unity as it had won in the previous one hundred and fifty-eight years since the Plains of Abraham."[11]

Allen had been reading the signs of the times. Soon after his book was published, when Remembrance Day came around again, Quebec's resurgent nationalism was in full flourish. An independence movement different from traditional defensive nationalism was gaining ground, building the momentum that would bear fruit in the following decades. Marcel Chaput, president of the new Rassemblement pour l'indépendance nationale, remarked, "For French-Canadians, Nov. 11 is the gloomy celebration of British and Anglo-Canadian imperialism." *Indépendantistes* would tally 8.8 per cent of the vote in the Quebec election of 1966. At the same time Quebec activists held a peace vigil to mark Remembrance Day. The pioneering feminist (and later senator) Thérèse Casgrain offered a lessons-learned commemorative message. "We want to make the public aware that our boys did not die for nothing," said the social democrat who had been a leader of Quebec's votes-for-women campaign after the Great War. "And that everything possible should be done to avoid further tragedies."[12]

*   *   *

Around the same time that Allen's popular book on Canada's ordeals by fire was appearing on store shelves, another look back at the country's war-torn decades was finding its way into the hands of tens of thousands of baby-boom teenagers.

In *Decisive Decades: A History of the Twentieth Century for Canadians* (1960), A.B. Hodgetts of the upper-crust Trinity College School in Port Hope, Ont., distilled Canada's involvement in the Great War into seventy deft pages.[13] The book, a standard Ontario Grade 10 history text well into the 1970s, was aimed at students who were being challenged to understand Canadian history alongside that of the "other English-speaking peoples," Great Britain and the United States—and was noteworthy for its frank discussion of French-English tensions in Canada, the challenge of U.S. cultural domination, a fear of nuclear war, and the urgent need for the country to undergo a process of spiritual and cultural growth. One of the subtlest and most candid reflections available on Canadian history, the well-crafted text can only be read in the twenty-first century with a sense of regret for the sharp decline in standards of historical understanding expected of secondary-school students.[14]

In Hodgetts's rendering, the Great War was not just a European War but a complicated worldwide conflict, a contest of rival economic empires. He placed particular emphasis on a theme obscured in later analyses: that much of the war was both about maritime power and decided at sea. The shape of the war, he persuasively argued, was determined in its first three months, when the British staged a display of sea power on a gigantic scale, overwhelming the German fleets, conquering all but one of the enemy's overseas possessions, and clamping the European coast "into an impassable blockade."[15]

Hodgetts's complexity of vision extended to his account of the general memory of the Great War. Instead of our "valiant" soldiers fighting for freedom, Hodgetts emphasizes "the courage and stoic endurance of the soldiers from every country"—those from both "our" side and "their" side—"who went through the holocaust of the First World War." Both sides demonstrated the "sacrifice, stoic courage and utter folly" of Passchendaele. (The martial vocabulary of "valour" is lacking.) He disputes the attributions to the Germans of a unique quality of atrocious beastliness in Belgium. With respect to the German recourse to chemical weapons, he observes that "warfare and human decency seldom go together" and wonders why a similar odium did not attach to burning men alive with flame-throwers. As for the claim that Canada was fighting for freedom against oppression, Hodgetts bluntly remarks, "No serious student of history now believes for one moment that the First World War was fought for any such reasons."[16]

Hodgetts reserves his toughest words of criticism for the legendary war of attrition, skilfully elucidating its implications for the rest of the conflict. Once the Battle of the Marne in 1914 spelled the end of the German dream of a swift capture of Paris, all hope for a quick victory on either side was removed. Yet the militaries of both France and Britain were unable to grasp the new realities of mechanized warfare. For Hodgetts, all eleven Entente campaigns in the war of attrition—the "mean ugly new phrase" that had "crept into the vocabulary of the western world"—were "utterly wasteful." If the subsequent celebrants of that war were right, he points out—that is, if the only way to Entente victory lay in "death on a vast scale," in a "grinding struggle to see which side could hold out longer against death and destruction"—then victory in 1918 came about "not because of brilliant leadership, not because of some superiority of human nature or the justice of the cause, but simply because the Allies had more material and especially more human beings to throw into the raging inferno."[17]

In Hodgetts's view the war was shaped by the socio-economic divisions and tensions of modern capitalism. So acutely was Germany's General Erich Ludendorff worried about his restive society that he set aside battalions ready for use against his own civilian population. During a period of amazing wartime profits in North America—as high as 47 per cent, according to the *Wall Street Journal*—the "sordid side of Canada's war effort," rising from "our somewhat grasping national outlook," was evident in the series of profiteering scandals: "The government and the consumers were overcharged time and again, with exorbitant profits proved in the sale of bread, milk, butter, meat, shells, fuses, clothing and a multitude of other commodities." Hodgetts pays special attention to the inequities of the soaring Canadian debt load: a burden of only $541,000,000 was increased more than five-fold, and forced Canadians to pay "heavy taxes for many years to come—not for the development of their country but to cover the costs of four years of organized destruction."[18]

The Great War also fractured the country's fragile unity—in what Hodgetts calls a "sad story of bungling mismanagement, intolerance and racial bitterness." Here was a Canada that was, more than commonly realized, "on the verge of civil war" in the summer of 1917. In that year's toxic federal election the Unionist government, egged on by prejudiced newspaper editors and politicians, ran roughshod over the opinions of *Canadiens*, "a people not steeped in the text-book romance of British history and the glory of the Empire." As for the country's achievement of a new status in the world, Hodgetts's verdict was nuanced. With the formation of the Imperial War Cabinet, the dominion prime ministers met "as absolute equals" with their British colleagues—which was "another landmark on Canada's road towards independence within the British Commonwealth of Nations." Still, his Great War was no war of independence. It merely hastened the "further development of those nationalist feelings that had become apparent, especially in Canada, long before 1914."[19]

Hodgetts devotes four sentences to the Battle of Vimy Ridge within a paragraph on the Battle of Arras, which was initiated as a "short campaign to attract the Germans away from the Aisne," the focus of a French offensive. Vimy proved to be the "best stroke yet made by the British," revealing "what careful planning and limited objectives could do," and scoring a lasting, and perhaps consequential, point against the Germans.

But, "Unfortunately, the Battle of Arras also got out of hand and was continued much longer than had been planned."[20]

Martial nationalism is more conspicuous in another Grade 10 textbook from 1960, *The Modern Era* by John C. Ricker, John T. Saywell, and Elliot Rose, all of the University of Toronto.[21] Paralleling the approach taken by Hodgetts, these authors emphasize "The War at Sea and the United States." They see the British blockade as a violation of "strict international law," which Prime Minister Lloyd George justified by remarking that "Nations fighting for their lives cannot always pause to observe punctilios." In the war's concluding one hundred days, the Dominion's troops won yet more "brilliant victories," with displays of "indomitable courage," as evidenced by 17,000 decorations, including no fewer than sixty-four Victoria Crosses. Nonetheless, these authors also do not emphasize Vimy, including it only in a discussion of the "brilliant victories" won by Dominion troops. They devote much more attention to the advent of tanks as a portent of modernity in warfare.[22]

As these textbooks indicate, the doctrine that Canada was born in the Great War as a consequence of the valour of our soldiers was not a "truth" widely disseminated among baby-boom students.

Although Remembrance Day was commemorated in the schools, well into the 1990s a regular feature was: "No More War!" In liturgical recitations of great Canadian battles, stretching back to the South African War and beyond, students were introduced to the notion of the sacrifices of Canada's soldiers and how much they owed their more comfortable lives to them. Yet it was also customary to include references to the incineration of Nagasaki and Hiroshima and even, sometimes, to Canada's role in the devastating fire-bombing of the German cities of Dresden and Hamburg in the Second World War. Vimy 1917 tended to figure, not as the "birth of the nation," but as one of a series of sad events that had robbed so many young Canadians, and people worldwide, of their lives.

*   *   *

In most respects Vimyism is a product of the 1980s and 1990s, decades in which the sprouts observable in 1936 and maturing in the 1960s flourished, nurtured by an enthusiastic and determined cohort of conservative nationalists.

In 1964, to mark the fiftieth anniversary of the start of the Great War, CBC-Radio produced an ambitious seventeen-hour series on Canada's experience in the conflict and its repercussions. The remarkable effort, entitled *Flanders Fields*, was based on eyewitness accounts of men—some two hundred veterans—soon to pass from the scene. It was broadcast just once before being consigned to the archives.[23]

The series provided listeners of the time with stories both tragic and heroic, in a tone ranging from the sardonic to the patriotic. The writer and producer was the eminent J. Frank Willis, a pioneer Canadian broadcaster whose rich voice also provides the narration. Willis speaks about "the ivory tower of a rear echelon dreamworld far from the reality of the trenches," a place where the "brass hats" planned battles. A survivor of Newfoundland's day of the dead, 1 July 1916, recalls, "Human life was so cheap, it was the most expendable of all military equipment." He tells the interviewer that after being wounded in the battle—"You could smell blood like a slaughterhouse"—he was judged no longer fit for active service and sent off to work in transportation, where he developed his understanding of military priorities. "There was more attention paid to a sick mule or a horse that died than a human being that died. There was more questions asked."[24]

The Vimy battle, says Willis, was "the shining page of Canada's war record." The Canadians advanced some 4,500 yards at a cost of 10,602 casualties—"3,598 of them lay dead." The segment about Vimy ends with several veterans describing their feelings of Canada's coming of age. "I think myself that was where Canada was born," says A.E. Wright. "I saw the Canadians . . . being tempered into a great nation," adds Elmore Philpott. "I have always felt that Canadian nationality was born on the top of Vimy Ridge," concludes E.S. Russenholt. Willis and his team end the segment with Russenholt's sense that April 1917 "welded" Canadian unity— a unity that the veteran said was just not possible "these days when we hear so much about division and all this sort of thing."[25]

The CBC chose Frank Underhill, a prominent and much-published Canadian historian, to write a conclusion to the fiftieth anniversary documentaries. He was a distinguished but in some ways peculiar choice. Underhill had always been a bundle of contradictions—someone who both bridled at British condescension towards colonials while often seeming to view his fellow Canadians with a certain condescension. Educated at the University of Toronto and Oxford University, he got a teaching job at the University of Saskatchewan in 1914 but then took time off to serve as an officer in the British army on the Western Front in the Great War. His contribution to the 1923 book *The Empire at War* affirmed that the war had made Canada.[26] But as the years passed Underhill became both increasingly sceptical that the war had accomplished anything and increasingly critical of the Empire for which he had fought. He regretted that Canada had involved itself in the Great War, and later declared that the country had gone into war "blindly," influenced by "the British propaganda about democracy."[27]

In the 1930s, as an intellectual godfather of the radical Co-operative Commonwealth Federation, Underhill had earned notoriety as a prominent critic of militarism and imperialism and an advocate for disarmament and world peace. Teaching at the University of Toronto from 1927 to 1955, Underhill was the "bad boy" of Canadian history. He had helped to write the CCF's *Regina Manifesto*, which supported the League of Nations but cautioned that the League needed to be rescued from "being mainly a League of capitalist Great Powers." In another widely read 1930s CCF-related publication, *Social Planning for Canada*, Underhill argued that Canadians who wanted to avoid war should resist not only capitalism and the imperialism it entailed, but also the international bodies that surreptitiously sustained the *status quo*. In a 1938 article called "In Flanders Field" and a subsequent unpublished memorandum on foreign policy, Underhill scandalously declared, "We should . . . make clear to London . . . that we intend to fertilize no more crops of poppies blooming in Flanders Fields."[28] Senior administrators at the University of Toronto considered firing him as a result of his statements, but encountered a storm of opposition.

By the 1960s and the time of the radio broadcast, though, Underhill had shifted to the right, moving close to the governing Pearson Liberals and back to the Underhill of 1923. He expressed a growing disillusionment with the ideals he had espoused in the 1930s. Now, speaking of the Great War, he suggested that it was "the point in our history at which we assumed the full responsibilities of a mature people in a world of autonomous nation-states." Underhill believed Canadians had been right to be proud of the Great War. In the broadcast he fondly remembers how it had helped him feel superior to the Americans.[29]

In his 1964 radio talk Underhill follows his bold statements about how the war made Canada with a host of qualifications. He laments the permanently damaging effects of the conscription crisis, and even argues that Sir Robert Borden had never received "sufficient condemnation for what he allowed to happen inside Canada in 1917." Underhill complains about the "inward-looking, tribal, particularist French-Canadian nationalism" that still menaced Confederation. Here was the unresolved "trauma of 1917." Echoing Russenholt, Underhill argues that the Great War had revealed that a Canada capable of "greater heroism, endurance and idealism" was also a Canada prone "to deeper social cleavages and more irrational forms of fanaticism than it is pleasant to contemplate." Canadians had grown up in a sheltered world, he argues, shielded by British power "from the unpleasant facts of world politics."[30]

This historian's summary of the Great War legacy suggests something of the contradictory ways in which the war was remembered in the 1960s. Underhill abandoned the well-worn notion of the nation coming to maturity almost as soon as he introduced it: Canada's "maturity" was, it becomes plain, not the product of 1918. Underhill was so unconvinced by the "making of the nation" trope that, after outlining all the ways in which the war undermined Canada, he concluded by suggesting that Canadians should get over their nationalism and identify with something bigger. For this thinker, the Great War thus did almost everything: it made the nation, dissolved the nation, and ushered in an era that rendered the nation redundant.

*   *   *

On Remembrance Day 1965 the full CBC-Television network broadcast a thirty-eight-minute war commemoration film supported by both Veterans Affairs and the Department of National Defence. Colour television would not come to Canada for another two months, so viewers did not have a chance to fully appreciate the 35mm cinematography. *Fields of Sacrifice*, a National Film Board production that had already been screened in theatres beginning two years earlier, was renowned writer-director Donald Brittain's breakthrough project.[31]

Viewers listened to an opening narration about "them." "The poppies of Flanders stand for them . . . they still echo across Vimy Ridge," Canadian actor Douglas Rains intones solemnly over a mournful musical score. "They have left their scars on the soil of Picardy. . . . They live in the minds of old men who still travel the roads of the Somme." The shot backing the last sentence shows an aged French farmer riding a plough horse.

"They are the dead."

In this case, the Canadian dead, 1914–18 and 1939–45.

Unlike John McCrae, Brittain did not presume to speak for the dead, though his film was certainly a poetic tour de force. Nor did he wrap the wars with patriotic gauze by instructing viewers that they were fought for freedom, democracy, or other noble causes. In the film the closest he comes to any of these traditional tropes is a sequence featuring Dutch schoolchildren in neat uniforms visiting a graveyard in orderly procession, holding flowers. The schoolchildren, he says, "are taken here so that they will know of the men who faced fear and death so that they would be born unafraid."

Brittain's script is spare. The sequence about Canada and the Netherlands, 1944–45, has a mere seven sentences in over three minutes. Viewed today, the film succeeds in part because its present-tense script brings past and present together. With its documentary film footage and a then-novel technique of panning a camera across a still photograph, the film gives war a sense of urgency and immediacy. Brittain works backwards in time. The movie's first half deals with the Second World War: the Battle of the Atlantic, Hong Kong, the aerial bombardment of Germany, Sicily ("the ancient land of death, a part of the ancient land of blood"), Monte Cassino, Ortona, Normandy, the Netherlands.

Then the picture moves to the Great War. Ypres in 1917 is "a city of death," by 1963 completely rebuilt. At a Menin Gate ceremony at dusk, in the days before battlefield tourism, the spectators are Belgian nuns. "The scars of 14/18 remain only on its soul." At Arras the crew treats an old lady to wine on the main square. A waiter pours another glass as she protests and shrugs. She was of an age to remember the war as a teenager. She did not, says the script, understand the songs the tipsy soldiers sang ("Mademoiselle from Armentières" plays in the background). "But she laughed along with them, for they would soon be dead."

As the Great War section makes its way to Vimy, a jump cut takes viewers to a German cemetery at the Nazi-mythologized Langemarck, now quiet. A few bars of the soundtrack suggest the German national anthem. "Time passes. Monuments and men grow mellow and there are no longer friends and enemies. Only victims." The people in Belgium and France now carry on with their lives, caught by the camera on peaceful streets.

"The world moves on," says Brittain. "Moving as the doomed men moved on their way to no man's land." *Fields of Sacrifice* is steeped in sadness—a blend of mournful reflection tinged with a mood of reconciliation.

Brittain chose Vimy to provide the dramatic denouement. He blends aerial shots of tourists wandering through restored trenches with generic Great War combat footage and roaring battle sound effects. "Easter Monday 1917. The Canadians throw themselves at Vimy Ridge." The battle sounds continue as the airborne camera makes its way up to Allward's monument. The sound effects fade out suddenly, giving way to a close-up montage of the grieving limestone figures. There is no hint or mention of victory or valour as the camera pans painstakingly over the names of the "missing" at the base of the monument. The film's final line of narration—"Eleven thousand names of Canadians who vanished. And they were joined in violent death by other Canadians until there were one hundred thousand memories of the two world wars over the fields of sacrifice"— gives way to more aerial shots as the camera, far above the scene, pulls away from the monument.

For Brittain and Mackenzie King, among others, Vimy offered rich visual symbolism. It provided a perfect place to lament the tragedy of war.

*   *   *

Don Shebib's *Good Times, Bad Times*, another Canadian documentary on war and remembering, followed five years after Brittain's *Fields of Sacrifice*. Employing Second World War footage (superior to the Great War moving pictures), this eminent Canadian director portrays Great War veterans at home, probing the great issues of war. Shebib's melancholic black and white production paints a sympathetic, emotionally shattering picture of Canadian men and war. Although it was made for CBC-Television, hence securing a mass audience, *Good Times, Bad Times* would most likely have been referred to as an "art film" when it aired in 1969. Film critic Peter Harcourt described *Good Times/Bad Times* as "magnificent" and Shebib's "most distinguished short."[32]

Shebib opens with shots of nineteenth-century toy soldiers over a stirring instrumental version of "God Save the Queen." The sequence ends with a lengthy close-up of a medal: "The Great War for Civilization, 1914–1919." The director shot the original footage himself. Contemporary images are dominated by close-ups of old men in Legion halls and veterans hospitals; the mood throughout is sombre. The sole mention of Canada comes in a passing reference to the Vimy battle during a televised Remembrance Day special being watched by a group of veterans. The announcer lists the stunning Great War casualty numbers. "There was something suggestive of tragic drama in this silent countryside where millions of men were waiting to kill each other." One of the veterans adds in voice-over, "It was wicked."

Good Times, Bad Times borrows its title from its remembrance theme—from what returned soldiers recall, what they repress. One man explains that they are inclined to think of war's good times, with the bad times retreating to the back of the mind. "They had so much of the bad and so little of the good."

Much of the archival footage focuses on death in war—soldiers killing, dying, burning, and rotting—over verses of "Marching Soldier," a lengthy 1945 poem by Irish writer Joyce Cary.[33] Although his film's themes are eternal, Shebib shuns all patriotic tropes. In one lengthy sequence, a Remembrance Day gathering in Toronto shows a crowd of Great War veterans marching to a cenotaph for a religious service. "Let us pray now for all to whom the war has brought sorrow and suffering," says the presiding minister.

> For men in wheelchairs, for those who go on crutches and on canes, for those who are blinded. For those who have the evident hurts of body. For those who have the more subtle hurts of mind and spirit. For those who wake up screaming in the night. For those who sit and look and yet see not with eyes that still have the power of sight but minds that are blank to all knowledge.

Shebib offers up a sense of irony that would have done Paul Fussell proud. He uses what film critic Harcourt calls "an ironically absurd war song" ("Auf Wiedersehen, My Dear," sung by Bing Crosby) along with Gustav Holsts's orchestral suite *The Planets* and a throbbing rock anthem by Iron Butterfly—"In-A-Gadda-Da-Vida." This last accompanies an intense bombing sequence. Scenes of joyous celebrations marking the end of the Second World War are followed by the mournful sounds of Samuel Barber's "Adagio for Strings." We see soldiers marching off, again accompanied by Cary's lines.

> *Goodbye. Goodbye, people.*
> *March, march, soldiers, follow away.*
> *We do not belong among these peaceful houses.*
> *Our foreheads are marked with a sign, we have looked at death too long.*

Within our eyes his picture sits. March, march soldiers.
For those who fear that face will put their curse upon us,
Those whom we set free will pay us with hatred,
Because we are guilty of action, of war, of blood.

In the end, old men in a veterans hospital sing together, with a double amputee offering a tune on his harmonica. Shebib concludes with a frail war survivor in his mealtime bib singing "God Save the Queen" in a quavering voice. He finishes and says, "Thank you very much. I'm all tired out. Now you can put me to sleep." The credits roll.

The reputation of the Great War had gone into a steep decline in the 1950s and 1960s—a turnabout sometimes attributed in part to the recoil of the sixties generation against what the Vietnamese would come to call "the American war," and, worse, the mangled minds of a marijuana-and LSD-infested generation, blind to the honour of the fallen and, as Jonathan Vance puts it, part of a "broader cultural turn" against "the idealism and principles of the First World War."[34] Undoubtedly many young activists in the 1960s were also saying no to war—as the exodus to Canada of forty-thousand-plus people escaping from the war in Vietnam suggested, as well as a vibrant peace movement.

Yet scepticism about the Great War—which accurately reflected the views of countless soldiers who fought in it—went far beyond such circles. Canadians who were interested in such things could read the work of British thinkers who, looking back on 1914–18, judged it severely. A.J.P. Taylor, one of the most widely read historians of the day, regarded it as a grim comedy in which railway schedules played a role as significant as any statesmen or generals.[35] The scepticism was also a sentiment shared by the two prime ministers who had first-hand experience of the conflict. No one would accuse John Diefenbaker, Conservative prime minister from 1957 to 1963, staunch monarchist, and holder of a fifty-year pin from the Canadian Legion, of being a secret sympathizer with sixties radicals, or of a want of enthusiasm for Great Britain. Yet in his memoirs, with respect to "the holocaust that was the First World War," he recalled a patronage-ridden military and officers who whiled away the hours on calculations of how many of their men would survive the year. Most of all he remembered the "incredible" carnage and the complete lack of territorial gains "worth mentioning." He remembered too the respectful way in which interwar critics of militarism had been treated: "J.S. Woodsworth was totally opposed to war, but he, too, was listened to with respect as he defended his views. The Hon. J.P.A. Cardin opposed conscription, but was listened to with respect. Both were sincere, and sincerity is the first qualification for an effective Member of Parliament."[36]

For Diefenbaker's successor as prime minister, Lester Pearson, the Great War, which for him consisted mainly of a stint in "the forgotten front" of Macedonia, was relatively uneventful, full of "disease, boredom, and mounting frustration" during a time in which his "college friends were falling in France."[37] Pearson elected not to travel to France for the fiftieth anniversary commemoration of Vimy in 1967. Instead the prime minister simply took the occasion to remind an audience of veterans of the war's "stupid bloodletting."[38] Significantly, neither of these prime ministers went so far as to suggest that Vimy provided the key to Canadian identity or that the Great War was the shining moment in which the country achieved its independence.

*   *   *

Anniversaries matter. Despite prevailing attitudes towards Canada's Great War, the seeds of late-twentieth-century Vimyism were being sown in the 1960s, and especially as part of the nationalistic fervor attending the celebration of Canada's centenary in 1967. Gregory Clark, for one, stepped forward in 1967 to express the opinion that it was at Vimy Ridge that he felt more Canadian than ever before, a sentiment he had not expressed three decades earlier.[39] During that same centennial year Col. Eberts Macintyre's book on Vimy was launched, and it not only helped to draw attention to the battle but also put Vimy at work to sustain relations between French and English Canadians during a period of considerable strain. It was a time, after all, according to the *Globe and Mail's* Paris correspondent, when Canada was having "difficulty in coming to terms with its own duality."[40]

Macintyre—age eighty-two in 1967—had joined the 28th Battalion as a junior officer in October 1914, fought at Vimy Ridge, and was a key organizer of the 1936 pilgrimage to the opening ceremony at the Vimy Memorial. As a native Montrealer who eventually settled on the Gatineau River near Wakefield, Que., Macintyre was acutely aware of the rapidly increasing French-English tensions (or "national unity" questions) of the 1960s. His *Canada at Vimy* was one of the early books on the subject, and it contains themes that would twenty years later be given more symphonic form by Pierre Berton. It includes the now canonical quotation from Brig.-Gen.

Alex Ross—"It was Canada from the Atlantic to the Pacific . . ."—that would become one of the prime statements of Vimyism.[41] Significantly, the author also acknowledged that the message of patriotism no longer seemed to be resonating with many Canadians.

For this Anglo-Montrealer, to be Canadian meant being British. Macintyre doubts that the volunteers went to Europe conscious of the rights or wrongs of the war. What they did know was that "Britain was at war with the most powerful and efficient army in the world and needed help." "Britain" was the ideal in a war whose causes and purposes were obscure. He adds convincing local detail to the overall thesis of an over-whelmingly British, foreign-born Canadian contribution. In Moose Jaw, at the start of the war, he picked out of the crowds the "Legion of Fron-tiersmen . . . some wearing parts of their old South African uniforms such as slouch hats or riding breeches." Macintyre himself points out the pre-dominantly British caste of the first volunteers, the majority of them with "no permanent attachments in Canada." They were men being pulled by the "magnetism of birth and history" back to the Mother Country.[42]

Well aware of the British nature of the First Canadian Contingent, Macintyre believes, "The mere fact that they had had the courage and enterprise to break away from their home environment and try their luck in a new land showed that they were of the type of men who had made the British Empire." They had come to Canada *because* they were more independent-minded; Canada in turn made them even *more* independent-minded, as they became the West's businessmen, farmers, lawyers, and engineers. Their apparent Britishness concealed a Canadian essence—as practical, down-to-earth individuals.[43]

Yet the Canadians were up against what was, in crucial respects, a mismanaged war—beginning with the deplorable conditions of the hous-ing provided for the 1,100 men and 35 officers of the 28th (North West) Canadian Infantry in Winnipeg before their departure for Europe. Once in Europe, the soldiers entered battles without detailed preparation—a "criminal folly." Macintyre saw thirty Highlanders, their tartan kilts still brightly coloured, lying dead in a straight line "as though on parade, mowed down by rifle and machine gun fire, killed while advancing with fixed bayonets against heavy wire and deep trenches and without the ben-efit of any effective artillery barrage." Without reaching the intensity of Will Bird, Macintyre also suggests that the high command was hopeless. The officials denied parachutes to the pilots of Royal Flying Corps planes on the grounds that supplying the equipment might be "considered bad for morale." For him, it was as sensible as denying lifebelts to sailors.[44] In these judgments he concurs with the critical observations made four decades earlier by historian and ex-artillery man W.B. Kerr: the Vimy victory was memorable in part because it had been squandered.[45]

Then again, in contrast to poorly planned battles, Vimy did stand out. It was no "hastily organized fight," but a masterpiece of planning and efficiency: "Never before in warfare had such an elaborate plan been prepared nor such a weighty concentration of artillery been assembled." Yet, to Macintyre's disappointment—still fixed in his mind after fifty years— the high command, never confident that the Canadians could take the ridge, did not follow through on the breakthrough. The Canadians were not allowed to take advantage of the "temporarily disorganized" Germans and "push on and exploit our success." When it quickly became apparent to the Germans that "we did not mean to follow up our victory," they simply stayed on in their positions.[46]

Macintyre is unusual in pointing out that, among an estimated 750,000 "young men who shed their blood on that historic hill," a large number were German. The statistic served to inspire him as "a mournful reminder of the utter futility of war," a phrase that twenty-first-century martial nationalists consistently avoid, but which he uses without self-consciousness. Even the timing of Vimy raised doubts in his mind. On the eve of battle, he writes, "It was nauseating to contemplate the horrors that the representatives of two Christian nations would inflict on each other at this time of the Easter festival, each side believing that he was in the right."[47]

Like Bird, Macintyre draws back from disavowing the war altogether. But his restrained yet powerful descriptions of the battlefield make tangible its daemonic power. He writes of a war-ravaged cemetery in Neuville St. Vaast:

> Every monument had been knocked down by the shelling, not a tombstone was left standing and all the vaults had been smashed open. Shattered coffins with their exposed skeletons covered the earth. Dead trees stood starkly, if they stood at all. Rank grass grew in scattered clumps. It seemed to me that in this troubled part of the world, not even the dead could be left in peace.[48]

The horses died in droves from overwork and cold: no fewer than six hundred in his division. Even Macintyre, no rebel, concedes that, towards the end of the war, Canadian soldiers were at times sent unwillingly into battle. He recycles a thought—citing an unnamed English colonel—that war had "lost much of its charm."[49]

Notwithstanding such nuances of interpretation, and writing at a time when Canadians' emotions were running high—and when Quebec seemed on the brink of dissolving Confederation—Macintyre went to new lengths to celebrate Vimy as the birth of the nation. It was high time that Canadians revived their sense of patriotism, a word they had seemingly forgotten. Vimy, a "glorious tribute to our past," gave them an appropriate way to do so. He reinforces the story-line that emphasized the great significance of the four divisions of Canadians coming together as one, fighting "shoulder-to-shoulder," with the capture of the ridge a "tremendous achievement" in which they "shared equally." Once Canada had been without a voice in international affairs. Its "baptismal blood bath" changed all that. Suddenly, here was a country that could sign the Peace Treaty at Versailles. And why? "Vimy had made all the difference! There our men had stood together, stood as Canadians, and at that moment the Canadian Corps, composed of men from every one of her nine provinces, speaking English and speaking French, represented a united and triumphant nation."[50]

Macintyre's suggestion of equal French- and English-Canadian enthusiasm for Vimy was a stretch, but then he was making this statement in 1967. Vimy was to be seen as a symbol of an understanding between the "founding peoples." The essence of the 1936 Vimy ceremony—as part of a broader campaign of Anglo-French cultural diplomacy, seeking symbolic patches for a diplomatic relationship that often seemed on the verge of coming apart—was now being put to somewhat similar use within Canada itself. Macintyre went so far as to redescribe Allward's pylons—which the sculptor had explained in 1936 were representative of Canada and France—as representing the "English- and French-speaking elements of Canada's people."[51]

*   *   *

In 1965 British-born John Swettenham took up the cause of General Arthur Currie in his book *To Seize the Victory: The Canadian Corps in World War I*.[52] As Swettenham tells it, as a result of a malicious conspiracy orchestrated by the despicable Sam Hughes, Currie's heroic war leadership had been callously disregarded upon the general's return to Canada. Even returned soldiers succumbed to "moral infection" and criticized their leader—a malady put right in 1928 with Currie's successful defence of his reputation against a libellous article in a famous trial in Cobourg. The "Spirit of the Canadian Corps" reasserted itself, and when Currie died in 1933 he received the funeral to which a national hero of his stature was entitled.

The Currie episode revealed, Swettenham points out, that even Canadian soldiers could waver in their support of their leaders. Yet the Canadian soldier, the author generalized, was a product of "a virile race of finest quality" nurtured in "a rigid climate." The soldier was a pioneer democrat and example of a "harder breed," unfazed by the rigours of the trenches. These staunch individualists were ultimately bound to see themselves reflected in their resourceful leader; bound to realize that Currie—also a son of the farm—was a selfless and practical leader, unlike the maniacal Hughes, a "tragic nuisance." Thanks to Currie, Canada had been able to write its name "large over the battlefields of France and Flanders." Not only that: the country ended the war with a fighting machine that was "the greatest national achievement of the Canadian people since the Dominion came into being." By defending himself in 1928, Currie had accomplished a deed at least as significant as the Battle of Mons itself—he had struck a blow against "the evil of unchallenged vilification" and henceforth no Canadian would be compelled to "turn in shame" from the country's glowing military record and the exploits of a noble "battle-leader."[53]

As for the Battle of Vimy Ridge—"Canada's Easter Gift to France," as Swettenham puts it—that well-planned operation had allowed the courage, will, and stamina of the Canadian soldier to shine.[54] Combining hero-worship and Nordic racialism with the exaltation of a "national army" fighting in union for freedom, Swettenham's well-researched and smoothly written account undoubtedly established key branches of the cult of the later Vimyism.

Yet, oddly, other parts of *To Seize the Victory* differ starkly from what would become the Vimyist mainstream. In his vivid description of the horrors of industrial warfare, Swettenham outdoes Harrison and Remarque, whom he approvingly cites. He contrasts the "chattering bright nonsense culled from optimistic newspapers," typical of the "war-madness of the time," with the "brutal truth" of the Front. In the "evil" Ypres Salient, Canadian soldiers "lived like beasts, more primitively than in Stone Age caves, in the blood-soaked, puzzling and filthy" trenches. One Canadian battalion took over a trench that was "still chocked with the decomposed bodies of Scottish soldiers." At Passchendaele, "Human remains, some like frozen swimmers, lay on every side. Not every dead face was caked with mud. Some of the recently killed were white; others grey, green, black or decomposed. A disgusting smell like marsh gas pressed heavily on the senses."[55]

Nor were such horrors simply the necessary price to pay for a better world. Rather, they were often the consequences of "futile" operations. The "true horror" of the war was not in its maimed and killed, or its length, or even its barbarism or atrocities—it was in how "*so many men died and achieved nothing by it.*"[56] Swettenham's Great War is a colossal catastrophe, worsened by arrogant, witless, and isolated senior officers trapped in their own assumptions, many of them frivolously engaged in their own schemes and subjected to the "widespread terror" perpetrated by Hughes. The Canadian war effort was shambolic in its corruption and confusion; and the British generals were fully culpable. British Field Marshal Douglas Haig in particular steered Canadians into "the great gamble of the Somme" and the muddy abattoir of Passchendaele, the second of which "served no useful strategic ends" and was not justifiable on any count. Haig and his advisors, ensconced in their château, driven by crass political motives, and unwilling to listen to Canadian reason, led the soldiers into these "horrors of mud and insane frontal assaults."[57]

Although in effect agreeing with Currie's accusers that "the great sacrifices made by Canadian troops had been unnecessary and that with wise direction they could have been avoided," Swettenham shifted the blame for the calamity onto Haig's shoulders. Although admitting that Currie saw himself as part of the British army, and the conquering Canadians as "young whelps of the old lion," Swettenham still highlights the Canadian general's independence of mind. Currie was only following orders, however irrational and murderous; he regarded the Battle of Passchendaele as a crazy scheme and could never understand why Haig thought it to be so important.[58]

To Seize the Victory is unlike more recent Vimyism in its acute sensitivity to the tragic ironies of the war. Anticipating Fussell, Swettenham notes "the contrast between the finely drawn plans of the belligerents of 1914 and their ultimate descent into colossal and bloody stalemate." Again echoing Harrison and Remarque, Swettenham warmly evokes the front-line soldiers' identification with their fellow sufferers on the other side of no man's land. He attends to many instances of Canadian-German co-operation in treating wounded soldiers and a pervasive "live-and-let-live" characterizing much of the Front. It was tragic that advocates of the peace plans of 1917 were drowned out by shouting war enthusiasts. One of the most haunting images in the book, "perhaps symbolic" of the "barren victory" of Passchendaele, is that of the two corpses, one Canadian and one German, found by stretcher parties clearing away the dead after the battle: "They had fought desperately and, sucked into the swamp, had died in one another's arms. All efforts to part them failed and so a large grave was dug in which to bury the pitiful remains."[59]

In 1967 another Vimy exposition appeared, this one by Lt.-Col. Herbert Fairlie Wood. In *Vimy!* Wood drew on the CBC recordings made earlier in the decade and on archival documents. A Foreword to the book by Maj.-Gen. F.F. (Frank) Worthington declares that before April 1917 "we" were "content to be Colonials with one thought in common—that of going 'home' to fight for the mother country." The description comfortably fits only his fellow Britons (at the outbreak of war, Worthington had been in Canada all of nine days). After Vimy—"a purely Canadian effort, planned and fought our own way"—it was no longer enough just to be British: "We were Canadian and could do a good job of paddling our own canoe."[60]

Yet the book that follows Worthington's opening salvo is much less categorical: it concedes that the "intangible results" of Vimy were difficult to assess, that the notion of Vimy as nation-maker had not really been the sentiment in 1917, and that romantic descriptions of a "tornado" of shell fire and the Canadian infantry pouring like a flood across the German lines were fanciful: "It had not really been like that, of course, but it was the sort of thing that G.H.Q. put out for consumption by the public." If ultimately Wood does say that Vimy was "for better or for worse" a milestone in "Canada's progress towards nationhood" or Canada's "Agincourt," he pounds relentlessly upon "the folly of war." With respect to the famous saying, "How sweet and honourable to die for one's country," Wood suggests it to be a "vast over-simplification." He asks: "Harness nations, turn them against each other, eliminate a generation in the process—can this possibly be ennobling?" Of other famous battles in the war, such as Festubert, St. Eloi, and Mount Sorrel, he concludes, "There was no victory here, no sense of achievement."[61]

Wood treats much of the Great War as being replete with tragic ironies for those who fought it. Tales of bloodthirsty Germans, blown out of proportion by our propagandists, did not correspond with the actuality of many of the German soldiers against whom Canadians fought—they were "essentially peace-loving rural peoples, wedded to their hills and mountain farms." At Vimy, after the Canadians' disastrous mid-February

gas raids—which Wood to his credit does not erase from his narrative—
the Germans arranged a truce, so that front-line soldiers, "at each other's
throats short hours before," managed to clear the battlefield of the Canadian dead. Again in line with Remarque, Harrison, and countless others,
Wood remembers the "gruesome humour" that allowed soldiers to survive the war, as in the fanciful treatment of skeletons as clothes racks or
in the comment of one veteran that he had been in the Vimy area long
enough "to know a lot of rats by their first names."[62]

An army run by authorities in love with "outworn tactics" lacked the
wisdom to provide adequate food for the soldiers, which led to some black
humour: "The cookhouse at the training camp near the Château de la
Haie had a hard-tack biscuit nailed to the door over a sign that read: 'A
square meal.'" Meanwhile, "The temporary inhabitants of the châteaux
behind the lines dined well, frequently and liquidly. The much abused
word 'cannon fodder' springs reluctantly to mind when food for soldiers is
considered. The guns got better attention than the men who died in front
of them." The soldiers had a "shrewd suspicion" that they were fed so
poorly and clothed so wretchedly because "the staff figured things on the
basis that most of the troops would die in the next attack and it was wasteful to issue good food or warm clothing only to see it disappear into the
mud." Wood is even scathingly sarcastic about the eight kilted battalions.
Its members wore the garment with "a fierce pride that made nonsense
out of reality": perhaps these Canadian soldiers' reputation for taking few
prisoners might be accounted for by the "discomfort of their costume."[63]

As for the Canadians' military leaders, he is appreciative of Lt.-Gen.
Byng—much more so than of Currie—and brutally dismissive of Haig,
this "very strange man" whose lack of foresight meant that victory at Vimy
did not in the end count for much and who was agonizingly slow to learn
the rudiments of the war: "The slaughter of a generation of his countrymen was a high price to pay to teach a general his job." The "bad management, sloth and indifference" with which the soldiers were treated was
complemented by the bleak fate of the Corps' fifty thousand horses, many
of them shot, bombarded with gas shells, or just worked to death. The fate
of the horses sickened many of the country boys at the Front.[64] For all
of Worthington's tub-thumping patriotism, and Wood's more qualified
nationalism, it would be hard for the average reader to come away from
Vimy! with anything but a keen sense of the savage ironies of the conflict.

In 1969 Lt.-Col. D.J. Goodspeed, a veteran of the Second World War
and senior historian in the Directorate of History of the Canadian Forces,

brought out *The Road Past Vimy: The Canadian Corps 1914–1918*. Goodspeed laments that "a whole generation of Canadians is growing up in almost complete ignorance of the events that did so much to shape their world," complaining that even though "war and military considerations have frequently been paramount" in Canadian history, they were often excluded from an academy averse to a subject considered "too brutal and barbarian." One of Goodspeed's sentences would prove especially influential: "No matter what the constitutional historians may say, it was on Easter Monday, April 9, 1917, and not on any other date, that Canada became a nation."[65] Here, then, Vimyism's core concept, enunciated by an official historian in a well-received book, found one of its first and most pugnacious expressions.

Yet the odd thing about this much-remembered sentence, whose argument was neither substantiated nor defended, is how discordant it is with Goodspeed's overall interpretation of the Great War. He argues that the Great War was "unnecessary"—it was not a fight for freedom or the prelude to any "permanent peace." The "futilities" of twentieth-century war "are not dissipated by ignoring them," he says, and the records of this pointless war are worth studying mainly as indications of how *not* to think about peace and war in a modern world. The Canadian war aims, so far as they were ever explicitly declared, did not include making the world safe for democracy—especially given that one of our allies was Czarist Russia. Rather, we went to war, in Borden's words, "to ensure the integrity and maintain the honour of our Empire." The notion that Canadians were battling against a totalitarian German juggernaut was not much in evidence in 1914, "for the very good reason that in both military and naval strength the Allies were overwhelmingly superior to the Central Powers, in quantity if not in quality." Still, that "juggernaut," Goodspeed writes, performed better than the forces against it because, contrary to "those brought up on legends of rigid Prussian militarism," the German system of command "was much more flexible than the British" and allowed for the capacity to "study, understand, and regularize what actually happened on most battlefields."[66]

Most of *The Road Past Vimy* is written in the key of critical realism, not romantic nationalism, and few readers will put it down admiring the supposed greatness of the Great War. We meet the brave Canadians massed "shoulder to shoulder in the attack formation they had practised in training camp," a formation "that might have been used at Waterloo," and we encounter the enthusiastic Canon Frederick George Scott, "shaking hands with the men and exclaiming over and over again: 'A great day for Canada, boys! A great day for Canada!'" But these are *ironic* figures, unaware—as

Goodspeed assumes his readers are all aware—that in the new world of war many of them are about to be torn apart by artillery shells or cut down by machine guns, often caught up, as in the Ypres Salient, in military campaigns defying "all military logic." Goodspeed remains impressed by the uncanny insanity and mass terror of this war. He pushes further British prime minister Lloyd George's somewhat belated and possibly self-serving critique of a secluded top brass surrounded by sycophants. If the conventional critique of senior commanders was that they made their plans "from the map without ever looking at the actual ground," in the case of Ypres, "it would almost seem as though the commanders did not even look at the map."[67]

Yet to dwell upon "the incompetence of individuals" risks "far too shallow an explanation," because at the base of it all was a military and ultimately political system that allowed such commanders "to act thus with impunity." A prime example of the irrational dysfunctionality of the political system was Borden's pledge of 500,000 men in uniform—a promise made without consulting even his cabinet colleagues in Canada or His Majesty's Government in England, and without consideration of the actual capacity of the country: an impulsive decision based on "emotion rather than reason."[68]

Still, even under these conditions, Goodspeed argues, Canadian soldiers did fight as best they could, and at Vimy Ridge they did score a modest success—and in that case, with "a sound plan" that "looked, by mere contrast, to be the product of military genius," the Canadian Corps was unified, not by hatred of the enemy, but by "common hardship and danger." Goodspeed was especially struck by the unwritten pacts that allowed Germans and Canadians to collaborate—culminating in arrangements that had Germans dressing Canadians' wounds on the battlefield and both sides exchanging wounded men. By 1916, "Most front-line soldiers had little hatred left for the enemy they fought so savagely; the causes of the war and the war aims of the statesmen alike seemed to belong to another world."[69] So, increasingly, did the causes and goals at home also seem to be in disarray. A time of profiteering scandals, the conscription crisis, the "gigantic gerrymander" of the 1917 election, hate-fuelled polemics against dissenters, and a country "as divided as never before in its history" was witnessing "a growing revulsion among the thoughtful at the facile slogans of the super-patriots."[70]

In the light of these observations, Goodspeed's own fleeting endorsement of a "super-patriotic" Vimyism seems all the more curious—the product, perhaps, not of his own very considerable powers of rational historical analysis, but of the ambient nationalism of Canada's centennial celebrations and his quest to redeem the field of military history by attaching it to a grander "colony-to-nation" narrative.

Indeed, the accounts of Macintyre, Swettenham, Wood, and Goodspeed all show that, before the advent of full-blown Vimyism in the last quarter of the twentieth century, it was still possible, even among the country's military historians, to see the Great War more as a cautionary tale about militarism run rampant than as the fount of true Canadianism. All four books—which built upon G.W.L. Nicholson's much-awaited official history, *Canadian Expeditionary Force, 1914–1919*, for the most part a sane and sensible operational history that occasionally strays into chest-thumping nationalism—contain elements that could be worked up into full-fledged Vimyism, yet each of them contained nuances and subtleties that told against any such mythical exaltation of the battle.[71] That would have to wait until the 1980s.

*   *   *

Much more significant in the rise of Vimyism was a book brought out, ironically enough, by a writer who had almost no use for militarism. Far more than any other author, in his book simply titled *Vimy* (1986), Pierre Berton reinvigorated the idea of that battle as a centrepiece of English-Canadian nationalism.

Berton was that rarest of rare birds, especially in Canada—a modern historian in command of a popular audience. Many Canadians would present "this year's Berton book" to their loved ones at Christmastime. At the peak of his career Berton might receive as much as $152,000 as an advance for a book.[72] Through his appearances on CBC-Television's *Front Page Challenge*, in countless newspaper columns, and in such widely discussed books on contemporary affairs as *The Comfortable Pew* (1965), a candid critique of institutional Christianity, and *The Smug Minority* (1968), a depiction of an elite-ridden Canada, Berton became one of the most influential English Canadians of his time.

In his well-conceived and generally well-researched histories Berton celebrated entrepreneurs and rebels who, in his mind, were the exact opposites of the distrusted and snobbish urban elites. His *Klondike: The Last Great Gold Rush* (1958) was not just about the gold rush but about free-spirited adventurers risking everything in the North and helping

Pierre Berton. One of English Canada's foremost twentieth-century mythmakers, the skilled storyteller chronicled the railway's role in creating Canada and also wrote *Vimy*, making a key claim for the battle as Canada's founding moment.

to stoke the great ambition that the twentieth century might belong to Canada. In 1970 Berton got his own birth-of-a-nation bandwagon rolling with *The National Dream*, a saga of the building of the Canadian Pacific Railway, following that with its companion piece, *The Last Spike* (1971). According to this telling, Canada came together with the construction of a strip of steel to the Pacific—over thirty years before Vimy Ridge.

Often disparaged by academics, with his optimistic sense of history as the unfolding of progress, Berton became the country's most popular historian by appealing simultaneously to patriotism and to rugged individualism, an onwards-and-upwards ascent he chronicled with a fine storyteller's panache.

Many of *Vimy*'s themes appeared earlier in his two popular books on the War of 1812. In *The Invasion of Canada 1812–1813* (1980), Berton argued—following in the footsteps of such intellectuals as George Grant and Gad Horowitz—that a distinctive "Canadian way of life" had arisen after 1814, one different from and even opposed to the "more individualistic American way," according to which "order imposed from above has advantages over grassroots democracy." In *Flames Across the Border* (1981), Berton argued that the War of 1812 had made Canada what it was because it had enshrined "national stereotypes" pitting regimented British redcoats against the Yankees, "vulgar, tobacco-chewing upstarts in loud suits, who had no breeding and spoke with an offensive twang." After 1812, with "the British colonial way" secured—"comfortable, orderly, secure, paternalistic"—came a "new nationalism," which meant that "few Canadians found it possible to consider, at least openly, the American way as a political choice for the future."[73]

Even so, in the midst of all of his exuberant nationalism, Berton managed to come up with an ironic conclusion in the first book: if the "Canadian way of life" was indeed so very different because of the conflict in 1812, that eventuality had arisen "because of a foolish war that scarcely anyone wanted or needed, but which, once launched, none knew how to stop."[74]

Berton's own attitudes towards war were ambiguous. He was no pacifist, having served in the Canadian Army in the Second World War, taught at the Royal Military College, and worked as an intelligence officer. Yet his books also revealed a man sharply attuned to the irrationalities and cruelties of war and dismissive of militarists who worshipped it. Repeatedly looking for the war that might serve as Canada's "foundational moment," and thus quite in keeping with Vimyism, he was also always keen to suggest, in a way unlike his successors, that the political outcomes of wars in no way outweighed their horrors. Canada's most prominent historian most likely captured the outlook of many of his fellow citizens.

Berton's vision of war and peace was also complex. Conscripted into the Canadian Army in 1942, he went overseas in March 1945, although to his frustration he never did engage in actual combat. Berton's stance was best conveyed in one of his last books, *Marching as to War: Canada's Turbulent Years* (2001), a grand narrative that treats all of Canadian history from the perspective of the country's four major twentieth-century wars (South Africa, the two world wars, and Korea). The glaring paradox of the book is that, while arguing that wars shaped Canadians as did nothing else, it opens on an emphatically non-militarist note:

> Were these wars necessary? In three cases the answer is unequivocal: certainly not! . . . Why were we risking Canadian lives to support the ambitions of an empire determined to impose its will on a peaceful community of Dutch farmers? Why did we cross the ocean again, in the face of opposition from one-third of our people, to sacrifice our youth in an ill-considered war that solved nothing and led only to another? Why, again, did we ship our youth to the Orient to help the new American empire support a corrupt Korean regime?[75]

Berton was not a celebrator of Canada's wars. At the same time, he was a significant figure in the shaping of the "big bang" theory of Canadian history that, after the 1980s, started to reimagine the Battle of Vimy Ridge as the country's real birthday. When Berton brought out *Vimy* in 1986—his thirty-third book and ninth major work in Canadian history[76]—the subject was guaranteed to gain a large audience.

The "Battle of Vimy Ridge" that has captivated many a Canadian mind—from Don Cherry to former prime minister Stephen Harper to historian Tim Cook—is, to a large extent, the Vimy of Berton's heroic story. Driven, as in so much of his writing, by a search for an essential "Canadian character," Berton found what he was looking for among the soldiers who took it upon themselves to raise Canada from youth to maturity on Vimy Ridge. After Berton this trope swiftly entered high-school textbooks and has ever since been a regular fixture in Vimy celebrations.[77]

As Berton outlines the story, Canada's soldiers, many as young and unformed as the land they epitomized, came from a "small country" with "scarcely any military tradition, no military aspirations, and little knowledge of war." Here was a peaceable frontier kingdom, an "unbelligerent nation" of "farms and villages, of outdoor plumbing and rutted concession roads," a place where "work was hard and pleasure innocent," where people "lazed on their front porches, or wound up the gramophone to listen to the great Al Jolson hit."[78] The soldiers sent off to fight had acquired most of their ideas about the glamour of war from boys' adventure stories. But, true sons of the frontier, they also had "guts and stamina . . . and a habit of self-reliance." With an echo of Macintyre's book, and drawing upon the romantic depictions of the capable, do-it-yourself westerners so beloved by readers of novelist Ralph Connor, Berton tells how many of Canada's soldiers were "the same adventurers who had poured into the pioneer West in the first decade of the century, determined to be unfettered by Old Country traditions."[79] Before Berton, Arthur Currie had also extolled the Canadian soldier as a man whose "broad shoulders, deep chest and strong, clean-cut limbs" bespoke the "invaluable gifts of our deep forests and lofty mountains, of our rolling plains and our great waterways, and of the clear light of our Northern skies." For Currie, it was all proof of evolution at work: the "laws of selection" had led to this "tenacious and indomitable will."[80]

Here, then, were Canadians possessed of "naïve enthusiasm" and "carefree indiscipline." They were on the brink of losing their "innocence." They were hard-working resourceful men used to long hours, uncomplainingly enduring the hardships of training on England's Salisbury Plain and remaining "irrepressibly cheerful and eager to exchange the mud of the training fields for the gumbo of Flanders."[81]

These high-spirited lads were often hard-drinking, hard-playing, hard-fighting. They were boys "whose arms and shoulder muscles had been toughened by years of playing the two indigenous Canadian games, lacrosse and ice hockey." As an admiring Berton writes, "There was nothing sheep-like about them." Pay nights were nights of drunken revelry. Rambunctious Canadian soldiers wrecked tents used for film screenings and messed up canteens on board the troopship *Sardinia*. Canadian soldiers occasionally shot unpopular British officers in the back. They were also deeply committed to one another, and performed their feats of bravery on behalf of "their closest friends—the half-dozen private soldiers with whom they slept, ate, laughed, worked, and caroused, the men in their own section . . . whom they could not and would not let down because in moments of desperation and terror their virtual existence was woven together as tightly as whipcord."[82]

When Berton first submitted his manuscript for his publisher's consideration, one assessor was shocked by his gung-ho, swashbuckling tone. So

Berton "cut away the overheated prose," enough to satisfy his critic that he had least turned "bad Kipling into good Kipling."[83] The reader had a point. There is something decidedly Kiplingesque about *Vimy*. Although the author exhibited none of Kipling's British imperialism, he did share a populist identification with the average soldier—the hard-working lads from the farm who made Vimy possible.[84] Gripping descriptions of the harsh conditions to which our boys were subjected became, in Berton's hands, additional proof of their frontier-induced independence and valour. It is no knock on a Christian saint if he must endure the heathens' arrows on his way to martyrdom, and it is no knock on Canada's staunch frontiersmen if, en route to the battle in which their manliness shone so brightly, they had to endure conditions, in the words of Andrew Macphail, "so unlike the pomp of war." Things were not always great, of course: death from poison gas was gruesome, the raids on German trenches were "vicious" and "ruthless," the cold was so severe that "bread froze after it came from the ovens and had to be cut apart with a hacksaw," pneumonia was rife.[85] But in Berton's narrative such details became, not signs of the senselessness of the war, but illustrations of the conditions to be heroically overcome by colourful Canadian frontiersmen.

Out of such a strong, free-spirited *Canadian* soldiery emerged inventive and heroic *Canadian* leaders.[86] One of them was Andrew McNaughton, who acquired his "self-reliance" from a lifetime of riding, shooting, hunting, and fishing. "At brigade headquarters he slept on the floor, spurning a mattress, perfectly content to open a tin of bully beef for his supper." Berton praises the artilleryman who would later organize relief camps and become a Second World War corps commander, but was clearly his own man. "What other senior officer on the Western Front," Berton asks, "kept a pet lion cub under the packing cases that did duty for his desk?" The controversial Arthur Currie was another such hero—"the greatest soldier in Canada's history—the man who more than any other had put the country on the map and given her an enviable international reputation."[87]

Unencumbered by the old doctrines and fusty elitism of Europeans, such stalwart frontiersmen fought a *Canadian* war. In three previous massive Vimy Ridge attacks from 1914 to 1916, the French had squandered 150,000 soldiers, "dead or mangled." The French were just like that. Bad at arithmetic, they tended to misjudge the trajectory of their own shells—quite unlike the Canadians, who brought "science to bear on the art of gunnery." The British were little better. They were so snobbish and hidebound in their thinking that, on one occasion, a "stiff-necked"

British officer marched proudly off to his demise, simply because he was too proud to listen to informed Canadians. The rank-obsessed British so little appreciated people of a scientific bent that they stigmatized them as "dangerous radicals," whereas the Canadians—sons of an egalitarian, class-free frontier—"made them welcome, looked to their comfort, and encouraged their experiments."[88]

Berton repeatedly contrasts Canadian frontier spirit and know-how with Old World inefficiency and fustiness. Among the Canadians, the distribution of detailed plans of the battlefield meant that every man understood his role in the greater scheme: "More than 40,000 maps were disseminated with the intention that all soldiers were to become familiar with their battalion's specific task." The immaculately planned attack was launched with a big bang to end all big bangs: "It is probable that with the exception of the Krakatoa explosion of 1883, in all of history no human ears had ever been assaulted by the intensity of sound produced by the artillery barrage that launched the Battle of Vimy Ridge on April 9, 1917."[89]

Here then was the Canada that emerged in France and Flanders— young, energetic, resourceful, independent-minded, gutsy. As a "good Kipling," Berton provides the reader with page after page of the Canadian exploits, often narrated from the soldiers' own point of view. The more harrowing the scene—and Berton does not shrink from gruesome detail— the more exemplary the Canadian achievement. Berton never loses sight of his great underlying theme—the emergence of a distinct Canadian identity. The Canadian soldiers "lost their innocence" but gained a mature sense of what had "to be endured by men who knew their job."[90]

In *Vimy* Berton, perhaps inadvertently, gave martial nationalism one of its most widely read founding texts. For Berton, Vimy was "clearly a milestone" on Canada's journey to "nationhood."[91] His opening epigraph comes from something Gregory Clark wrote in 1967: "As far as I could see, south, north, along the miles of the Ridge, there were the Canadians. And I experienced my first full sense of nationhood."[92] Berton relates the scene as Canadians readied themselves for the great assault:

As they passed they called greetings to each other: 'There go the 13th! Good old 13th!' and the answering greeting: 'Good luck, Toronto!' For the first and the last time all four Canadian divisions would be attacking in line, British Columbia side by side with Cal- gary, Ottawa next to Vancouver, the Van Doos of Quebec shoulder to shoulder with the Highlanders of Nova Scotia.[93]

At Vimy, Berton explains, "From the moment he enlisted to the day of his discharge the Canadian soldier was under Canadian control." This condition had far-ranging cultural implications:

> There were certain things that were *theirs* and nobody else's, certain things they knew about that others did not know: Cyclone Taylor and Newsy Lalonde; Eaton's catalogue and Marquis wheat, CPR strawberries and Labatt's India Pale Ale; Tom Longboat, Kit of the *Mail*, Big Bear, and Louis Riel; Mackenzie and Mann; the Calgary *Eye Opener* and *Saturday Night*; Nellie McClung, Henri Bourassa, Pauline Johnson, and the Dumbbells. This was the glue that held them together and made them peacock proud. The British had done their best to frustrate this—to scatter the Canadian units through the British army; but the Canadians would have none of it.

Even soldiers from the "Old Country"—as in the case of future major-general Frank Worthington—now understood themselves to be "Canadian all the way."[94]

Such soldiers would come back to Canada as bearers of a new national identity, and the world would look at Canada in a new way, regarding the typical Canadian as "a brawny two-fisted frontiersman, independent in action and thought, tough, bold, inventive, and hard as the impermeable granite of the Precambrian Shield. He had rolled back the frontier, opened the West, and prevailed against the Hun through daring and ingenuity." Thanks to Prime Minister Borden, Canada achieved autonomy, exemplified by its representation at the Peace Conference at Versailles and in the League of Nations. But thanks were equally owed to Canada's soldiers: "Canada had won her independence on the battlefields of Flanders and in the conference rooms of Downing Street."[95]

As Berton tells the tale, after 1918 Vimy became the pervasive, untouchable symbol of the entire country—as he puts it in another book, "that shining, unifying moment when old quarrels were forgotten, had given the country a sense of purpose and confidence."[96] In the postwar years, Berton says in *Vimy*, the battle took on a mythic quality, which was of immense importance in a country "short of myths":

> Canadians could grumble that Ypres, the Somme, and Passchendaele were bungled by the British. But Vimy! That was Canada's, and nobody could take that victory away. In the years between the

two World Wars, every schoolchild, every veteran's son, every immigrant was made aware of it.[97]

Even Canadians who afterwards felt disillusioned about the war could never shake "Vimy Fever" and found in the battle the inspiring story the country had been lacking. This vision "still illuminates our folk memory. We carry it with us, for it has been drilled into our minds by constant repetition, a tale retold, like a looped movie—the heart-thumping spectacle of the entire Canadian Corps clambering up that whale-backed ridge." In the "drumfire repetition" of the very word "Vimy," one could sense the "longing to tell the world and ourselves that we had passed through the fire and not been found wanting." No wonder that in 1936 the unveiling of the massive and immodest war monument perched atop Hill 145 at Vimy Ridge—the Canadian shrine—entailed a ceremony focused on the victorious Canadians' extraordinary feat of arms.[98]

For Berton, the triumphalist martial message of Vimy, as later typified by the monument, would remain constant over the long decades. Vimy was the "single magical word" that stood for Canada's "Great War victories." As such, it "made us cocky." Apparently, "There were few Canadians, at least in English-speaking Canada, who could resist the thrill of pride in the much-heralded victories of their famous corps. Foreign newspapers had praised it to the skies; statesmen and generals had echoed those plaudits." Vimy "became part of the cultural baggage that every loyal Canadian carried." Anyone who served at Vimy was a "Vimy veteran." Children were named "Vimy." Innumerable parks, schools, and city streets would bear the name.[99]

*   *   *

Berton's gripping account in *Vimy* exerted a lasting influence, and over the following decades Vimyism itself became firmly entrenched on the Canadian landscape of memory. But critics complained about Berton's book for years; and the evidence and arguments of more recent historians suggest that his "riveting" and accessible account does not exactly represent anything close to the full truth with respect to the battle.

Far from being a fan, Major John R. Grodzinski of the Royal Military College wrote in 2009 that *Vimy* was "execrable" and "distorted this battle beyond anybody's ability to repair the damage." His condemnation came in the midst of a discussion of how journalistic and academic writing on the war constituted a "relatively immature" historiography that was sacrificing accuracy to nationalism. In particular, Grodzinski wrote, writers had overlooked the heavy losses incurred in taking the ridge, which were "proportionally the same as several of the worst battles of the war."[100]

In the opening pages of *Vimy Ridge: A Canadian Reassessment* (2010), Arthur Currie biographer A.M.H. Hyatt rather nervously reassures readers that the battle remains a "Canadian epic."[101] Yet the detailed articles that follow his Foreword deliver an unmistakable message: on key points the "epic" that Berton was so instrumental in developing bears only an indirect relation to the historical record. Berton's story of Vimy may work as a ripping yarn, but it fails in three important ways: in mistaking the nature of the force that took Vimy Ridge; in overstating the battle's significance; and in failing to understand the wider context in which the battle took place.[102] Not only that, the writers in *Vimy Ridge: A Canadian Reassessment* point out that Berton's narrative of "Canadian innocence"—of our side being pure while confronting enemy viciousness—misrepresents the realities of twentieth-century warfare. His "Vimy, birth of the nation" trope entails the invention of a tradition that defies the facts, contributing to a particularly narrow conception of the "nation" under discussion.

A key assumption in Berton—and one now widely accepted in the Vimyist narrative—is that the event represented a *Canadian* victory. In this regard Berton was picking up on the "classic" treatment of Vimy by writers ranging from Lord Beaverbrook to Colonel Archer Fortescue Duguid. In 1935 Duguid, the official Canadian army historian, stated that Vimy was "almost exclusively" a Canadian show, which forged the Canadian Corps into "one homogeneous entity."[103] Yet the majority of the Canadian Corps consisted of first-generation British immigrants; and, as military historian Paul Dickson points out, only about a third of the troops sent overseas in the fall of 1914 were born in Canada. Even the native-born, according to Dickson, "were often only one generation removed from Britain," and six months after Vimy, Jean Martin shows, 55.48 per cent of the Canadian Corps was "foreign," that is, born outside Canada.[104] Offered a chance to serve in the military, most eligible men in Canada had given it a pass. Vimy, from this perspective, was a British victory.

Nor was this force made up of Berton's sturdy sons of the frontier. Most soldiers came from the cities. About 65 per cent were manual labourers and a further 18.5 per cent were clerical workers. Even though Canada would remain about 50 per cent rural down to 1921, the CEF was overwhelmingly drawn from non-rural areas.[105] It was not dominated by frontiersmen but by some white-collar employees and many more blue-collar workers, such as coal miners from Nova Scotia, Alberta, and British Columbia, who registered in droves. For miners, and other working-class Canadians, a tale stressing "innocents" suddenly plunged into a world of high-handed bosses and unpredictable accidents is off base, to say the least.[106]

The Canadian Corps was not autonomous. Functioning as an integral part of the British Expeditionary Force, it was not an independent national army. At most, the Canadian Corps was a "proto-national army." Canadian soldiers were governed by British military law and subject to British military discipline. As Gary Sheffield points out, "the key role played by British units and formations and individual British officers in the 9 April 1917 attack" at Vimy Ridge cannot be ignored. The simple reason why Canadian soldiers found themselves north of Arras in early 1917 was that "the Canadian Corps was then part of the First British Army."[107] Berton's firm declarations of Canadian exceptionalism—although flamboyant and fun—are well off the mark.

The Canadian soldiers also depended, for the most part, on British leadership, as Patrick Brennan shows. British support—in planning, artillery, leadership, and fighting—was instrumental to the battle.[108] A narrow martial nationalism has meant, as Sheffield adds, that the British elements of the force that fought in the battle were airbrushed out of popular memory. Berton's focus on McNaughton and his treatment of Currie, real estate speculator and embezzler, as "Canada's greatest soldier" are difficult to reconcile with the very real leadership of Britain's Julian Byng, who, in the words of Currie's own biographer, "moulded the Corps into a cohesive unit" and steered the entire enterprise, none of which would have happened without British politicians, strategists, planners, gunners, and infantrymen. Or, perhaps it should be said, it was a *somewhat* cohesive unit: although the "disorganized rabble" of the First Canadian Division, legendary for tensions between native-born and others, had attained a degree of coherence and homogeneity through extensive training, not all such divisions would have disappeared by the second week of April 1917. As Andrew Iarocci argues, the impression of a unified corps functioning with a flawless unity—and standing proudly apart, at least in Berton's account, from the less-evolved Brits—does not match the record of "the experiences of those who fought on the battlefield," which testifies to levels of chaos and confusion similar to those of many other Great War encounters. With respect to the Fourth Division's attack, it "quickly became confused and appeared to stall." But rather than attending to such mundane facts, operational assessments have tended to repeat the same old story of Canadian brilliance. "The reason" for that inclination "is obvious," writes Andrew Godefroy: "Canadians consider Vimy Ridge an icon of national achievement."[109]

Contrary to interpretations claiming that Canadian soldiers were trained to be exceptionally free-thinking and free-standing, in contrast to the servile, tradition-bound Brits, both Canadian and British soldiers, as members of the same army under the same general, were (unsurprisingly) "prepared to fight in a similar way." If, as Brennan maintains, the barrage plans of the Canadian artillery were important to the Vimy assault, then some credit for them must surely go to Major Alan Brooke, staff officer of the Royal Artillery, who was ultimately responsible for that facet of the attack. Instead Brooke is conveniently written off as a "haughty Englishman." Even the widespread dissemination of maps to soldiers was not so very original to the Canadians: the practice had already become standard within the BEF, having also been tried out by the French command.[110]

Berton's account of the Canadians' individualism carried its own internal contradictions. His narrative strategy of exalting particular personnel clashes with his detailed description of the tightly integrated industrial apparatus within which such people moved. Berton describes a vast Vimy war machine, one that functioned best on the basis of precision timing and the integration of each soldier into the collective—something combining many of the attributes of Henry Ford's system of mass production. The men buried 21 miles of electrical cable in trenches 7 feet deep. They put up 1,100 miles of telephone wire, some of it on aerial supports. They built a 20-mile-long tramway system, complete with a hidden terminus, and a vast labyrinth of subways, whose total length was almost 6 miles (much of it dug by coal miners from Nova Scotia and the West). They constructed a water system serviced by a 4-inch water main fed by a 1,500-gallon tank. "They were like automatons, trained for months to respond instantly to any order," says Berton—in other words, rather more like the industrial workers that so many of them were, rather than the rugged frontiersmen he wanted them to be.[111]

The French, for their part, also had more than a little to do with the victory, such as it was, at Vimy. The French army had learned valuable lessons after the "bloody Somme offensive," and revised their age-old linear tactics that called for straight lines of soldiers moving forward, brandishing bayonets, instead adopting a more "flexible" strategy "employing self-reliant platoons" and fostering "innovation and initiative on the part of junior officers and non-commissioned officers (NCOs)," all of it with the aim of solving the riddle of the trenches.[112] The French had also seen "two long years of ferocious attacks and counterattacks, supported by prolonged bombardments," which had "transformed the terrain of Vimy Ridge." The result of these earlier offensives had been to confine the Germans to "a small yet densely fortified perimeter on Hill 145 and its adjacent defences," which meant that when the heavy artillery was unleashed in April 1917, against the heavily outnumbered German defenders, it found a highly concentrated target.[113]

Was this battle, as Berton states, the "greatest victory of the war"? As Sheffield remarks, with due scholarly gravitas, "It is not easy to see how this claim can be substantiated." Vimy Ridge marked "only the northern flank of the Battle of Arras," which was in turn an attempt only to divert German strength from the much bigger struggle to uproot the German army from France. Indeed, even the very identity of the particular, or overall, victor at Vimy is in some doubt. At least some of the German defenders, according to evidence gathered by Godefroy, thought that they had scored a victory or at least a draw. The Germans were not necessarily deluded. In April 1917 the German high command had "adopted a largely defensive strategy in the west, designed to hold on to ground already won, while the war on the Eastern Front was decided." From this perspective, the Germans were mainly able to hold their line in the Battle of Arras and repel a concerted Allied offensive in one of the most significant (if often forgotten) battles of the war. The BEF mounted the northern offensive as a diversion from the more fundamental and even more titanic French struggle going on further south. In April 1917 the Germans even gave out awards to those in the 261st Prussian Reserve Infantry Regiment who had engaged in the "fierce fighting at Vimy Ridge" and "prevented a British breakthrough of the German lines between April 9 and 13 April 1917." One German wrote of how the "memory of the days of heroic glory and deepest sorrow glows indelibly at the Battle of Vimy Ridge, that patch of earth sanctified by the rivers of noble blood and uncountable heroic graves."[114]

As Godefroy points out, the idea that the German army did not at the time consider Vimy Ridge a defeat, and perhaps even saw it as a victory, made sense given the bigger picture: "After all, no massive breakthrough followed this attack and perhaps to the German Army the loss of a few kilometres of vital ground meant little in the grand scheme of things."[115] Far from constituting a brilliant victory that broke the deadlock of the Western Front and constituted "a big turning point in the war,"[116] the

Battle of Arras, along with the struggle for Vimy Ridge, "ultimately reinforced what British and Dominion soldiers had already experienced for two years"—a grinding war of attrition. Neither the capture of the ridge nor the overall Battle of Arras constituted a "strategic breakthrough." If the "intention was to inflict a crushing defeat on the German forces, and to demonstrate to the world that we now had the strength in men and munitions to go on and win the war," to cite Macintyre from 1967, it did not really succeed.[117]

Berton liked the image of the great explosion that had initiated Vimy and which, by symbolic implication, provided the fireworks announcing the birth of the nation. Yet the down-to-earth consequences of the big bang were a big disappointment because such bombardment so churned up the ground that neither heavy artillery nor horses could be easily moved through it. Capturing the ridge, it turned out, meant little if you could not move beyond it. It promised to deliver to its conquerors a strategic command of a vast countryside; but, under the conditions of modern warfare, at least according to the impressive cohort of military historians who have rigorously assessed the available evidence, it did not deliver.[118]

In the end Berton's sovereign theme of rough-hewn country boys bringing their can-do independence and resilience into the European theatre of war does not pass muster. The formula renders Canadians more as victims of someone else's war than as active makers of it. Berton's observation that Canada in 1914 had "scarcely any military tradition, no military aspirations, and little knowledge of war"[119] is difficult to square with the historical evidence: the cult of General Wolfe, a record-high arms budget, and the militia units and cadet corps to be found coast to coast—plus the forcible occupancy of the second-largest land mass claimed by any country on the planet, much of it acquired through the application of either direct or indirect pressure upon indigenous peoples—pressure exerted by newcomers integrated into the greatest empire the world had ever seen.

Yet, in Canada, a mid-twentieth-century emphasis on the "peaceable kingdom" as the passkey to the "Canadian character" has gradually been overtaken by the considerable evidence of violence in the conquest of British Columbia, of Canadian "ethnic cleansing" on the Plains, and the less than peaceful acquisition of Quebec and Acadia.[120] Moreover, as historian Paul Maroney demonstrates, a widespread and deep-seated Canadian celebration of imperial militarism and violence helps to explain much of the initial enthusiasm that swept up many urban English Canadians in 1914.[121] Berton's "innocence lost" can become a kind of shell game: all

the good things about empire (peace, order, good government) we grate-
fully claim, whereas all the bad things (conquest, exploitation, genocide)
belong to somebody else. The Canada that went to war in 1914 was, by
and large, a modern country that was very much part of a global order.
The "Frontier" may never have been, as Berton imagined, the font of egalitarian democracy and can-do individualism—that, at least, was the argument of a legion of Canadian historians who from the 1930s to the 1960s
wrestled with the idea. Even so, by 1921 the majority of Canadians would
be residents of cities. Most Canadians came from places fully integrated
into worldwide systems of production, distribution, and exchange—even
when they emerged from the wheat fields of the Prairies, so closely tied to
the markets of the world.

Berton's emphasis on youthful country boys absolves Canadians of
any responsibility for the war's enormities. His innocents abroad remain
innocents to the end. They suffer in the trenches. They do not—or only
rarely—make other people suffer. They are killed, but they are not themselves killers.[122] They are boys out for a time on the town—never pillag-
ers, looters, or rapists. Only rarely, and almost never in Berton, do we
imagine them as part of an army of occupation, imposing often unwel-
come demands upon the communities they occupied. Tavern-owners and
shopkeepers might rejoice at the influx of new trade; many other residents might feel themselves to have been invaded by aliens they did not
understand or particularly like.[123] Historically, such armies of occupation
accentuate long-standing patterns of assaults on women.[124] Canadian soldiers may have been outstanding figures in the Battle of Arras, but they
were also the looters of the town of Arras. Although Berton's book does
touch lightly upon some of this history, it does so in a forgiving indulgent
"boys will be boys" tone, in keeping with the theme of the high-spirited
hijinks of farm boys out on a tear.

To its credit, Berton's *Vimy* does introduce factual evidence that helps
to build a less one-sided and more critical construction of the Canadians at
war. While a certain gung-ho spirit enters into his description of Canadians
hurling drums of burning oil at the enemy, Berton is unusual among Vimy
celebrants in highlighting the unintended consequences of gas warfare.
Following the original plan for a preliminary attack at Vimy in the weeks
before the main assault in April, clouds of poison gas (chlorine and phosgene) were "released from cylinders in the Canadian trenches to smother
the German positions." It was hoped that the gas would corrode the enemy's weapons and render his positions vulnerable—an example, writes Ber-

ton, of how dangerous it is "for generals to believe in magic." It actually turned out to be a potent killer of Canadian soldiers who, seeking cover from enemy fire in shell holes, found the pits fatally full of gas. "The human details of the gas attack are heart breaking," writes Berton. "The poisonous clouds were released in two waves, the phosgene first at three that morning, the chlorine two hours later. It was more than ineffective; it killed the men it was supposed to cover." The innovation condemned Canadians to die painful deaths lasting as long as forty-eight hours, as they slowly drowned in their own body fluids. Would the story have been less heartbreaking if the chemical weapons had been used successfully against the Germans?[125]

Berton also notices the Canadians' brutal tactics of prisoner-killing and trench-raiding. He writes of how "some of the Calgarians" remembered the "gruff advice" given them in England by Major J.R.L. Perry, their battalion's second in command: "I don't want any *angels* in my battalion, when you get to France. I don't want you to take any *prisoners*! I hope you understand." One twenty-two-year-old soldier was haunted by his bad memories of prisoner-killing. He had "war in his blood," since his ancestors had arrived in England "with the Conqueror," yet felt guilty about killing a German who was probably about to surrender.[126]

Berton satisfies the demands of realism by introducing such details, but generally weaves them into his narrative without significantly disrupting its sense of nationalistic triumphalism. Canadians could be enthusiastic truce-breakers, prisoner killers, and wielders of chemical weapons of mass destruction, but that did not stain their intrinsic boyish innocence—and we are reassured that some of them disapproved, at least in retrospect, of such goings-on.

Vimy is actually a subtly self-subverting text, one that affirms the noble nation-building camaraderie of the soldiers on one page and the futility and cruelty of their endeavour on the next. The largely artificial formula of the "frontier thesis" allows Berton to have his cake and eat it too. Our country boys can remain innocents abroad, even as they murder prisoners, because Canadians themselves bore no ultimate responsibility for the shape or conduct of the war. This narrative has become an enduring aspect of Canadian war remembrance: we disclaim responsibility for its enormities and take credit for our achievements.

Finally, Berton's book is fascinating because it reveals how Canadian commemoration of the war can, in effect, function as an anti-modernist escape from the realities of Canadian history. Somehow, victory upon this one ridge cleansed Canadians of their original sins of religious division,

French-English incomprehension, regional alienation, or racial prejudice—and induced, not just in the participating soldiers but in Canada
as a personified entity, a deep sense of collective belonging. At last, we all
became one. As the saying goes, "We went up Vimy Ridge as Albertans
and Nova Scotians. We came down as Canadians."[127]

Most likely, out of 100,000-odd Canadian soldiers, some did actually
feel a greater sense of kinship with their fellow Canadians as a result of
having together attained the ridge. Certainly some of them said so. One
determined historian has unearthed a letter suggesting that one soldier
felt a new sense of being Canadian.[128] A number of veterans, prompted by
interviewers in the 1960s to remember how proud they now felt that their
battle had paved the way to Canada's centennial, obliged their question-
ers. A few, like Gregory Clark, found in themselves new sentiments of
nationalism that they had not expressed three decades earlier. In the case
of a soldier who had been in Canada a scant nine days, just what was meant
by "feeling Canadian" remains unclear, especially because he was part of
an army whose majority was born outside the country and that went out of
its way to celebrate Scottish traditions while simultaneously maginalizing
racialized outsiders, including French Canadians.

*   *   *

The ultimate irony of Berton's *Vimy* is that rather than provoking a fever-
reducing remedy, it aggravated the very condition of militarism that the
writer usually wanted to cure. If Berton was, thanks to his energetic editors,
transformed from a "Bad Kipling" into a "Good Kipling," a twenty-first-
century reader might be forgiven for wondering if any sort of "Kipling" is
at all appropriate in a world no longer besotted with imperial nationalism,
racial reasoning, or heroic warfare.

Vimy had perhaps one quite unexpected consequence. After Prime
Minister Borden went to France to visit the wounded of Vimy Ridge, he
returned home to Canada in May convinced that the country should move
ahead on compulsory military service. Shortly after that, on 24 May, Montreal became the scene of anti-conscription riots.[129] Rather than leading
the country almost magically to attain new levels of unity and together-
ness, Vimy Ridge was the prelude to an unprecedented conflict in Canada
so serious that it raised the prospect of the country's violent dissolution.

8

VIMY:
THE EMERGING MYTH

Yeah, yeah. Vimy-fucking-Ridge. I was there. "Birth of a Nation"
they called it on TV, but I didn't see nobody being born, just a lot of
people dying so we could sit there on top of another shithole of mud with
Captain Rutherford pushing for that DSO or the MC or the YMCA
with Triangles . . . just give him a fucking medal, will ya?

— DAVID FENNARIO, *Bolsheviki: A Dead Serious Comedy*

B Y THE SECOND DECADE of the twenty-first century, Vimy had
become Canada's national fable. Particularly under the reign of the
Harper Conservatives, through carefully selected words and images,
the Canadian state worked overtime to re-enchant Canadians about the
war—to encourage us to remember it as a time of gallant mounted cav-
alrymen, determined macho generals, submissive women, and undivided
national purpose: the "Canada" that "shared in the triumph and tragedy
of the Western Front" is not so much a complicated modern country as a
heroic person in her (or his?) own right, as solid and real and alive as a new-
born babe. And not just the state: a glance through what is known as "civil
society" will turn up many of the same themes, in part orchestrated by the
state and in part an element of a much broader resurgence of conservative
values and ideals.

The federal government's citizenship guide's now-inevitable quotation from Brig.-Gen. Ross about "Canada from the Atlantic to the Pacific
on parade" figures on the web pages advertising "1914 Honour" and "1914
Valour," both wines from the Diamond Estates Winery. Meanwhile, the
Canadian Legion markets a full line of "Vimy 1917—Birth of a Nation"
merchandise. The Vimy Commemorative T-Shirt, "made from 100%

pre-shrunk 10 ounce cotton and durably printed," can be had for $17.95 ($21.95 if you happen to be a somewhat larger Vimyist). A commemorative lapel pin can be yours for $6.95. The Vimy Ball Cap, "*aussi disponible en français*," is available for just $13.95. The Vimy Car Magnet can be attained for $4.95. The online Legion catalogue also includes an interpretation of both the battle and the monument. The battle, the "impossible victory at Vimy Ridge," was an "overwhelming success," while the monument—with its allegorical figures now imagined to stand for Canadian soldiers—stands in tribute to their martial valour and the "principles they gave up their lives for."[1]

Strangely enough, the most authoritative words come from Don Cherry, the "Prime Minister of Saturday Night," the flamboyant clown who once finished first in a *National Post* poll that asked Canadians "to name the country's leading public intellectual."[2] Cherry gives voice, it seems, to a down-to-earth nationalism that appeals to many. "Truck drivers give me the thumbs up. The professors and the guys who drink Perrier water and white wine don't like me. I don't care about them." For Cherry's vast following, here stands a man unafraid to affirm the values of a "moral Canadian nation." Along with the war in Afghanistan, which he unequivocally supported, Cherry has repeatedly emphasized Vimy Ridge—the "birth of a nation"—and on at least one occasion managed to connect the battle of 1917 to Canada's war in Kandahar almost a century later.[3]

What stands out throughout so many of these proud statements of Vimyism is the aggressive editing of the historical record to produce the effect most desired today. The more often it is repeated, the truer it seems: Vimy—birth of the nation.[4] The effect is to erase all the people—such as a legion of returned soldiers *from* Vimy—who thought it was no such thing.

In all their diversity, contemporary statements of Vimyism work to romanticize war and make militarism a core value of all true Canadians. They all drastically oversimplify a far messier, more contentious record—one in which war in general, and the Great War in particular, were often not a model of nationhood but a problem that humanity had to overcome. They all attempt to make official, indeed unquestionable, an ethereal, almost religious national narrative at odds with persuasive historical evidence.

*   *   *

How did a war dismissed in the 1960s by both John Diefenbaker and Lester Pearson as a pointless bloodbath come to be venerated some fifty years later? The experience of another Commonwealth nation, Australia, provides a valuable clue. According to its newly refurbished history, Australia was born (or forged or baptized) in Turkey.[5]

The Anzac Phenomenon is named for the Australian and New Zealand Army Corps, formed in 1914. The Battle of Gallipoli began on 25 April 1915 with the Entente forces, including the Australian and New Zealand Army Corps (Anzac), seeking to take hold of the Gallipoli peninsula. Eventually, after eight months of fighting, they were pushed out of the country by the Turks. This big battle against the Ottoman Empire provides a fascinating parallel with the rise of Vimyism in Canada. Like Vimyism, the Australian mythology existed in fragmentary form before the 1960s, gaining some traction in that decade; but it was only in the last quarter of the twentieth century that the myth-symbol complex attained prominence.[6]

As in Canada, a Great War battle came to be seen as not *just* a Great War battle, but as the foundation of Australian identity, the birthplace of Australian freedom and democracy—and indeed of Australia itself. A visitor to Australia on the 25th of April, the anniversary of the Battle of Gallipoli, may well encounter vast commemorative celebrations in the larger cities' cathedral-like war memorials (which far outdo anything in Canada). Dignitaries make speeches. Some of them travel all the way to Turkey to make similar speeches. In 2011 the saturation media coverage included an hour-long radio special focused on the donkeys involved in the battle. So revered has Gallipoli become that, as historian Marilyn Lake ruefully observes, "To write about what's wrong with Anzac today is to court the charge of treason."[7] Since the 1980s, some say, April 25 has come to be regarded as holier in the national calendar than December 25.

To a non-Australian all of this might seem bizarre. The Anzacs fought a battle designed by the British keen to find an alternative to the Western Front. Military historians remain divided, and will most likely long remain so, about whether this attack, backed emphatically by Winston Churchill, was a good or bad idea. The British sought to unsettle the Ottoman Empire, allied with the Germans, thus opening the way to what they hoped was the Central Powers' soft southern underbelly. They also wanted to show their support for their allies, the Russians, whose troop mobilization in July 1914 did so much to catapult Europe into war. The Russian Empire coveted Constantinople, much of Turkey, and great swathes of Southern Europe.[8]

That Australians glamorize a losing battle fought on another continent for strategic objectives having little to do with Australia does seem passing strange; and for a certain generation of Australians Gallipoli epitomized the pointlessness of wars ostensibly fought over grand principles but in fact mere reflections of the struggles of empires. The Gallipoli story was memorialized in a poignant anti-war song, "And the Band Played Waltzing Matilda," written in 1971 by Eric Bogle, a Scot who had immigrated to Australia two years earlier. Paul Keating, the country's prime minister from 1991 to 1996, defined what he saw as the "truth" of Gallipoli: "Dragged into service by the imperial government in an ill-conceived and poorly executed campaign, we were cut to ribbons and dispatched—and none of it in the defence of Australia."[9]

Keating was a contentious figure. He represented an Australia that would acknowledge past genocide against indigenous peoples, move past its racist White Australia immigration policy, and make room for advocates of gender equality; and he articulated a foreign policy somewhat independent of that of the United States. For his enemies, he became a threat to their values—and to the Australian history they had learned. Schoolchildren might no longer be able to tell their parents about the heroic pioneer exploits. Disturbing accounts of massacres and land grabs had to be avoided.

A counteroffensive against Keating's approach took the form of a renovation of Australian history. Instead of celebrating equality-seekers and trade unionists, Australians should celebrate their warriors. Instead of reflecting on Australians' involvement in the war in Vietnam, they should find inspiration in Australians' martial prowess. Instead of worrying about the claims of women, gays and lesbians, and others, they should focus on valiant men, the tough-minded, swaggering diggers and their down-to-earth practicality. As right-wing politician and future prime minister John Howard explained, they should replace the "history of shame promoted by the left."[10]

As a result, Australia Day on 26 January—the anniversary celebration of the 1788 arrival of the first fleet of British ships, a day protested by indigenous activists—was progressively supplemented, and partly displaced, by 25 April, Anzac Day. "On this day," Howard proclaimed in 2003, "we *enrich* ourselves . . . a nation reveals itself not only by the *men* it produces but by the *men* it honours, the *men* it remembers."[11] Such timeless masculine virtues came to be exalted as the essence of Australianism as right-wing historians and their political supporters attacked on a number of fronts: critics who did not want Australia involved in the endless wars of empire; indigenous activists who wanted Australians to acknowledge responsibility for the genocidal massacres that accompanied the European invasion of the continent; and social democrats who, while admiring Australia's early traditions of female enfranchisement and enlightened labour legislation, also believed that the country had to come to terms with its legacy of racism. In a sustained and systematic campaign to militarize Australian history, an inherently improbable story—that Australia was born thanks to the invasion of Turkey by Entente forces in 1915 and a subsequent defeat—came to be a noble symbol central to what it meant to be Australian.

Gallipoli 1915—Birth of a Nation. As Prime Minister Julia Gillard explained in April 2012, as she stood at a podium in Turkey, Australia was born at Gallipoli. Here was "our first act of nationhood in the eyes of a watching world, an act authored not by statesmen or diplomats, but by simple soldiers. The Anzacs."[12] The Australians who died attempting to take a height of land on a distant continent did more than lay down their lives for Empire; they embodied the spirit of a new nation. They may have ascended that height as the residents of Sydney, Perth, and Adelaide, from a vast country encompassing many regions and interests, but they came back from Gallipoli as Australians. The country emerged from the war deeply divided, but no matter. The episode became regarded as Australia's veritable "War of Independence," in which hardy Australian men stood firm against their ineffectual and condescending British commanders a theme brought to the fore in Peter Weir's 1981 film Gallipoli.

Since the late 1980s the spirit of Anzac, once regarded as the province of eccentric old-timers, has become something akin to a state religion, disseminated by a vast army of mass media outlets, liberal and conservative politicians, and the state's own memory-enhancing apparatus. Australians are taught a new way of seeing their history through a military lens via campaigns to link the "history from below" of ordinary families with military history, in Lake's words, "an enterprise made possible by the vast new genealogical resources, including Nominal Rolls, available at the Australian War Memorial and the Department of Veterans' Affairs."[13] To question the Anzac Phenomenon as the birth of the nation would be to disparage the grandfathers and great grandfathers who fought so valiantly, alongside their donkeys, at Gallipoli. Who are we, the complacent and comfortably situated beneficiaries of their heroism, to question their decision? By presenting only "the most general reasons for going to war" rather than dwelling upon the actual objectives of the states that went to war in 1914, which would open up awkward inquiries into the success or failure of the enterprise, the promoters of the Anzacs can declare the campaign "unsullied by political calculation," emphasizing character and courage. Through the alchemy of words and images, a battle fought for autocratic empires becomes transformed into a struggle for freedom—for, as we all know: "It is the soldier, not the reporter who has given us freedom of the press. It is the soldier, not the protest organiser who has given us freedom of speech."[14]

The Australian epic is, with minor variations, eerily similar to the Canadian stories of soldiers going up hills and becoming purveyors of freedom and exemplars of nationality—except, of course, the Australians did not gain their objective, suffering a disastrous defeat.[15] When "we" win, as at Vimy, it is thanks to our free-standing initiative. And common to both Vimy and Gallipoli is the presumption of colonial innocence—with a history, as Mark McKenna puts it for the Australian case, "free from the 'blemishes' and 'stains'" of the colonial past. As in Canada, the sanctified Australian soldiers came to be primarily seen, not as killers and invaders, but as victims and "mates," remembered for their courage and sacrifice rather than their "obedience to orders and a capacity to kill people."[16] A military event that accomplished little takes on the sheen of one of the great turning points of history.

While to a Canadian Gallipoli might appear to be an odd event to celebrate, and Vimy doubtless looks just as strange to an Australian, the absurdly overwrought treatment of both distant battles looks even odder to the people who actually live in Northern France and Flanders, who have developed forms of remembrance light years removed from such provincial nationalisms. While the Europeans might take care to say so in the most diplomatic of ways, the evidence suggests that those centrally involved in Great War commemoration in the lands devastated by the war have come to believe that the "British Dominions" are more or less out of their minds in celebrating as a war of independence what was for those Europeans, and much of the world, a descent into catastrophic ruin.[17]

*   *   *

In Canada one of the founding texts of a new martial nationalism is Jonathan Vance's *Death So Noble: Memory, Meaning, and the First World War*.[18] Drawing upon a wide diversity of sources, Vance explores the commemorative practices of Canadians as they struggled to come to terms with bereavement in the immediate aftermath of the Great War. These people confronted a painful dilemma: that of mourning 60,000-plus men, many of whose bodies had been blown to bits or lost in the craters of Flanders Fields.

Like Britons and Germans confronting the same dilemma, Canadians understandably mobilized their own familiar cultural forms.[19] As the story of the war took shape, according to Vance, the sacrifices of those killed in the war were elevated into an ennobling myth that inspired (and should still inspire) the nation. The bereaved found ways of handling their grief in traditional sources, derived above all from the Christian religion and the British Empire. Of their own free will, in a grassroots and un-coerced form of grief management, they constructed their own version of the High Diction of wartime sacrifice and honour. For them, the "sanctity of the fallen" was paramount. Vance writes: "No truth was so important to discover, no fiction so important to puncture, that it could justify calling into question the sacrifices of the dead. In this regard, we must take care not to underestimate the profound grief occasioned by the war."[20]

For Vance, High Diction became an enduring, entrenched response to the conflict and the overwhelmingly predominant Canadian view from 1918 to 1939—so much so that it can be called "Canada's myth"— the explanation for the inexplicable that stood out above all others. Canadians who had experienced tragedy in the war could take comfort in the idea that their losses constituted the necessary price of patriotism; the sacrifices of soldiers could inspire the creation of a united country grounded in the sanctified memories of a noble war. The force of Canada's myth was readily apparent throughout interwar Canada in the memorials that communities raised to "the fallen." It persists in Remembrance Day, wherein the inspiring democracy of death in wartime is honoured with "a national funeral in which the nation re-enacts the burials of the dead so grieving relatives can experience the funeral that was held a continent away, if at all."[21]

The central place of the Great War in Canada is confirmed by how (in the words of one appreciative reviewer, writing in 1998) we "still honour the fallen from that conflict—more so than those from any other." Another key was a sense of solidarity with the British Empire, to which Canada was indissolubly linked. In the underpinning belief that the victory of the Allies in the Great War constituted, in Vance's own words, "a victory over the forces of barbarism," Canada's myth seemingly found its political and moral foundations: Great War commemorations in turn become true reflections of the Canadian people rather than the manipulations of history by an elite.[22]

Vance often strikes a somewhat sceptical distance from this presentation of the "myth of Canada." He is far from unequivocally admiring of its expressions, and particularly of what he sees as a lack of realism embedded in the practice; but he repeatedly asserts that most mainstream members of the population upheld the myth. Canadians appreciated romantic visual and written representations of the war because those messages transformed the chaos of modern battle into "a rational and comprehensible activity." Rather than choosing to "wallow in the horrors of war," interwar Canadians for the most part decided to remember the war as an uplifting experience. Rather than showing interest in "a faithful rendering of the horrors of the war," Canadians preferred paintings that displayed heroic men on horseback, the inspiring words of the heroic General Currie urging his men into battle in March 1918, or veterans' cheerful recollections of evenings in cafés and the rollicking performances of entertainers. In "Canada's memory," the Great War became not "a technological nightmare of man-destroying machines," but a "contest between human beings. . . . Virtually everything in the canon points towards this interpretation. The individual is celebrated; the machine ignored."[23]

In Canada's myth, then, the war was not a dehumanizing and futile exercise in mass slaughter but a noble enterprise in which individuals gave freely of the best of themselves in a "citizen army" fighting for "democracy, freedom, justice, [and] Christianity." In Canada's myth, citizen-soldiers enjoyed a special status. Their victory at Vimy Ridge—a demonstration of Canadian unity because it was achieved by battalions from across the country—quickly became an inspiring myth of its own. "They are distillations of the essence of Canada," says Vance of the soldiers. "Compelling and larger than life, they reveal the degree to which the myth had made the soldier and Canada virtually interchangeable." The citizen-soldiers transcended "the unnatural economic and class divisions that rent society" and created in France and Flanders an esprit de corps that was nothing less than "an organic communion based on the innate worth of the individual."[24]

"Deeply rooted in the Canadian consciousness by the time of the Armistice," Vance maintains, "the idea that the war meant nothing less than the birth of the nation flourished afterwards." From this nationalistic perspective, American attempts to claim victory were indignantly refuted by opinions drawing upon "the wellspring of anti-Americanism that lies in the Canadian psyche." Canadians in vast numbers had come to accept not only that they had brought a nation into being, but that "the war had been a just one, fought to defend Christianity and Western civilization, and that Canada's sons and daughters had done well by their country and would not be forgotten for their sacrifices."[25]

While much of Vance's work is concerned with specific moments of public history such as monumentalization, behind the commemorative phenomena in his account is a remarkably cohesive "collective" or "social" memory. Although he does not define this memory's nature and logic, he constantly affirms its homogeneity and continuity.[26] The problem in this approach is that "collective memory" is not something that actually exists, except in the minds of individuals, characteristically mobilized in social groups and intent on making their particular interests appear to be general interests. As one analyst puts it, "memory"— once placed above the flux of politico-historical change and struggle—can easily become "a quasi-mystical soul existing independently of human beings."[27] For Vance, "Canada's memory" and "Canada's myth" come to be interchangeable terms. The implicit, inherently unlikely proposition is that, by and large and across their many divisions of language, religion, race, ethnicity, and gender, Canadians came to think in more or less the same way, in both official languages, about the Great War and its consequences. When living Canadians loudly dissent from Canada's memory when they raise questions about Currie's heroism, query the motivations of profiteering armaments manufacturers, or question the militarization of Remembrance Day, for instance—they are depicted as inadvertently strengthening the all-conquering myth they oppose. They become exiled from "Canada's myth."

In the end, Vance came not to critique the myth he describes, but rather to celebrate it. In *Death So Noble*, despite his distanced irony in reflecting on certain manifestations of this myth-symbol complex—and on the Victorian earnestness with which it was often expressed—Vance actually subscribes wholeheartedly to its tenets. His criticism of the war is muted.

While recognizing the existence of large constituencies of Canadians—French Canadians most obviously—alienated from his "myth of Canada," Vance nevertheless both describes and celebrates what he sees as the overwhelmingly dominant "memory" of the war.[28] Yet the historical record suggests how contested, perhaps even marginalized, this martial nationalist interpretation of the war had become in the 1920s and 1930s.

Vance's insistence on Canada's (singular and static) "memory" is question-able. If counter-memories were sometimes implicit and implied, at other times, as suggested by the responses to the 1934 photo-spreads, they were expressed in full-volume declarations. It is true, as Vance has valuably shown, that in funerals, remembrance services, and most monuments, participants stressed the nobility of sacrifice. Yet to go from such funerary moments to a bold generalization about one overwhelmingly dominant "memory" seems hazardous. Just as the obituary pages of newspapers sel-dom have probing critiques of the dearly departed, and funeral orations seldom itemize the failings as well as the strengths of the deceased, so we might well expect commemorations designed to honour the war dead to exclude much in the way of critical voices. It is possible—indeed, it is surely a typical experience—to go to a funeral and praise a lovable, kind-hearted, and unselfish soul while nurturing more complicated and con-tradictory sentiments, better expressed at other times and in other places.

Vance insists that, for full two decades, the sacralization of the soldiers who had suffered "death so noble" insulated the memory of the Great War from substantial, influential critique. He imposes upon the past a pat-tern that is far too neat, and which considerable evidence explicitly rebuts. While his interpretation of the strategies and motives of local commu-nities has its strengths, as a sympathetic if somewhat condescending understanding of local practices of bereavement, his implied thesis—that Canada's myth as he defines it overwhelmed all other ways of representing the war—is on shaky ground. That is especially so given the ironic com-ments made in countless letters sent home while the war was going on, in descriptions of trench-raiding as "a mad enterprise," and in all the black humour brought back by soldiers. Soldiers sometimes treated patriotic propaganda about their supposed crusade for civilization with clear con-tempt. One wrote ironically of the gas that was "sent over to strike terror into the black heart of the enemy," and another, with tongue in cheek, referred to the Germans as "beastly body-boiling Sausage Eaters," mak-ing fun of a sedulously propagated false report about a German propensity to transform corpses into soap. In 1917 one ambulance driver estimated that if a peace settlement emerged, "I guarantee it would be passed by a majority of 9 to 1."[29]

Veterans and non-veterans alike strongly resisted the redemptive "nation-building" narrative of the Great War and called sharply into question those who put it to work for their own purposes. Many people, including soldiers and their families, went beyond bereavement and trauma to develop an intense, and often critical, curiosity about the events of 1914–18 that had plunged the world into chaos. A war commemorated in one context might well be critiqued and analysed in another—and views also shifted over time as they entered into conflict and dialogue with other perspectives.

Many Canadians have been perfectly able to withstand a jingoistic appeal to the memory of the Great War. The federal election of 1926, for example, pitted the Liberal Party's Mackenzie King against Conservative Arthur Meighen, renowned as the Father of Conscription, with Lt.-Gen. Julian Byng, a hero of Vimy Ridge and governor general, at his side.[30] In a land transfixed by Vance's myth, the Quebec-bashing patriotic legacy of Meighen and Byng's stature and war record would surely have walloped anything King might have put up against them. Here was a showdown between the heroism of Vimy and a pusillanimous, portly, and pontificating peace-lover. Yet in the course of actual events, Mackenzie King won the 1926 election, and Byng and Meighen were humiliated. A year later, in 1927, when the prime minister addressed a giant gathering in Ottawa—on the occasion of the sixtieth anniversary of Confederation—the core doctrine that Canada was born on Vimy Ridge was, on this most nationalistic of occasions, almost completely absent. Canadian independence, such as it was, was grasped only partially and incoherently in the mid-1920s. The 1926 Imperial Conference, the prelude to the 1931 Statute of Westminster, seemed to augur full Canadian independence—yet the Canadian constitution remained unamendable in Canada, the Judicial Committee of the Privy Council remained in place as the court of last appeal, and the country embarked but tentatively upon the stormy seas of international diplomacy, with a minimal diplomatic corps down to the 1940s.

Instead of there being one big memory of the war—"Canada's myth"— the remembered war was always a tangled mix of twisted, knotted, and often unsavory memories. There never was one overwhelmingly predominant Canadian memory of the war—and especially one that remained impervious to all change for decade after decade, one that, as Vance says, crossed "boundaries of gender, class, religion, ethnicity, and region," with "few groups or individuals" failing to accept it, at least in part.[31] Indeed, those supposedly "few groups and individuals" who did not accept it, in whole or in part, were seemingly often in the majority from the late 1920s and into the 1930s. Not only were they made up of the usual suspects—women, leftists, pacifists, Québécois—but they also included many mainstream liberals concerned to defend their tradition's well-developed pacificism. Most problematically of all for Vance's thesis, these people also contained a very large number of the veterans who fought in the war.

If "Canada's memory" of the war was imperiled by those who actually fought in it, can we really say it was "Canada's memory"? For if veterans in the tens of thousands gravitated to positions critical of the Great War and its repercussions, on what grounds apart from ideological bias can twenty-first-century historians discredit their words and rule their deeds inadmissible? Vance curiously presents Will Bird as a "folklorist" and one of Canada's most important soldier-writers, as someone who "came closest to capturing the proper balance" on the war. But this is the same Bird who has his lead character say, "This war is wrong."[32] Rather than touting the deep-seated unity of the leaders and the led in the military, Bird devoted considerable energy to a critique of the military brass on behalf of the rank-and-file, going so far as to mock the histories that made the senior officers into such heroes and to question the integrity of many of the medals they wore.

Careful students of commemorative sites—"public memory," not "collective memory"—strongly disagree with Vance's contention that "Canada's memory" shielded Canadians from strenuous, at times anguished, debates over what the Great War had meant.[33] Vance does make a slight allowance for these debates: a "few faint voices tried to shape an alternate vision," to be overheard in such "rarefied" elite circles as the Canadian Institute of International Affairs; they posed "little real threat to the just war theory." But this stance essentially leaves unscathed his primary claim about "Canada's memory" being that of a noble struggle for "democracy, freedom, justice, [and] Christianity."[34] The historical evidence indicates that critiques of the war flourished outside elite circles, and did so *massively*, in ardent interwar debates about peace and war.[35] Vance's discomfort with Canadian peace-lovers, including the prime minister, is understandable: in their demonstrated hundreds of thousands, they sharply contradict any thesis requiring the "myth of Canada" to exclude a realistic critique of the mass mechanized slaughter of the Great War.

*   *   *

If Vance was interested in documenting the memory of the Great War from a cultural and historical perspective, Tim Cook's massive two volumes—*At the Sharp End: Canadians Fighting the Great War 1914–1916* (2007) and *Shock Troops: Canadians Fighting the Great War 1917–1918*

(2008)—reflect an attempt to combine traditional military history with techniques and insights generated by social historians of the 1970s and 1980s who advocated "history from the bottom up."[36] At the core of Cook's well-researched and well-presented work is an unresolved contradiction. No less than Berton—indeed, sometimes even more than Berton—Cook praises the Great War as Canada's valorous war of independence, as a time when excellent individuals proved themselves in the test of battle and pushed Canada, in Arthur Lower's famous expression, from colony to nation.[37] Yet, as a good historian—a scholar who played a central role in designing the Canadian War Museum—Cook introduces a vast amount of evidence that fatally complicates this story of martial nationalism.

Perhaps Cook's most valuable discovery—which goes against the grain of Vance's argument—is the pervasiveness of sardonic critiques of wartime patriotism by the very soldiers fighting it. It turns out that abrasive wartime irony—about patriotism, profits, martial valour, and military leadership—was as Canadian as maple syrup. In many respects Cook's opus contains so many of these sceptical appraisals of this war and all war that it sometimes reads like Harrison's *Generals Die in Bed*, this time with endnotes.

To be sure, this is emphatically not the spin on the Great War that Cook wants to provide. In his martial nationalism he again often outdoes Berton—taking that writer's feel-good melodies and turning them into a thundering national anthem. The first verse of this anthem hails the supreme virtues of war heroes serving under intrepid leaders; the second signals their achievement of new heights of national unity that swiftly inspired Canadians as a whole; and the third announces the world's recognition of Canada's newly found confidence. Oddly, none of these themes harmonizes easily with Cook's own evidence.

The first verse rings most loudly in Cook's six chapters about the Battle of Vimy Ridge—or seven chapters, if we include the one about the lead-up to the battle. Some one hundred densely packed pages rival Berton's book in their copious detail.[38] Cook's heroic Canadians, bucking those who said it could not be done, just went ahead and did it—they took the ridge, a "milestone along Canada's slow march to nationhood." They were, once again, rugged fellows performing amazing acts. They confounded the more conformist Germans with unprecedented acts of ingenuity, tenacity, and courage. The most heroic among the Canadians won medals.[39] Beneficiaries of a newly evolved "Canadian Way of War," our soldiers were the well-informed executors of brilliantly conceived plans. They fought stoically on, against high odds. Ultimately, as Canada's heroes, they prevailed.

"Heroes" is a complicated word. In classic times a hero was often invested with god-like capacities of strength and wisdom (often accompanied by an only-too-human weakness, as was the case with poor Achilles and his heel). Later on romantic heroes were extraordinary individuals who demonstrated excellence in their responses to adversity (in rags-to-riches stories, for instance). In today's world, we often mean something else by heroes. When we describe a neighbour's heroic struggle with cancer, we do not mean she was endowed with superhuman abilities or that her struggle allowed her to develop her excellence. We mostly mean that, caught up in dire circumstances, she responded in an admirable way, with composure and dignity, as we ourselves would hope to respond in a similar situation. Like refugees fleeing in their millions from the Middle East, today's heroes are generally neither tragic nor romantic figures, but often just people responding as best they can to extremely difficult circumstances. We usually sympathize with them.[40]

Although applying the discourse of heroism to Canada's Great War soldiers often signifies this compassionate sense of identifying with people caught up in a situation not of their choosing,[41] Cook takes us well beyond this—to more old-fashioned heroes displaying their individual excellence under testing conditions. He relishes the tales of kilted pipers and bayonet-wielding trench raiders. We find a fighter peppered with shrapnel "fighting to the death" as he "disappeared into history," Canadians who are sometimes "hard-as-nails" and sometimes "tough-as-nails," who fight "like hell," like "British bull-dogs" or (perhaps if they are *really* aroused) "Canadian pit-bulls." Iron individuals can prevail against a hail of bullets or a cloud of poison gas; just one man can turn a battle's tide of defeat into one of victory. Those with special "grit and determination" and "thrusting leadership" win medals; those without such gifts might lose their mental balance.[42]

Yet the evidence keeps getting in the way of this theme of heroism. At the very top, the search for the equivalent of Canada's heroic George Washington in this war of independence comes to grief, in part because throughout the war Canadians were answerable to leaders who were not Canadian. The British commanders included secretary of state and army organizer Lord Kitchener, dismissed as a better poster-boy than actual minister. British field marshal Earl Haig, though acquitted of being a wilful mass murderer, still seems to be one of the duller knives in the drawer. Lt.-Gen. Julian Byng, although said to be the man who unified the Canadian Corps as a team, is no less British; indeed, he even expressed his displeasure at being asked to lead the Canadians. As for the Canadians in charge, Cook's Sir Sam Hughes—or "Sir Sham Shoes," as he was elsewhere named because of the scandals surrounding army boots—appears to have been deranged. Sir Arthur Currie, for Cook the best candidate of them all, comes burdened with a guilty history of embezzlement—a buried and forgotten episode after it briefly crops up in Cook's volume one. Although Currie sometimes remonstrates with his British higher-ups, he rarely prevails against them. Moreover, a hero to many historians, Currie was, by 1918, generally reviled by many of his men, who "blamed their corps commander for the losses suffered in the war and now for their delay in getting home." It did not help matters that, at a time when his troops were complaining of inadequate rations, he had grown quite portly on "better food" and was residing "in royal palaces."[43]

Currie had also grown fat off rank-and-file soldiers in a more direct way. In 1913, while he was trying to raise a new militia regiment in Victoria, he confronted a situation familiar to many Western Canadian speculators. His real estate promotions had almost bankrupted him. He had also been offered the command of the 50th Regiment (the Gordon Highlanders of Canada), which as lieutenant-colonel he would be expected to equip with new pseudo-Scottish regalia while entertaining with food and drink. He diverted government funds intended for the troops, to the total of $10,833.34, to his own pocket. Currie's never-prosecuted crime was an "open secret" in Ottawa, where it was discussed in cabinet. That Canada's "greatest soldier" would have been penitentiary-bound in a less elitist order is rarely mentioned in contemporary martial nationalist celebrations of his excellence.[44]

Cook may nevertheless have set out to find, and then struggled to discern, classically conceived heroes—but, for want of convincing evidence, was forced to retreat and brand all the Canadian soldiers as heroes simply because they struggled to survive the war and at times helped each other out. For anyone who does not wholly identify with British imperialism, their heroism must consist only in this—and not in the cause for which they fought.

But—to go on to the second verse of this anthem—at least, even if only inadvertently, the soldiers surely founded Canada, achieving new heights of pan-Canadian unity in both Europe and back home? Cook, no slouch in the colony-to-nation department, amplifies every murmur in which it seemed that Canadians were beginning to think as one unified team. By the end of *Shock Troops*, with its account of the "epoch-changing role its veterans had played in shaping their country and the modern world, and of the courageous sacrifice made by all who took up arms for their country *in any war*"[45]—that is, from Acadia in 1710 to Canada's engagements in Afghanistan and the Middle East in the early decades of the twenty-first century—loyal readers must surely feel obliged to stand to attention and salute them. In all such wars, soldiers making courageous sacrifices defend Canada's freedom and reshape the planet, presumably for the good of Canadians and all the world's people. Compared with Berton's folksy and somewhat ambivalent rendition, this patriotic Vimyist anthem reached an ear-splitting level.

But—is it true? Take, first, the bonds of unity attributed to all of the fighting Canadians after January 1917.[46] Cook's own evidence reveals deep divisions among the troops over the wisdom of the gas raids preceding Vimy, with subaltern officers lodging ineffective protests against an attack that the writer himself considers folly. Although he has the good sense to avoid the militarists' more unbelievable statements implying that actual soldiers at Vimy paused after their days of wading through corpses and toxic mud to reflect on their role in solidifying Canadian unity, he does play up the scarce "hooray-for-Canada" quotations that are conventionally—and repeatedly—cited. Many of them are more ambiguous than they seem, and as conclusive evidence of the soldiers' general attitudes they are frail.[47] Moreover, Cook consistently underplays the clear signs of French-English strife in the Canadian Corps and does not apparently recognize that, from a Quebec perspective, the Great War can never have the "birth of the nation" aura that other Canadians want to place around it.[48] The evidence that soldiers had an increased sense of fellow-feeling for each other after Vimy is tenuous at best. Some of the French Canadians, dramatically underrepresented at Vimy, continued to express resentment against the arrogance and presumption of their British/Canadian counterparts, who had never warmed to the notion of a bilingual Canada.[49]

Good historian that he is, Cook delivers fresh and compelling evidence of how sharply the war divided Canadians. He notes the members of hard-working labour battalions who slaved away, with "scarcely a word of thanks or encouragement from on high." He notices the astonishingly severe sentences meted out to soldiers, sometimes for minor offences. He allows himself to wonder if executing soldiers for fleeing from deadly fire was really such a good idea. Most unusually, he notices the many times the rank-and-file were seemingly sent off to be butchered for no apparent reason, except perhaps to straighten out a line on a map or to satisfy some unfounded theory of the high command. He returns, again and again, to "hopeless and cruel battles," to inexcusably "rushed and callous operations," to examples of the "worst sort of generalship," to examples of leaders utterly unaware of the conditions of the front-line troops. He brings forward new evidence of the acute rebelliousness of the Canadian soldiers, typified by their refusal to advance over the Rhine to occupy Germany until they had been properly fed—an act of defiance the Brass blamed upon the "strong socialistic tendencies" infecting the soldiers, whom Cook himself describes as being "more willing to kick against a system that was increasingly failing them."[50] At such moments, his national anthem starts to sound a bit like "Solidarity Forever."

Nonetheless, to move on to the third verse, surely the war, if it did not unify Canadians in Europe and at home into one big team, at least secured recognition of our prowess and our autonomy from the world at large? Here was a "decisive event in pushing 'the nation' towards full autonomy and international recognition." Thanks to this war of independence, Canadians gained respect as serious players in global affairs. The Great War "forged Canada like no other event in the young country's history." Among the familiar quotations from admiring Brits, Lloyd George's encomium to the Canadians after the Battle of the Somme—"they were marked out as storm troops"—inspired the title of Cook's second book. In anxious pursuit of international recognition of this point, Cook seemingly quotes from every German he can find who expresses awe at the Canadians' fighting prowess and every Briton who can be found to say something along the lines once meted out to a sceptical General Haig, that is, to treat them as "junior but sovereign allies."[51]

The "junior" part of this formula is very much in evidence. But the "sovereign" bit? Not so much. Direct evidence of British or U.S. deference to Canada's presumed new stature is slender. Currie did not think Passchendaele worth the body of a single Canadian soldier. Haig disagreed. The result? A mud-spattered butcher's bill—astounding even by Great War standards—for Canadians. As many other "martial races" can attest, being favourably written up as staunch fighters for the Empire is not the same thing as being accorded respect and status within it.[52] Nor did merely signing the Treaty of Versailles—as a subaltern member of the British Empire—vault the Canadian team into the first division. Such matters are based upon power relations and the calculation of politico-economic interests. Many countries that signed the Treaty of Versailles—Ecuador, Guatemala, Haiti, Honduras, Liberia, Nicaragua, Panama, Romania (which declared war on the Central Powers just in the nick of time in November 1918)—had made a minimal contribution to fighting the war. As Nicaragua (invaded by the United States in 1927) would soon discover, power in a world of big empires did not come from the barrel of a pen. Empires are not scout troops awarding good members with badges for their good behaviour. In 1922 Lloyd George would blithely assume that Canada would fall in when the British Empire declared a new war on Turkey. He had apparently not received the memo about Canadian independence.

At the root of these observations about Cook's magisterial two volumes is our critical distance from his decision to place his hard-earned and invaluable evidence in a conventional colony-to-nation narrative—rather as though Picasso had placed *Guernica* in a gilded Victorian frame and titled it "Valorous Times in Spain." What Cook so convincingly brings forward are not indications of the Great War as a Canada-making breakthrough, but rather how strikingly the years of conflict exemplified industrial modernity in its most radical form. Many Great War battle sites such as Vimy entailed the creation of vast, artificial cities, larger than most in Canada, fixed on either side of a no man's land, with complex networks of trenches, roads, rail lines, and telephone systems; and a system of mass death that increasingly relied upon such weapons as massive artillery bombardments and toxic gas, rendering the old days of individualized combat an anachronism.

Yet he also shows us a world of military men who still believed, even into 1918, that courageous fellows on horseback and heroic soldiers, bayonets drawn, could somehow win the day.[53] Rather than seeing "their" side as being driven by a logic wholly foreign to "our" side, Cook resists the notion of a stark moral chasm dividing the combatants.[54] As both sides responded to the challenges of killing masses of people in the age of mechanized warfare, they came, increasingly, to resemble each other.

Had he placed modernity rather than nationalism at the core of his study, Cook might have emphasized not the team spirit of the Canadian Corps under Currie, but the tendency of the army to duplicate and intensify the ethnic and class divisions found in Canada. Here was a political project drawing upon a diversity of groups, classes, and interests—and never a collective person being born or coming of age. A tremendous merit of Cook's book is that it provides compelling evidence that all Canadians at the Front were by no means apologists of the war.

Cook stresses its horrors. In a description strikingly reminiscent of Varley's *For What?* he describes a battlefield that "looked like an abattoir, with the Canadians literally stepping over red soil, long loops of intestines, and other shredded body parts of men who had been killed and then dismembered by shellfire." Like Bird, he wants us to smell this war. He imagines trench raiders crossing "garbage-strewn ground" in which "foul-smelling craters filled with fouler-smelling bodies of the dead" were passed without comment. He introduces us to the Somme with a comment from James Kirk of Summerside: here was "some awful looking place. . . . The stink would turn a skunk sick." Near Courcelette was a field strewn with rotting, maggot-ridden corpses: one nauseated gunner remarked that the "odor from the dead bodies is something fierce." Near Hill 70, one German soldier described the smell of the corpses as "almost unbearable." A Canadian agreed with him, while worrying that the "distinct smell of gas" suggested the toxicity of the "pulverized battlefield."[55] In effect Cook reveals what can still be disconcerting when reassuring official narratives of "everybody pulling together" are contrasted with pervasive evidence of the fatal conflicts of "entrenched and opposing interests."

Therein lies a basic contradiction of Cook's irreplaceable works—ones seeking to harmonize the sufferings and deaths of the many with the schemes and ambitions of the few. A measure of the acuteness of this contradiction comes in Cook's scathing treatment of *Generals Die in Bed*. The Harrison that Cook introduces us to is a vulgar polemicist and coarse realist—even though, paradoxically, Cook's own descriptions of battlefields outdo in shock value anything to be found in Harrison, and the novelist's treatment of officers is often nuanced and complex.[56] Harrison's crime, though, was to use his considerable literary gifts to convey, in post-Victorian words and images, his first-person impressions of the war. While some of his military interlocutors thought he had accurately captured their reality, the problem was that he did so from an unabashedly rank-and-file point of view.

Cook sternly rejects the "liturgy of hate and spite directed against the generals and high command," which he sees as one of the "most enduring legacies of the war." Startlingly, as though forgetting all his own similar insights, Cook commends Brig.-Gen. Archibald Macdonell's response to Harrison. Macdonell hoped to "live long enough to have the opportunity of (in good trench language) shoving my fist into that s. of a b___ Harrison's tummy until his guts hang out of his mouth!!!" So, although Cook often writes as if those at the Front should have the last word on difficult topics, here he endorses the posthumous silencing of one of the most articulate of the soldiers who witnessed the war.[57]

For all their differences in tone and method, Vance and Cook both became caught up the entrapments of Vimyism. Both advance the arguments of an integral nationalism—one that imagines "Canada" as a person, whose identity and interests should proceed all others. For Vance, notwithstanding a brief six-page eruption of realism close to the end of *Death So Noble*, Canada's myth (or Canada's memory) becomes a living entity, a quasi-mystical essence that repels all critique (even the assessments seemingly shared by a majority of Canadians). For Cook, notwithstanding all of his evidence of division in Europe and Canada, the country was "forged in the fire of war," even though—in a mind-boggling twist—it was also "nearly consumed by it."[58]

Both authors might have been well advised to refresh their memories of the colony-to-nation thesis that underlies both their works. For Arthur Lower's argument was not that the Great War had made a nation; when commenting on the release of the war photographs in 1934 he had complained that nothing had been accomplished in Canada to "deepen national sentiment." In *Colony to Nation* (1946), Lower sought to explore the "underlying principles of our evolution and to characterize succinctly the men and peoples who have constituted and moulded our nation—our nation yet to be."[59] Unlike Vance and Cook, Lower's Canadian nationalism did not require Canadians to share a collective memory of their supposed "war of independence"—a big bang theory of Canadian history.

*   *   *

The militarist's overarching argument, which Vance has the merit of making explicit, is that the Great War was fought for decency, democracy, and freedom, to defend "our" values against "their" values, civilization against barbarism. From this point of view it was not, then, J.L. Granatstein's "battle of rival imperialisms," but a national display of our moral as well as technological excellence.[60] In response to Varley's question, "For What?" the correct response, for a Vimyist, is: "*So that Canada could be born and attain its stature as a stalwart defender of liberal democratic values against their enemies.*" This argument echoes the propaganda of the day—when symphony orchestras in North America moved to ban the playing of music by those barbarians Bach and Beethoven, and citizens mounted keen efforts in Berlin, Ont., and the Province of New Brunswick to extirpate all hints of German influence.

The mid-1960s saw a large centennial-related boom in Vimy books. Textbook writers reflected their emphasis on Vimy's nation-building significance, even though—as in the case of both of the historians William Kilbourn and J.M.S. Careless—they also conceded that the war constituted one of the country's bigger "challenges." Nonetheless, many proclaimed, here was an end to Canada's "colonial childhood." This patriotic theme persisted into the early 1970s, with high-school textbooks still celebrating "the most perfectly organized and most successful battle of the whole war."[61] After that, new styles of history writing came into vogue, with contradictory results. Writers tried to go beyond the conventional patriotic recitation of heroic battles to describe war's deeper cultural implications—which meant attending to its social and economic costs. They also—perhaps responding to provincial curriculum requirements—progressively "Canadianized" the war to make it more and more narrowly a national event. That trend doubtless contributed to Vimy being seen as planned and fought by Canadians under Canadian command.[62]

Over time the consensus about the war began to shift. With the Quebec question front and centre in the 1970s and 1980s, attitudes towards a war that had pitched Quebec-centred *nationalistes* against Empire-focused nationalists became quite complicated. Heather Robertson's *A Terrible Beauty: The Art of Canada at War* (1977) emphasized both Canadians' European exploits and the war's disuniting effects within Canada. The Great War, she said, had been fought "as bitterly at home as abroad." J.L. Granatstein and H.L. Hitsman's *Broken Promises: A History of Conscription in Canada* (1977) offered a sober and reasonably sympathetic evaluation of the French-Canadian perception of, and resistance to, the imposition of conscription in 1917. It revealed Vimy not to have been the "battle that made Canada" but the "battle that incited conscription," the country's most serious and divisive crisis.[63] Military historians themselves warned that claims about Canadian nationhood arriving at Vimy Ridge were simplistic. Writing in 1982, Stephen Harris, among the most thoughtful, agreed that Canadian military prowess had contributed to national autonomy, but also noted how Vimy as a symbol came lumbered with the conscription crisis, which followed so closely on its heels (and to which, in good measure, it contributed). Considering it highly unlikely that Vimy could ever serve as "the symbol of national pride, spirit and identity," Harris reasoned that coming Canadian generations were likely to find "other things to celebrate" and "other symbols of unity."[64]

The conservative campaign to reclaim an unadulterated Vimy—and return to the Great War as the birth of the nation—flourished only in the 1990s. It went beyond the works of Vance and Cook to include textbooks used in high schools. The texts—especially those aimed at Grade 10 students in Ontario—were startling in their new emphases. The Great War as a world war had now shrunk in size, geographically speaking. At the epicentre of this war—to an extent that textbook writers in 1960 would have considered bizarre—was Vimy.

In their text *Canada: Our Century, Our Story* (2000), for example, John Fielding and Rosemary Evans elevated Vimy to an epochal nation-forming event. Perhaps responding to new demands for the inclusion of a wider diversity of Canadians, the authors applied a politics of affirmative action to the memory of the Great War—as a time when Canada was "in many ways a racist society . . . as was the rest of the world," with few people possessing much "understanding of prejudice, stereotyping, discrimination and racism, despite the abolition of slavery in the nineteenth century." Happily, many plucky Canadians from racialized backgrounds had bucked this trend, including William Semia, a member of the Cat Lake Band in Northern Ontario, who learned how to speak English after enlisting and "used it later to drill platoons." Capt. Reverend William Andrew White, a son of ex-slaves, studied theology at Acadia University and rose to become the "only Black chaplain and the only Black officer in the Canadian Army." Less happily, German and Ukrainian Canadians were singled out for persecution, placed in internment camps. Rather than being "unpatriotic, even treasonous," opponents to conscription were "patriotic, and their reasoning was clear-sighted."[65]

The depiction of the war now came with a more explicit "realism." Earlier texts had relied upon words to convey, in general descriptions, the hardships and sufferings of the war. In 2000 Fielding and Evans placed greater emphasis upon gory graphics—including human bodies strewn through no man's land—and first-person testimonies. Once again Gregory Clark came to the fore, effectively called upon to convey the wretchedness of living conditions on the Western Front: "Trenches is too romantic a name. These were ditches, common, ordinary ditches. As time went by they became filthy. We had no garbage disposal, no sewage disposal." Will Bird was the subject of a lengthy profile titled "An Ordinary Soldier," with a gripping account of the death of a fellow soldier at Passchendaele. To illustrate the "cost of war" the authors introduced a misdated reproduction of Frederick Varley's *For What? Canada: Our Century, Our Story*, then—although at times straying from factual accuracy—did not try to shield students from the bitter hazards and sufferings of the war.[66]

Yet the end result of the acknowledgement of dire hardships and deaths is to validate the achievements of Canadians in arms, who become in the telling all the more extraordinary and selfless by virtue of their sufferings. Students are expected to balance the "devastating toll" of the battles with the "valour and courage of many thousands of Canadian soldiers." The text strongly implies that every Canadian now lives under a strong moral obligation to remember not just the Great War but also all Canadian wars rolled into one. "What do you think?" the text asks students in one subsection. "In the 1990s, Dan Murphy had a poppy pinned on his motorcycle before leaving on a cross-country adventure. Why is it important for him and all of us to think about those who fought in wars for Canada before we were born?" Even bloody, muddy Passchendaele gets a positive spin: as the caption to one photograph explains, "More than 15,000 Canadian soldiers were killed or wounded in the Battle of Passchendaele. They won the battle, and nine Victoria Crosses." Following the lead of its soldiers, Canada, presented with "the greatest challenge it had ever faced," came through with flying colours, in a coming-of-age saga that culminated in its signing of the Treaty of Versailles as a "separate nation." Although the authors do point out that Canada was allowed to send two delegates to Versailles, neither of whom could vote, they do not advise students that Canada's signature on the treaty was highly ambiguous—since it signed as a sub-unit of the British Empire.[67]

The battle that A.B. Hodgetts in 1960 reduced to a mere four sentences in the midst of a realistic description of the Battle of Arras now becomes the pith and essence of Canadianism. So original, and so effective, was the brand new *Canadian* strategy of the creeping barrage that even the British army adopted it in 1918, and it "made a major contribution to the Allied victory."[68] Vimy Ridge marked the "turning point" for Canada in the war, providing "the soldiers of the Canadian Corps [with] something they had never had—a sense of nationhood." Just the very words "Vimy Ridge" could work a peculiar magic upon Canadians, it seems—and even before they had even arrived there. One volunteer of Japanese descent from British Columbia remarked that as soon as he heard he would later be taking part in this particular battle, "he felt proud, and like a true Canadian for the first time." Even though, as the text says, "little ground was captured, and no great strategic advantage was gained," nationhood was nevertheless established. In textbook fashion, after they digest these passages, students are asked to reflect on why, nonetheless, Vimy is "so important for Canadians."[69]

Making History—The Story of Canada in the Twentieth Century, from a team of historians, was also published in 2000 and destined for roughly the same market. It follows many of the same strategies. Although it makes less of an effort to insert racialized minorities into the story of the Great War and has a fleeting reference to the role of imperialism, it reduces the war's scope to a conflict almost entirely fought in Northwestern Europe. It offers the same realistic descriptions, mentions soldiers executed for desertion and cowardice, internment camps, the divisive election of 1917, and divisions of opinion between war-supporters and pacifists.[70] Varley's *For What?* makes another appearance.

Yet, despite these realistic concessions to the hardships and pain of war, the text makes the upbeat suggestion that all such sacrifices worked to gain Canada "recognition as an independent country in world affairs." The Canadian forces not only thoroughly "distinguished themselves" but contributed "to a growing sense of national identity." Indeed, the Canadians began "to think of themselves in a new way." The text makes the remarkable observation that before the war, "most Canadians had no contact with each other," but once they got to Europe and started fighting they began to develop a "sense of national identity, of being distinctly Canadian and separate from Britain." It is simply the case that, even in the depths of the Great War, "national pride grew." The text offers accounts of the usual heroes and anti-heroes—from that dubious character Sir Sam Hughes to the hopeless and hapless Haig, from the passionate heroic prime minister Borden to flying ace Billy Bishop, "Canada's best-known hero." Students are enjoined to "use a computer" to calculate the top flying aces by country.[71]

In this text, too, Vimy becomes the epicentre of Canada's war. Even topics that are not centrally related to Vimy—such as war weariness in spring 1917—are somehow related to it. The "stunning four-day victory" resulted in the capture of an amazing number of German artillery pieces and dealt a blow to Germany's Hindenburg Line of defence. No wonder the Canadians who took Vimy, depicted in a large photograph, are so jubilant: "This photograph became one of the most famous images of Canadians in World War I. Why do you think this was so?" The text supplies its own answer: because this was "an important turning point for Canada." In one remarkable passage, with a resolute determination to correct a veteran's memory that might not quite live up to nationalistic expectations, a soldier's harrowing first-person account of the actual battle is followed by a passage that puts him in his place: "Private Fraser recalled the horrors of war. Historians would later take a somewhat different view of the Battle of Vimy Ridge, identifying it as one of the defining events of Canadian history."[72]

McGraw-Hill Ryerson's 2000 entry in the Grade 10 history sweepstakes, *Canada: A Nation Unfolding*, by yet another team of authors, pushed the contradiction of sober realism and nationalistic celebration to a new pitch of intensity—so much so that it is difficult not to imagine the writers strenuously disagreeing among themselves. No fewer than 65 of its 452 pages focus on the Great War and in themselves reveal the impact of new trends in history writing, such as closer attention to the average person and to popular culture.[73] In an unusually distanced manner the writers take time to discuss the war's economic origins—how Britain and Germany were in conflict because, after the Industrial Revolution, both countries aimed to dominate the world economy by acquiring colonies for resources and markets. Diplomats and governments shared responsibility for failing "to arrive at a peaceful compromise." Militarism and nationalism also served to make the war much more likely. The text asks students to consider whether any one country or group of countries can be blamed for the war—with the obvious hint that the better answer would be that its origins sprang from several factors, including the "aggressive competition resulting from the Industrial Revolution." The text even implies through one question—what if the assassin Gavrilo Princip had missed?—that the dirty deed did not explain the war. The description of the conduct of the war has an equally realistic tone, debunking "the myth of civilized war," graphically describing the effects of chlorine gas, and outlining how the new industrial technology meant that honourable warfare, entailing lines of soldiers advancing across the battlefields, was replaced by mechanized warfare.[74]

Canada: A Nation Unfolding also outperformed its rivals in demographic inclusivity.[75] It described the role of women in munitions work and as nurses. A detailed section on "A White Man's War: Racism in the Canadian Military" notes that Black Canadians were mostly restricted to a Black-only, non-combat division, which then receives a two-page section. Thus the history of the Great War can be used to address questions of racism in the broader society. The text takes due notice of anti-German rampages and oppressive acts against Canada's "Enemy Aliens." It mentions the resistance of Québécois and the Easter resistance of 1918. It has the by now familiar information on Hughes and Haig and descriptions of the less than honourable wartime "greed and corruption." Almost nothing was "won" on either side when the war finally ended; but "much had been lost." Of those who "lost" from the war, foremost were the returned soldiers themselves, promised "full re-establishment" by the Borden government, but consistently frustrated by a regime keen to keep their pensions low and reluctant to compromise with an increasingly aggressive veterans' movement.[76]

The section on the Great War begins with a quote from Timothy Findley's novel *The Wars* (1977):

> Someone once said to Clive: do you think we will ever be forgiven for what we've done? They meant their generation and the war and what the war had done to civilization. Clive said something I've never forgotten. He said: I doubt we'll ever be forgiven. All I hope is—they'll remember we were human beings.[77]

The overall lesson that the authors hope students will attain from the Great War is insight into how "future conflicts between nations" might best be avoided.[78]

Yet, almost without skipping a beat, the account combines its sober portrayal of the war with a stirring account of the valiant heroes who won it for Canada, including Currie, who, having performed brilliantly at Vimy, demonstrated to the whole world that "Canadians were capable of devising and carrying out a well-planned and successful attack." Currie's heroism was typical of the Canadian soldiers as a whole, whose wholesome recreations are listed without any acknowledgement of some of the less inspiring aspects of the army's activities in Northwestern Europe.[79] An account that earlier had declared that the Great War had put to rest all talk of "honourable war" ends up hailing the "gallant efforts of Canadian soldiers and the supreme sacrifice made by thousands of young Canadians." Once again, Canada became a nation thanks to that supreme sacrifice. It had fully earned "the right to stand as a nation on its own." It had taken an enormous step towards independence, establishing a sense of "pride and patriotism" that would carry over in "the post-war years as Canadian politicians came to demand a place for Canada on the international stage." It follows that "Canada's wartime experience would be a defining period in its history."[80]

*   *   *

Yet another purveyor of war memory—and a different kind of site altogether—came with the 2005 opening of the Canadian War Museum (CWM) on the banks of the Ottawa River, just a bit down from Parliament Hill.

"This is your legacy," the CWM explains to visitors in bold characters. "It is the memory of how war has affected your life in Canada today. It is preserved here so that you can share it and remember." Not only that, "This is your Museum. It is for people like you, ordinary Canadians, who have made history."

The price tag for the 45,000-square-foot museum was $135.75 million. Like so many other museums developed since the 1970s, the focus is not on collections of artifacts. Rather, the institution seeks to promote an interactive, participatory visitor "experience" so that its space becomes "fluid, performative and theatrical."[81] The CWM is selling a particular set of ideas about Canada and war. It also tries to mould a sense of the Canadian self "inseparable from the nation's military history."[82]

The CWM's presentation starts with "you-ism," a notion familiar in marketing circles. Marketers often use "you" as they attempt to convince customers that the seller really *is* thinking about them. "You" draws you in. An outfit selling cruises in 2015 headlined its trademarked pitch "Your world, your way,"™ with a plentiful supply in the following copy of the words "you" or "your."

These days a war museum cannot afford to be overtly bellicose. A glory-of-war, flag-waving narrative would be insensitive to many visitors, especially in a country to which so many have fled from war and armed men in uniform. War museums need to carefully underline the horror of war, the lives lost, ruined buildings and landscapes, war on the home front.

Few visitors will emerge from the CWM's Great War exhibit feeling nostalgic for the good old days on the Western Front. A striking full-scale diorama of Passchendaele complete with mud, fog, and a dead body— or so we imagine, seeing a helmeted mannequin lying face down in the mire—does not make the average visitor regret having missed the battle. The displays reflect an admirable determination to remind us of the suffering caused by war. The Great War is not validated as a campaign against German wickedness. To its credit, the museum invests no energy in allegations of unilateral "German War Guilt." Rather, a board headed "A World War Unleashed" explains that pre-1914 Europe was "a powder keg. Mutual grievances, opposing alliances, and secret treaties divided the heavily armed great powers."

The CWM offers fascinating artifacts and works of art. Its Beaver-brook war art collection includes some 13,000 works. At the start of the Great War centenary the museum mounted a special exhibit, "Ordinary People in Extraordinary Times," free of charge, highlighted by nine bronze figures created by Florence Wyle and Frances Loring. Wyle's *Munitions Worker* and *Noon Hour* and Loring's *The Shell Finisher*, *The Rod Turner*, and *The Furnace Girl* pay tribute to the women who undertook risky work in munitions factories. The museum's permanent Great War exhibit features Loring's *Girls with a Rail*. The CWM describes women who became Great War industrial workers as a "reserve army of labour," employing a phrase borrowed from Karl Marx.

At the heart of the Great War exhibit is, of course, Vimy Ridge. The film *Vimy Ridge: The Soldiers' Story* (2005) plays non-stop. Visitors seated in the centrepiece video section learn that the soldiers on Vimy Ridge came "from every hamlet in Canada"—once more hearing the satisfying if false tale of their deep roots in Canadian soil. "After Vimy, we were invincible," one respondent tells the audience, hailing Canada's "Greatest Achievement," which would have come as news to many Canadian soldiers at Passchendaele. Vimy, as has become customary, is shortened to the days immediately following 9 April: the earlier gas attacks that killed so many Canadians are omitted. Once again, the taking of Vimy Ridge, "the linchpin of German defences in the region," is vested with a military significance completely out of keeping with the evidence of the days following its capture. The great Vimy Memorial too undergoes a transformation—it is not Allward's "sermon against war," or the peace monument so many people thought it was in 1936, but a war memorial paying tribute to Canada's soldiers.

The CWM's treatment of the Great War is, in its details, an exercise in studied ambivalence. Visitors learn of the "terrible price of WWI." Of the 420,000 who served overseas, more than half were killed or injured. The staggering figures are hard to even imagine in the twenty-first century. This, the museum's story has it, was "Canada's Sacrifice." The description of the slaughter as a national sacrifice, however, stands in the way of a full understanding of Canada as a complex, conflict-ridden polity.

Canada did indeed emerge from the terrible war "an unfinished country . . . proud and victorious, and with a new standing in the world. It was also a grieving and divided country." The museum dedicates a section to "turmoil on the home front," with part of this display exploring conscription and the way it ripped the country apart. This overwhelmingly important aspect of the war and its political legacy is mixed in with photos, artifacts, and text dealing with conscientious objectors and the treatment of visible minorities. Afro-Canadians were banned from bearing arms and segregated into separate military units. The CWM describes the racist policy blandly, explaining that "most served with No. 2 Construction Battalion, which carried out essential support activities behind the front lines."

The section on home-front turmoil also looks at the police killing of labour activist/pacifist Ginger Goodwin and the resulting general strike in Vancouver. With respect to the conscription crisis, the curators included a panel on the Quebec City riots of 1918 in which troops fired on civilians. The CWM conscription display also reveals that the idea of going to war in 1917 was far from popular with those who were required to register for military service. Of the 400,000 men registered, some 380,000 appealed.

Another ambivalent treatment of a controversial part of the war is the CWM display on what was known at the time, with refreshing directness, as "shell shock"—subsequently dubbed "combat fatigue" and now post-traumatic stress disorder (PTSD). The shell-shock display includes a one-minute film of a twitching, gibbering victim under the caption "Shell Shock: Trauma and Shattered Minds."

"The horror of war could shatter a mind. . . . The military and medical communities initially believed shell shock resulted from physical damage to the brain by the shock of exploding shells, but prolonged exposure to stress was the true cause." But the "communities" themselves sometimes had a different view. Soon after the war Andrew Macphail defined shell shock in men who had experienced combat as a "manifestation of childishness and femininity." A much less often cited conclusion about the nature of shell-shocked men came from a panel of prominent medical men convened by Militia Minister Sir Edward Kemp as the war was drawing to an end. The experts viewed men with psychological trauma as "individuals of a constitutionally inferior type (who) will form a class of tramps, ne'er do wells and criminals that history shows has always followed a war."[83]

Any suggestions that Canada might have housed people with different interests and values are dealt with dismissively. This is particularly evident in the museum's almost scandalous treatment of wartime profiteering, treating what was a major public issue almost as an unbalanced conspiracy theory: "A focus on wartime manufacturing, inflation and product shortage led to continuous price increases on the home front. Looking for explanations, angry Canadians blamed the 'profiteers.' They believed these unscrupulous businessmen—who remained largely unnamed and unknown—were conspiring with the government to raise prices." In addition to the syntactical problem of a "focus" that somehow creates "price increases," the caption is dishonest. A good many of the unscrupulous businessmen were not just named and known but became subject to extensive investigations that looked into such colourful topics as lame horses, defective boots, and lamentable potatoes. These subjects would surely have made for interesting museum displays. The implication that only "angry Canadians" found them objectionable is unfounded.[84] By implying that only emotional Canadians harboured vaguely based suspicions of a cloudy conspiracy, the curators obscured a core contradiction of the war.

A similar evasiveness haunts the CWM's discussion of the oppression of racialized minorities—not just Afro-Canadians—during Canada's Great War. "As war pressure mounted, some turned on their neighbours and persecuted Canadians of German and Ukrainian descent." True, but this way of putting it places responsibility for their victimization upon "some" and not upon the "state," which passed the legislation and created the concentration camps that made it possible. (Raymond Moriyama, architect of the CWM, was himself a victim of state internment during the Second World War.) Xenophobic "war fever" thus seems like the foible of a few, not the result of a campaign calculated by the state and orchestrated by the mass media to achieve certain social and political results. "Some 107 internees died in confinement; many others suffered from ill-health and shattered spirits." The display encourages visitors to imagine this death and suffering as something that simply happened, not as something that identifiable people and agencies made to happen. The account also does not establish that some prisoners were physically abused and shot in what were officially known as "concentration camps"—an expression the museum avoids. While gesturing towards the repression of Quebec, in its mention of the Easter resistance the museum does not draw upon the far more extensive historiography documenting state repression in the Great War. The Canadian penchant for killing German prisoners receives no mention at all.

The museum, wedded as it is to the nationalist theme of Canada as a collective person, strains under its contradictory burden: realistic depiction and patriotic commemoration. "The Royal Canadian Hall of Honour" depicts "Canada's rich history of honouring and remembering"—with the phrase "rich history" steering us away from reflection on what it is we are honouring and remembering. The writing informs readers, "At the turn of the twenty-first century, honouring has once again become part of Canadians' public and private worlds." Had such honouring been abandoned for a time? If so, when and why?

The exhibition presents visitors with a gripping photograph of a "Gas Attack"—although exactly which side is attacking which is not made clear—together with a denunciation of this "Filthy Loathsome Pestilence." The focus is, perhaps inevitably, on the first unleashing of poison gas by the Germans at the Second Battle of Ypres. The "Allies responded to this terror weapon with a series of respirators (gas masks) that offered partial protection, as well as with gas of their own." The passing gesture towards shared responsibility for this novel way of killing offers no sense of how extensively and enthusiastically Canadians embraced this new "terror weapon" and put it to work on the Western Front.

The paintings chosen for its permanent Great War gallery from the CWM's massive collection understandably reflect the museum's perspective on the war. The display is not an exhibition of war art, making no claim to be such. The paintings assist in guiding the visitor along, telling a story of Canada and the war. There is nothing by A.Y. Jackson. Other Group of Seven members Arthur Lismer (a Halifax convoy in a small display devoted to the devastating Halifax explosion of 1917) and Manly MacDonald (*Land Girls Hoeing*, as part of the war-at-home display) contribute to the exhibit's narrative.

The conventionally patriotic representations of the collection feature *Canada's Answer*, a canvas by Royal Navy paymaster Norman Wilkinson, inventor of naval camouflage, who portrays Canada's first contingent on the way to England, a jaunty representation of powerful ships sailing the high seas. The huge, panoramic canvas *The Battle for Courcelette* by Louis Weirter depicts the frenzied chaos of battle, complete with a destroyed tank, a burning factory, and aircraft swooping through puffs of shell fire. Although the piece is rather old-fashioned, the artist had personally witnessed the battle before painting it two years later.

Not so with the billboard-size canvas by Richard Jack, who painted the *2nd Battle of Ypres* without having travelled across the English Channel to Flanders. His depiction of a battle he had not seen offers a dose of realism, with dead and wounded soldiers amidst the rubble of battle, a dynamic trench scene with puffs of exploding shells, and the enemy in retreat. As its centrepiece the painting has a gallant officer, his head bandaged, standing well above what might be a trench line, gesturing boldly to his men, urging them forward to the fight. Nearby two admiring soldiers look fierce, ready to respond to the call. But it would have been a rare, indeed foolhardy, act for a Western Front combatant to stand up in such an exposed manner, making himself an easy target and violating a (vital) principle of combat—it is not advisable to "skyline" yourself. One art historian criticized Jack for employing "every hackneyed nineteenth century war art convention"—the sort of thing that gives "traditional battle paintings a bad reputation."[85] Nevertheless, CWM curators feature the painting prominently, choosing it over a wide selection of more sophisticated works in the collection.

Another canvas that deals with the same battle, *The First German Gas Attack at Ypres* by William Roberts, a former artilleryman, does not duplicate Jack's attempt at detailed realism. He provides an abstract view of the war's global nature, portraying soldiers from France's North African colonies being seared by poison gas. "Which painting," the CWM asks, seeking to get people to reflect on two differing approaches, "better conveys the brutal nature of the battle?" In contrast to the conventional story of the Canadians alone standing fast in the face of the gas, the painting shows one Canadian fleeing alongside the Zouaves from the 45th Algerian Division. The art provides a tangible sense of the war's horrific chaos.[86]

One of the last canvases on the winding path that ushers visitors through the Great War section is Varley's emblematic masterpiece *For What?* Before the new CWM opened, the sombre burial scene had been a staple of two major CWM travelling exhibitions, one in the late 1970s and the other, called *Canvas of War*, in the early 2000s. *Canvas of War* attracted a half-million visitors in nine cities. Laura Brandon, the CWM's war art curator until 2015, assembled the exhibit, and describes *For What?* as "devastating." Brandon's 2006 book on the forgotten history of Canadian war art discusses art historian Barry Lord's 1974 Marxist-nationalist perspective on Varley's painting. Lord's view of some war art as part of a popular struggle for liberation, with many works, such as Mabel May's

Women Making Shells, showing workers toiling on the home front, moved him to suggest that workers and artists had much in common. "Advancing together in the common struggle of the war, artist and worker here take a long step forward toward a people's art." Lord, a museum curator and art critic, understood the context of Varley's landscape: "*For What?* was a question many Canadian veterans were to ask as they came back to a Canada of exploitation, repression and unemployment."[87]

Varley himself provided a straightforward statement about the painting's meaning: "We'd be healthier to forget [the war], & that we never can. We are forever tainted with its abortiveness & its cruel drama." The words reflect the artist's reaction to what he had just witnessed, the question that haunted so many others searching for a shred of meaning in the wake of the war.[88]

Recent visitors to the CWM's Great War gallery could find Varley's canvas near the end of the exhibit, consigned to a corner without the benefit of the careful lighting and high profile enjoyed by other paintings in the exhibition. The didactic text accompanying *For What?* prods readers to question Varley's feelings about the war. The caption asks: "What do you think that Frederick Varley is suggesting with this evocative work and title?" It continues, "Was the war pointless? If the war had been pointless, why had more than 400,000 Canadians continued to serve and fight overseas?"[89] But, to respond with some leading questions of our own: Do we not find in Varley's quiet integrity and solemn realism, so emphatically marginalized in this museum, an eloquent rebuttal of the Vimyism that surrounds it? Is it not a reminder of a more balanced time when an honest observer, gazing upon the Great War's blood-soaked fields, could only marvel at the cruel insanity of modern war?

Then there is the War Museum's final query. If the war was pointless, why did soldiers fight on? This is yet another fascinating question that the CWM does not address in any significant way.

Many soldiers resisted. Mutinies were not uncommon, though they were ruthlessly repressed, along with word of their outbreaks. The French army was hit by 27,000-odd desertions in 1917. The force handed out hundreds of death sentences, though most were commuted. British army troops rioted at the Etaples base in France in 1917.[90] The Russian army fell apart that same year, and the war in that country subsequently gave rise to revolution, the end of the Czarist empire, and the transformation of the history of the twentieth century.

Why, then, did so many fight on? For one thing, if they did not continue to follow orders they risked being condemned to death by their officers and shot—which was the fate of twenty-two Canadians who were executed for desertion during the war. The British executed 335 men. Military justice, like martial music, is often an oxymoron. The CWM itself does mention courts martial as being rudimentary and brusque: "The odds against an accused soldier were heavy." Archival records show, the museum says, that "accused soldiers rarely gave long or detailed statements, and cases could be settled after only a few witnesses had been called. The vast majority of accused soldiers were found guilty."[91]

A more common and less formal way of enforcing discipline—with discipline being absolutely central to the culture of the military as an institution—was to torture offenders who might be perceived as slackers or guilty of the crime of disrespecting the army hierarchy through "insubordination." Officers of the Canadian contingent often applied "Field Punishment No. 1," known by soldiers as "crucifixion." Soldiers were tied to a large wheel for hours, splayed out so that their comrades would take note. The helpless offender would be baked by the sun, soaked by cold rain, and unable to scratch the lice that were endemic to trench life.[92]

The answer to the CWM's puzzling query about Varley's *For What?* is complex. Many soldiers on both sides did fight on because they truly believed in the cause. Others fought on because, in one of the oldest insights about men and war, they were there for each other—so-called "bands of brothers" welded together by sharing the horrific experience of combat. But perhaps, as is so often the case, the search for an answer leads to the insights of eyewitnesses who, like Varley, dealt with their anguish by making art.

Vera Brittain was a nurse at the British army camp at Etaples in 1917, the year of the mutiny. She later became a peace activist, and in her seventies was carried off by police after sitting down on a street during a demonstration. Brittain wrote one of the most important memoirs to emerge from the Great War. Her explanation of why people persisted is at once poignant and nuanced. In her 1933 classic *Testament of Youth*, she wrote:

Between 1914 and 1919 young men and women, disastrously pure in heart and unsuspicious of elderly self-interest and cynical exploitation, were continually rededicating themselves—as I did that morning in Boulogne—to an end that they believed, and went on trying to believe, lofty and ideal. When patriotism "wore threadbare," when suspicion and doubt began to creep in, the more ardent and frequent was the re-dedication, the more deliberate the self-induced conviction that our efforts were disinterested and our cause was just. Unfortunately, this state of mind was what anti-war propagandists call it—"hysterical exaltation," "quasi-mystical idealistic hysteria"— but it had concrete results in stupendous patience, in superhuman endurance, in the constant reaffirmation of incredible courage. To refuse to acknowledge this is to underrate the power of those white angels who fight so naively on the side of destruction.[93]

Varley painted *For What?* soon after returning from the trenches just as the war was ending. Brittain, who lost her fiancé, her brother, and two of her closest friends to the war, published her insights fifteen years after Varley completed his wartime canvas. By 1933 the canon of Great War literature was well established, though little of the art had been produced by women. Brittain captured the war's great irony, its jarring contrasts— of romanticism and insanity.

Rather than indulging their unreflecting Vimyism, CWM curators might better have considered the existence of other, far more complex, ways of getting visitors to think about the question of *For What?*

*   *   *

"What is war?" the War Museum asks visitors as they enter the Canadian Experience galleries that comprise its permanent exhibitions. "War is organized, armed conflict. Virtually every human society, past and present, makes war." The CWM, hedging bets with the word "virtually," informs its audience that war is a constant in the realm of human endeavour, pretty well an eternal verity.

In his twelve-volume *A Study of History* (1934–61) Arnold Toynbee offers a rather more thoughtful note on the matter. "Wars are exhilarating when fought elsewhere by other people," suggests the historian, who served in political intelligence for the British Foreign Office during the Great War before becoming a delegate to the Paris peace talks. "Perhaps most exhilarating of all when over and done with; and historians of all civilizations had traditionally regarded them as the most interesting topic in their field."[94]

Peace, apparently, would never have such a high place. At least that is what a group of Ottawa peace promoters learned during a campaign to have Canada's new war museum focus on peace as well as war. The "Make Room for Peace" activists began their efforts after construction of the CWM was underway. As it turned out, they were stonewalled. Their suggestions were politely received, duly considered, and shelved for future consideration. In this war museum, peace is an afterthought.

The group acknowledged that the new museum showed the human costs of war and the inhuman conditions endured by soldiers. They were encouraged by the explanations of the tragedy of so many Canadians killed and by a CWM question about what young Canadians could have accomplished had they not perished. But they were dismayed by what they called "a pervasive feeling of the inevitability of war throughout," pointing to the CWM's opening what-is-war question.

Why, they asked, could a new museum not also ask wider questions to suggest broader understandings of war? It could raise issues of prevention and disarmament, for instance; or the role of diplomacy or of international law and treaties aimed at eradicating war. At one Make Room for Peace meeting a woman who had arrived in Canada from Vietnam summed up her concerns.

> The Canadian War Museum aroused compassion in me for the people who suffered due to wars, mostly for the soldiers who fought in the war and sacrificed their life or part of their body. It also gave me some knowledge of Canadian history but it failed to create an understanding of war, of how to deal with conflicts among groups and nations without using force. It also does not help me reflect on how we can live our life to promote peace and avoid war. . . . How can we know about war if we don't learn about peace?[95]

Some eight years after the CWM opened, it did mount a temporary effort, *Peace: The Exhibition*, with creatively designed, interactive features. Visitors could fashion their own protest buttons and sit down at a negotiating table to settle a conflict. The Six Nations Confederacy and its Great Law of Peace received substantial attention along with other indigenous traditions. The exhibition featured Lester Pearson's Nobel Peace Prize and Canada's role in helping to establish United Nations peacekeeping in 1956 through the United Nations Emergency Force. Under the heading

"Lessons from a War for Peace" was the explanation that one artifact—a sculpture of a dove on an artillery shell—was provided on Armistice Day 1918 by a munitions manufacturer.[96]

One of the CWM's proudest features is its Regeneration Hall, part of what is described as "an Architecture of Hope." The hall, a vaulted passage, would seem to speak to the concerns of peace activists. "Nature may be ravaged by war," explained architect Raymond Moriyama, "but inevitably it survives, hybridizes, regenerates and prevails. From the healing process emerges hope."[97]

Regeneration Hall reflects this optimism. The highest point in the museum, it is a soaring passage lined with maquettes for Allward's dramatic statues that adorn the Vimy Memorial. It is a space intended to invite reflection, the "hope for a peaceful future."

"Here the eye is drawn skyward along a sharp triangle of glass and steel," explains a CWM video that describes Allward's art as representing the caring nature of the human spirit. "A small balcony overlooks the hall and offers a glimpse of the Peace Tower through the narrow window."[98]

The CWM routinely highlights the view of the Peace Tower from Regeneration Hall. On a visit to the museum in 2007 Debbie Grisdale, a peace activist who had been involved in the Make Room for Peace effort, talked about her concerns about the role of peace with a volunteer guide, a former teacher. The guide told Grisdale that she especially liked to talk to children about peace and the importance of working for peace in their schools and communities. Regeneration Hall, she said, was the ideal spot to do this because she could point out the Peace Tower through the window in the east wall. As they talked, a school tour with two teachers and ten- and eleven-year-olds entered the hall. Grisdale's guide turned to the visitors, offering to point out the Peace Tower and explain the importance of the hall; but the group hurried on down the stairs before she could make her explanation.

"They did not have time to hear about peace—the children wanted to get downstairs to see the tanks and artillery," Grisdale recalled. "Too bad, I thought. Another opportunity to teach about peace, lost to the allure of weapons."

Around the time of Remembrance Day 2015, visiting children inevitably wandered into the museum's gift shop. The offerings featured the "Baghdad 2003" model of a U.S. Abrams tank, part of the complete *Forces of Valour* series of "combat proven machines." The shop displayed soft rubber hand grenades suitable for indoor use—and a Legion- issued CD ("A Tribute to Wartime Valour") with children's choirs singing "Onward Christian Soldiers," "Fight the Good Fight," and "The Maple Leaf Forever." The shop is in good measure aimed at young warriors who might be keen to have a "Smith & Wesson Tactical Stylus & Pen" made of aircraft aluminum.

9

THE LANDSCAPES OF
GREAT WAR MEMORY

*The passions that we bring to war can be brought just as well to
the struggle against war. . . . I myself would be unable to imagine
the passions of war if I had not, at various times in my life, linked arms
with the men and women around me and marched up, singing or
chanting, to the waiting line of armed and uniformed men.*

— BARBARA EHRENREICH, *Blood Rites:*
Origins and History of the Passion of War

A MONTH before storming Vimy Ridge the Canadian forces launched
a chemical attack on the German foe. Over a distance of four miles,
sappers carried phosgene and chlorine gas in tanks weighing 160
pounds. The attack was a fiasco. The gas hung in the air and then blew
back at the Canadians, killing the very soldiers it was supposed to cover.
The ravages were so extreme that, two days later, the Germans offered a
truce to help the Canadians retrieve their dead.

Some ninety years later, in 2007, Jack Granatstein remembered
Canada's chemical warfare: "We used it because it worked—there is simply
no doubt that it eased the way." The statement might well be nominated
as the daintiest euphemism yet for a technique of war that leaves its victims
to die slowly, agonizingly coughing up a steady stream of yellow fluid.[1]
Still, at least Granatstein was honest in acknowledging the extent to
which Canadians made war using all the technology on offer. Many stories
imagine Canadians *suffering*—but fail to register how they *cause others to
suffer*. The notion that our Empire bore any responsibility for either the
war or its catastrophic aftermath is also kept firmly at bay. "As a rule,"

Margaret Atwood remarks of people in general, "we tend to remember the awful things done to us, and to forget the awful things we did."[2]

In 2015 the annual Veterans Affairs Canada (VAC) publication *Canada Remembers Times* featured Filip Konowal, "A Ukrainian-Canadian War Hero." Konowal won the Victoria Cross in 1917 after he "personally took out" sixteen Germans with his "gun, bayonet and explosives." Though wounded, Corporal Konowal survived the war and is "still admired as a true hero by many proud Ukrainian Canadians." Here is Vimyism in action. In its video-game lingo, such as "taking out," the article airbrushes away the killing while ignoring Corporal Konowal's Ukrainian compatriots back home—a good many of them destined for Ottawa's concentration camps.[3]

Conflict is an indispensable, compelling ingredient of war stories, from ripping yarns to highbrow literature. Heroes and their adventures make for great reading. From the *Odyssey* through the *Holy Bible* to *Lord of the Rings*, battles provide inspiring stories; and, far beyond its actual importance, Vimy has been mythologized with a zeal worthy of Homer. Allward's Vimy monument, intended to be a sermon against war, has been reimagined as a cathedral-like monument to Canadian valour. McCrae's "In Flanders Fields," ambiguously lamenting war *and* exalting the Empire's war effort, has become an official nationalist scriptural reading—sufficiently exalted to feature on Canada's currency. A century after Allward conceived his monument and McCrae wrote his poem, the Vimyist narrative is heavily indebted to the deployment of the first-person plural: *us, we, our.* ("Take up our quarrel with the foe.")

A focus on a single battle (or a single Great War) that somehow united Canada obscures just who *we* were, in all *our* complications. It is a version of history that drastically oversimplifies the past.[4] Indigenous men joined up en masse. They returned home, if they were lucky, to a country where they were barred by law from voting for a government that denied them pension benefits for which their fellow veterans were eligible.[5] To adopt Vimy Ridge as their founding myth, French Canadians would not only have to sideline Cartier and Champlain, Bishop Laval and Marguerite Bourgeoys. They would also need to forget how fiercely most of their forbears resisted conscription, and the contempt they faced from a legion of aroused Anglo commentators.

A history that honestly represents a complicated past refuses such oversimplifications. In her landmark study *Landscapes of War and Memory: The Two World Wars in Canadian Literature and the Arts*, Sherrill Grace explains how storytellers after 1977 (the year Timothy Findley published

The Wars) have refused pat explanations of the shattering events experienced by their characters. "I do not understand, I don't. I won't. I can't. Why is this happening to us?" cries the bereaved mother of Findley's leading character. She "wept—but angrily," asking, "What does it mean—*to kill your children*?" Findley's "devastatingly honest" portrayal of the Great War, concludes Grace, "shatters the myth of 'death so noble.'"

Grace came across the idea of "landscapes of memory" in a piece written by Findley, and she asks:

> What happens if there are blank expanses in the landscape or areas of the map without familiar signposts? What if the story is interrupted, erased, forgotten or buried? What if another story—one that is widely accepted, sanctioned, dominant and official—already occupies the available space so that one's memories and stories can find no room, location, grounding, or accepted place in the landscape?[6]

What if Canada's "landscapes of Great War memory" will always defy the attempts of an official martial nationalism to make them stand for a single, buoyantly patriotic, conception of history?

*　　*　　*

Some eighty years after the dedication of the Vimy monument in France, Vimyist patriots were attempting to hijack the "Mother Canada" image—and motherhood symbolism in general—by erecting an uber-patriotic statue on a remote Nova Scotia shoreline, Green Cove, within Cape Breton Highlands National Park.

For the Never Forgotten National Memorial Foundation (NFNMF), Allward's *Canada Bereft* (or "Mother Canada") would soon be reborn. Now the basic idea would no longer be part of his sermon against war. It had become a romantically maternal symbol of Canadian patriotism. "Beneath stormy seas and in distant lands lie men and women who never returned home. The Never Forgotten National Memorial will be a place for visitors to reach back through the generations and forge a very real connection with this young nation's Fallen Heroes."[7]

The brash scheme envisaged a huge war memorial. Added to a lofty, eight-storey statue of a woman staring out to sea with arms outstretched—to be called "Mother Canada"—would be an ambitious commercial development, including a "Procession Pathway Bridge," a "Commemorative

Ring of True Patriot Love," a "With Glowing Hearts National Sanctu-ary," and, of course, a gift shop. As a 2012 application to the Canadian Intellectual Property Office revealed, the organizers also had in mind tank tops and underwear, fanny packs and golf balls, toy figures and toy pistols. The NFNMF and its lawyers, working from a Toronto bank tower, regis-tered exclusive rights to label over a hundred such items emblazoned with the words "Mother Canada."[8]

Such a "surreal list of souvenirs" constituted "retail remembrance," said critics—but the statue planners had even broader plans to turn a reimagined icon from the Vimy monument into a martial spectacular. For March 2017, the 150th anniversary of Confederation, the Big Statue planners envisaged a cross-country "Homecoming Tour" culminating on 1 July, Canada Day. What was to come "home" were "capsules" of "repatriated soil and seawater," shipped to Ottawa for "respectful public viewings" before travelling on to Victoria and then back east for a "grand arrival" in Halifax. People unable to visit the Big Statue in person would have a chance to "experience the symbolic return of Our Fallen firsthand." And so, "we" would "proudly commemorate Our Fallen across the very heart of Canada, creating an unprecedented link of love and respect embracing all corners of this young nation."[9]

The Big Statue garnered an impressive list of supporters, from a Calgary Flames hockey team executive and other corporate bigwigs to former provincial premiers and a posse of retired military men. Military historians Jack Granatstein and David Bercuson predictably put their shoulders to the wheel, as did CBC-TV news host Peter Mansbridge. Peter MacKay, former defence minister and leading Conservative, explained: "This Memorial is a wonderful initiative that will give Canadians a steadfast symbol here in our country, to honour the unsurpassed bravery in the name of freedom and liberty, that Canadian soldiers displayed."[10] Although the support group was overwhelmingly male, it did include Mila Mulroney, wife of a former prime minister, and Lisa LaFlamme, a prominent anchorwoman.

All of this was too much for Cape Breton peace activists Lee-Anne Brodhead and Sean Howard, who organized a group called the Friends of Green Cove. They were joined by a group of twenty-eight former senior Parks Canada executives, who were astounded that a commercial operation could be insinuated into a national park without a stringent environmental assessment. "It is clear," they charged, "that the proposed 'Mother Canada' statue for Cape Breton Highlands National Park will not enhance ecological integrity." Friends of Green Cove further pointed out that the minimal impact study had been carried out by a company that NFNMF listed as a stakeholder. The Vimy Foundation, a charity dedicated to preserving Canada's "First World War legacy as symbolized with the victory at Vimy Ridge," and normally a strong backer of the birth-of-a-nation thesis, raised a more surprising voice of alarm. It worried that the project for the Big Statue—"disrespectful and unsavoury"—was going to muddy the waters (and—although this remained unspoken—perhaps grab some of its own share in the "retail remembrance" marketplace).[11]

Investigative reporter Tim Bousquet, running a feisty independent news site called *The Halifax Examiner*, spotted Defence Minister MacKay's hyperventilating rhetoric about "unsurpassed bravery in the name of freedom and liberty." Bousquet took issue with the particular landscape of memory being constructed by the project's proponents.

> World War I was about a lot of things, but one thing it wasn't about was defending freedom and democracy. It was a stupid, vile war—perhaps the most stupid and vile war ever, which is saying a lot—fought for pointless, vainglorious "honour" at best, and nationalistic breast-beating at worst. . . . There's a place for monuments to the victims of war. It's important that we remember our past indifference to humanity and mourn those lives so casually given up. Such monuments should be somber, reflective places, places where we confront the devil that is ourselves and lament the harrowing loss of so many young people. What monuments to the victims of war should not be is gaudy roadside attractions run by trinket sellers.[12]

In 2015, with the defeat of the Conservative government and the energetic organizing of the Friends of Green Cove, some of the impetus behind projects like the Big Statue declined. "Mother Canada" would not soon set foot at Green Cove as Parks Canada backed away from a project that was an apparent anathema to a new Liberal government.[13] Yet although the demise of a government committed to a bellicose narrative spelled a reversal for Vimyism, in the long war of attrition for the hearts and minds of Canadians, its boosters had not quite been chased from the field.

*   *   *

Indeed, Vimyism is likely to persist as a powerful complex of myths and symbols even as some of its more flagrantly kitschy initiatives bite the dust. Perhaps most fundamentally, militarism is the cultural counterpart of a vast array of economic institutions, operating nationally and globally, with a vested interest in war. "Worldwide," peace scholar Ernie Regehr points out, "military forces spend more in just three days, about $14 billion, than is available for the entire United Nations (UN) operating budget, plus peacekeeping, for a full year ($13 billion)." The annual price tag for the world's military spending is around $17 trillion.[14] Nor are Canadians laggards in cashing in on militarism: under Justin Trudeau, Canada gained the distinction of being the second-biggest exporter of arms to the Middle East.[15]

George Drew was simplistic in the 1930s when he blamed the global armaments trade for single-handedly accelerating the rush to war, yet his theory gestures towards a larger truth: as long as a capitalist world economy featuring a war-promoting armaments business continues to reign unimpeded, it will encourage people to think that military policies and military hardware constitute solutions to a vast diversity of problems. Although formal empires have declined markedly since 1918, with the demise of many of them accelerated by the Great War itself, imperialism as a fact of power politics has scarcely vanished.

We live in a world still shaped and reshaped by the forces of empire. When the terrorist forces of the Islamic State (also known as ISIS) publicized their success in operating on either side of the Syria/Iraq border, they showcased the demolition of a sand berm that had once marked the division, then panned their cameras to a cardboard sign lying on the sand. Words on the sign read: "End of Sykes-Picot." The Sykes-Picot Agreement was concluded behind closed doors by British and French diplomats just as the generals were preparing for the deadly Battle of the Somme. With Russian concurrence but without any consultation with the peoples of what was then "Asia Minor," the empires drew up arbitrary borders, handing Syria and northern Iraq to the French and the rest of Iraq, Transjordan, and Palestine to the British. When the war was over the British exercised their Great War mandate by attacking Arabs seeking self-government; senior ministers, including Winston Churchill, favoured bombing raids because they promised to be a cheaper alternative to the boots-on-the-ground repression of Arab dissent. Said Arthur Travis Harris, later to become a "hero" in the Second World War as he undertook what he himself called "terror" attacks on German cities, Arab discontent could be tamped down by dropping "one 250 lb. or 500 pound bomb in each village that speaks out of turn."[16] Today's ISIS is very much a product of yesterday's Great War, which was in large part a clash of empires, each seeking to gain or to preserve its position in the world.

But the logic of war goes beyond questions of capitalist political economy to a vast culture of war. War remains deeply embedded in our ways of thinking.[17] Above all, it remains a potent force within nationalism— all those things that tell us who we are (and who we aren't). If today the word "myth" is often used dismissively—to denote an account of an event which is simply untrue—mythical stories, no matter how far-fetched, can hold nations together. The concept of "Canada's myth" of the Great War is often used crudely, in efforts to imagine a loyal uniformity in a country rocked with stormy debates about the war and its consequences. Yet those who stress the real need of bereaved contemporaries to find *some* noble meaning in the war do, nonetheless, have a point.[18] Those who lost loved ones in the twentieth century's wars—some ninety million violent deaths— have an interest in believing that a greater good or cosmic purpose was served by their loss.

Bereaved and injured Canadians struggled in the 1920s and 1930s. The myth that a war had been fought to free the world of war and autocracy was extremely difficult to maintain in the face of all the glaring contrary evidence—much of it offered first-hand by soldiers who had actually been engaged in it. Among most historians today, a key foundation stone of that myth—Germany's sole and unqualified responsibility for the war, of the sort intimated by the Versailles Treaty—has decisively crumbled.[19] That rationale was, indeed, already considerably the worse for wear by the late 1920s, and many Canadians knew it.[20] Yet without the certainty that the British, French, and Russian empires stood for democracy and right, and the Central Powers for autocracy and wrong, much of the cosmic justification for the deaths of Canadian soldiers vanished. In the early twenty-first century few well-informed people find themselves able to harbour a nostalgic reverence for the British Empire as a fount of civility.

Yet it was precisely when the British Empire had entered its unmistakably steep decline in the 1950s and 1960s that the myth of "Vimy, birth of the nation" was starting to take root. In retrospect this Vimyism allowed its partisans both to celebrate the Empire and to distance Canada from it because it set Canadians apart from the British under whom they served. The Canadians were, to use the familial analogies, youthful sons of the Motherland, more vigorous and imaginative than their aged parent. The soldiers of the CEF, as part of the British army, could then be imagined to be the free-standing founders of our "imagined community," to use the famous phrase of political analyst Benedict Anderson.[21] Nations, on his reading, allow each of their members to imagine themselves bound with their fellows by deep bonds of communion, regardless of the actual inequality and exploitation that may prevail. By affirming a solid emotional bond with the soldiers at Vimy, we declare that we share common ties with them—far stronger ties of solidarity than with other victims of empire such as, for instance, the Kenyan peasants tortured in British concentration camps in the 1950s.

In 2000, during a state ceremony at Ottawa's National War Memorial, Canada buried its own unknown soldier, unearthed from a former battlefield in France. Thousands looked on. The prevailing sentiment, expressed in *Legion Magazine*, drew upon the rhetorical resources of Fussell's High Diction. It was fervently Vimyist. Canada's Unknown Soldier was returned to the country "with tremendous dignity. . . . It is a powerful story . . . it endures so long as we—and generations to come—remember his symbolic sacrifice and pause long enough every day to think about the hope and the fear associated with preserving the kind of peace and freedom he fought and died for." As Anderson remarks, "No more arresting emblems of the modern culture of nationalism exist than cenotaphs and tombs of Unknown Soldiers." The unknown soldiers and their tombs are "saturated with ghostly *national* imaginings."[22]

The NFNMF's capsules of dirt and water are attempts to accomplish the same objective: to inspire Canadians to imagine their country as unified by the blood and soil of a great battlefield, united in the face of a common enemy, real or imagined. Like Serbian nationalists who revere the Battle of Kosovo as the birthplace of their nation in 1389, so too Canadian martial nationalists enjoin their fellow Canadians to revere Vimy Ridge, or sometimes Passchendaele and the Hundred Days.[23] Less important is the need to identify the empires that went to war in Europe in 1914 or explain why they did so. Born in a great battle, the nation acquires an inspiring national narrative. Whatever its fearful costs in human suffering wherever it has taken root, such blood-and-soil nationalism, with its ability to inspire people with a sense that their lives are heroic and meaningful and that the lives of other people are far less worthy, has shown few signs of disappearing: contemporary Europe, a hotbed of xenophobia and nativism, bears witness to its powerful resurgence.

Such a formula for nationalism has a strong appeal to many Canadians, paradoxically because their country has so often frustrated any attempt to impose one unifying nationalism upon it. Canadians do not now share, and are unlikely in any foreseeable future to share, a single sense of "the nation." Canadians have never consolidated as a nation in Anderson's strong sense of identifying with the same myths, heroes, villains, or turning points in their history. For many people, and at certain times, this lack of clarity can seem a grievous burden. Among them, a yearning for the certainties of blood and soil becomes a palpable force. Especially among what is now the British-Canadian minority, accustomed to ruling the roost yet worriedly perceiving how complicated and cantankerous that roost has become, the impulse to find one authoritative Canadianism came to be strongly felt in the early twenty-first century.[24] The Vimy phenomenon, arising at the same time as challenges to British imperial supremacy, offers a birth narrative free of any taint of the actual processes of acquisitive European colonialism whereby the country was established. Vimy stands out as that moment when "we" performed so brilliantly as shock troops for our Motherland, our "Maple Leaf Empire." It is naturally and inevitably our defining moment. We came to realize who we were, separate from the Empire, by fighting for the selfsame Empire at Vimy.

In the proclamations and dreams of the "Mother Canada" statue boosters, for example, we find a relentless emphasis on Canada as a "young nation." Such a way of thinking allows us, if we are so motivated, to remember the Great War self-centredly, as though a world conflict was really all about us, fighting for freedom (and not, say, also about Belgium, keen to keep German hands off its vast and lucrative killing fields in the Congo). To this tale of immaculate conception we add one of an equally unblemished youth. That Canadian soldiers looted farms and cities, raped women, spread venereal disease, killed German prisoners, and deployed chemical weaponry cannot be anything but a minor footnote to the story. The Vimy myth allows us to have it both ways: to be both the Empire's hardened, skilled "shock troops," hard men making war on the unwashed and the ungodly, and innocents abroad, removed from the power politics of empire.

*　　*　　*

The Canadian state presides over three (at least) distinct cultural communities, two separate major language groups, and multiple regions. Since the 1960s it has been periodically seized by crises that have seemingly challenged its very existence.

These realities tell against Vimyism. It is difficult, for instance, to imagine the majority of Québécois spontaneously warming to the history of a Canadian army that marched into occupied Germany in 1918 singing "The Maple Leaf Forever"—that anthem to the "dauntless hero" James Wolfe who in 1759 vanquished New France, that is, their ancestors. It is just as hard to imagine francophone Quebeckers cheering on, in their imaginations, the enforcers of armed conscription pursuing French Canadians into the woods or shooting them down in the streets of Quebec City.[25] It is equally hard to imagine today's Ukrainian Canadians concluding, on reflection, that their unemployed ancestors had only themselves to blame for their sufferings in Canada's concentration camps. Or Afro-Canadians persuading themselves to identify with the CEF when they were initially excluded from the war and later admitted—but only into construction battalions, with the proviso that they serve under white officers. Or indigenous Canadians, who after serving with distinction returned to blatantly racist policies with respect to resettlement and their pensions.[26]

Vimy as the national origin story can be welcomed without inner reservations mainly by those Anglo-Canadians who retain a fond regard for the British Empire. Since the 1960s the members of this group have become a minority—yet one retaining vast political resources and cultural power. In a country of minorities, without a commanding set of myths and symbols that authoritatively advise the young about who they are, a clearly articulated minority nationalism can be highly seductive, especially for those anxious to integrate into what are still Canada's established elites. Vimyism— promoted by a powerful, determined, and affluent minority—fills a cultural void. Indeed, members of other less privileged minorities can be told that they have a place in this tale. Rather than dwelling on the vast majority of Québécois who opposed the war, we can focus on the valiant Vandoos and the unusually pro-British Talbot Papineau. While remembering (fleetingly) the glaring racism of the CEF and its celebrants, we can focus on plucky Aboriginal Canadians, such as the much-bruited indigenous snipers who succeeded by dint of their individual get-up-and-go. Or, in what is perhaps the most glaring contradiction of all, a Great War in which child soldiers laid down their lives on both sides can be spun as a "coming of age" tale of brave lads finding the inner strength to do their bit.

Vulnerable schoolchildren unequipped to place nationalistic tales in critical perspective are increasingly preyed upon by aggressive campaigners for blood-and-soil nationalism. These advocates clothe their militaristic propaganda in child-friendly tales about furry creatures doing cute things. For years the Veterans Affairs Canada website, in "Information for Students," has been offering a *Veterans Week Teachers' Guide* to help small children learn about war via "Tales of Animals in War." Colour illustrations portray talking animals wearing poppies. In the 2015 guide, Squeaker, Bonfire Jr., Gandy, Win, and their pals are "pretty amazing animal heroes," members of the "Remembrance Club." Rats, detested by Great War combatants because they grew fat on the corpses of dead soldiers and heightened trench life misery, are reimagined to be furry friends in 2015: "Rats *still* serve soldiers today!" the guide exclaims, and cites African rats that help out in efforts to clear land mines—and win peanuts as awards. Not a single rat, the guide reassures children, perishes in the process.[27]

Meanwhile, the Vimy Foundation, keen to promote McCrae's "In Flanders Fields," urged all Canadian schools to mark the poem's centenary by having classes recite it to "pass the torch of remembrance." The luckiest were eligible for an iPad and even a "Vimy Prize Pack." A poem that over the course of its long career has been used to attack pacifists and war profiteers, comfort the bereaved, sell surgical dressings, inspire Americans uncertain about entering the war, and shame French Canadians in 1917— "I hope I stabbed a Fr. Canadian with my vote," exclaimed McCrae in that election year—gains a fresh lease on life: as a sacrament within cash-strapped educational systems, administered by teachers drawing upon the time saving pedagogical resources thoughtfully provided by the state.[28] In Ontario, students in high-school history classes were now finding themselves working on the reconstruction of trenches.

Vimyism thus offers Canadians an uplifting and sacred story of their origins—something to believe in. Inculcated in the very young, it can become accepted as part of the taken-for-granted common sense of the country's history. Yet, in a further paradox, American patterns of consumption and patriotism drive this way of rethinking Canadian history—as that of a unified, uncomplicated, homogeneous people welded together by a war of independence won in a decisive battle. In an ever-more-Americanized culture, pervasive patterns of historical thought feature clashes between heroes and villains, freedom and unfreedom, clear beginnings and decisive outcomes. The martial nationalism of the early twenty-first century contains much that is "Made in the U.S.A."— from its exalted if historically unfounded rhetoric about the freedom fighters of 1914, engaged in our very own "war of independence," to the mass-marketing techniques persuading us that Vimy really was "the birth of the nation."[29] As Arthur Lower complained as early as 1958, there was something drab about a country that did not have a founding revolution or war.[30]

The packaging of Vimy is attractive, and it fits within a much wider culture of war. Hollywood and X-Box do not want for customers. Classic war games such as *Call of Duty* boast sales in the millions. Players interested in refighting the Great War have been able, since 1980, to dive into dozens of games, including titles such as *Verdun* (2013), *1916: Der Unbekannte Krieg* (2012), and *Trenches* (2009). Blasting away at villains and aliens opposed to rights and freedoms, the heroes of today's "shooters" have replaced the mounted cavalry that thrilled Kipling's generation—but they offer players much the same experience of a black-and-white world, with "our" side serving up forceful lessons to "them." In 2014 British historian Joanna Bourke concluded that war-themed video games "come heavily freighted with ideological messages," with players embedded in political space. The space they occupy, however, is "remarkably sanitized: games rarely mention politics, hint about the legitimacy of killing, or admit to "collateral damage." They are saturated with talk of "our troops."[31]

By the mid-2010s an Ottawa-area firm that designs software and training material for the military was hard at work in an effort to provide Canadian aficionados of virtual reality with an enjoyable experience of the Great War in the comfort of their living rooms. SimWave Consulting's virtual reality booth aimed to reproduce trench life during Canada's historic Great War battle using life-like simulations, even "4D effects like wind, heat, cold, a vibrating platform, and soon, smells from the battlefield." Promoters promised that Canadians could enjoy "a history lesson they will never forget." The young would be reminded that the Battle of Vimy Ridge constituted a "big turning point in the war."[32]

For such enterprisers, war is entertaining and spectacular. It can also, as so many video games subtly imply, be part of attaining maturity. The war games indirectly proceed on the assumption that, in Martin Ceadel's words, war is "necessary to development, and that it is thus a positive good."[33] You do not win as a "shooter" if you cannot demonstrate your excellence as a killer and win the great goal—if not securing a glowing future for the British Empire, then at least advancing to the next level.

A romanticized Great War offers a suitable venue for the perpetual restaging of male coming-of-age stories. In his film and novel *Passchendaele* (2008) writer-director-actor Paul Gross emphasizes the mud and mayhem of this most notorious of Canada's Great War battles. Yet such details are not a prelude to a critique of a battle that even General Currie thought a futile waste. Instead, they are but a warm-up to the celebration of the stalwart, brave soldiers who endured it. Their sacrifice—in the words of actor Gross, whose character at one point is depicted as a handsome if beleaguered Christ-like figure carrying his cross on the battlefield— "shaped what it meant to be Canadian. Proud. Strong. Resolute."[34] Just as the Stations of the Cross focus intently on Jesus' tribulations, so that we may all the better appreciate the moral grandeur of His sacrifice, so too do we come to appreciate the nobility of Michael Dunne, the soldier Gross plays. Dunne prevails, complete with cross, over the blood-soaked, exploding mud of Passchendaele. Indeed, the more spectacular the details of our soldiers' suffering, the more sacred their sacrifice.

The membrane between the remembrance of war's hardships and the glorification of those who prevailed over them is, as Michael Enright observes, indeed very thin—especially in a culture that reveres the go-getting individual.[35] The gutsy war hero, winning his spurs, overcoming his fear, undergoing heart-pounding adventures and emerging triumphant over his enemy, has been a staple figure in a multitude of cultures, ours emphatically included. He is not going to exit the stage any time soon.

War remains profoundly attractive, especially to vulnerable minds addicted to its romance and spectacle. It appeals especially to immature young males with short attention spans. It offers a chance for people to imagine themselves as heroic adventurers fighting against evil. And, to a certain sensibility, it is ravishingly beautiful. David Bercuson is hardly alone, although he may be extreme, in his almost orgasmic descriptions of the "sensual experience" of war. He celebrates "the seeing and hearing of sights and sounds that no one else will see or experience."

> It is the "lust of the eye," as the biblical phrase has it. It is the awful beauty of tracer fire at night, of a horizon lit by the gun flashes of a thousand field pieces, of a formation of hundreds of bombers droning through the sky despite bursts of anti-aircraft fire and the wanton attacks of enemy fighters. It is the experience of comradely love so strong as to cause men to sacrifice their lives without a moment's hesitation to save their fellows.[36]

Bercuson's rhapsody recalls the similarly lusty Canon Frederick George Scott, who revered the "true Christian knights" fighting for Canada and a dramatic battlefield that gave him an "electric thrill." He went on to exclaim, "The display of fireworks was magnificent."[37]

*   *   *

When it comes to the Great War, authors are often assigned a pro-war or anti-war position. For some, Will Bird is plainly an anti-war writer because he dwelt upon the sufferings of soldiers; Canon Scott is a pro-war writer because he never ceased to take the side of Canadian soldiers and plainly loved the pyrotechnics of battle.

The trouble with the handy and popular anti-war/pro-war dichotomy is that it imposes a rigid pattern on historical processes of remembering the war that were instead nuanced, dynamic, and contested.[38] Ceadel's helpful categories that sort out how people understand questions of war complicate this discussion, but allow a subtler appreciation of the responses of Canadians to the political and ethical challenge of the Great War.[39] Canada in 1914 was crowded with militarists—people who, like McCrae, "ached for war." For McCrae's friend Macphail, who also enlisted in 1914, "the justification of war" was "the concomitant training, with its regenerative effects on the trainees and ultimately on society at large."[40] Such militarists were joined by crusaders, such as Samuel Chown and Canon Scott, for whom war with Germany was a struggle for Christian values against an ungodly and brutal aggressor. They were accompanied in this belief by more secular thinkers, such as H.G. Wells, who coined the popular phrase "The War That Will End War," and U.S. president Woodrow Wilson, whose "Fourteen Points" foresaw a world order governed by covenants of peace, openly arrived at, always provided that Germany first be militarily defeated. Their pro-war stance was also shared by many defencists, who saw in German espionage and U-boat attacks dangers to the British Empire, to which they (unlike many French Canadians) owed their primary allegiance. Certainly down to 1917, in the majority pro-war camp, these three stances were often combined in pro-war arguments that convinced a good many people.

Yet over the course of the war such arguments suffered a dramatic erosion. Militarists fond of the romantic adventure of war found the Great War's mechanized realities the antithesis of the character-building individualism they revered. For some, the romance of war died on the Somme, where neatly arrayed men, lined up in military tradition, were mowed down by German machine-gunners. For others it died with the gas warfare at Ypres, in which the chemicals destroyed the brave and the cowardly alike; or at the mass grave that was Passchendaele. At home they confronted the squalid realities of a grossly mismanaged war, with its rank profiteering and corruption. After the war, such militarists then engaged with the realities of mass mutilation and shell shock. As for their crusading partners, they too often found the war highly unsettling. The righteous crusade seemed increasingly to require ungodly measures—including what was for many of them the ultimate contradiction of conscription. Forcing men into the army contaminated the purity of the Allied cause. Overseas, many began to mutter that despotism in the British military was little less objectionable than Kaiserism. In the trenches, as innumerable documents suggest, the "Othering" of the Germans as the subhuman pawns of a tyrannical regime waned as Allied soldiers came to see the soldiers on the other side as people more or less like themselves. Both sides worshipped the same God. They were beleaguered with the same lice and mud. They often took the trouble—and the risk—of moving injured enemies from harm's way. The others did not look like monsters. They looked like fellow soldiers.

Both pacificists and pacifists were in a small minority during the early years of the war. But as the war proceeded, their numbers swelled. If hard-line pacifists like Alice Chown were a rarity, pragmatic pacificists were, increasingly, thick on the ground. At home, this stance towards the war took the form of mounting resistance to profiteering and workplace tyranny—provocatively called Canada's own version of "Kaiserism." At the Front, it involved a fast-accelerating grassroots struggle against militarism itself—against meaningless inspections, cruel punishments, and badly botched battles. All of those tendencies called into question not just *how* the war was being fought but the very *why* of the war. An open disrespect for military authority, sometimes erupting into outright mutiny, was a Canadian commonplace in 1918 and 1919. In one of the largest, and least-explored, mass movements in Canadian history, veterans repeatedly rose up angrily against a system that had promised them much and given them little. The novels and memoirs written by soldier-writers (apart from the writers of official regimental histories) routinely included abrasive critiques of the military brass. Many featured striking attacks on the war itself.

Scepticism about the Great War deepened through the 1920s and 1930s. It was by no means limited to the left (indeed, some leftists spurned all such peace talk and hoped for a class war that would end the class system). Arthur Meighen, former Conservative prime minister and nobody's idea of a leftist, explained in 1930 that the one overriding lesson of the

Great War was that it had been won "chiefly by pressure of blockade" applied until the "civil population cracked." For Meighen, war had "lost its efficacy." It could "leave nothing behind but victors in reaction and vanquished in revolution, and all alike impoverished." He argued that war no longer "served a human purpose . . . it solves no problem; it affords no security; it offers no prizes to the victor." Civilization was called upon to end war, Meighen proclaimed, or "war will end civilization."[41]

Meighen and the countless veterans who wrote in response to the release of war photographs in the 1930s were saying that the Great War had taught them something about the dangers of war. But it was not, in its most general sense, "war"—political conflicts that have turned violent, involve state military forces, and entail a considerable loss of life[42]—that so many returned soldiers and so many interwar politicians were rejecting. They were rejecting *this* particular war—which they interpreted as a sign of war's transformation in a modern, mechanized world. For in such a world the very word "war" had changed its meaning. Spatially, it now meant a conflict whose local beginnings—one assassination in a Balkan city—were pregnant with global consequences, endangering people from New Zealand to Siberia. Temporally, it meant a conflict whose formal duration—four years, three months, and fourteen days, by one reckoning— did not correspond to its span as a shaping force in human history: Germany paid its last reparation payment in September 2010.[43] Meighen thought the "groanings" of veterans would extend for two generations. But the burdensome "legacy costs" of the Great War were still weighing upon the Canadian treasury into the 1960s.

Critical, hard-nosed appraisals, including Meighen's, also made reference to a newly obvious condition: war is an incredibly expensive tool of statecraft that can be almost guaranteed not to attain proposed objectives. As Ernie Regehr observes, on the basis of an impressive arsenal of global statistics, armed force is a "highly overrated investment for conflict management." Since the 1970s efforts by states' militaries to impose political objectives have failed about 90 per cent of the time. Back in 1934, when Gregory Clark beheld the sight of German veterans with amputated limbs, part of an "international brotherhood" of some twenty million wounded soldiers on both sides, he exclaimed: "Winners take nothing, losers take less!"[44] This critical, realistic lesson about war, that its costs bear little relationship to its dubious benefits—a belief shared by Meighen and Bennett on the right, Woodsworth on the left, and Mackenzie King in the middle—was driven home ten-fold in a thermonuclear age.

Yet Vimyists work overtime to silence this critical assessment of the Great War. In contemporary Canada, especially in journalistic treatments of peace and war, hard-nosed realists who know the difficult ways of the world are pitted against starry-eyed idealists, deluded products of the age of naive peaceniks, profoundly ignorant of the "real world." To be a realist is to be someone willing to resort to state-sanctioned violence to attain political objectives. But from a different perspective, realists are those willing to measure the intended consequences of a recourse to arms against the likelihood—and the costs—of its achieving its intended objectives. Only a few of those who tried to shape the memory of the Great War before the 1960s—before it began to be subjected to ministrations of romantic militarism—were interested in a wide-ranging philosophical discussion about war in general. But a vast number of such Canadians, from right to left, combatants and non-combatants, the religious and the irreligious, burned with the need to impress the next generation with the vital lesson they had learned from this particular war. The imagined war and the actual war—its bungling mismanagement, harsh despotism, immeasurable cruelty, disappointing outcome, and stupendous long-term costs—were two completely different things. Taking the measure of this new thing called war, people from all sides had drawn critical and realistic conclusions. They now had a far more accurate sense, sometimes abstract and sometimes written into the very texture of their damaged bodies, of what war actually entailed in a twentieth-century world.[45]

Our sense of Vimy as a trap stems in part from our recoiling from the official history's celebration of a bloody and mismanaged war. Might Canadians be well served to reflect upon a Great War record of prisoner-killing and chemical warfare and consider whether such tactics proceed from values we want to perpetuate? After a half-century of ardent struggle for gender parity and racial justice, is it not bizarre to erect as a collective hero the figure of the embezzler Arthur Currie, the archetypical general who died in bed?

Our more substantive objections to Vimyism, however, stem from its childish irrationalism. Our argument that Vimy is a trap proceeds primarily from the critically realistic criteria laid out by Meighen: Vimyism distorts the historical record and falsifies the actual character of modern warfare.

The official Vimy narratives falsify the record through the omission of the events outside the four-day assault on the ridge itself. They erase the *imperial* nature of the war, turning Vimy Ridge into a "Canadian selfie."

They overemphasize Vimy as an event that encouraged Canadians to overcome their country's internal divisions—making an almost total imposition of present-day hopes upon historical complexities. They are naive in imagining that Canada "earned" its autonomy in the Empire because of widespread gratitude for wartime services rendered.[46] They attempt to lure us into a trap of perpetual childhood, of toy soldiers, *Boy's Own Annual*, and gallant men accomplishing great deeds. In essence, they seek to erase the hard-won lessons of actual Great War soldiers and the difficult insight that had percolated even into the hard head of an Arthur Meighen. War had changed; its protagonists were no longer only the soldiers and generals in the field but entire societies. Tens of thousands of Germans died as a result of the Allied blockade, *after the armistice*—an eventuality that in turn helped to poison interwar German politics.

All that was solid had melted into air—to remember Karl Marx's fine old aphorism about the brash new world aborning all around him.[47] How we think about time, space, history, peace, and war has been altered dramatically in a modern capitalist world in which distances are easily conquered by mechanical devices, as so many victims of machine-gun and artillery fire discovered, and by new techniques of communication, as the pervasive use of propagandistic images and stories deployed throughout the war still echo in many a present-day Great War reconstruction.

If we take one last look at Varley's *For What?*—still quietly offering its critique of the war on an obscure wall of a War Museum that has no time for its message—we notice that in Varley's landscape of memory, much that was solid—bodies, the sodden earth, our old martial certainties—has dissolved. Using a conventional landscape form, Varley intuited an unconventional social message: in modern war, even the bodies of the individual dead are no longer easily distinguished from each other.[48] The ideals of pastoralism are upended: the "farmer" in his field, with his folksy cart and white picket fence, is a gravedigger in a blood-soaked terrain planting not a life-giving crop, but dead men. From 1918 onwards, many Canadians looked upon *this* landscape of modernity. And they dared to dream of another.

*   *   *

A short distance away from the War Museum a very different landscape of war was made public on Parliament Hill in 2014. Just before Remembrance Day, the Canadian government unveiled seven new bronze figures that together comprise Parliament Hill's first-ever war memorial. The authorities solemnly deposited some dirt—now inevitably described as "sacred soil"—from War of 1812 battlefields at the base of the fighting figures cast in bronze. The memorial sits in a prominent spot in front of the East Block.

The monument recalls action figures in a toy soldier set marketed to small boys. One fellow is firing a cannon, another a musket. One figure brandishes a knife; another raises a fist. Two of the fighters seem to be Aboriginal (one may be Métis). A woman is bandaging an arm. The statue is not just about patriotism but inclusiveness and diversity. "Canada's Newest Monument Evokes the Memory of War of 1812 Heroes," proclaimed the official press release. "This new landmark on Parliament Hill will forever remind us of the courage and bravery of those who served and successfully defended their land in the fight for Canada more than 200 years ago," intoned Heritage Minister Shelly Glover, failing to mention that the Aboriginal peoples who fought for the Crown were betrayed by the British and lost their land. For sculptor Adrienne Alison, who had previously known little about the War of 1812, the commission was all about history. "After this, I really feel like we, as Canadians, don't know our own history," she said as she began work on the piece. "It's an important thing, to popularize this. It's nation-building." Glover then situated this new monument in the now-sanctified setting of the Great War: "To me, now, this is as important as Vimy Ridge."[49] In martial nationalism, *all* of Canada's wars—even, in this case, one fought before there even *was* a Dominion of Canada—are rolled into one: wherever and whenever the forces of empire were engaged, there we should find our meaning as a people.

On the other side of the ocean, carved in stone, in a German military graveyard at Vladslo, near Ypres, sits a very different memorial. The grave markers lie flat, shaded by mature deciduous trees. A tall rhododendron hedge forms the cemetery boundary, sculpted to grow higher behind two mournful statues that kneel on low pedestals, overlooking the grave of their son. *Musketier* Peter (Pieter) Kollwitz was killed just weeks after the war began. He was eighteen years old.

"It seems so stupid that the boys must go to war," Käthe Kollwitz wrote in her diary shortly before learning of her son's death. "The whole thing is ghastly and insane. Occasionally there comes a foolish thought: how can they possibly take part in such madness?"[50]

When Kollwitz visited the Roggevelde graveyard in 1926 to plan a memorial to her son, she and her husband Karl decided to place the

Käthe Kolwitz's "Grieving Parents." The eminent Expressionist's poignant memorial to her son Pieter, 18, killed in 1914, adorns a German military graveyard near Vladslo, Belgium. "It seems so stupid that the boys must go to war," she wrote. "The whole thing is ghastly and insane."

memorial that would become known as "The Grieving Parents" directly across from the entrance so that the kneeling figures would have the whole cemetery before them. Kollwitz's work—"The Mother" and "The Father"—has no trace of patriotic bombast. Unlike Allward's Vimy Memorial, its scale is modestly human. Many visitors approaching the famous work know that the grave of the artist's son lies a few steps from the statues. Some may sense something else, no less profound than parental grief. It had taken Kollwitz seven years to complete the project. "The memorial begun for Peter had grown to encompass all the victims of the war," suggested one biographer. "It had been the most difficult trial of Kollwitz's life."[51] We are reminded of the anguished question that resounds in Findley's *The Wars*: "What does it mean—*to kill your children*?"

By the time the granite statues were installed in Flanders in 1932, Kollwitz had become one of Germany's leading artists. Her *Revolt of the Weavers* lithograph series graphically illustrates a struggle in which working people organize and carry out an uprising, only to suffer defeat. A dark vision animated much of Kollwitz's work, shaped as it was with the defeat of revolutionary hopes in Germany. Yet it coexisted with a Christian humanism and the conviction that hope lay in resistance. By 1943, after much of her art had been destroyed by the Nazis and her Berlin home reduced to rubble by Allied bombing, she could still note in her diary the creed of an activist artist.

> Every war carries with it the war which will answer it. Every war is answered by a new war, until everything, everything is smashed. . . . That is why I am so wholeheartedly for a radical end to this madness, and why my only hope is for world socialism. . . . Pacifism simply is not a matter of calm looking on; it is hard, hard work.[52]

Kollwitz's work often dwelt with the theme of sacrifice, while avoiding conventional patriotic tropes of soldiers sacrificing themselves for the nation. For Kollwitz, sacrifice often meant women giving themselves up for their children. With respect to the war, it meant that her son had been sacrificed for nothing. Pieter had marched off to the front as an eager volunteer. "Is it a break of faith with you, Peter," Kollwitz wondered, "if I can now see only the madness of the war?" Once she had finished "The Grieving Parents," Kollwitz searched for an exhibition in Berlin where they would be safe. She was worried that they "might be scrawled over with swastikas."[53] After two weeks at the National Gallery, the statues were moved by train to Flanders.

Although the notion of "breaking faith" echoes through McCrae's "In Flanders Fields," the clash between the German Expressionist and the Canadian militarist could not be sharper. McCrae implored his readers not to break with those who die—which meant to continue the killing. Kollwitz, who had done nothing to deter her son from signing up, in part because she accepted the argument that Germany had no choice but to defend itself, was bereft because she believed that her generation had failed to prevent the catastrophe. As Jay Winter explains:

> He had died believing; how could his mother not honour that belief? But to feel that the war was an exercise in futility led to an even more damaging admission that her son and his whole generation had been "betrayed." This recognition was agonizing, but she did not flinch from giving it artistic form. This is one reason why it took her so long to complete the monument, and why she and her husband are on their knees before their son's grave. They are there to beg forgiveness,

to ask him to accept their failure to find a better way, their failure to prevent the madness of war from cutting his life short.[54]

After Kollwitz got the news of her son's death, she wrote: "There is in our lives a wound which will never heal. Nor should it." The message on the principal plaque at the graveyard ends with these words (translated): "The dead of this cemetery cry out for peace." One of the last entries in Kollwitz's diary proclaims: "One day, a new ideal will arise, and there will be an end to all wars. I die convinced of this. It will need much hard work, but it will be achieved. . . . The important thing, until that happens, is to hold one's banner high and to struggle. . . . Without struggle there is no life."[55]

As official Canada bedecked Parliament Hill with a permanent homage to the glories of war, the president of France and the German chancellor together inaugurated a new European war memorial not far from Canada's Vimy Ridge monument. On a far larger scale than Kollwitz's quiet, grief-laden meditation in stone, this European monument is a massive elliptical "Ring of Remembrance" 129 metres long and 75 wide. Part of the ring appears to balance precariously out over the ground, symbolizing the fragile nature of peace. The ring has five hundred panels of bronzed stainless steel that invite visitors to ponder a list of 579,606 names, German and French alike. The Great War killed that many people in Northern France alone. Architect Philippe Prost explained that it is all about reconciliation, to "unite yesterday's enemies." He added, "The Ring is synonymous with unity and eternity. Unity, because the names form a sort of human chain, and eternity because the letters are joined without an end, in alphabetical order without any distinction of nationality, rank or religion."[56]

Canadian actor, playwright, and director R.H. Thomson also turned his back on national distinctions. Having lost five great uncles, killed between 1914 and 1918, he based his play *The Lost Boys* on their letters home. He went on to initiate *The World Remembers/Le monde se souvient*, which entailed the creation of a database of the names of as many of the war dead as possible. "The challenge of Remembrance Day is to honour the dead in ways that communicate the immensity of the loss," Thomson explained. "And surely we must have multiple narratives about the problems of war and the challenges of peace."[57] In 2014 *The World Remembers* began projecting their names in public places—schools, libraries, churches, the walls of public buildings. The display would terminate every 11 November in each of the centenaries of the war years. *The World Remembers* embraced the approach of the transnational Ring of Remembrance. The projected database display featured a Canadian at the centre of the moving image, circled by the rapidly changing names of people from other countries. In 2015 the name of Robert Keenan, for instance, remained on the screen for five minutes. Every twenty-three seconds a ring of names surrounding the Canadian name faded away to be replaced by another group: Ali Mustafa, Turkey. Charles Parker, Great Britain. Otto Weideke, Germany. Alphonse Leroux, France.

Nearly eight decades after the unveiling of Allward's majestic sermon against war at Vimy, in nearby Ablain-Saint-Nazaire, the name of Canadian nurse Katherine Maud McDonald of Brantford, Ont., appeared on the Ring of Remembrance. She was killed at the First Canadian General Hospital in 1918. Placing her name together with those of the German dead, perhaps those who fired the guns that killed her, reflects the transnational spirit of mature mourning and painful reconciliation that suffuses *The World Remembers*.

From Varley and Kollwitz to Prost and Thomson, post-patriotic commemorations take us beyond the narrow nationalisms that have for so long claimed to speak authoritatively about the meanings of state-orchestrated mass death from 1914 to 1918. Archaic, romanticized talk of valour and glory fades away, as does the strutting jingoism of those who would still speak with a glib enthusiasm of wars that they did not directly experience, and the likes of which they themselves will most probably never suffer. Instead, we find realistic, compassionate memorials to the losses of war—and the resolve that such dark and painful days will never again be experienced.

Notes

PROLOGUE

1 Fred Varley to Maud Varley, 19 Oct. 1936; and Varley interview with Lawrence Sabbath, 1960, in Maria Tippett, *Stormy Weather: F.H. Varley, A Biography* (Toronto: McClelland and Stewart, 1998), 85.

2 Quoted in Tippett, *Stormy Weather*, 92, 93.

3 Laura Brandon, *Art or Memorial: The Forgotten History and Canada's War Art* (Calgary: University of Calgary Press, 2006), 18–19.

4 Quoted in Tippett, *Stormy Weather*, 93.

5 Brandon, *Art or Memorial*, 19–20, quoted in C.C. Hill, *The Group of Seven: Art for a Nation* (Toronto: McClelland and Stewart, 1995), 65. The letter is undated but probably written 13 Oct. 1918.

6 Quoted in Tippett, *Stormy Weather*, 108.

7 Dominic Hibberd, *Wilfred Owen: A New Biography* (London: Phoenix, 2003), 346–47.

8 Varley's sister Lilian was visiting London from Sheffield when he got the idea for a title of the grim scene. "We had been talking about war and she said, for what reason Fred?" he recalled in 1964. To which the painter replied, "Thanks Lil— For What?" Tippett, *Stormy Weather*, 109.

I: MYTHS, MEMORIES, AND A CREATION STORY

1 Citizenship and Immigration Canada, *Discover Canada: The Rights and Responsibilities of Citizenship* (Ottawa, 2011).

2 The Corps was formed in September 1915 on the basis of the CEF; the two terms are used interchangeably by many authors.

3 Pierre Berton, *Vimy* (Toronto: McClelland and Stewart, 1986), 45.

4 "Coach's Corner with Don Cherry & Ron MacLean," *Hockey Night in Canada*, 5 April 2014, YouTube, https://www.youtube.com/watch?v=Gjy4cA4kOxk.

5 Citizenship and Immigration Canada, *Discover Canada, 21;* D.E. Macintyre, *Canada at Vimy* (Toronto: Peter Martin Associates, 1967), viii. In the original, Ross's second sentence is: "I thought then, and I think today, that in those few minutes I witnessed the birth of a nation." The "few minutes" he refers to were those following "zero hour" at 5:30 a.m. At that dark hour, in a gale of sleet and snow, he would certainly not have been able to receive any visual impression of seeing Canada "on parade." He clearly uses the term retrospectively; the statement suggests not how the battle was experienced by any actual soldier, but how it was reconstructed in the imagination of someone identifying with the top brass, for whom inspecting a parade would be a normal occurrence. Moreover, the guide's excision of the first two original phrases makes it seem that Ross is describing what would objectively be the case for any normal observer, while he was initially qualifying the experience by telling us that this is what he thought then and thinks now: a much less hubristic, timeless, and totalizing statement than that to be found in the contemporary slogan: "Vimy 1917: Birth of a Nation." D.E. Macintyre was the brother-in-law of the grandfather of one of the present authors, known to him in the 1950s as "Uncle Eberts."

6 *National Post* (Toronto), 9 April 2012.

7 Jonathan Vance, "Remembrance," *Canada's History*, October–November 2014, 32, 37; Vance, *Death So Noble: Memory, Meaning, and the First World War* (Vancouver: UBC Press, 1997), 136; Vance, *Maple Leaf Empire* (Oxford: Oxford University Press, 2012), 103, 132.

8 Tim Cook, *Shock Troops: Canadians Fighting the Great War 1917–1918* (Toronto: Viking Canada, 2008), 625.

9 Sue Malvern, *Modern Art, Britain and the Great War: Witnessing, Testimony and Remembrance* (New Haven, Conn.: Yale University Press, 2004), 5, quoted in Sherrill Grace, *Landscapes of War and Memory: The Two World Wars in Canadian Literature and the Arts, 1977–2007* (Edmonton: University of Alberta Press, 2014), 82.

10 We intend no offence to the students of the Vimy schools in Port Colborne, Ont., and Edmonton, Alta.; to those who live in the hamlet of Vimy Ridge, 59 kilometres north of Edmonton, or Vimy Ridge, Ont., near Highway 11 between Kirkland Lake and Cochrane, or Vimy Ridge, Que., not far from Thetford Mines; nor do we intend any disrespect for fans of the mountain ridge in east-central British Columbia, a sub-range of the Cariboo Mountains, which bears the name "Vimy Ridge." The name has also been applied to countless streets, avenues, roads, and boulevards; the address of the Canadian War Museum is 1 Vimy Place. Many of these places, we are sure, are commodious resorts, not confining traps.

11 It is even possible that the term "Great War" was invented in Canada: see *Maclean's*, October 1914, 53, for the saying, "Some wars name themselves. This is the Great War." The *Oxford English Dictionary*, entry for "Great," led us to this reference.

12 Cook, *Shock Troops*, 433.

13 *Globe and Mail* (Toronto), 17 Nov. 2015.

14 For Donald Schurman, in 1990, it was "almost impossible to imagine Canadian writers protesting in print, either against World War One or its successor. Support for the military goals of the war was a hallmark of the colonial English Canadian." For Mark Sheftall, in 2009, while the interwar years witnessed the rise of cultural works that "emphasized the disillusioning human, material, social and spiritual cost of the conflict," in Canada (along with New Zealand and Australia) the "dominant narrative for the duration of the inter-war period focused on what was achieved between 1914 and 1918 by the nation and its soldiers, rather than on what was lost in the process"(2). See Donald Schurman, "Writing about War," in *Writing about Canada: A Handbook for Modern Canadian History*, ed. John Schultz (Scarborough, Ont.: Prentice-Hall, 1990), 241; Mark Sheftall, *Altered Memories of the Great War: Divergent Narratives of Britain, Australia, New Zealand and Canada* (London: I.B. Taurus, 2009), 57–58. Quite the contrary, we argue: from 1918 to today, and especially from the 1920s to the 1970s, the Great War was a site of contestation, not consensus, in Canada and Quebec.

15 Arthur R.M. Lower, "The Character of Kingston," in *To Preserve and Defend: Essays on Kingston in the Nineteenth Century*, ed. Gerald Tulchinsky (Montreal and Kingston: McGill-Queen's University Press, 1976), 19–20.

16 Jay Winter, "Introduction," to Paul Fussell, *The Great War and Modern Memory* (Oxford: Oxford University Press, 2013), electronic edition, x.

17 Jay Cassel, "Making Canada Safe for Sex: Government and the Problem of Sexually Transmitted Disease in the Twentieth Century," in *Canadian Health Care and the State: A Century of Evolution*, ed. C. David Naylor (Montreal and Kingston: McGill-Queen's University Press, 1992), 122. The use of the sardonic "VD" refers to the greatly elevated levels of venereal disease found in the CEF. See also Desmond Morton, *When Your Number's Up: The Canadian Soldier in the First World War* (Toronto: Random House, 1993), who goes so far as to call VD "the largest public-health issue facing the CEF" (202).

18 "Why I Support the Creation of Valour District," Mayor Paterson's Community Update, 8 May 2015, mayorpaterson.com (September 2015).

19 City of Kingston, *Kingston Commemorations Strategy 2015–2024*, final draft, 14 May 2015.

20 See, for instance, Grace, *Landscapes of War and Memory*. The Kingston discussion provides a fascinating example of Grace's "Landscape of Memory," the contested terrain on which the cultural politics of commemoration get played out.

21 City of Kingston, *Report to Council No. 15-242*, 5 May 2015, Comments 37 and 36.

22 City of Kingston, *Report*, Comment 21.

23 City of Kingston, *Report*, Comment 7.

24 City of Kingston, *Report*, Comment 30.

25 City of Kingston, *Report*, Comments 46, 82.

26 City of Kingston, *Report*, Comment 30.

27 "Kingston—Great War Memorial," 17 Aug. 2013, Ontario War Memorials, ontariowarmemorials.blogspot.ca/2013/08/kingston-great-war-memorial (16 Sept. 2015).

28 Gavin Stamp, *The Memorial to the Missing of the Somme* (London: Profile Books, 2007), 103.

29 Quoted in Sandra Gwyn, *Tapestry of War: A Private View of Canadians in the Great War* (Toronto: Harper Collins, 1992), 399. According to Geoff Keelan, the memory of Talbot Papineau was "constructed entirely by Canada's English-speaking majority," in search of a reassuring image of a rare French-Canadian "patriot" who signed onto their "wartime nation-building exercise." For Keelan, the invention of Papineau as a significant "voice of francophone Québec" constitutes not only the retrieval of a forgotten history but also the deliberate use of an atypical story to achieve political objectives—an "abuse of history." See Geoff Keelan, "The Forgotten Few: Quebec and the Memory of the First World War," in *The Great War: From Memory to History*, ed. Kellen Kurschinski, Steve Marti, Alicia Robinet, Matt Symes, and Jonathan F. Vance (Waterloo, Ont.: Wilfrid Laurier University Press, 2015), 236.

30 Grace, *Landscapes of War and Memory*, 213–14, 215.

31 A popular spot with visitors remains the execution site at Poperinge, Belgium, where the British routinely shot their own men. The local tourist bureau ("Centre of hops and beer") describes it with characteristic distaste. "One can still visit the restored cell block with audiotape and the execution pole as a symbol of the insanity of war." See "Death Cells and Execution Spot," http://www.toerismepoperinge.be/en/pagina/1211-1220-1254/executieplaats-en-dodencellen.html (November 2015).

32 Maarten Van Alstein, *The Great War Remembered: Commemoration and Peace in Flanders Fields*, Report, Flemish Peace Institute, Brussels, November 2011, 51.

33 Quoted in Van Alstein, *Great War Remembered*, 16.

34 Van Alstein, *Great War Remembered*, 9, emphasis added.

35 Grace, *Landscapes of War and Memory*, 31.

36 Van Alstein, *Great War Remembered*, 12.

37 Van Alstein, *Great War Remembered*, 30, 41.

38 Van Alstein, *Great War Remembered*, 30.

39 Van Alstein, *Great War Remembered*, 30.

40 W. Erauw, *Herinneringscultur, herenkingsplicht en de historici in onze democratie* (2006), quoted in Van Alstein, *Great War Remembered*, 28.

41 George L. Mosse, *Fallen Soldiers: Reshaping the Memory of the World Wars* (New York: Oxford University Press, 1990), 70–71.

42 Mosse, *Fallen Soldiers*, 72.

43 Adolf Hitler, *Mein Kampf* (New York: Reynal and Hitchcock, 1941), Internet Archive, http://www.hitler.org/writings/Mein_Kampf/; https://archive.org/stream/meinkampf035176mbp/meinkampf035176mbp_djvu.txt.

44 Mosse, *Fallen Soldiers*, 72–73.

45 "Sassoon's Public Statement of Defiance," 31 July 1913, All Poetry, http://allpoetry.com/Sassoon's-Public-Statement-Of-Defiance (December 2015); emphasis added.

46 Interview with Piet Chielens, April 2014, www.youtube.com/watch?v=ODcQ7Io6vzs (September 2015).

47 Van Alstein, *Great War Remembered*, 66.

48 P. Chielens, D. Dendooven, and A. Vandenbilcke, *In Flanders Fields Museum Guide* (Ypres: IFFM, 2014), 7, 15.

49 Jay Winter, *Remembering War: The Great War between Memory and History in the Twentieth Century* (New Haven, Conn. and London: Yale University Press, 2006), 227.

50 Chielens, Dendooven, and Vandenbilcke, *In Flanders Fields Museum Guide*, 121–37.

51 Kip Pegley, "Music and the 'Feminized' Peacekeeper at the Canadian War Museum," Queen's University Cultural Studies Colloquium Series, Kingston, Ont., 20 March 2013.

52 IFFM, Script: Third Ypres, "'Memory, let all slip . . .' The Battlefield & the Hospital Ward." La Motte's book *The Backwash of War* was based on diaries she kept at a field hospital in Flanders. Published in 1916, it was powerful—and unpalatable—enough to be suppressed until 1934. Ellen N. La Motte, *The Backwash of War: The Human Wreckage of the Battlefield as Witnessed by an American Hospital Nurse* (New York: G.P. Putnam's Sons, 1916), available archive.org.

53 Quoted in Van Alstein, *Great War Remembered*, 16.

54 Van Alstein, *Great War Remembered*, 12.

55 Interview with Chielens, April 2014.

2: A GREAT WAR OF ATTRITION AND FUTILITY: A CAPSULE HISTORY

1 See, with respect to the debates within the British cabinet, Douglas Newton, *The Darkest Days: The Truth Behind Britain's Rush to War, 1914* (London and New York: Verso, 2015). John Morley, Gladstone's biographer and a towering intellectual among liberals in the Anglosphere, was among those who believed the case for the war to be weak. What might have happened if these debates within the British cabinet had swung the other way—which they almost did—is one of the great "what ifs?" of history. Many historians are allergic to such counterfactual propositions; yet they arise almost irresistibly when pondering each of the component decisions that led so many statesmen, who seemingly had little to gain from war, into so vast a cataclysm. See Niall Ferguson, *The Pity of War: Explaining World War I* (New York: Basic Books, 2000). J.L. Granatstein et al., *Twentieth Century Canada* (Toronto: McGraw-Hill Ryerson, 1983), 93, persuasively argue the case that "Britain bore some of the responsibility" for the war, having contributed to "the intrigues of European diplomacy."

2 For the team of Protestant ministers, M.F. McCutcheon et al., eds., *The Christian and War: An Appeal* (Toronto: McClelland and Stewart, 1926), 8; loss of civilians, N.P. Howard, "The Social and Political Consequences of the Allied Food Blockade of Germany, 1918-19," *German History* 11, 2 (1993), 166. The blockade contravened international law, traditionally solicitous of civilians caught up in war. Overall estimates of the German lives cost by the British blockade sometimes run as high as a million. All estimates of deaths caused by blockades then and now are subject to debate because they generally rely upon demographic data, not direct reports of deaths. An estimated 271,000 civilian deaths occurred in 1918.

3 George Perley, Acting Prime Minister, Armistice Day Statement, 11 Nov. 1930, LAC, Bennett Papers, MG 26 K, M-1463, 506073.

4 Christopher Clark, *The Sleepwalkers: How Europe Went to War in 1914* (New York: Harper, 2012), 553. The details of the coming of the Great War will always be worth studying in depth, and they have greatly enriched many a course in international relations and diplomacy.

5 J.L. Granatstein, *The Last Good War: An Illustrated History of Canada in the Second World War, 1939–1945* (Vancouver and Toronto: Douglas and McIntyre, 2005), viii.

6 Quoted in Jeffrey Keshen, *Propaganda and Censorship during Canada's Great War* (Edmonton: University of Alberta Press, 1996), 14. Keshen's book is an indispensible guide to the state's manipulation of public sentiment

7 For a Canadian adaptation of this argument, and an illustration of some of its rhetorical consequences, see J.L. Granatstein, "Thirty Years of War," *Canada's History*, October–November 2014, 20–29.

8 See Margaret MacMillan, *Paris 1919: Six Months That Changed The World* (New York: Random House, 2003), in which an accomplished story-teller and Lloyd George's granddaughter develops the best case imaginable for the Versailles negotiations. That many of the most powerful participants believed they had put off a further war by a mere twenty years goes unemphasized; as does Lloyd George's own corrosive scepticism about the conference and treaty.

9 Hew Strachan, one of the most eminent of the British World War historians, argues that with the withdrawal of the Russians from the conflict in 1917, its underlying issue—lawful liberty against lawless tyranny—was more sharply posed. Strachan, *The First World War* (New York: Viking, 2004).

10 David Stevenson, *The First World War and International Politics* (Oxford: Oxford University Press, 1988), addresses the role of the armaments race in accelerating the war.

11 Tim Cook, *At the Sharp End: Canadians Fighting the Great War 1914–1916* (Toronto: Viking Canada, 2007), 455.

12 See, for example, Edward Paice, *Tip & Run: The Untold Tragedy of the Great War in Africa* (London: Phoenix, 2008), 392–94; according to British colonial officials, "The full scale of the mortality among [the] native carriers will never be told." For an estimate of 90,000 African porters killed in Britain's Great War, see Hew Strachan, *The First World War in Africa* (Oxford: Oxford University Press, 2004), 641, 548; the death toll on the German side is more difficult to compute. Including deaths from famine and disease connected to the war would push the statistics even higher.

13 For the Canadian statistics, see Cook, *At the Sharp End*, 612, 708, n.6. The worldwide numbers assume even more astronomical levels under the plausible theory that the influenza pandemic of 1918–20 (believed to have killed more than 50,000,000 people) was directly related to the war. For an accessible account, see John M. Barry, *The Great Influenza: The Epic Story of the Greatest Plague in History* (New York: Viking Penguin, 2004).

14 As Strachan points out, from the perspective of Helmuth von Moltke, chief of the German general staff, it was "progressively clearer that any war would be fought

by coalitions," a condition that "reduced to vanishing point the chances of a quick decisive victory. If one power defeated another in short order, the victory would not end the war. The conquered power would be bailed out by its ally." Strachan, *First World War*, 42.

15 Robert Craig Brown and Ramsay Cook, *Canada 1896–1921: A Nation Transformed* (Toronto: McClelland and Stewart, 1974), 226; Hughes quoted in Tim Cook, *The Madman and the Butcher: The Sensational Wars of Sam Hughes and General Arthur Currie* (Toronto: Allen Lane, 2010), 16.

16 Kenneth Kingston of Alma, N.B., to S.D. Chown, 25 Nov. 1916, Chown Papers, United Church of Canada Archives (UCA), Box 1, File 13.

17 Ernest J. Chambers, *The Governor-General's Body Guard* (Toronto, 1902), 121, as quoted in Carl Berger, *The Sense of Power: Studies in the Ideas of Canadian Imperialism 1867–1914* (Toronto: University of Toronto Press, 1970), 234. Militarist arguments predicated on war's evolutionary benefits for humanity as a whole are explored in Mark Moss, *Manliness and Militarism: Educating Young Boys in Ontario for War* (Don Mills, Ont.: Oxford University Press, 2001), ch.3.

18 "Why Is Canada at War? The Essays That Won the Prizes in the Competition Conducted by the Herald and Mail," *Halifax Herald*, 26 Dec. 1914, 20 Jan. 1915.

19 Ian McKay, "The 1910s: The Stillborn Triumph of Progressive Reform," in *The Atlantic Provinces in Confederation*, ed. E.R. Forbes and Del Muise (Toronto: University of Toronto Press and Fredericton, N.B.: Acadiensis Press, 1993), 207.

20 Quoted in McKay, "The 1910s," 203.

21 D.E. Macintyre, *Canada at Vimy* (Toronto: Peter Martin Associates, 1967), 6.

22 Keshen, *Propaganda and Censorship*, 76.

23 Normally depicted as a purely aggressive strategy—such was certainly the consensus among Canadians in 1914—the Schlieffen Plan was probably a more complicated defensive concept, calculated to create a counterattack in the event of a French invasion—although debate about it has been extremely arduous, especially since the uncovering of new documents in the archives of the now-defunct German Democratic Republic.

24 See, for instance, Strachan, *First World War*, 163–64.

25 See Col. G.W.L. Nicholson, *Canadian Expeditionary Force 1914–1919: Official History of the Canadian Army in the First World War* (Ottawa: Queen's Printer, 1962). The Currie Building in the Royal Military College, Kingston, also has a plaque listing the battles.

26 A.J.P. Taylor, *The First World War: An Illustrated History* (London: Penguin, 1966), 194.

27 D.J. Goodspeed, *The Road Past Vimy: The Canadian Corps 1914–1918* (Toronto: Macmillan of Canada, 1969), 135, notes: "The popular vote . . . reflected far more accurately the real split in the country. The civilian vote in Prince Edward Island, Nova Scotia, Quebec and the Yukon went against the government, and the total civilian vote for all Canada was 841,944 for the government and 744,849 against it, giving the conscriptionists a civilian majority of only 97,095. The soldiers' vote, however, was 215,849 in favour of the government and 18,522 against. In any case, the country was divided as never before in its history." The debate

over conscription is not reducible to a squabble between English and French Canadians.

28 David Tough, "A Better Truth: The Democratic Legacy of Resistance to Conscription, 1917–1921," in *Worth Fighting For: Canada's Tradition of War Resistance from 1812 to the War on Terror*, ed. Lara Campbell, Michael Dawson, and Catherine Gidney (Toronto: Between the Lines, 2015).

29 Brown and Cook, *Canada 1896–1921*, 249. In Cook and Brown's summation, "In the name of preserving 'civilization'—a civilization that was rooted in the assumed continuance of a *laissez-faire* style of economic life in pre-war Canada—. . . the government of Canada had changed it almost beyond recognition."

30 Tim Cook, *Shock Troops: Canadians Fighting the Great War 1917–1918* (Toronto: Viking Canada, 2008), 207, 583, 593.

3: IN THE WAKE OF WAR: EXPERIENCING AND REMEMBERING

1 S.D. Chown, "My Life," manuscript biography, United Church Archives (UCA), Toronto, File 16-457, 77–78.

2 Chown, "My Life," 77–78.

3 Grace MacInnis, *J.S. Woodsworth: A Man to Remember* (Toronto: Macmillan, 1953), 104–5.

4 Chown, "My Life," 85.

5 Chown, "My Life," 91–92.

6 Chown, "My Life," 90–91.

7 McCrae "ached for war" in Tim Cook, "Forged in Fire," in *In Flanders Fields: Writing on War, Loss and Remembrance*, ed. Amanda Betts (Toronto: Alfred A. Knopf Canada, 2015), 34; Macphail in Ian Ross Robertson, *Sir Andrew Macphail: The Life and Legacy of a Canadian Man of Letters* (Montreal and Kingston: McGill-Queen's University Press, 2008), 192.

8 Robertson, *Sir Andrew Macphail*, 191, 192, 157, 177.

9 S.D. Chown to Ministers, Members and Adherents of the Methodist Church, n.d. [1917], UCA, Chown Fonds, Box 1, File 13; S.D. Chown to Rev. S.D. Chown to Members and Adherents of the Methodist Church of Canada, 8 Dec. 1916, UCA, Chown Fonds, Box 1, File 13; Draft of Sermon on Psalm 4.1. "Thou has set me at large when I was in distress," n.d. [1915], UCA, Chown Fonds, Box 3, File 71.

10 S.D. Chown, "A Call to Prayer," *Christian Guardian*, 3 April 1918; Chown to Rev. J.C. Reid, 28 Feb. 1917, and Chown to Rev. Kenneth Kingston, 30 Nov. 1916 (personal), both UCA, Chown Fonds, Box 1, File 13; Michael Bliss, "The Methodist Church and World War I," *Canadian Historical Review* 49 (1968), 217, 218–19. Chown said that Kingston-area officers were putting down as "Church of England" all who said they were Protestant.

11 Pierre Berton, *Marching as to War: Canada's Turbulent Years 1899-1953* (Toronto: Anchor Canada, 2002), 199, citing the Toronto *News*; in a similar vein, a Unionist politician attacked Quebec as "a plague spot on the whole Dominion."

12　H.P. Almon Abbott, *The Religion of the Tommy: War Essays and Addresses* (Milwaukee: Morehouse Publishing, 1918), 36, 34.

13　S.D. Chown, "Outline of Address—British Wesleyan Conference," July 1917, UCA, Chown Fonds, Box 12, File 309.

14　S.D. Chown to Hon. George P. Graham, 4 June 1918, UCA, Chown Fonds, Box 1, File 16.

15　S.D. Chown to Hon. George P. Graham, 4 June 1918, UCA, Chown Fonds, Box 1, File 16; Paul Fussell, *The Great War and Modern Memory* (Oxford: Oxford University Press, 2000 [1975]), 21–23. In Fussell's witty examples of High Diction, for example, a horse becomes a "steed, or charger," the enemy is "the foe, or the host," and danger is "peril." To enlist is to "join the colors" and the sky is "the heavens." As Fussell puts it: "Every war constitutes an irony of situation because its means are so melodramatically disproportionate to its presumed ends. . . . But the Great War was more ironic than any before or since. It was a hideous embarrassment to the prevailing Meliorist myth which had dominated the public consciousness for a century. It reversed the Idea of Progress" (7–8).

16　Alice Amelia Chown, *The Stairway* (Boston: Cornhill Company, 1921), 12.

17　Chown, *Stairway*, 68; M. Conway Turton, "An Outrageous Idealist," *Canadian Comment*, October 1935, 8.

18　Thomas P. Socknat, *Witness Against War: Pacifism in Canada 1900–1945* (Toronto: University of Toronto Press, 1987), 56. The women pacifists in Canada included Rose Henderson, Frances Benyon, Gertrude Richardson, and Laura Hughes. See Peter Campbell, *Rose Henderson: A Woman for the People* (Montreal and Kingston: McGill-Queen's University Press, 2010), ch.6; Barbara Roberts, *A Reconstructed World: A Feminist Biography of Gertrude Richardson* (Montreal and Kingston: McGill-Queen's University Press, 1996); and Francis Marion Beynon, "Woman and War," *Grain Growers' Guide*, 31 July 1912, 9, as cited in Ian McKay, *Reasoning Otherwise: Leftists and the People's Enlightenment in Canada, 1890–1920* (Toronto: Between the Lines, 2008), 310. As early as 1912 Beynon's sceptical appraisal of war was drawing the hostile notice of her more militaristic readers.

19　Quoted in Roberts, *A Reconstructed World*, 186.

20　Alice Chown, "Open Letter to Pacifists," *Christian Guardian*, 1 March 1916 (letter and response).

21　W.L.M. King, Diary, 24 Dec. 1916, Library and Archives Canada (LAC), Ottawa, MG26-J13.

22　Chown, "Open Letter to Pacifists."

23　Alice Chown, "Miss Chrystal MacMillan," *Toronto World*, 4 Nov. 1916 (letter); "Miss Chrystal MacMillan," *Toronto World*, 4 Nov. 1916 (editorial).

24　Alice Chown, "The Paxist Gospel," *Toronto World*, 10 Nov. 1916 (letter); "The Anti-War Blindness," *Toronto World*, 10 Nov. 1916 (editorial).

25　Alice Chown to S.D. Chown, 17 Dec. 1918, UCA, Chown Fonds, Box 1, File 6.

26　As Fussell, *Great War and Modern Memory*, points out, "modern irony"—stimulated by the stark contrast between expectation and experience—was one of the great cultural legacies of the Great War. Fussell focuses on famous, upper-class writers—which, his critics argued, meant that his generalizations did not apply to the war in general, fought as it mainly was by unlettered servicemen cheered along by equally unlettered patriots. See, for example, Rosa Maria Bracco, *Merchants of Hope: British Middlebrow Writers and the First World War, 1919–1939* (Providence and Oxford: Berg, 1993); and Janet S.K. Watson, *Fighting Different Wars: Experience, Memory, and the First World War in Britain* (Cambridge: Cambridge University Press, 2004). Yet the evidence of many Canadian soldiers' letters suggests that, in appropriate contexts—that is, *not* in letters of condolence and *not* in terms that would bring down the wrath of the censor—they waxed as ironically about the war as many of its best-known disillusioned poets.

27 Tim Cook, *Shock Troops: Canadians Fighting the Great War 1917–1918* (Toronto: Viking Canada, 2008), 183.

28 Tim Cook, *At the Sharp End: Canadians Fighting the Great War 1914–1916* (Toronto: Viking Canada, 2007), 263, 185, 304; Cook, *Shock Troops*, 323. Cook suggests that most soldiers would have agreed with these sentiments.

29 Cook, *Sharp End*, 15, 201. For a prime example of "trench irony," see Marcelle Cinq-Mars, ed., *L'Echo du front* (Outremont, Que.: Athéna, 2008), which mines little-consulted trench newspapers for cartoons—including one from the *Listening Post* in which a man asks another man who is nervously going into the trenches for a loan of five dollars because the man being asked would probably not be in any further need of money.

30 Cook, *Shock Troops*, 290.

31 Cook, *Shock Troops*, 290, 396.

32 David Marshall, "'Khaki Has Become a Sacred Colour': The Methodist Church and the Sanctification of World War One," in *Canadian Churches and the First World War*, ed. Gordon L. Heath, McMaster Divinity College Press, McMaster General Series 4 (Eugene, Ore.: Pickwick Publications, 2014), 119.

33 S.D. Chown, "Outline of Address—British Wesleyan Conference," July 1917, UCA, Chown Fonds, Box 12, File 309.

34 Pierre Berton, *Vimy* (Toronto: McClelland and Stewart, 1986), 120, 121. For Canadian soldiers killing prisoners, see, for instance, Cook, *At the Sharp End*, 451. On Germans and the reputation of Canadians for prisoner-killing, see Robert Engen, "The Canadian Soldier: Combat Motivation in the Second World War, 1943–1945," Ph.D. dissertation, Queen's University, Kingston, Ont., 2014. For "mad enterprise," Cook, *At the Sharp End*, 297. Engen, "Canadian Soldier," ch. 7, presents convincing documentation of prisoner-killing, looting, and sexual assaults committed by Canadian troops in Europe in the Second World War. This thesis has since been published: *Strangers in Arms: Combat Motivation in the Canadian Army, 1943–1945* (Montreal and Kingston: McGill-Queen's University Press, 2016). Documentation of prisoner-killing and German reprisals against Canadians on that account can be found in J.L. Granatstein, *The Greatest Victory: Canada's One Hundred Days, 1918* (Don Mills, Ont.: Oxford University Press, 2014), 30–31; 152–53, which indicates Currie's knowledge of the slaughtering of German POWs.

35 Quoted in Andrew Iarocci, "The 1st Canadian Division: An Operational Mosaic," in *Vimy Ridge: A Canadian Reassessment*, ed. Geoffrey Hayes, Andrew Iarocci, and

Mike Bechthold (Waterloo, Ont.: Laurier Centre for Military Strategic and Disarmament Studies, 2010), 160.

36 Cook, *Shock Troops*, 306, "penalty for killing," 253.

37 W.H. Roberts to Borden, 26 Sept. 1919, LAC, Borden Papers, MG 26 H1, C-4414, 134205-06; Jack Kavanagh to Borden, 7 July 1919, LAC, Borden Papers, MG 26 H1, C-4365, 83130. For Flavelle, see Michael Bliss, *A Canadian Millionaire: The Life and Business Times of Sir Joseph Flavelle, Bart., 1858–1939* (Toronto: Macmillan of Canada, 1978). For a useful re-examination of wartime profiteers, see Ryan Targa, "From Governors to Grocers: How Profiteering Changed English-Canadian Perceptions of Liberalism in the Great War of 1914–1918," M.A. thesis, Queen's University, Kingston, Ont., 2013. Contrary to the line peddled by the Canadian War Museum, the profiteer was hardly a figure of the "emotional" imagination of overheated Canadians: there is a wealth of evidence showing how thoroughly well-connected businessmen and politicians used the old tricks of patronage in the new world of total war.

38 "Some Gains in This War," 4 Aug. 1916, UCA, Chown Fonds, Box 11, File 306.

39 S.D. Chown to Rev. Kenneth Kingston, 30 Nov. 1916 (personal), UCA, Chown Fonds, Box 1, File 13.

40 See Sigmund Freud, *Civilization and Its Discontents*, trans. J. Strachey (New York: Norton, 1962). For a discussion of the impact of the Great War upon Freud and the "death drive," see David Reynolds, *The Long Shadow: The Legacies of the Great War in the Twentieth Century* (New York and London: W.W. Norton, 2014), 193–94. For the attitudes of U.S. historians with respect to the war, see Charles A. Beard and Mary Beard, *The Rise of American Civilization* (New York: Macmillan, 1930), who view the conventional account of the Central Powers' unmitigated guilt as "the story for babes" (617); and Sidney Bradshaw Fay, *The Origins of the World War*, 2 vols. (New York: Macmillan, 1929), a temperate and measured work concluding: "All the European countries, in a greater or less degree, were responsible. One must abandon the dictum of the Versailles Treaty that German and her allies were solely responsible" (548–49). For contemporary evaluations of their work, see Ernst A. Breisach, *American Progressive History: An Experiment in Modernization* (Chicago and London: University of Chicago Press, 1993); and Ellen Fitzpatrick, *History's Memory: Writing America's Past 1880–1980* (Cambridge, Mass., and London: Harvard University Press, 2002). For J.M. Keynes's still influential critique of the Versailles Treaty, see J.M. Keynes, *The Economic Consequences of the Peace* (New York: Harcourt, Brace and Howe, 1920).

41 Robertson, *Sir Andrew Macphail*, 189, 182, 184, 188, 211.

42 John Buchan (Lord Tweedsmuir), *Canadian Occasions* (Toronto: Musson Book Company, 1940), 213. For Buchan's view of the war as a "folly," see Andrew Lownie, *John Buchan: The Presbyterian Cavalier* (Toronto: McArthur and Company, 2004), 126. The protagonist in the last of Buchan's many adventure novels reflects on how the "memories of the war in which he had fought raced before him like a cinema show" and decides: "It had been waste, futile waste, and death, illimitable, futile death." John Buchan, *Sick Heart River* (Toronto: Musson, 1941), 295. For Buchan's grief-saturated reflections on the friends he lost in the Great War, see *These for Remembrance: Memoirs of 6 Friends Killed in the Great War* (London:

Buchan and Enright, 1919). As Peter Vansittart remarks in his Introduction: "John Buchan did not look back on the Great War as a romantic crusade. His brother Alastair had been killed at Arras in 1917. . . . His closest friends had perished. He knew that behind optimistic headlines were men with blood bubbles instead of eyes, or reduced to a hand thrust from the mud, or a muddled shape crucified on barbed wire. Amongst much else, Buchan would have remembered Canadian soldiers ordered to dig their own graves, before assaulting Vimy Ridge, 1917" (np).

43 S.D. Chown, "World Reconstruction: An Address Delivered at the Methodist Centenary Celebration, Columbus, Ohio, July 10th, 1919, by the Rev. S.D. Chown, D.D, L.L.D," UCA, Chown Fonds; S.D. Chown, Sermon, 30 Aug. 1923, on the text "John 12:21—'Sir, we want to see Jesus.'" UCA, Chown Fonds, Box 3, File 73.

44 S.D. Chown, "The Abolition of War," n.d. [c.1924], UCA, Chown Fonds, Box 5, File 113; Chown, "World Reconstruction."

45 Chown, "Abolition of War."

46 For Creighton's about-face on war—"a hideous, utterly unchristian, unforgivable crime"—see Donald Wright, *Donald Creighton: A Life in History* (Toronto: University of Toronto Press, 2015), 59. The historian Donald Creighton was W.B. Creighton's son.

47 Jonathan Vance, *Death So Noble: Memory, Meaning, and the First World War* (Vancouver: UBC Press, 1997), 263; Berton, *Vimy*, 295.

48 Robert Service, "Only a Boche," and "My Foe," in *Rhymes of a Red Cross Man* (Toronto: William Briggs, 1916). This book was number one on the U.S. nonfiction list for both 1917 and 1918, outselling John McCrae's *In Flanders Fields*. Klay Dyer, Denis Saint-Jacques, and Claude Martin, "Best-Sellers," in *History of the Book in Canada*, vol.3, *1918–1980*, ed. Carole Gerson and Jacques Michon (Toronto: University of Toronto Press, 2007), 460. Brian Douglas Tennyson, in his excellent resource *The Canadian Experience of the Great War: A Guide to Memoirs* (Lanham, Md., Toronto, and Plymouth, UK: Scarecrow Press, 2013), lists no fewer than 37 books of poetry published from 1916 to 1919, which is almost certainly an underestimate; for instance, he misses Alfred Gordon, *'Vimy Ridge' and New Poems* (Toronto: Dent, 1918). These books, and probably most of the others he lists, were celebrations of the war effort, not critiques.

49 Many of the dogs were killed on orders of the high command, in a move not calculated to mitigate tensions between the Brass and the enlisted men. See Cook, *At the Sharp End*, 250. Even Canon Frederick George Scott's beloved terrier Alberta was executed by a sergeant of the French police; the renowned padre dissuaded the dog's many fans from exacting revenge by reminding them that "we had a war on with the Germans, and that we had better not start another till it was finished." Canon Frederick Scott, *The Great War as I Saw It* (Kingston: Legacy Books Press, 2009 [Toronto: F.D. Goodchild, 1922]), 220.

50 Jack Munroe, *Mopping Up! A Dog Story of the Princess 'Pats'* (New York: H.K. Fly Company, 1918), 163–67. Bobbie goes on to distinguish the "Canadian brand of ruthlessness" from the more treacherous and dissimulating ruthlessness of "Fritz" (293).

51 Quoted in Dorothy Farniloe, *The Legend of Jack Munroe: A Portrait of a Canadian Hero* (Windsor: Black Moss Press, 1994), 185.

52 Munroe, *Mopping Up!* 119.

53 Harold R. Peat, *Private Peat* (Indianapolis: Bobbs-Merill, 1917), 175, 85, 132, 162, 154, 219. A similarly propagandistic anti-German tone was struck by Ralph Connor in *The Major* (New York: George H. Doran, 1917). For the film version (1918) see silenthollywood.com/privatepeat1918 (January 2016).

54 Philip Gibb, *Now It Can Be Told* (New York and London: Harper Brothers, 1920), 505.

55 Harold R. Peat, *The Inexcusable Lie* (Chicago: R.R. Donnelly and Sons, 1923), 36.

56 Peat, *Inexcusable Lie*, 126.

57 In *The Inexcusable Lie* Peat remembers reading about the British prime minister pressing the button that sets off the great explosion that inaugurated "the famous ridge of Passchendaele," and dwells upon the ease with which the word "annihilation" was applied to "the death of possibly three thousand men" (164–66). His "memory" thus enhanced the Vimy story with a button-pushing prime minister and seemingly confused Vimy with Passchendaele.

58 James H. Pedley, *Only This: A War Retrospect, 1917–1918* (Ottawa: CEF Books, 1999 [1927]), 13 ("real curtains"), 182 ("not a bad war"), 194 ("getting out of bed"), 30 ("Guts-and-Gaiters"), 125 (block quotation).

59 Pedley, *Only This*, 168, 167.

60 Wilfred Kerr, *Shrieks and Crashes: The Memoir of Wilfred Kerr, Canadian Field Artillery, 1917* (Ottawa: CEF Books, 2005 [Toronto: Hunter Rose, 1929]), Foreword; 111 (quoting Herodotus), 138, 33, 92–93, 99 (the necessity of orders).

61 Tim Cook, "'Literary Memorials': The Great War Regimental Histories, 1919–1939," *Journal of the Canadian Historical Association* 13, 1 (2002): 167–190 (especially 183n61).

62 Kerr, *Shrieks and Crashes*, Foreword ("There was a gulf"), 101–2.

63 Kerr, *Shrieks and Crashes*, 137.

64 Kerr, *Shrieks and Crashes*, 138 ("asses"), 156, 25 (Vimy). In a second book, Wilfred Kerr, *Arms and the Maple Leaf: The Memoir of Wilfred Kerr, Canadian Field Artillery, Canadian Expeditionary Force, 1918* (Ottawa: CEF Boos, 2005 [Seaforth, Ont.: Huron Expositor, 1943]), Kerr brings out what is implicit in this passage, which is that the dull British general staff had required instruction by Ludendorff, "instructor to our Generals in the new tactics" (104).

65 M.F. McCutcheon, Allan P. Shatford, W.A. Gifford, Richard Roberts, W.D. Reid, and T.W. Jones, eds., *The Christian and War: An Appeal* (Toronto: McClelland and Stewart, 1926), 13 (aims), 99–100 (disease germs).

66 McCutcheon et al., eds., *Christian and War*, 105, citing an article by St. John Ervine in *The Nation*, 21 July 1921. For a sober reflection on this question, see Tim Cook, "The Politics of Surrender: Canadian Soldiers and the Killing of Prisoners in the Great War," *Journal of Military History* 70,3 (July 2006): 637–65. As Cook concludes: "It might be tempting to ascribe these unlawful actions to undisciplined or inexperienced soldiers, but they appear to have happened throughout the war,

in almost every battle from 1915 to 1918, and were recounted in official reports and personal memoirs, carried out by the lowest private to junior subalterns, and sanctioned by senior officers from lieutenant-colonels to the corps commander" (664–65).

67 McCutcheon et al., eds., *Christian and War*, 106.

68 McCutcheon et al., eds., *Christian and War*, 117.

69 The label "Literature of Disillusionment" might be queried for implying that its key figures wrote purely out of their own emotional letdown by the war; and both in Canada and internationally it has become fashionable to view these writers as out-of-touch personalities who disparaged the ordinary soldier and took liberties with the facts. Yet our brief overview of Service alone suggests a more cautious verdict. See especially Brian Bond, *The Unquiet Western Front: Britain's Role in Literature and History* (New York: Oxford University Press, 2002); Allyson Booth, *Postcards from the Trenches* (New York and Oxford: Oxford University Press, 1996); R.M. Bracco, *Merchants of Hope: British Middlebrow Writers and the First World War, 1919–1939* (Oxford: Oxford University Press, 1993); Modris Ecksteins, *The Rites of Spring: The Great War and the Birth of the Modern Age* (London: Bantam Press, 1989); Allen Frantzen, *Bloody Good: Chivalry, Sacrifice, and the Great War* (Chicago, 2004); Mark Sheftall, *Altered Memories of the Great War: Divergent Narratives of Britain, Australia, New Zealand and Canada* (London: I.B. Taurus, 2009); and Dan Todman, *The Great War: Myth and Memory* (London: Hambledon Continuum 2005). For a judicious overview, see Adrian Barlow, *The Great War in British Literature* (Cambridge: Cambridge University Press, 2000).

70 For interesting appraisals, see Modris Ecksteins, "All Quiet on the Western Front and the Fate of a War," *Journal of Contemporary History* 15 (1980): 345-66, which is reflected in the same author's *Rites of Spring*; and David Reynolds, *The Long Shadow: The Legacies of the Great War in the Twentieth Century* (New York and London: W.W. Norton and Company, 2014), 199, who sagely observes that "the tenth-anniversary book boom is often cited as shaping public attitudes, but the movies reached a far wider audience and did so with much greater power." Also, Jay Winter, *The Experience of World War I* (Edinburgh: Southside, 1988), 266; and Patrick Sauer, "The Most Loved and Hated Novel about World War I," www.smithsonianmag.com/history/most-loved-and-hated-novel-about-world-war-I-180955540/?no-ist (March 2016).

71 For the challenges confronting Canadian cultural producers in the face of continental and international market competition, see Mary Vipond, "Canadian Nationalism and the Plight of Canadian Magazines in the 1920s," *Canadian Historical Review* 58 (March 1977): 43–63; Janet B. Friskney and Carole Gerson, "Writers and the Market for Fiction and Literature," in *History of the Book in Canada*, vol. 3, *1918–1980*, ed. Carole Gerson and Jacques Michon (Toronto: University of Toronto Press, 2007), 131–42; Mary Vipond, "Major Trends in Canada's Print Mass Media," in *History of the Book*, ed. Gerson and Michon, 242–47; and Sarah Brouillette and Jacques Michon, "Control and Content in Mass-Market Distribution," in *History of the Book*, ed. Gerson and Michon, 404–11, who write: "In the decade following the First World War, Canadian magazines were scarcely

visible on newsstands and in drugstores and local shops. In 1926 it was estimated that of the 25 million American magazines sold in Canada each year, 14 million were purchased from newsstands" (405). Such statistics make it dangerous to overlook the influence of U.S. publications with respect to the Great War, especially given the strength and depth of the pushback against it in the 1920s and 1930s.

72 See Jonathan Vance, "The Soldier as Novelist: Literature, History, and the Great War," *Canadian Literature* 179 (Winter 2003), which takes issue with Harrison's accuracy.

73 Jonathan Scotland, "Getting It Right? Charles Yale Harrison's *Generals Die in Bed* as a Representative Example of Canadian Postwar Disillusion," paper delivered to the Canadian Historical Association, June 2014, 5. For a more detailed analysis of both this novelist and the wider Canadian debate about the war, see Scotland, "And the Men Returned: Canadian Veterans and the Aftermath of the Great War," Ph.D. thesis, Western University, London, Ont., 2016.

74 Charles Yale Harrison, *Generals Die in Bed* (Toronto: Annick Press, 2014 [New York: Morrow, 1930]), 47–48.

75 Harrison, *Generals Die in Bed*, 56.

76 Quoted in Vance, *Death So Noble*, 194.

77 The jabs at Harrison in conventional treatments of the public memory of the Great War in Canada are innumerable, and often proceed on the naive assumption that his novel can be judged on the same criteria as a news report—as though Franz Kafka might be blamed for not giving us a fair-minded interpretation of Czech bureaucracy rather than indicating what is strange and alienating about modern life. Nonetheless, on almost all the points about which Harrison is conventionally indicted—on Canadian prisoner-killing and looting, for instance—recent archive-based investigations have borne him out.

78 Harrison, *Generals Die in Bed*, 29.

79 Harrison, *Generals Die in Bed*, 105.

80 Cook, *At the Sharp End*, 451.

81 Annick Press, www.annickpress.com/Generals-Die-in-Bed-Special-Edition (June 2016).

82 Norm Christie, "Introduction," in Will R. Bird, *Private Timothy Fergus Clancy: A Novel of the Great War* (Ottawa: Graphic Publishers, 1930 [Ottawa: CEF Books, 2005]), n.p.

83 Will R. Bird, *And We Go On: A Story of the War by a Private in the Canadian Black Watch; a Story Without Filth or Favor* (Toronto: Hunter Rose, 1930), 5. The book is listed as a "memoir" in Tennyson, *Canadian Experience of the Great War*, 46; in the opening pages of Will R. Bird, *Ghosts Have Warm Hands* (Toronto and Vancouver: Clarke, Irwin, 1968), Bird lists it as fiction. Much of *And We Go On* describes psychic events and inner states of mind that go well beyond a strictly factual account, and the text has clear overlaps with Bird's copious fiction (he published more than eighty stories about the war from 1927 to 1945).

84 Bird, *And We Go On*, 333.

85 Bird, *And We Go On*, 147.

86 The articles in *Maclean's* ran from January to October 1932 and were later gathered together in a book: Will R. Bird, *Thirteen Years After: A Great War Veteran Revisits The Old Battlefields* (Ottawa: CEF Books, 2001 [Toronto: MacLean Publishing, 1932]). These opening paragraphs draw upon Ian McKay and Robin Bates, *In The Province of History: Tourism and the Romance of the Past in Twentieth-Century Nova Scotia* (Montreal and Kingston: McGill-Queen's University Press, 2010), ch.2. On the international trend to turn Great War battlefields into tourist destinations, see David W. Lloyd, *Battlefield Tourism: Pilgrimage and the Commemoration of the Great War in Britain, Australia and Canada, 1919–1939* (Oxford and New York: Berg Press, 1998).

87 "Says Officers Misrepresented," *Maclean*'s, 1 Sept. 1932; "Brickbats and Bouquets," *Maclean*'s, 1 June 1932, 68. Canon Frederick George Scott wrote to the magazine saying he thought Bird had enabled old soldiers to join together once again "in the sacred memories of the past by the spiritual revisiting of the war zone." "Canon Scott to Mr. Bird," *Maclean's*, 15 Aug. 1932, 24.

88 Bird, *And We Go On*, 326; Bird, *Thirteen Years After*, 225, 42.

89 Bird, *Thirteen Years After*, 76, 219–20.

90 Bird, *Thirteen Years After*, 213.

91 Bird, *Thirteen Years After*, 76.

92 For a strikingly different interpretation of Bird as someone who simply celebrated Canada's Great War and saw the Vimy Memorial as something that "affirmed in stone the searing martial rite of passage that helped transform Canada into a nation," see Sheftall, *Altered Memories of the Great War*, 1, which proceeds on the assumption of a near-unanimous Canadian endorsement of the "birth of the nation" narrative. That Bird was an unrelenting critic of less than intelligent commissioned officers and the biased histories that celebrated them, and wrote "This war is wrong," somehow escapes Sheftall's attention.

93 Bird, *Thirteen Years*, 93, 120.

94 Peter Neary, "'Without the Stigma of Pauperism': Canadian Veterans in the 1930s," *British Journal of Canadian Studies* 22,1 (2009): 31–62, queries the thesis—developed in Desmond Morton and Glenn Wright, *Winning the Second Battle: Canadian Veterans and the Return to Civilian Life 1915–1930* (Toronto: University of Toronto Press, 1987), that their struggles constituted, even if advertently, the beginnings of a more humane social policy in Canada—as does Lara Campbell, "'We Who Have Wallowed in the Mud of Flanders': First World War Veterans, Unemployment and the Development of Social Welfare in Canada, 1929–1939," *Journal of the Canadian Historical Association* 11,1 (2000): 125–149.

95 Morton and Wright, *Winning the Second Battle*, ch. 7. Hastily conceived and sometimes ill-executed back-to-the-land schemes for veterans were constant bones of contention through the 1920s and 1930s. For discussions, see James Murton, *Creating a Modern Countryside: Liberalism and Land Resettlement in British Columbia* (Vancouver: UBC Press, 2007); Dawn S. Bowen, "'Forward to a Farm': Land Settlement as Unemployment Relief in the 1930s," in *Social Fabric or Patchwork Quilt: The Development of Social Policy in Canada*, ed. Raymond B. Blake and Jeffrey A. Keshen (Peterborough, Ont.: Broadview, 2006), 123–42.

96 Report of the Fifth Annual Dominion Convention, 17–22 Oct. 1931, LAC, Cana-
    dian Legion Fonds, MG28 I 298, vol. 74, file 9.

97 Interview with Gregory Clark, Canadian Broadcasting Corporation, "Flanders'
    Fields," 17-part documentary, vol. 6, LAC, RG 41; Mrs. Jean McDonald to R.B.
    Bennett, 4 Aug. 1931, LAC, Bennett Papers, MG 26 K, M-1264, 325734–35.

98 Interview with Gregory Clark; Bernard Rose to King, 5 Dec. 1929 (enclosing
    letter from Arthur Currie), LAC, W.L.M. King Papers, MG 26 J1, C-2313,
    132186–90.

99 See Peter Barham, *Forgotten Lunatics of the Great War* (New Haven, Conn.: Yale
    University Press, 2004), esp. ch.15. As Mark Humphries remarks: "The very act
    of seeking an escape from the battlefield or applying for a postwar pension for
    psychological traumas transgressed masculine norms that required men to be
    aggressive, self-reliant, and un-emotional." Humphries, "War's Long Shadow:
    Masculinity, Medicine and the Gendered Politics of Trauma, 1914–1939," *Cana-
    dian Historical Review* 91, no.3 (2010), 503. Artilleryman Edward Turquand Ches-
    ley, one of the most eloquent of the veterans critical of the war, described "the
    multitude of the draggle-tail men who peddle from house to house and from office
    to office and even accost you on the street with requests to buy three cakes of soap.
    What is to be done about these folk? Well, the obvious course is to slam the door
    or walk quickly by them. Bums are bums whether returned soldiers or not, and
    some of them have certainly just recovered from an alcoholic jag." Edward Tur-
    quand Chesley ["An Unknown Soldier"], "The Vice of Victory," in *Open House*,
    ed. William Arthur Deacon and Wilfred Reeves (Ottawa: Graphic Publishers,
    1931), 27–28.

100 David Thompson, "Working-Class Anguish and Revolutionary Indignation: The
    Making of Radical and Socialist Unemployment Movements in Canada, 1875–
    1928," Ph.D. thesis, Queen's University, Kingston, Ont., 2014, ch.10.

101 Jeffrey Keshen, *Propaganda and Censorship during Canada's Great War* (Edmonton:
    University of Alberta Press, 1996), 204.

102 C.G. MacNeil to King, 25 Jan. 1922, LAC, W.L.M. King Papers, MG 26 J1,
    C-2247, 65734–35; C.G. MacNeil to King, 2 Feb. 1922, LAC, W.L.M. King
    Papers, MG 26 J1, C-2247, 65736–38; "Sedition: Bolsheviki Literature," Lieuten-
    ant-Colonel G.E. Burns, District Intelligence Officer, 24 Jan. 1921, LAC, RG-
    24-c-8, 4472, file part 1, MD4 20-1-44.

103 "One veteran," in Cook, *Shock Troops*, 604; Article Prepared by Brig.-General
    Alex. Ross, 5 June 1934, LAC, Canadian Legion Fonds, MG28 I 298, Vol.8, Mas-
    ter Circulars, June to January 1934.

104 *Herald* (Halifax), 20, 21, 24 Feb. 1919.

105 Quoted in Thompson, "Working-Class Anguish and Revolutionary Indignation."

106 Scotland, "And the Men Returned," 263; Thompson, "Working-Class Anguish
    and Revolutionary Indignation," ch.10; Sir Percy Lake to King, 26 April 1926,
    LAC, W.L.M. King Papers, MG26 J1, C-2289, 113193–95.

107 Lake to King, 26 April 1926.

108 LAC, Robert Boyer Inch Fonds, MG30-C187, Vol. 5, file 25, Chown, Alice—
    Women's League of Nations Association, Toronto, 19 Dec. 1934.

4: THE WOUNDS OF MEMORY, THE PUSH FOR PEACE

1 See, for instance, *Winnipeg Free Press*, 6 Feb. 1934. Canadian soldiers were forbidden to take pictures while serving on the Western Front, although some disobeyed this order. For additional work on the Great War as it was photographed, see Carl De Keyer and David Van Reybrouck, eds., *The First World War: Unseen Glass Plate Photographs of the Western Front* (Chicago: University of Chicago Press, 2015).

2 Laurence Stalling, *The First World War: A Photographic History* (New York: Simon and Schuster, 1933). The series ran in the *Toronto Star* from 25 Jan. to 22 March and in the *Winnipeg Free Press* (and associated publications) from 3 Feb. to 24 Feb. 1934. The *Star* also drew upon 14 images from Frederick Barber's extremely graphic *The Horror of It: Camera Records of War's Gruesome Glories* (New York: Historical Foundation, 1932) and the official British war photographs.

3 Despite the *Star*'s statement, war photography did exist in more limited form in the mid-nineteenth century, as seen in the U.S. Civil War. On the impact of Canadian war photography, see Ann Thomas, Anthony Petiteau, and Bodo von Dewitz, *The Great War: The Persuasive Power of Photography* (Ottawa: 5Continents Editions, 2014). Both this book and Amber Lloyd Langston and Laura Brandon, *Witness: Canadian Art of the First World War* (Ottawa: Canadian War Museum, 2014), place much less emphasis—as compared to the 1930s—on the bodily harm caused by the war.

4 R.E. Knowles, "Wartime Photos Have Great Appeal to Heart States Sir Wm. Mulock," *Toronto Star*, 26 Jan. 1934, 1, 3.

5 "War Photographs Lauded by Christie St. Sufferers," *Toronto Star*, 29 Jan. 1934, 1,2.

6 In the 1960s Clark would write a piece on Vimy that repeated many of the much-celebrated themes of Vimyism. (Yet he went to say, "Symbols are costly.") Gregory Clark, "The Symbol," *Weekend Magazine*, 4 April 1967, 2; and see ch.7 here.

7 *Toronto Star*, 10 Feb. 1934; 16 Feb. 1934.

8 *Toronto Star*, 13 Feb. 1934.

9 *Toronto Star*, 10 Feb. 1934.

10 *Toronto Star*, 25 Jan. 1934; 23 Feb. 1934. The captions with the *Star* and *Free Press* photos for Figures 1 to 8 are the original newspaper cutlines.

11 *Toronto Star*, 26 Jan. 1934.

12 *Toronto Star*, 9 Feb. 1934. "Strangely, we never refer to the Germans as our enemy. In the week-old newspaper which comes up from the base we read of the enemy and the Hun, but this is newspaper talk and we place no stock in it. Instead we call him Heinie and Fritz." Charles Yale Harrison, *Generals Die in Bed* (Toronto: Annick Press, 2014 [New York: Morrow, 1930]), 23.

13 *Toronto Star*, 16 Feb. 1934. The division of labour at the newspaper is uncertain. We do not know whether Clark or an editor—or both—wrote the headlines that accompanied the photographs.

14 *Toronto Star*, 28 Feb. 1934.

15 *Toronto Star*, 26 Feb. 1934; 14 Feb. 1934; 23 Feb. 1934.

16 *Toronto Star*, 30 Jan. 1934.

17 "Easy to Make Scrapbooks Now of War Photos," *Toronto Star*, 29 Jan. 1934, 1;
"War's Horror Made Clear by Pictures, Say Readers," *Toronto Star*, 2 Feb. 1934,
30; "Wants Star's War Pictures in Libraries of Schools," *Toronto Star*, 15 Feb.
1934, 26.

18 "Readers Praise War Photos as Great Lesson to Youth," *Toronto Star*, 1 Feb. 1934,
3; "Publishing War Pictures Held National Service," *Toronto Star*, 10 Feb. 1934,
3; "Legion Votes Commendation of War Photos as Peace Aid," *Toronto Star*, 8
Feb. 1934, 12; "'Original' Says True Horror Is Depicted in War Photos," *Toronto
Star*, 14 Feb. 1934; "Legion Members Like War Photos," *Toronto Star*, 2 March
1934, 12. One assembly of the "Native Sons of Canada," the Riverdale Assembly
No. 80, a nationalist group in which many veterans were active, also wrote in to
endorse the series. A. McGregor, "Native Sons Approve," *Toronto Star*, 19 Feb.
1934, 6; "Readers Praise War Photos as Great Lesson to Youth," *Toronto Star*, 1
Feb. 1934, 3. Zone 4 covered St. Thomas, West Lorne, Belmont, Aylmer, Inger-
soll, Woodstock, Tillsonburg, Delhi, Otterville, and Norwich.

19 "Pictures of World Conflict Hailed as Aid to Peace," *Toronto Star*, 29 Jan. 1934,
27. Two of them did say that veterans would rather forget the horrific events of the
war, in the general context of endorsing the series as an educational tool.

20 "Readers Praise War Photos as Great Lesson to Youth," *Toronto Star*, 1 Feb. 1934,
3 (letter from "Ex. R.S.M., 27th Battalion").

21 "War's Horror Made Clear by Pictures, Say Readers," *Toronto Star*, 2 Feb. 1934,
30; "Publishing War Pictures Held National Service," *Toronto Star*, 10 Feb.
1934, 3; "Veterans Praise War Views as Aid in Promoting Peace," *Toronto Star*, 6
Feb. 1934, 8. It was highly unlikely that the paper was *manufacturing* such letters
because many of them came with names, addresses, and sometimes institutional
affiliations, all of them subject to verification. The papers, as a matter of course,
would have received more letters than they printed and made editorial choices
about which ones to display. In this case, by making choices about which letters
to print, newspapers were actively engaged in reshaping the public memory of the
war. Of course, the *Star* wanted to sell papers. It was also prone to idealistic pro-
nouncements: "The universality of the dread nature of war cannot be realized until
friend and foe, stranger and brother, are shown to be all in the same boat, the same
storm-tossed boat headed for the rocks." "Pictures of All Nations Show Friend
and Foe during Stark Tragedy," *Toronto Star*, 5 Feb. 1934, 1, 2.

22 "False Glamor of War," *Toronto Star*, 30 Jan. 1934, 6, a letter to the editor from
William Howey of Owen Sound; "Legion Votes Commendation of War Photos
as Peace Aid," *Toronto Star*, 8 Feb. 1934, 12. The Howey letter was probably from
William H. Howey, regimental number 502661, who gave his occupation as
"Methodist Minister"—see http://www.canadiangreatwarproject.com/searches/
soldierDetail.asp?ID=138961; and Library and Archives Canada (LAC), http://
www.bac-lac.gc.ca/eng/discover/military-heritage/first-world-war/first-world-
war-1914-1918-cef/Pages/item.aspx?IdNumber=474679.

23 Ethel Iris Wax, "All Against War," *Toronto Star*, 8 March 1934, 6; "Readers Praise
War Photos as Great Lesson to Youth," *Toronto Star*, 1 Feb. 1934, 3; "Canadian,

'Reorganizing the World,'" *Toronto Star*, 1 March 1934, 6. All cities or towns cited are in Ontario unless otherwise indicated.

24 R.E. Knowles, "Dr. Fallis Found Own Face in Star's War Photographs," *Toronto Star*, 30 Jan. 1934, 1, 3. For Fallis's own reflections on his peace activism in the 1930s, see George O. Fallis, *A Padre's Pilgrimage* (Toronto: Ryerson Press, 1953).

25 "Star War Pictures Praised by Officials," editorial, *Toronto Star*, 21 Feb. 1934, 22.

26 "Veterans Praise War Views as Aid in Promoting Peace," *Toronto Star*, 6 Feb. 1934, 8; "Pictures of World Conflict Hailed as Aid to Peace," *Toronto Star*, 29 Jan. 1934, 27. The letter writer did go on to say that he thought military training still important. It was imperative, said Richard Anderson of Gananoque, Ex-Gunner 23rd Howitzer Battery, that people think back to those "dark days, with plenty of mud and water that we were walking and laying in." As for his 11-year-old son, "may I state that I never want him to put a uniform on to leave this country to fight." "Veterans Praise War Views as Aid in Promoting Peace," *Toronto Star*, 6 Feb. 1934, 8. The details fit Gananoque's Richard Anderson, regimental number 342945, and a machinist by trade.

27 "War Photographs Lauded by Christie St. Sufferers," *Toronto Star*, 29 Jan. 1934.

28 "Veterans Praise War Views as Aid in Promoting Peace," *Toronto Star*, 6 Feb. 1934, 8.

29 "Publishing War Pictures Held National Service," *Toronto Star*, 10 Feb. 1934, 3.

30 Internationalist, "A Super-State," *Toronto Star*, 9 March 1934, 6; "'Original' Says True Horror Is Depicted in War Photos," *Toronto Star*, 14 Feb. 1934, 48.

31 "Soldier Sees Self on Way to Blighty," *Toronto Star*, 7 Feb. 1934, 5; "Pictures of World Conflict Hailed as Aid to Peace," *Toronto Star*, 29 Jan. 1934, 27; W. Livingston, "War's Insanity," *Toronto Star*, 24 Feb. 1934, 4. Another letter writer, "Ex-Soldat," in and out of hospitals since the war, praised the *Star* for removing "the false idea of pomp and glory of war. . . . I would hate to see the flower of young Canadian manhood again become cannon fodder for the enrichment of the ammunition trusts and other war-mongering profiteers who glorify war for monetary profits and huge dividends." "Readers Praise War Photos as Great Lesson to Youth," *Toronto Star*, 1 Feb. 1934, 3.

32 "Recognized Himself as Man on Stretcher," *Toronto Star*, 13 Feb. 1934, 11; "Veterans Praise War Views as Aid in Promoting Peace," *Toronto Star*, 6 Feb. 1934, 8; "Readers Praise War Photos as Great Lesson to Youth," *Toronto Star*, 1 Feb. 1934, 3.

33 "Legion Votes Commendation of War Photos as Peace Aid," *Toronto Star*, 8 Feb. 1934, 12; "'Original' Says True Horror Is Depicted in War Photos," *Toronto Star*, 14 Feb. 1934, 48. R.C. Hays wrote, "We old crocks of the great war haven't talked much about things we saw because it wasn't pleasant to try and discuss war with people who couldn't visualize it." "Publishing War Pictures Held National Service," *Toronto Star*, 10 Feb. 1934, 3.

34 "'Original' Says True Horror Is Depicted in War Photos," *Toronto Star*, 14 Feb. 1934, 48; "War's Horror Made Clear by Pictures, Say Readers," *Toronto Star*, 2 Feb. 1934, 30.

35 "War's Horror Made Clear by Pictures, Say Readers," *Toronto Star*, 2 Feb. 1934, 30; "Readers Praise War Photos as Great Lesson to Youth," *Toronto Star*, 1 Feb.

1934, 3; "'Original' Says True Horror is Depicted in War Photos," *Toronto Star*, 14 Feb. 1934, 48. This man, along with two brothers and all his cousins, had gone to war.

36 "Legion Votes Commendation of War Photos as Peace Aid," *Toronto Star*, 8 Feb. 1934, 12. Where, pointedly asked Ralph Naylor of Oshawa, were the "patriots" who had "gained and prospered" thanks to war? "Are they willing to show their patriotism now? We do not want something for nothing, but we should be entitled to live?" "Veterans Praise War Views as Aid in Promoting Peace," *Toronto Star*, 6 Feb. 1934, 8.

37 For the veteran from Scotland, Ont.: S.S. Harry Slaight, "Real War Pictures," *Toronto Star*, 8 March 1934, 6. Capt. Rev. T. Allan Paterson, war chaplain from 1915 to 1918, did mention his experiences at Ypres and Vimy Ridge, which, he said, "convinced me that common sense had ceased to function. Change and decay in all around I saw. God forbid war should ever function again anywhere." "Veterans Praise War Views as Aid in Promoting Peace," *Toronto Star*, 6 Feb. 1934, 8.

38 *Winnipeg Free Press*, 1 Feb. 1934.

39 If, as a source, the *Star*'s letters sometimes make us wonder how much weight we can safely give to anonymous sources, of the *Free Press* responses, 101 are signed, leaving only 13 letters signed by pen names (and even among these, writers sometimes added details that would have allowed contemporaries to identity them with some confidence).

40 *Winnipeg Free Press*, 3 Feb. 1934.

41 The *Winnipeg Free Press* found endorsers from political figures such as Premier John Bracken, the presidents of the Women's Conservative Association and Women's Liberal Club, Manitoba's minister of education, and two MLAs, S.J. Farmer and John Queen; from church people, including the Archbishop of Winnipeg, Archbishop of Rupert's Land, president of the Women's Missionary Society, rector of Holy Trinity Church, head of the Ukrainian-Greek Catholic Church in Canada, and a good assortment of United Church ministers; from the bench, the chief justice of Manitoba; among educationists, two star professors of Wesley College, Watson Kirkconnell and Arthur Lower, along with the college's principal, as well as the registrar of the University of Manitoba and the principals of St. John's Technical School and Cecil Rhodes Schools; from clubs and associations, the presidents of the University Women's Club and the Junior League of Winnipeg, and peace activists including the president of the Women's International League for Peace and Freedom and the vice-president of the League for Peace and the deputy of the Grand Lodge of B'Nai Brith. Outside Winnipeg it won the support of the mayors of Morris, Boissevain, Oak Lake, Selkirk, and the mayors of Canora and Kamsack, Saskatchewan; school teachers and principals in The Pas, Brandon, Deloraine, and Straithclair; an assortment of crown prosecutors; businessmen including William Voss, the president of the Dauphin Board of Trade, and Finley Yellowless, a general merchant in Ninette.

42 *Winnipeg Free Press*, 1 Feb. 1934; 7 Feb. 1934.

43 *Winnipeg Free Press*, 1 Feb. 1934.

44 *Winnipeg Free Press*, 1 Feb. 1934; 14 Feb. 1934.

45 *Winnipeg Free Press*, 24 Feb. 1934

46 *Winnipeg Free Press*, 19 Feb. 1934; *Toronto Daily Star*, 25 Jan. 1934.

47 *Winnipeg Free Press*, 3 Feb. 1934. On Kirkconnell's racial thought, see Daniel
    Meister, "Which Cultures Count? Re-assessing the 'Father of Canadian Multi-
    culturalism,' 1919–1943," unpublished paper, Queen's University, 2014; "Young
    Watson Kirkconnell and 'Canadian Futurities': Excavating the Early Racial and
    Political Thought of the Father of Canadian Multiculturalism, 1918–1920," M.A.
    cognate essay, Queen's University, Kingston, Ont., 2014.

48 *Winnipeg Free Press*, 3 Feb. 1934; 10 Feb. 1934. Fully 20 per cent of the *Free Press*
    respondents were women—in contrast to 10 per cent in the case of the *Toronto
    Star*—perhaps a reflection of the further strides taken by women on the Prairies.
    Yet, surprisingly, few of them made a "maternal case" for peace, although for Mrs.
    Norman Young, who had just finished reading Vera Brittain's classic *Testament of
    Youth*, the photographs were enough to convince every woman "of the utter and
    cruel futility of war." *Winnipeg Free Press*, 3 Feb. 1934. All cities or towns cited are
    in Manitoba unless otherwise indicated.

49 *Winnipeg Free Press*, 10 Feb. 1934. Cameron remembered coming upon a "fine,
    young, clean-shaven Princess Pat," with a "lovely photo held tight in his hand, a
    woman and a child of three, but the soldier's eyes had closed in death." The pres-
    ent generation needed to be pounded with the truth about the war.

50 *Winnipeg Free Press*, 10 Feb. 1934.

51 *Winnipeg Free Press*, 10 Feb. 1934. As in Toronto, some suggested the series be
    printed on one side of the page only, to facilitate the creation of scrapbooks. Of
    the solicited opinion-givers, 13 [14 per cent] claimed first-hand knowledge of
    the Great War; among the letter-writers, 13 [54 per cent] also claimed first-hand
    knowledge of the Great War.

52 *Winnipeg Free Press*, 8 Feb. 1934; 15 Feb. 1934.

53 Stefan Epp-Koop, *We're Going to Run This City: Winnipeg's Political Left after the
    General Strike* (Winnipeg: University of Manitoba Press, 2015), 25.

54 *Winnipeg Free Press*, 3 Feb. 1934. Webb had earlier figured among the critics of
    Generals Die in Bed, whose descriptions of looting in Arras he dismissed as "tom-
    myrot." For him, Harrison was a "downright liar trying to sell a book," on a
    subject about which he was uninformed. "Local Veterans Say Latest War Book Is
    'Pack of Lies,'" *Winnipeg Tribune*, 14 May 1930, 3.

55 A. Cairns to Bennett, 27 July 1935, LAC, Bennett Papers, MG 26 K, M-983,
    86880-1.

56 *Winnipeg Free Press*, 6 Feb. 1934; 15 Feb. 1934.

57 *Winnipeg Free Press*, 15 Feb. 1934. "A Returned Soldier" from St. Vital took issue
    with Mayor Webb. The average soldier was pleased to see such depiction of the
    "horrors of war," and the Mayor's interest in seeing "funny" or "interesting"
    depictions of the war just revealed how out of touch he was. So did "A Reader,"
    who remarked that both returned soldiers and widows and children were "glad to
    see the photos," so that "everyone see 'what the boys went through.'" *Winnipeg
    Free Press*, 9 Feb. 1934.

58 *Winnipeg Free Press*, 9 Feb. 1934. The newspaper rightly challenged his insinu-
ation that the photographs only came from safely behind the lines. As "War
Shadowed" complained, the pictures might "form entertainment for quite a few
people," generate revenues for the newspaper, but only cause pain to those for
whom "they represent their very heart's blood." The soldiers had done "what any
red-blooded man would do—went to his country's aid at a time when the very
civilization of the world was threatened." *Winnipeg Free Press*, 9 Feb. 1934.

59 *Winnipeg Free Press*, 7 Feb. 1934; 14 Feb. 1934; 17 Feb. 1934.

60 *Winnipeg Free Press*, 3 Feb. 1934. Osborne implicitly criticized the *Free Press* captions, which in comparison to Clark's, were particularly graceless.

61 *Winnipeg Free Press*, 3 Feb. 1934; 15 Feb. 1934.

62 Dr. D.C. Davidson in Cartwright was an exceptional case as someone who
defended what we would now consider the "mainstream position" on the Great
War. He thought the pictures, valueless as propaganda for either peace or war
preparation, were of value in reminding Canadians of "the courage, the heroism
and endurance of Canadians of 1914-18. . . . In times like these we should turn
often to the records of the Canadians in Flanders for inspiration that will enable
us to fight, if necessary, with our backs to the wall, with the same grim determination to win through to prosperity." *Winnipeg Free Press*, 10 Feb. 1934. Presumably
Mayor Webb felt this way as well.

5: THE CONTESTED POLITICS OF PEACE AND WAR

1 Lita-Rose Betcherman, *Ernest Lapointe: Mackenzie King's Great Quebec Lieutenant*
(Toronto: University of Toronto Press, 2002), 274.

2 Quoted in Betcherman, *Ernest Lapointe*, 265.

3 Betcherman, *Ernest Lapointe*, 274, states that in the months leading up to the war,
"King would not take a step without clearing it with Lapointe." John MacFarlane,
Ernest Lapointe and Quebec's Influence on Canadian Foreign Policy (Toronto: University of Toronto Press, 1999), ch. 8, presents a slightly less categorical interpretation of the King-Lapointe relationship, pointing out issues on which King differed
with Lapointe and calling attention to Lapointe's frequent battles with anglophone ministers.

4 Quoted in MacFarlane, *Ernest Lapointe*, 151.

5 This account draws directly on MacFarlane, *Ernest Lapointe*, 150–51.

6 Ian Miller, "Toronto's Response to the Outbreak of War, 1939," *Canadian Military History* 11, 1 (Winter 2002), 8, 21.

7 In September 1934 the Department of National Defence received sobering statistics relating to the percentages of veterans on relief in Edmonton and Calgary:
49.8 per cent and 56 per cent respectively. In January 1936 A.E. Nightingale of the
Red Chevron Club for veterans in Edmonton wrote that many of the numerous
veterans in the relief camps were resentful of their lot: "They cannot compete with
youth—and are not wanted . . . the veterans are in their forties, but actually they

are at least 10 years older . . . one by one their ranks are thinning, the strain prov-
ing too great." For younger workers, going on relief could seem to be a bump on
the road; for older veterans, often considered unemployable, it could bring a sense
of never being wanted as a worker again. A.E. Nightingale to King, 4 Jan. 1936,
W.L.M. King Papers, MG 26 J1, C-3692, 193470; 1934 statistics in "Subversive
Activities," H.H. Matthews, District Officer Commanding, 2 Oct. 1934, LAC,
RG 24 vol. 4685 MD13-CS11, vol. 1; Alexander Ross to Bennett, 7 Jan. 1935,
LAC, Bennett Papers, MG 26 K, M-983, 86835-46.

8 Re: Conference of Psychiatrists and Neurologists, 2 Dec. 1936, LAC, Canadian
Legion Fonds, MG28 I 298, vol. 8, Master Circulars, 1936. One estimate of the
cost of war-related pensions in Canada came to about $41,953,036.79 in 1934–35:
"Amount of Pension Payments," n.d., LAC, Bennett Papers, MG 26 K, M-1464,
507211. By some estimates, such Great War "legacy costs" reached their peak in
the 1960s, fully a half-century after the war. See also chapter 3 here, note 94.

9 H.A.E. Coo to King, 30 June 1931, LAC, W.L.M. King Papers, MG 26 J1,
C-2325, 157313–16; Thomas Burkes to Bennett, 20 Dec. 1933, LAC, Bennett
Papers, MG 26 K, M-1263, 324833–37; Thomas Burkes to Bennett, 13 Jan. 1934,
LAC, Bennett Papers, MG 26 K, M-1263, 324831–32; J. King to King, 8 June
1936, LAC, W.L.M. King Papers, MG 26 J1, C-3689, 199376–77.

10 "Subversive Activities," H.H. Matthews to the DND, 6 June 1933, LAC, RG 24,
vol. 4685, MD13-CS11, vol. 1; B. Liss to King, 10 Nov. 1936, LAC, W.L.M. King
Papers, MG 26 J1, C-3689.

11 Alex Ross to All Branches, 21 Aug. 1934, LAC, Canadian Legion Fonds, MG28
I 298, vol. 8, Master Circulars, June to December 1934. In June 1935 the British Empire Service League—with which the Canadian Legion was affiliated—
declared it to be "the duty of the nations of the Empire to maintain adequate forces
for use on sea and land and in the air, that our Imperial heritage may be adequately
safeguarded. . . . It is its plain duty to express its opinion that the present compara-
tive weakness of the Defence Forces of the Empire imperils national security and
is provocative of war." See Donald Simpson to Bennett, 30 June 1935, LAC, Bennett Papers, MG 26 K, M-1094, 272231–32.

12 League of Nations Society to Bennett, January 1932, LAC, Bennett Papers, MG
26 K M-1093, 271327–33; for press coverage, see "Conscription Seen by Prime
Minister as Source of War," *Globe*, 13 Jan. 1932. Evidence indicates that this mass
movement indeed pressured the Conservative government to beef up and maintain Canada's presence at the Disarmament Conference: see Sir George Perley to
Bennett, 13 March 1932, LAC, MG 26 K M-1094, 27909; Perley to Bennett, 14
March 1932, 271991–93. The country's population at the time was officially estimated at 10,376,379.

13 For these groups, see Thomas P. Socknat, *Witness Against War: Pacifism in Canada
1900–1945* (Toronto: University of Toronto Press, 1987). For a fierce indict-
ment of pacifist *Canadiens* who supposedly "killed the Canadian military," see
J.L. Granatstein, *Who Killed the Canadian Military?* (Toronto: HarperPerennial
Canada, 2004), 97.

14 Alice Chown, for example, addressed a Toronto meeting of the Women's Labor
League on the subject "Is There a War Danger?" and was sternly critiqued in the

left-wing *Woman Worker* because she had expressed her hopes that the League would create "the spirit among nations that would make war impossible. The abolition of War depended on how quickly we could educate the people to this feeling of love and goodwill." Comrade Florence Custance set her straight, arguing that the "League never was and never could be an instrument of Peace, that it was formed in those days of bitter class conflict to offset the revolutionary wave that was sweeping across Europe after the war and when the workers of the whole world were in ferment." Margaret Hobbs and Joan Sangster, eds., *The Woman Worker 1926–1929* (St. John's, Nfld.: Canadian Committee on Labour History, 1999), 157. By the mid-1930s Chown was hobnobbing with Communist leader Tim Buck.

15 See Christine Elie, "The City and the Reds: Leftism, the Civic Politics of Order, and a Contested Modernity in Montreal, 1929–1947," Ph.D. thesis, Queen's University, Kingston, Ont., 2015.

16 Anna R. Gray to Bennett, 3 July 1931, LAC, Bennett Papers, MG 26 K, M-1093, 270897.

17 Rt. Hon. Arthur Meighen, "To Get Rid of War," *Maclean's*, 15 Jan. 1931, 26; Robert L. Borden, "In the Kindergarten of Peace," *Interdependence* 8:1 (January 1931), 1–15, LAC, Meighen Papers, Series 5, MG 26 I, vol. 98, C-3562,0104246-61; Official Report of Debates, House of Commons, 2nd Session, 17th Parliament, vol. 4, 1931 (Ottawa: King's Printer, 1931), 3553.

18 George Drew, *Salesmen of Death: The Truth about War Makers*, 3rd ed. (Toronto: League of Nations Society, 1933).

19 "Brickbats and Bouquets," *Maclean's*, 15 Sept. 1931, 40–41; F.M. Hearn to Bennett, 7 Dec. 1931 and A.L. Lockwood to Bennett, 26 Dec. 1931, LAC, Bennett Papers, MG 26 K, M-1093, 270731-33 and 270871-72.

20 Brooke Claxton, *Keeping in Step with Mars*, n.p. [Toronto], n.d. [1934] (reprinted from *Canadian Business*, June 1934). For Claxton, see David Bercuson, *True Patriot: The Life of Brooke Claxton 1898–1960* (Toronto: University of Toronto Press, 1993), which observes that Claxton "had picked up the pieces of men who had been blown to bits. He knew that war was a base, dreadful, and dirty business, without glory. He rejected the romanticism expressed on war memorials and in Armistice Day speeches about the 'glorious dead'" (40). Yet somehow this insight into Claxton's realist and critical stance with respect to war gets lost in the remainder of a volume that waxes eloquent on his ardent defencism. Another significant Liberal figure in the movement for disarmament was future foreign affairs minister Paul Martin, who served as the president of the Border Cities Branch of the League of Nations Society. For Martin's activism and a detailed vision of peace from his Windsor group, see Miss M.C. Straith to Bennett, 19 Dec. 1931, LAC, Bennett Papers, MG 26 K, M-1093, 270841-42.

21 Chown, Alice—Women's League of Nations, LAC, Robert Boyer Inch Fonds, MG30-C187, vol.5, file 25.

22 Neville Thompson, *Canada and the End of the Imperial Dream: Beverley Baxter's Reports from London through War and Peace, 1936–1960* (Don Mills, Ont.: Oxford University Press, 2013), 109.

23 Irvine C. Sutton to Bennett, 9 Dec. 1931, LAC, Bennett Papers, MG 26 K, M-1093, 270745–46; C.W. Morrow to Bennett, 27 Nov. 1931, LAC, Bennett Papers, MG 26 K, M-1093, 270677; R.H. Clarke to Bennett, 10 Dec. 1931, LAC, Bennett Papers, MG 26 K, M-1093, 270757–58; Charles Heisterman to Bennett, 14 Nov. 1931, LAC, Bennett Papers, MG 26 K, M-1093, 270669; Olive Matthews to Bennett, 19 Dec. 1931, LAC, Bennett Papers, MG 26 K, M-1093, 270844; Mrs. R.H. Brotherhood to Bennett, 15 Dec. 1931, LAC, Bennett Papers, MG 26 K, M-1093, 271228–29; "To the Statesmen," October 1935, LAC, Bennett Papers, MG 26 K, M-1464, 507333–42.

24 Rev D.H. McLachlan to Bennett, 22 Jan. 1932, LAC, Bennett Papers, MG 26 K, M-1093, 271408-271413; Effie A. Jamieson to Bennett, 8 Dec. 1931 (Women's Missionary Society of the United Church, advising Bennett they had secured 100,000 signatures to add to the Disarmament Declaration), LAC, Bennett Papers, MG 26 K, M-1093, 270740.

25 Mrs. R.W. Angus to Bennett, 22 Oct. 1931, LAC, Bennett Papers, MG 26 K, M-1093, 270960–62; T.H. Hutchinson to Bennett, 1 Dec. 1931, LAC, Bennett Papers, MG 26 K, M-1464, 507221; M.J. Dilger to Bennett, 6 April 1932, LAC, Bennett Papers, MG 26 K, M-1093, 271134–35; Rev. W.L. Palframan, 5 Aug. 1935, LAC, Bennett Papers, MG 26 K, M-1464, 507320–21. For good measure, these Baptists also declared their unswerving opposition to divorce, "intoxicating drinks," and publicly funded Catholic schools.

26 G. Brown to Bennett, 5 May 1933, LAC, Bennett Papers, MG 26 K, M-1093, 271629–30.

27 Peter Campbell, *Rose Henderson: A Woman for the People* (Montreal and Kingston: McGill-Queen's University Press, 2010), 159.

28 Allison Ward, "The Woman Who Would Not Meet the King: Using Agnes Sharpe to Explore Omissions in Political History," paper presented to the Canadian Historical Association, 2015; for a fuller exposition, see Allison Ward, "Guarding the City Beautiful: Liberalism, Empire, Labour, and Civic Identity in Hamilton, Ontario, 1929–1953," Ph.D. thesis, Queen's University, Kingston, Ont., 2014.

29 Socknat, *Witness Against War*, 114. His research suggests an anti-cadet training movement that enjoyed limited success in the 1920s; ours suggests that the movement scored some surprising victories in the 1930s.

30 F. Stanley Measley, "Should My Boy Play War?" *Maclean's*, 1 March 1931; A. Marsh to Bennett, 23 March 1933, LAC, Bennett Papers, MG 26 K, M-1464, 507239.

31 For more discussion about peace and war in human history, see Azar Gat, *A History of Military Thought from the Enlightenment to the Cold War* (New York: Oxford University Press, 2001); Hans Joas and Wolfgang Knöbl, *War in Social Thought: Hobbes to the Present*, trans. Alex Skinner (Princeton, N.J., and Oxford: Princeton University Press, 2013); John Keegan *A History of Warfare* (Toronto: Vintage Canada, 1994); John U. Nef, *War and Human Progress: An Essay on the Rise of Industrial Civilization* (New York: W.W. Norton, 1950); Alfred Vagts, *A History of Militarism: Civilian and Military* (New York: Free Press, 1959); and Martin Van Creveld, *A History of Strategy: From Sun Tzu to William S. Lind*

(Kouvala, Finland: Castalia House, 2015). Of outstanding interest for its reflections on war and modernity is Daniel Pick, *War Machine: The Rationalisation of Slaughter in the Modern Age* (New Haven, Conn., and London: Yale University Press, 1993).

32 Martin Ceadel, *Thinking about Peace and War* (Oxford and New York: Oxford University Press, 1987), 4–6.

33 A perusal of Brian Douglas Tennyson, *The Canadian Experience of the Great War: A Guide to Memoirs* (Lanham, Md., Toronto, and Plymouth, UK: Scarecrow Press, 2013), indicates that, of the nine war novels published by Canadian combatants in the 1930s, six were emphatically pacificist in tone; the other three were ambivalent. Of these ambiguous cases, even *Arm of Gold* (Toronto: McClelland and Stewart, 1932) by Ralph Connor, who was one of the most enthusiastic boosters of the Great War while it was happening, features a doomed wounded veteran and makes no argument that the war was beneficial in fortifying Canadian manhood or making Canada a nation. Our thanks to Richard Allen for drawing Connor's novel to our attention. Our point is not that *some* soldier-novelists did not emphasize Vimy Ridge—it is the more striking one that militarist themes are missing in action in virtually all Canadian soldiers' novels of the 1930s.

34 Norman Hillmer, *O.D. Skelton: A Portrait of Canadian Ambition* (Toronto: University of Toronto Press, 2015), 209–10.

35 Ferdinand Mount, "Parcelled Out," *London Review of Books*, 22 Oct. 2015, 7.

36 See Susan Pedersen, *The Guardians: The League of Nations and the Crisis of Empire* (Oxford: Oxford University Press, 2015).

37 Pedersen, *Guardians*, 6.

38 Quoted in Hillmer, *O.D. Skelton*, 219, which provides a brilliant and accessible introduction to the quandaries confronting Canadian foreign-policy makers in the 1930s. King's frustration with the League was evident in his Diary, 14 Jan. 1936: "The league of Nations must be transformed into a peace agency to work by a peaceful means towards peaceful ends. It cannot be an instrument of war and an instrument of peace at one and the same time." Vincent Massey, King's appointee as Canadian High Commissioner in London, told his diary in 1937: "I am increasingly conscious of the futility of my existence in Geneva. . . . In fact I cannot help feeling that I might more appropriately hold a visitor's ticket . . . than a delegate's." Quoted in Richard Veatch, *Canada and the League of Nations* (Toronto: University of Toronto Press, 1975), 174.

39 W.L.M. King, Diary, 5 May 1937; Diary, 31 Aug. 1938. It figured as part of the scandal that one of the principal figures was of German descent—"though of a very respectable and old-time family in Toronto." For the details, see David Mackenzie, "The Bren Gun Scandal and the Maclean Publishing Company's Investigation of Canadian Contracts, 1938-1940," *Journal of Canadian Studies* 26, 3 (Fall 1991): 140–62.

40 Eugene Forsey to Mackenzie King, 14 Feb. 1937, LAC, W.L.M. King Papers, MG 26 J1, C-3725, 2012135.

41 The evidence comes from consulting ten influential English-language newspapers from Halifax to Vancouver: *Halifax Herald*, *Gazette* (Montreal), *Toronto Star*,

Globe and Mail (Toronto), *Ottawa Citizen*, *Winnipeg Tribune*, *Leader-Post* (Regina), *Edmonton Journal*, *Calgary Herald*, and *Vancouver Sun*. The research revealed precisely two—muted and minor—editorial references to Vimy.

42 "Canada's Position: An Editorial," *Halifax Herald*, 4 Sept. 1939, 1; "Who Is the Enemy?" *Calgary Herald*, 4 Sept. 1939, 4; Harry J. Walker, "When Soldier-Settlers Left Their Fields to Fight Invasion," *Ottawa Journal*, 9 Sept. 1939, 19; "Canada's Entry into War Welcomed by French Papers," *Ottawa Journal*, 11 Sept. 1939, 1; "Canada to Play Important role in War," *Ottawa Journal*, 15 Sept. 1939, 1; "Will This Be Repeated?" *Winnipeg Tribune*, 1 Sept. 1939, 9; "Troops Are Landing in France 'Rapidly,' Paris Announces," *Globe and Mail*, 7 Sept. 1939, 1. See also "1939 Contemptibles 'Stand To' in France," *Toronto Star*, 7 Sept. 1939, 9.

43 "Tranquil Courage: An Editorial," *Halifax Herald*, 2 Sept. 1939, 1. For anyone with a sense of history, it was a bit rich for the demagogic *Halifax Herald*—which pounded the war drum with deafening insistence from 1914 to 1918, doing its best to incite mass panic about foreign conspiracies and Liberal ne'er-do-wells—to strike this tone.

44 "Canada's Spirit," *Leader-Post* (Regina), 11 Sept. 1939, 4.

45 "The War Reviewed," *Toronto Star*, 4 Sept. 1939, 1, 2.

46 "Hospital Vets Show Fatalistic Courage," *Toronto Star*, 1 Sept. 1939, 30.

47 "Winnipeg Reaction to War News Contrast to 1914 Celebration," *Winnipeg Tribune*, 1 Sept. 1939, 4; "The City Hears the News," *Winnipeg Tribune*, Extra, 3 Sept. 1939, 1, 2.

48 "Reginans Spend Sleepless Night Waiting for War News," *Leader-Post* (Regina), 1 Sept. 1939, 3.

49 "Calm, Grim City Hears of Conflict," *Edmonton Journal*, 4 Sept. 1939, 1, 2.

50 Gus Siverts, "Lend Me Your Ears," *Vancouver Sun*, 4 Sept. 1939, 6.

51 Gus Sivertz, "Vancouver Citizens Hear Fateful Words with Calm Determination," *Vancouver Sun*, 4 Sept. 1939, 16.

52 "Woodsworth Opposed to Entering War," *Halifax Herald*, 9 Sept. 1939, 4; "Woodsworth Personally against Canada Entering European War," *Leader-Post* (Regina), 9 Sept. 1939, 11: "Woodsworth Takes Stand against War," *Vancouver Sun*, 9 Sept. 1939, 11.

53 "Canada at War," *Vancouver Sun*, 11 Sept. 1939, 4.

54 "C.C.F. Oppose Canadian Conscription for War," *Vancouver Sun*, 9 Sept. 1939, 8.

55 "Stop Them! An Editorial," *Halifax Herald*, 2 Sept. 1939, 3 (see also "Stop Them Right Now: An Editorial," *Halifax Herald*, 5 Sept. 1939, 1); "No Profiteering!" *Winnipeg Tribune*, 4 Sept. 1939, 13 (thus, the profiteering that today's Canadian War Museum considers an illusion of "emotional" people was seen in 1939 as one of the paramount phenomena of the Great War that Canadians were enjoined to remember); "Time to Prepare," *Vancouver Sun*, 1 Sept. 1939, 10; "War Supplies First Need from Canada," *Toronto Star*, 4 Sept. 1939, 1, 2 (reprinted more or less verbatim in Winnipeg: W.W. Murray, CP Press, "Will Pay High If War Is Long," *Winnipeg Tribune*, 4 Sept. 1939, 18); "Canada's War Bill near $3,000,000,000," *Toronto Star*, 4 Sept. 1939, 6; "Work for All to Do: An Editorial," *Halifax Herald*, 6 Sept. 1939, 1; "Warns against Enlisting Men Who Are

Unfit," *Calgary Herald*, 2 Sept. 1939, 3. The *Toronto Star*'s "Canada's War Bill" story was a Canadian Press article that was also picked up by the *Calgary Herald* and *Edmonton Journal*: see A.W. Murray, "First World War Has Cost Canada $3,000,000,000," *Calgary Herald*, 4 Sept. 1939, 4; "A.W. Murray, "Recall Great War of 1914–18 Cost Canada $3,000,000,000," *Edmonton Journal*, 4 Sept. 1939, 12. See also "Last War's Mistakes Costly to Canadians," *Toronto Star*, 7 Sept. 1939, 2; and "Experience of Great War to Benefit Munitions Board," *Edmonton Journal*, 4 Sept. 1939, 7.

56 "Raymond Repeats Anti-War Appeals," *Gazette* (Montreal), 9 Sept. 1939, 10.

57 "Few Oppose Dominion's Entering War," *Leader-Post* (Regina), 11 Sept. 1939, 9.

58 Campbell Carroll, "Paul Gouin, at Anti-War Meeting, Suggests Own Participation Plan," *Gazette* (Montreal), 5 Sept. 1939, 11, 13. The slogan attributed to Lord Tweedsmuir, formerly John Buchan, to the effect that a Canadian owed his first allegiance to Canada was for a time a feature of the masthead of *Le Devoir*.

59 "Canada's War Entry Opposed," *Vancouver Sun*, 5 Sept. 1939, 3; "Ottawa and Paul Gouin," *Gazette* (Montreal), 6 Sept. 1939, 8; "Canada Maps Its Course," *Vancouver Sun*, 9 Sept. 1939, 4; "Wanted—At Once," *Calgary Herald*, 6 Sept. 1939, 4; "Canada to Assume Big Role in War," *Gazette*, 11 Sept. 1939, 5; "Canada's Part," *Vancouver Sun*, 4 Sept. 1939, 6. Gouin held rallies across Quebec and circulated a petition. See "Quebec Town Cool to Anti-War Plea," *Gazette* (Montreal), 6 Sept. 1939, 6.

60 "Reginans Spend Sleepless Night Waiting for War News," *Leader-Post* (Regina), 1 Sept. 1939, 3; "No Senseless Intolerance," *Calgary Herald*, 7 Sept. 1939, 4. The article was reprinted from the *Winnipeg Free Press*; "We Face It Now," *Vancouver Sun*, 2 Sept. 1939, 6; "Who Is the Enemy?" *Calgary Herald*, 4 Sept. 1939, 4. The *Winnipeg Tribune* did quote one resentful 31-year-old man in a local café who exclaimed, "They should have finished the job last time . . . and kept these damn Germans under control. "The City Hears the News," *Winnipeg Tribune*, Extra, 3 Sept. 1939, 1, 2.

61 "Intolerable," *Halifax Herald*, 1 Sept. 1939, 6; "Work for All to Do: An Editorial," *Halifax Herald*, 6 Sept. 1939, 1.

62 When King did attempt to rouse the Liberal cabinet with a master narrative, it was one that dwelt not upon the nation-building righteousness of the Great War but the inevitability and goodness of liberalism, stretching from Papineau and Mackenzie and culminating in himself. W.L.M. King, Diary, 12 Sept. 1939.

63 W.L.M. King, Diary, 3 Sept. 1939. There is general agreement that most Canadians shared King's apprehension and that there was very little jubilation that fall.

64 Ian Miller, "Toronto's Response to the Outbreak of War, 1939," *Canadian Military History* 11, 1 (Winter 2002), 21. Miller notes Granatstein's complaint that Canadians were unenthusiastic about the war, on account of "neutralists, isolationists, and League supporters, as well as the vast majority of Québécois." Miller's arch rejoinder: "Only a Canadian historian would condemn Canadians for having learned lessons from the past."

65 *Winnipeg Free Press*, 15 Feb. 1934.

66 Thompson, *Canada and the End of the Imperial Dream*, 109–10.

6: SCULPTING THE JAGGED EDGES OF WAR:
MOMENTOUS QUESTIONS, MONUMENTAL DECISIONS

1 "Canada's Wonderful Memorial to Her Missing," *British Empire Service League*, 9, 1933, cited in Jacqueline Hucker, "Vimy: A Monument for the Modern World," *Architecture Canada* 33,1 (2008), 43.

2 Hucker, "Vimy: A Monument," 43. Hucker served as the historical consultant to the conservation team.

3 Glenbow Museum, Noel Adair Farrow Papers, cited in Jonathan Vance, *Death So Noble: Memory, Meaning and the First World War* (Vancouver: UBC Press, 1997), 218, fn.34.

4 Katherine Hale, "Walter S. Allward: Sculptor," *Canadian Magazine* 52,3 (1919), quoted in Lane Borstad, "Walter Allward: Sculptor and Architect of the Vimy Ridge Memorial," *Architecture Canada* 33,1 (2008), 26.

5 *Star Weekly* (Toronto), June 23, 1934; in clipping file of Allward fonds, Queen's University Archives (QUA), Kingston, Ont.

6 Walter Allward to A.E. Kent, Jan. 19, 1917, in Allward Papers, Fonds 5055, Box 1, QUA.

7 Borstad, "Walter Allward," 26; and *Saturday Night*, 13 Nov. 1920, quoted in Borstad, "Walter Allward," 27.

8 For details on Sam and Garnet Hughes, see Tim Cook, *The Madman and the Butcher: The Sensational Wars of Sam Hughes and General Arthur Currie* (Toronto: Allen Lane, 2010); Hughes letter to Beaverbrook is quoted in Vance, *Death So Noble*, 68.

9 Allward to Col. H.S. Osborne, Canadian Battlefield Memorials Commission ("an Agency of the Imperial War Graves Commission"), 27 Sept. 1926, in Allward Fonds, 5055, Box 1, File 9, QUA.

10 Col. H.S. Osborne to Walter Allward, 19 Aug. 1925; Allward to Osborne, 27 Oct. 1925, Allward fonds, File 8, QUA.

11 Osborne to Allward, 23 March 1931, file 16, QUA; Allward to Osborne, 16 June 1931, file 16, QUA.

12 *Star Weekly*, 23 June 1936; undated clipping, Allward fonds, File 19, QUA.

13 Jane Urquhart, *The Stone Carvers* (Toronto: McClelland and Stewart, 2001), 377.

14 "The King at Vimy Ridge; Eleven Years' Work Completed; 'Moonlit' Pylons on Douai Plan; A Protest against War," *The Observer*, 21 May 1936.

15 Nathan Greenfield, *Baptism of Fire: The Second Battle of Ypres and the Forging of Canada, April 1915* (Toronto: HarperCollins, 2007), 356. Greenfield is reverently quoting Robert Borden.

16 Alan Gordon, *Making Public Pasts: The Contested Terrain of Montreal's Public Memories, 1891–1930* (Montreal and Kingston: McGill-Queen's University Press, 2001), xv.

17 On war and commemoration in Canada, see Stephanie Martell Browness, "Site, Space, and Memory: The Construction of Meaning in Commemorative Public Space," M.A. thesis, Carleton University, Ottawa, 2010; Malcolm Ferguson,

"Canada's Response: The Making and Remaking of the National War Memorial,"
M.A. thesis, Carleton University, 2012; David L.A. Gordon and Brian S. Osborne,
"Constructing National Identity in Canada's Capital, 1900–2000: Confedera-
tion Square and the National War Memorial," *Journal of Historical Geography* 30,4
(October 2004); Gordon, *Making Public Pasts*; Alan Gordon, "Lest We Forget:
Two Solitudes in War and Memory," in *Canadas of the Mind: The Making and
Unmaking of Canadian Nationalisms in the Twentieth Century*, ed. Norman Hillmer
and Adam Chapnick (Montreal: McGill-Queen's University Press, 2007), 159–173;
Jacqueline Hucker, "'After the Agony in Stony Places': The Meaning and Signifi-
cance of the Vimy Monument," in *Vimy Ridge: A Canadian Reassessment*, ed. Geof-
frey Hayes, Andrew Iarocci, and Mike Bechthold (Waterloo, Ont.: Wilfrid Laurier
University Press, 2007), 279–290; Hucker, "'Battle and Burial': Recapturing the
Cultural Meaning of Canada's National Memorial on Vimy Ridge," *The Public
Historian* 31,1 (Winter 2009); Hucker, "Lest We Forget: National Memorials to
Canada's First World War Dead," *Journal of the Study of Architecture in Canada* 23,3
(1998); Susan Phillips-Desroches, "Canada's National War Memorial: Reflection
of the Past or Liberal Dream?" M.A. thesis, Carleton University, Ottawa, 2002;
Katie Pickles, "Claiming Cavell: Britishness and Memorialization," in *Canada and
the British World: Culture, Migration, and Identity*, ed. Philip Buckner (Vancouver
and Toronto: UBC Press, 2006), 157–73; John Pierce, "Constructing Memory:
The Vimy Memorial; Photo Essay: The Vimy Pilgrimage," *Canadian Military
History*, 1 (Autumn 1992): 4–14; Robert Shipley, *To Mark Our Place: A History of
Canadian War Memorials* (Toronto: NC Press, 1987); Denise Thomson, "National
Sorrow, National Pride; Commemoration of War in Canada, 1918–1945," *Journal
of Canadian Studies* 30,4 (Winter 1995–1996): 5–27; Jonathan Vance, "Tangible
Demonstration of a Great Victory; War Trophies in Canada," *Material History
Review* 42 (Fall 1995): 47–56; Vance, "The Great Response: Canada's Long Strug
gle to Honour the Dead of the Great War," *The Beaver* 76,5 (October/November
1996); Vance, "Sacrifice in Stained Glass: Memorial Windows of the Great War,"
Canadian Military History 5,2 (Autumn 1996): 16–24; Vance, *Death So Noble*. In
many respects, Angus Calder remarks, monuments are as much a sign of the times
in which they are constructed as they are a reflection of what they intend to commemorate. Angus Calder, *Disasters and Heroes: On War, Memory and Representation*
(Chicago: University of Chicago Press, 2004).

18 This observation is made by former Canadian War Museum curator Laura Brandon, *Art and War* (New York: Palgrave Macmillan, 2007), 115.

19 Jay Winter, *Remembering War: The Great War between Memory and History in the
Twentieth Century* (New Haven, Conn., and London: Yale University Press, 2006),
20.

20 As suggested by Allyson Booth, *Postcards from the Trenches: Negotiating the Space
between Modernism and the First World War* (New York and Oxford: Oxford University Press, 1996), ch. 1. As Booth notes, contemporary journalism singled out
the Canadians at Vimy Ridge for their foresight with respect to the European
burial of the dead: "According to the *Times*, the Canadian attack on Vimy Ridge
established the pattern for burial of the dead. Before the attack, '[O]f their own
initiative and with the assistance of the Directorate [of Graves Registration and

Enquiries] . . . [the Canadians] had marked out land, dug trenches, and made all arrangements for the burial of the killed in the forthcoming action. Within twenty-four hours of that brilliant and successful feat of arms the graves were each marked and recorded" (25).

21 See Vance, *Death So Noble*; Vance, Vance, "Sacrifice in Stained Glass," 16-24; Vance, *A History of Canadian Culture* (Don Mills, Ont.: Oxford University Press, 2009), 265. For similar themes in patterns of remembrance in Europe, see Stefan Goebel, *The Great War and Medieval Memory: War, Remembrance and Medievalism in Britain and Germany, 1914–1940* (Cambridge: Cambridge University Press, 2007).

22 Shipley, *To Mark Our Place*, 56–63.

23 W.L.M. King, Diary, 4 Aug. 1914; 2 Aug. 1914, Library and Archives Canada (LAC), Ottawa, MG26-J13.

24 H.S. Ferns and Bernard Ostry, "Mackenzie King and the First World War," *Canadian Historical Review* 36,2 (1955), 101, drawn from Proceedings of the Canadian Club, Toronto, 1912–1913, 10 (Toronto, 1913), 221.

25 W.L.M. King, Diary, 1, 2 Aug. 1914. In this regard King was anticipating a major theme in the recent historiography on the Great War.

26 W.L.M. King, Diary, 5 Aug. 1914.

27 W.L.M. King, Diary, 19 July 1917.

28 Mackenzie King, *Debates of the House of Commons*, 1922, 181; Mackenzie King, *Debates of the House of Commons*, 1926, III, 2355.

29 Tim Cook, *Warlords: Borden, Mackenzie King, and Canada's World Wars* (Toronto: Allen Lane, 2012), 203. But the King Diary reveals a number of friendly interactions with military men, including General Arthur Currie, none of which support this interpretation.

30 A point articulated most clearly by Norman Angell (1872–1967), a founding father of liberal internationalism, in *The Great Illusion: A Study of the Relation of Military Power in Nations to their Economic and Social Advantage* (New York: G.P. Putnam's & Sons, 1910); see also Angell, *The Foundations of International Policy* (London: William Heinemann, 1914).

31 W.L.M. King, Diary, 1 Jan. 1915; 5 Aug. 1914.

32 The only excuse for calling King a "warlord," as Cook does, would be to test the politician's spiritualist conviction that the dead revisit the living—since King's spirit would surely exert itself to correct any such attribution. Given that Cook sees King as a man who believed that "war had to be avoided at nearly any cost" and that "Another generation should not be marched into the trenches and the horror that they represented" (199), it is not clear in what sense the prime minister was in any way a "warlord"—a term that the book never defines.

33 Pierre Berton, *Marching as to War: Canada's Turbulent Years, 1899–1953* (Toronto: Doubleday Canada, 2001), 244. Berton was not the first writer to express qualms about King's ambiguous sexual identity. Henry Ferns and Bernard Ostry, in *The Age of Mackenzie King* (Toronto: James Lorimer, 1976), wrote with evident disdain of King's "strained emotional relationship" with Henry Albert Harper, whose exploration could be "safely left to the study of those interested in psychology" (50). In a 1960 letter politician A.K. Cameron declared, "If you would know a man

you must know the women in his life," and exclaimed: "There were no women in his life except: mediums, soothsayers and crystal gazers. As to sex consciousness he was as immune to temptation as a eunach [eunuch] or a hermorphidite [hermaphrodite]. So it would seem he ratted on nature." A.K. Cameron to D.C. Harvey, 22 March 1960, Public Archives of Nova Scotia (PANS), D.C. Harvey Fonds, vol. 437. C.P. Stacey spent much of his book *A Very Double Life: The Private World of Mackenzie King* (Toronto: Macmillan of Canada, 1976), attempting to prove, without clear evidence, that King was sexually involved with prostitutes.

34 W.L.M. King, Diary, 8 June 1919.

35 Formally the Peace and Victory Tower, it is colloquially and tellingly known as the Peace Tower.

36 Ferguson, "Canada's Response," 1.

37 Canada, *House of Commons Debates*, 11 May 1923, 2687–88, quoted in Ferguson, "Canada's Response," 22.

38 Quoted in Ferguson, "Canada's Response," 31–32.

39 Ferguson, "Canada's Response," 36–38, 47.

40 Quoted in Ferguson, "Canada's Response," 42.

41 Ferguson, "Canada's Response," 42; Thomson quoted, 71.

42 Ferguson, "Canada's Response," 80; King quoted, 52. Throughout much of Canada, as Gordon finds in Montreal, the "discourse of victory" was subordinated to the "discourse of peace." Gordon, *Making Public Pasts*, 92.

43 "I had thought, at one time, that I might have occasion to prepare a speech to deliver myself, if when the time of the unveiling came, I should then be in office. Little did I dream that the speech which I would write would be one for the King himself to deliver." W.L.M. King, Diary, 27 Feb. 1939, 4–5. Our thanks to Malcolm Ferguson for drawing this passage to our attention.

44 Ferguson, "Canada's Response," 17. The following discussion is indebted to Ferguson's thesis.

45 Gordon, *Making Public Pasts*, ch.5, and 99.

46 Malcolm Ferguson, "The Winnipeg War Memorial Controversy, 1924–1928," unpublished paper, Queen's University, Kingston, Ont., 2014. For insights into how Anglo-Winnipeggers dominated the city's public history in 1926, see Robert Cupido, "Public Commemoration and Ethnocultural Assertion: Winnipeg Celebrates the Diamond Jubilee of Confederation," *Urban History Review* 38,2 (Spring 2010): 64–74.

47 Victoria Baker, *Emanuel Hahn and Elizabeth Wyn Wood: Tradition and Innovation in Canadian Sculpture* (Ottawa: National Gallery of Canada, 1997), 28.

48 Baker, *Emanuel Hahn*, 30; reviewers quoted, 31.

49 Ferguson, "Winnipeg War Memorial Controversy." Like elsewhere in Canada, Winnipeg had seen private commemorations by groups such as the Women's Canadian Club and Soldiers' Relatives Memorial Association; and monuments erected by businesses such as the Canadian Pacific Railway and Bank of Montreal; but no general monument commemorating the war. In addition to the primary sources cited, this account relies upon Marilyn Baker, "To Honor and Remember:

Remembrances of the Great War, the Next-of-Kin Monument in Winnipeg," Manitoba Historical Society, http://www.mhs.mb.ca/docs/mb_history/02/nex-tofkinmonument.shtml (February 2016); Ferguson, "Winnipeg War Memorial Controversy"; and James Gray, "The Battle of the Winnipeg Cenotaph," in *The Roar of the Twenties* (Toronto: Macmillan of Canada, 1975), ch.12.

50 "Vets Oppose Using $10,000 for Cenotaph," *Winnipeg Tribune*, 3 June 1920, 1; "Amiens Anniversary Brings Score of Fresh Memorial Tokens to Cenotaph's Base," *Winnipeg Tribune*, 11 Aug. 1920, 6; "Catholics will Rebuild Rheims as a Memorial," *Winnipeg Tribune*, 16 Sept. 1920; Winter, *Remembering War*, 142.

51 "No decision on Cenotaph Site," *Winnipeg Tribune*, 21 Dec. 1923; "Cenotaph Site Not Located," *Winnipeg Tribune*, 14 Feb. 1924; "New Committee to Choose Site for Cenotaph," *Winnipeg Tribune*, 2 May 1924.

52 "Board of Trade Protests Award Cenotaph Plan," *Winnipeg Tribune*, 9 Feb. 1926, 1; "Veterans Protest Cenotaph Award," *Winnipeg Tribune*, 12 Feb. 1926, 6; "GWVA Regret Award in Cenotaph Competition," *Winnipeg Tribune*, 17 Feb. 1926, 5.

53 C.D., "The War Memorial," *Winnipeg Tribune*, 20 Feb. 1926, 5; "Protest against Cenotaph Design to Be Reviewed by War Memorial Committee," *Winnipeg Tribune*, 25 Feb. 1926, 9.

54 M.N., "Bury Old Hates," *Winnipeg Tribune*, 27 Feb. 1926, 9.

55 "The Cenotaph Design," *Winnipeg Tribune*, 10 March 1926, 4; "ILP Supports Attitude Taken by Ald. Durward," *Winnipeg Tribune*, 12 March 1926, 2. See also Edgar J. Tarr, "Winnipeg Canadian Club Urges Acceptance of Hahn Memorial Design," *Winnipeg Tribune*, 10 March 1926, 1, 3.

56 Victoria Baker, *Emanuel Hahn and Elizabeth Wyn Wood: Tradition and Innovation in Canadian Sculpture* (Ottawa: National Gallery of Canada, 1997), 51–52.

57 "Mrs. Hahn Thinks Husband's Nationality Lost Her Award," *Winnipeg Tribune*, 5 Dec. 1927, 1.

58 "Design a Failure," *Winnipeg Tribune*, 24 Nov. 1927, 9.

59 Both Hahn and Wood were involved in further commemorative activities—the stunning Welland-Crowland War Memorial is one of Wood's most memorable—but not in Winnipeg.

60 "Legion Demands Improvement of Cenotaph Site," *Winnipeg Tribune*, 10 Oct. 1929, 3; $2,500 Voted to Clean Up Cenotaph Site," *Winnipeg Tribune*, 15 Oct. 1929, 3.

61 A Soldier's Widow, "A Widow's Protest," *Winnipeg Tribune*, 11 Oct. 1930, 4.

62 Mrs. Jack Thom, "Woman's Opinion of Armistice," *Winnipeg Tribune*, 9 Dec. 1932, 12.

63 J.H. Gray, "Battle of the Winnipeg Cenotaph," *Canadian Forum*, November 1934, 60–64; subsequently included in Gray, *Roar of the Twenties*.

64 For contemporary articles on Allward, see Hale, "Walter S. Allward, Sculptor"; H.C. Osborne, "Allward of Vimy," *Saturday Night*, April 1937. See also Dennis Duffy, "Complexity and Contradiction in Canadian Public Sculpture: The Case of Walter Allward," *American Review of Canadian Studies* 38,2 (Summer 2008): 189–206; and Duffy, "Among the Missing: Mass Death & Canadian National-

ism at the Vimy Memorial," *disClosure: A Journal of Social Theory* 18,10 (2009), 159–180.

65 "Mr. Henry: Re: Vimy Ridge," n.d., LAC, W.L.M. King Papers, Memoranda and Notes, MG 26 J4, vol. 225, C-4287, C-153290.

66 Pierce, "Constructing Memory," 5.

67 Quoted in Hucker, "'After the Agony in Stony Places,'" 282.

68 Quoted in Hucker, "'After the Agony in Stony Places,'" 279.

69 W.L.M. King, Diary, 13 April 1926; 5 Oct. 1928.

70 "Would Abrogate Cenotaph Plan and Build Memorial Home for Mentally Unfit," *Winnipeg Free Press*, March 8, 1926, as cited in Ferguson, "Winnipeg," 30. The Communist Party of Canada critically observed that by 1926, $195.312.95 had been spent on "Battlefield memorials." See "Great War Still Costing Canada Many Million Dollars Yearly," *The Worker* (Toronto), March 20, 1926, cited in Ferguson, "Winnipeg War Memorial Controversy," 31.

71 All these examples are drawn from David Thompson, "Working-Class Anguish and Revolutionary Indignation: The Making of Radical and Socialist Unemployment Movements in Canada, 1875–1928," Ph.D. thesis, Queen's University, Kingston, Ont., 2014, ch.10; see also, for Macphail, Canada, *House of Commons Debates*, 23 April 1926, 2757, as cited in Vance, *Death So Noble*, 263.

72 Canada, *House of Commons Debates*, First Session – Fifteenth Parliament, vol. 173, March 12, 1926, 3260.

73 Quoted in Ferguson, "Canada's Response," 104.

74 W.W. Murray, comp. and ed., *The Epic of Vimy*, 2nd ed. (Ottawa: The Legionary, 1937); D.E. Macintyre, *Canada at Vimy* (Toronto: Peter Martin Associates, 1967), 100. For descriptions of the 1936 event, see both of these books, and also W.W. Murray, "The Vimy Pilgrimage," *Canadian Geographical Journal* 13,8 (1939); Lt. Col. Graham Seton Hutchison, *Pilgrimage* (London: Rich and Cowan, 1936), Walter S. Woods, *The Men Who Came Back: A Book of Memories* (Toronto: Ryerson Press, 1956), 106–21.

75 John Hundevad, "The Origin," in Murray, *Epic of Vimy*, 6.

76 Macintyre, *Canada at Vimy*, 160; Murray, *Epic of Vimy*, 13.

77 Macintyre, *Canada at Vimy*, 175, 178.

78 Hucker, "'After the Agony in Stony Places,'" 284; Hundevad, "The Origin," 6. This is also the tone struck in a volume of 1930s verse devoted to Vimy: see Leonard Fels-Charlick [Charles Leonard Flick], *The Ballad of Vimy Ridge* (Dawlish, Devon: The Canning Press, 1937).

79 Hucker, "'After the Agony in Stony Places,'" 287–88.

80 Murray, *Epic of Vimy*, 75, 88.

81 Hucker, "'After the Agony in Stony Places,'" 288; Macintyre, *Canada at Vimy*, 189–90.

82 Murray, *Epic of Vimy*, 79.

83 Macintyre, *Canada at Vimy*, 187.

84 Murray, *Epic of Vimy*, 93–94.

85 Macintyre, *Canada at Vimy*, 165–66.

86 Murray, *Epic of Vimy*, 97. The exploits of early French explorer Samuel de Champlain and Louis-Joseph de Montcalm, the French commander during the Seven Years War who died at the Battle of the Plains of Abraham in 1759, are well known. The lesser-known "Maisonneuve" refers to Paul de Chomedey, Sieur de Maisonneuve (1612–76), the French officer who contributed to the foundation of Montreal.

87 Murray, *Epic of Vimy*, 67.

88 See Murray, *Epic of Vimy*; David Inglis, "Vimy Ridge: A Canadian Myth Over Seventy Five Years," M.A. thesis, Simon Fraser University, 1995, 69, 71; Canadian Battlefields Memorials Commission quoted in Hucker, "'After the Agony in Stony Places,'" 279.

89 For the text, see Murray, *Epic of Vimy*, 93; for one story that highlighted the phrase, see "'A World at Peace Only True Memorial," *Halifax Herald*, 27 July 1936, 4.

90 Sandra Gwyn, *Tapestry of War: A Private View of Canadians in the Great War* (Toronto: HarperCollins, 1992), 345.

91 George Perley to Bennett, 24 March 1932, LAC, Bennett Papers, MG 26 K, M-1093 271114-3.

92 One of the great unanswered questions about Vimy is why the monument still exists. In June 1940 word reached Canada that the Nazis had destroyed the monument—which provoked outrage at such a "wanton" act of destruction. The story turned out to be untrue. The full story of the Nazis and Vimy has yet to be written, but it seems unlikely that the Nazis spared the monument out of fondness for the British Empire or a chivalric attitude towards memorials for dead soldiers from adversary countries. For the story, see Serge Durflinger, "Safeguarding Sanctity: Canada and the Vimy Memorial during the Second World War," in *Vimy Ridge*, ed. Hayes, Iarocci, and Bechthold; and "Chronology of Vimy Memorial," n.d., LAC, W.L.M. King Papers, Memoranda and Notes, MG 26 J4, vol. 345, H-1528, C-238307. To our knowledge, no one has really answered *why* the Nazis spared the monument. See Kirrily Freeman, "The Battle for Bronzes: The Destruction of French Public Statuary, 1941–44," Ph.D. thesis, University of Waterloo, 2005, for indications of how other monuments in France were handled in the period of Nazi domination.

93 For the inscription of names, see Pierce, "Constructing Memory," 6; Randal Marlin, *Propaganda and the Ethics of Persuasion*, 2nd ed. (Peterborough, Ont.: Broadview Press, 2013), 340.

94 Fallis quoted in Macintyre, *Canada at Vimy*, 189–90; and in Murray, *Epic of Vimy*, 91–92; Deschamps in Murray, *Epic of Vimy*, 93.

95 Hucker, "'After the Agony in Stony Places,'" 283.

96 Pierce, "Constructing Memory," 6. The reference given for this information in Hucker is imprecise.

97 See, for an illuminating German-British comparison, Goebel, *The Great War and Medieval Memory*.

98 Victor Huard, "Armageddon Reconsidered: Shifting Attitudes towards Peace in English Canada, 1936–1953," Ph.D. thesis, Queen's University, Kingston, Ont., 1996, 53–54.

99 Huard, "Armageddon Reconsidered," 54.

100 Macintyre, *Canada at Vimy*, 178. See Pierce, "Constructing Memory," 11, for a photograph of the Honour Guard of Canadian Great War Veterans.

101 Quoted in Huard, "Armageddon Reconsidered," 54 (*New Outlook*), 55 (*Winnipeg Free Press*, 27 July 1936).

102 Hucker, "Vimy: A Monument," citing *British Empire Service League*.

103 W.L.M. King, Diary, 26 July 1936.

104 "'A World at Peace' Only True Memorial," *Halifax Herald*, 27 July 1936, 4, quoted in Huard, "Armageddon Reconsidered," 55; R.L.F, "Notes re: Resolution of Thanks to the Canadian Battlefields Memorials Commission," 11 June 1936, LAC, W.L.M. King Papers, Memoranda and Notes, MG 26 J4, vol. 225, C-4287, C-153298–307. In certain moods King tends towards a nation-forged-in-war narrative but even here he links it to the war's horrors and the need for peace. Note, too, that he does not confine his narrative to soldiers but widens it to include the people as a whole.

105 "Message from the Prime Minister of Canada on the Occasion of the Unveiling of the Memorial at Vimy," 26 July 1936, LAC, W.L.M. King Papers, Memoranda and Notes, MG 26 J4, vol. 225, C-4287, C-153365–70. At least one Vimy veteran told him that "the troops, who are pretty critical, thought it admirable in content and length." Sgt. W.J. Garvock to King, 26 July 1936, LAC, W.L.M. King Papers, MG 26 J1, C-3688, 187150.

106 Hector Charlesworth to King, 19 Aug. 1936, LAC, W.L.M. King Papers, MG 26 J1, C-3686, 185045–47.

107 G.R.L. Potter, Ottawa, untitled poem, in Murray, *Epic of Vimy*.

108 Murray, *Epic of Vimy*, 62.

109 Macintyre, *Canada at Vimy*, 187.

110 Alex Ross to King, 16 Sept. 1937, C-3729, 207193; Alex Ross to King, 13 May 1937, C-3729, 207195–98, LAC, W.L.M. King Papers, MG 26 J1.

111 See Pierce, "Constructing Memory," 5, for the claim that the event was meant to "symbolize Canada's coming-of age as a nation." Yet evidence for the assertion is missing.

112 Quoted in Hucker, "'After the Agony in Stony Places,'" 283. King certainly saw himself as the man who, next to Allward himself, deserved the credit for the monument. As he told the story in 1922, ever since 1919 he had been pushing for preservation of the ridge as a permanent memorial; as a record of "Canadian genius and bravery," this "tract of consecrated ground in the heart of Europe" must be preserved. A century and a half in the future, when Canada had attained an "important position . . . as a nation," its people would greatly appreciate it. The acquisition of the 250-acre site from the French was the "outcome of my agitation and persistent efforts to secure this land for Canada." King to P.C. Larkin, 22 July 1922, LAC, W.L.M. King Papers, MG 26 J1, C-2246, 64456–58; W.L.M. King, Diary, 5 Dec. 1922, Library and Archives Canada (LAC), Ottawa, MG26-J13. Channeling the spirit of 1936, Prime Minister Lester Pearson used the Ottawa ceremony in 1967 to remind listeners that all of the soldiers at Vimy wore their maple leaf emblems, and that the Great War as a whole confirmed the dire need for "collective action

towards peace." *Winnipeg Free Press*, 10 April 1967, 1, 8, as quoted in Inglis, "Vimy Ridge," 92.

113 "Address of Welcome by the Prime Minister of Canada on the occasion of the Visit of President Roosevelt to Quebec," 31 July 3 1936, LAC, W.L.M. King Papers, Memoranda and Notes, MG 26 J4, vol. 225, C-4287, C-153365–70.

114 Inglis, "Vimy Ridge," 116; the preceding points in this paragraph draw on Inglis, "Vimy Ridge," 58, 56, 71.

115 This discussion builds upon similar reflections in Pierce, "Constructing Memory," 7.

116 For details, see Suzanne Evans, *Mothers of Heros, Mothers of Martyrs: World War I and the Politics of Grief* (Montreal and Kingston: McGill-Queen's University Press, 2007), 103–5, 161–63. See also Veteran Affairs Canada, "1936 National Memorial (Silver) Cross Mother—Charlotte Susan Wood," http://www.veterans.gc.ca/eng/remembrance/memorials/books/silver/1936 (June 2016).

117 *Illustrated London News*, 1 Aug. 1936.

118 "His Majesty Voices Hope 'It Shall Never Happen Again' to Mrs. Wood," *Winnipeg Free Press*, 28 July 1936, as quoted in Evans, *Mothers of Heroes, Mothers of Martyrs*, 162–63. See also Veteran Affairs Canada, "1936 National Memorial (Silver) Cross Mother—Charlotte Susan Wood."

7: THE LONG AND WINDING ROAD TO VIMYISM

1 M.J. Scott, "Stirs Deep Spiritual Emotions," *Globe and Mail*, 11 Nov. 1950.

2 Claxton in *Globe and Mail*, 13 Nov. 1950. Claxton's views about military spending had changed since the 1930s. Having served briefly as Canada's first minister of National Health and Welfare during an early phase of the federal welfare state, he moved into the National Defence portfolio in 1946, a position he held until 1954. He had a key role in shaping foreign policy in the early Cold War period. The phrase "good war" is borrowed from the title of a Studs Terkel book: *The Good War: An Oral History of World War Two* (1984). There has been much mythologization of the war. It was, of course, an epic struggle against fascism and militarism, a war that had to be fought. Yet, as Fussell, himself a Second World War veteran, suggests: "The Allied war has been sanitized and romanticized almost beyond recognition by the sentimental, the loony patriotic, the ignorant and the bloodthirsty." Paul Fussell, *Wartime* (New York: Oxford University Press, 1989), ix. For the ambiguity of Canada's Second World War and the difficult and contradictory aspects of Canada's "good war," see Sherrill Grace, *Landscapes of War and Memory: The Two World Wars in Canadian Literature and the Arts, 1977–2007* (Edmonton: University of Alberta Press, 2014), Part IV.

3 "Aviation History," G.E. Aviation, http://www.geaviation.com/company/aviation-history.html (June 2016).

4 J.S Keefler, "Proposes Youth Get Compulsory Army Training," *Globe and Mail*, 10 Nov. 1950.

5   Ian McKay and Jamie Swift, *Warrior Nation: Rebranding Canada in an Age of Anxiety* (Toronto: Between the Lines, 2012), 96.

6   Gwynne Dyer, *Canada in the Great Power Game 1914–2014* (Toronto: Random House Canada, 2014), 311.

7   "Past the Eleventh Hour," *Winnipeg Free Press*, 11 Nov. 1960.

8   J.A.D., "Uncomfortable Thought," *Winnipeg Free Press*, 11 Nov. 1960.

9   Ralph Allen, *Ordeal by Fire: Canada 1914–1945* (Toronto: Doubleday Canada, 1961), 97. For Currie's statement to the troops, see chapter 3 here.

10 Allen, *Ordeal by Fire*, 143–44, 107. When Ottawa finally expropriated the Ross factory in 1917, it paid the owner $2 million for a venture with an initial capitalization of half that amount.

11 Allen, *Ordeal by Fire*, 172, 149, 157.

12 *Globe and Mail*, 13 Nov. 1961.

13 A.B. Hodgetts, *Decisive Decades: A History of the Twentieth Century for Canadians* (Toronto: Thomas Nelson and Sons, 1960). Hodgetts would later become well known as the author of a highly critical assessment of the teaching of Canadian history.

14 For an insightful analysis of Hodgetts' text, see José E. Igartua, *The Other Quiet Revolution: National Identities in English Canada, 1945–71* (Vancouver and Toronto: UBC Press, 2006), 151–53. As Igartua points out, like many of his generation, Hodgetts still used the category of "race" for "culture" or "people," but his consistent argument was that in order for Canada's two main linguistic groups to coexist, they needed to understand and accommodate one another.

15 Hodgetts, *Decisive Decades*, 159.

16 Hodgetts, *Decisive Decades*, 222, 174, 161, 168, 208 ("no serious student"), 162, 222. Flame-throwers went on to become a favoured weapon of Canadian troops in Italy in the Second World War.

17 Hodgetts, *Decisive Decades*, 162, 222, 171–72 ("raging inferno"). Hodgetts also eschews the individualistic Haig-bashing that has allowed some Canadian historians to imagine the British field marshal to be the singularly dense culprit responsible for the mass deaths of attritional warfare.

18 Hodgetts, *Decisive Decades*, 199, 207, 203. Much of the additional wartime debt load was caused by the government's decision to bail out the "misguided private ventures" of bankrupt railway companies, with a $700-million price tag borne not by their shareholders but by Canadian citizens, forced to pay almost $150 million a year in interest charges. The war years thus revealed "a story of greed, selfishness and sometimes of complete dishonesty," which forms an "unpleasant, indeed a disgraceful, chapter in our history." Hodgetts, *Decisive Decades*, 206.

19 Hodgetts, *Decisive Decades*, 208, 212, 213, 225.

20 Hodgetts, *Decisive Decades*, 180. Hodgetts does use the term "amazing achievement" in reference to the war, but only when he speaks of the five Victory Loan drives during the conflict. Hodgetts, *Decisive Decades*, 204.

21 John C. Ricker, John T. Saywell, and Elliot E. Rose, *The Modern Era* (Toronto: Clarke, Irwin, 1960).

22 Ricker, Saywell, and Rose, *Modern Era*, 118, 136, 108–10.

23 Some 50 years later veteran CBC-Radio producer Steve Wadhams condensed the tape into a five-part *Ideas* series, *The Bugle and the Passing Bell*, which ran from 22 June to 26 June 2015.

24 *The Bugle and the Passing Bell*, CBC-Radio *Ideas*, Part 3, "Siege Warfare and Newfoundland's Day of the Dead," June 24, 2015, http://www.cbc.ca/radio/ideas/the-bugle-and-the-passing-bell-part-3-siege-warfare-and-newfoundland-s-day-of-the-dead-1.3124810 (June 2016).

25 *Flanders Fields*, CBC-Radio, Part 9, *The Battle of Vimy Ridge*, mimeo transcript, 1964, NAC, RG 41, vols. 6–22; a seventeen-part series of interviews conducted between 1962 and 1964. This extensive collection includes over 830 hours of interviews.

26 Frank Underhill, "The Canadian Forces in the War," in *The Empire at War*, vol. 2, ed. Sir Charles Lucas (Toronto: Oxford University Press, 1923), 81–294.

27 Quoted in Kenneth C. Dewar, *Frank Underhill and the Politics of Ideas* (Montreal and Kingston: McGill-Queen's University Press, 2015), 98.

28 Dewar, *Frank Underhill and the Politics of Ideas*, 99–100.

29 *Flanders Fields*, vol. 6, ch. 17, Frank Underhill, "The Aftermath."

30 *Flanders Fields*, vol. 6, ch. 17, Frank Underhill, "The Aftermath."

31 *Fields of Sacrifice*, dir. Donald Brittain, 38 min., National Film Board of Canada, 1964, https://www.nfb.ca/film/fields_of_sacrifice (October 2015).

32 *Good Times, Bad Times*, dir. Don Shebib (also photography and editing), 40 min., CBC, 1974; Peter Harcourt, "Men of Vision: Some Comments on the Work of Don Shebib," in *Canadian Film Reader*, ed. Seth Feldman and Joyce Nelson (Toronto: Peter Martin, 1977), 211, 209.

33 Cary, a Great War veteran, fought with a Nigerian regiment against the Germans in Cameroon.

34 Jonathan Vance, "A Moment's Perfection," in *In Flanders Fields: Writing on War, Loss and Remembrance*, ed. Amanda Betts (Toronto: Alfred A. Knopf Canada, 2015), 204.

35 A.J.P. Taylor, *The First World War: An Illustrated History* (Harmondsworth, U.K.: Penguin, 1967). For a critical assessment of the impact of Taylor's notoriously sarcastic book, see Dan Todman, *The Great War: Myth and Memory* (London: Continuum, 2011), 137–39.

36 John G. Diefenbaker, *Those Things We Treasure: A Selection of Speeches on Freedom and in Defence of Our Parliamentary Heritage* (Toronto: Macmillan of Canada, 1972), 106, 55; Diefenbaker, *One Canada: Memoirs of the Right Honourable John G. Diefenbaker*, vol. 1, *The Crusading Years, 1895 to 1956* (Toronto: Macmillan of Canada, 1975), 82, 89, 87. On receiving an honour in London in 1963 Diefenbaker referred to the city as the "cradle of freedom in the Motherland of liberty and self-government." Diefenbaker, *Those Things We Treasure*, 106. Diefenbaker did not actually proceed to the Front, but this hardly influences how he chose to "remember" it, based on his own experiences.

37 *Mike: The Memoirs of the Right Honourable Lester B. Pearson*, vol. 1 (Toronto: University of Toronto Press, 1972), 28.

38 *Toronto Star*, 10 April 1967.

39 Gregory Clark, "The Symbol," *Weekend Magazine*, 4 April 1967, 2.

40 *Globe and Mail*, 10 April 1967.

41 Alex Ross, "Introduction," to D.E. Macintyre, *Canada at Vimy* (Toronto: Peter Martin Associates, 1967), viii.

42 Macintyre, *Canada at Vimy*, 4, 12–13, 206–7. In his own battalion in Saskatchewan, 80 per cent were British-born, 18 per cent Canadian, and 2 per cent American.

43 Macintyre, *Canada at Vimy*, 211.

44 Macintyre, *Canada at Vimy*, 70, 25–26, 69.

45 W.B. Kerr, "Historical Literature on Canada's Participation in the Great War," *Canadian Historical Review* 41 (1933): 412–36.

46 Macintyre, *Canada at Vimy*, 70, 116, 118.

47 Macintyre, *Canada at Vimy*, 50, 103.

48 Macintyre, *Canada at Vimy*, 62–63.

49 Macintyre, *Canada at Vimy*, 84, 28, 77–78.

50 Macintyre, *Canada at Vimy*, 196, 206, 215.

51 Macintyre, *Canada at Vimy*, 154.

52 John Swettenham, *To Seize the Victory: The Canadian Corps in World War I* (Toronto: Ryerson Press, 1965). After serving in the Second World War with the Royal Engineers, Swettenham immigrated to Canada and joined the Army Historical Section; he became one of three historians responsible for preparing the official history of Canadian Army operations.

53 Swettenham, *To Seize the Victory*, 26 ("virile race"), 241 ("harder breed"), 107 ("hard climate"), 239 ("tragic nuisance"), 145, 239 ("greatest national achievement"), 20 (vilification), 84 ("battle-leader"). The quotation "the greatest national achievement . . ." references the 1923 words of imperial historian Sir Charles Lucas.

54 Swettenham, *To Seize the Victory*, 145.

55 Swettenham, *To Seize the Victory*, 151 ("nonsense"), 106 (Ypres), 105 ("decomposed bodies"), 185 (Passchendaele).

56 Swettenham, *To Seize the Victory*, 93, citing Richard M. Watt, *Dare Call It Treason* (London: Chatto & Windus, 1964), 84.

57 Swettenham, *To Seize the Victory*, 127 (Hughes), 113 ("great gamble of the Somme"), 189 (Passchendaele), 190 ("frontal assault").

58 Swettenham, *To Seize the Victory*, 20 ("great sacrifices"), 234 ("young whelps"), 185.

59 Swettenham, *To Seize the Victory*, 61 ("stalemate"), 189 ("barren victory").

60 Maj.-Gen. F.F. Worthington, "Foreword," in Herbert Fairlie Wood, *Vimy!* (Toronto: Macmillan of Canada, 1967; London: Corgi, 1972), 5. Page references here refer to the Corgi edition.

61 Wood, *Vimy!* 154, 158 ("Canada's progress towards nationhood"), 159 ("Agincourt"), 158 ("folly of war"), 156 ("Harness nations," "sense of achievement").

62 Wood, *Vimy!* 33 ("essentially peace-loving"), 103 ("throats"), 147–48 (rats).

63 Wood, *Vimy!* 44 ("square meal"), 45 ("dined well," "shrewd suspicion"), 46 ("discomfort of their costume").

64 Wood, *Vimy!* 62 ("strange man"), 63 ("slaughter of a generation"), 45 ("bad man-
    agement"), 43 (fate of horses).

65 D.J. Goodspeed, *The Road Past Vimy: The Canadian Corps 1914–1918* (Toronto:
    Macmillan of Canada, 1969), 173 ("war and military considerations"), 93 ("Canada
    became a nation").

66 Goodspeed, *Road Past Vimy*, 173 ("futilities"), 7 ("to ensure the integrity," "jugger-
    naut"), 55 ("Prussian militarism"), 151–52 ("most battlefields").

67 Goodspeed, *Road Past Vimy*, 25 ("used at Waterloo," Scott, "shaking hands"), 36
    ("all military logic," "look at the map"), 122–23, 53, 67, 122. Almost three decades
    later Robin Prior and Trevor Wilson were of the same mind: "The delusions of the
    military command, and the waywardness of the political leadership, brought dire
    consequences upon Haig's army in the Flanders campaign of 1917," leaving it so
    weakened that the ground fought for desperately from July to November 1917 was
    relinquished in just three days. Prior and Wilson, *Passchendaele: The Untold Story*
    (New Haven, Conn., and London: Yale University Press, 1996), 200. That Haig
    was allowed by politicians—including Lloyd George—to undertake the offensive
    "beggars comprehension" (196). Frederick George Scott was an Anglican clergy-
    man and poet who served as the senior chaplain of the 1st Canadian Division in the
    Great War. A zealous imperialist and ardent war supporter, his book *The Great War
    as I Saw It* (1922) is a useful first-hand account of the war by a man wounded in 1918.
    It describes his 1916 search for the body of his son at the Somme. Another son,
    F.R. "Frank" Scott, enjoyed considerable success as a poet. The younger Scott was a
    prominent social democrat, and together with Frank Underhill would help to found
    the Co-operative Commonwealth Federation, co-authoring key party publications.

68 Goodspeed, *Road Past Vimy*, 48 ("incompetence"), 129 ("emotion").

69 Goodspeed, *Road Past Vimy*, 93 ("military genius"), 124 ("common hardship"), 74
    ("little hatred"). True, fired up by propaganda in 1918, "a few Canadian units lost
    much of their inclination to take prisoners" (170).

70 Goodspeed, *Road Past Vimy*, 133 ("gigantic gerrymander"), 135 ("as divided"), 128
    ("super-patriots").

71 G.W.L. Nicholson, *Canadian Expeditionary Force, 1914-1919* (Ottawa: Queen's
    Printer, 1962 [Montreal and Kingston: McGill-Queen's University Press, 2015]).
    In his perceptive and critical introduction to the reprinted version, historian Mark
    Osborne Humphries remarks: "In the conventional nationalist telling we lose
    much of the nuance to the story. The Canadian Corps was never an autonomous
    formation capable of independent action. . . . For those who fought between 1914
    and 1918, the war was not about national independence or coming of age: this
    claim is an historical imposition. Canadians were doing their bit for King and
    Empire because it was ultimately an Imperial war effort to safeguard a British
    Empire that most believed was indestructible" (xxxv).

72 A.B. McKillop, *Pierre Berton: A Biography* (Toronto: McClelland and Stewart,
    2008), 637.

73 Pierre Berton, *The Invasion of Canada 1812–1813* (Toronto: McClelland and Stew-
    art, 1980), 314; Berton, *Flames across the Border* (Toronto: McClelland and Stewart,
    1981), 428–29.

74 Berton, *Invasion of Canada*, 314.

75 Pierre Berton, *Marching as to War: Canada's Turbulent Years, 1899–1953* (Toronto: Doubleday Canada), 3–4.

76 McKillop, *Pierre Berton*, 595.

77 Berton, *Marching as to War*, 157. Throughout we feel comfortable blending quotations from Berton's *Vimy* with his *Marching as to War* because Berton—an early apostle of recycling—repeated many ideas in the second book that he had expressed 15 years earlier.

78 Pierre Berton, *Vimy* (Toronto: McClelland and Stewart, 1986), 27 ("pleasure innocent"), 26 (Jolson). For Berton, Stephen Leacock's *Sunshine Sketches of a Little Town* (1912) perfectly captured *fin-de-siècle* Canada; Berton, *Vimy*, 27. That Leacock also wrote *Arcadian Adventures with the Idle Rich* (1914), a blistering satire of class-riddled Montreal, did not—and arguably could not—register within Berton's frontierist framework.

79 Berton, *Vimy*, 29 ("self-reliance"), 298 ("Old Country").

80 Quoted in Paul Dickson, "The End of the Beginning: The Canadian Corps in 1917," in *Vimy Ridge: A Canadian Reassessment*, ed. Geoffrey Hayes, Andrew Iarocci, and Mike Bechthold (Waterloo, Ont.: Laurier Centre for Military Strategic and Disarmament Studies, 2010), 32.

81 Berton, *Vimy*, 294 ("naïve enthusiasm"), 52 ("gumbo of Flanders").

82 Berton, *Vimy*, 28 ("lacrosse and ice hockey"), 48 ("sheep-like"), 160 ("whipcord").

83 McKillop, *Pierre Berton*, 592–93.

84 Mark Leier, "Kipling Gets a Red Card," *Labour/Le travail* 31 (Spring 1993), 163–68. Leier argues that Kipling, although an imperialist, was not just an imperialist, but a staunch defender of the rank-and-file soldier; newspapers of the Industrial Workers of the World (the "Wobblies") published poems that drew directly upon his poems, thus putting the imperialist's work to new, unintended uses.

85 Berton, *Vimy*, 85; Macphail quoted, 86.

86 Although Berton also writes, in populist mode: "No overall hero emerged from the Canadian Corps. . . . The real heroes were the masses of ordinary soldiers who fought and died in the belief they were making the world a better place, and their inventive leaders who stubbornly refused to follow the old rules of war." Berton, *Vimy*, 295.

87 Berton, *Vimy*, 109, 163. Currie as "the greatest soldier," Berton, *Marching as to War*, 226.

88 Berton, *Vimy*, 15 (French had squandered), 167 ("art of gunnery"), 165 ("encouraged their experiments"); "stiff-necked" British officer, Berton, *Marching as to War*, 206.

89 Berton, *Vimy*, 14; "40,000 maps . . . disseminated," Mark Osborne Humphries, "'Old Wine in New Bottles': A Comparison of British and Canadian Preparations for the Battle of Arras," in *Vimy Ridge*, ed. Hayes, Iarocci, and Bechthold, 77.

90 Berton, *Vimy*, 294.

91 Berton, *Vimy*, 314.

92 Berton, *Vimy*, frontispiece; Clark, "Symbol," 2.

93   Berton, *Vimy*, 200.

94   Berton, *Vimy*, 17 ("certain things"), 292 (Worthington).

95   Berton, *Marching as to War*, 240 ("daring and ingenuity"), 263 ("Downing Street").

96   Berton, *Marching as to War*, 305–6.

97   Berton, *Vimy*, 295.

98   Berton, *Marching as to War*, 178; Berton, *Vimy*, 296, 302.

99   Berton, *Marching as to War*, 2; Berton, *Vimy*, 305 ("echoed those plaudits"); 33 ("Vimy veteran").

100 Major John R. Grodzinski, "The Use and Abuse of Battle: Vimy Ridge and the Great War over the History of the First World War," *Canadian Military History* 10,1 (2009), 85. Grodzinski argued, for instance, that writers had not only overestimated the battle's military significance but also juxtaposed enterprising Canadians and Australian corps commanders with supposedly donkeyish, aristocratic, and château-bound British generals. He attached considerable weight to the question of the high casualty rate—leading him to suggest that, had Vimy been a sustained offensive (like Passchendaele) rather than a strictly limited engagement, "our perspective of that battle might well be different" (85).

101 A.M.J. Hyatt, "Foreword," in *Vimy Ridge*, ed. Hayes, Iarocci, and Bechthold, xi–xii.

102 Gary Sheffield, "Vimy Ridge and the Battle of Arras: A British Perspective," in *Vimy Ridge*, ed. Hayes, Iarocci, and Bechthold, 17.

103 Quoted in Andrew Iarocci, "The 1st Canadian Division: An Operational Mosaic," in *Vimy Ridge*, ed. Hayes, Iarocci, and Bechthold, 155.

104 Dickson, "End of the Beginning," 33; Jean Martin, "Vimy, April 1917: The Birth of *Which* Nation?" *Canadian Military Journal* 11,2 (Spring 2011), 34. According to Martin, as late as October 1917—that is, a half-year after Vimy—of the "438,806 men enlisted in the CEF, 194,473 (44.3 percent) were Canadian born, 215,749 (49.2 percent) were born in Britain and 26,564 (6 percent) were born in other countries."

105 Dickson, "End of the Beginning," 34.

106 Adrian Gregory, *The Last Great War: British Society and the First World War* (Cambridge: Cambridge University Press, 2008), makes this point in the British context, noting in particular that an environment of recurrent explosions and autocratic authorities would hardly have come as a great novelty to the thousands of British miners who enlisted.

107 Humphries, "'Old Wine in New Bottles,'" 80; Dickson, "End of the Beginning," 33; Sheffield, "Vimy Ridge and the Battle of Arras," 15; Geoffrey Hayes, Andrew Iarocci, and Mike Bechthold, "Afterthoughts," in *Vimy Ridge*, ed. Hayes, Iarocci, and Bechthold, 313.

108 Patrick Brennan, "Julian Byng and Leadership in the Canadian Corps," in *Vimy Ridge*, ed. Hayes, Iarocci, and Bechthold, 87. As Tim Cook remarks in *Shock Troops: Canadians Fighting the Great War 1917–1918* (Toronto: Viking Canada, 2008), 147: "In our elevation of the Battle of Vimy Ridge to the status of icon and

our reverence for it as a milestone along Canada's slow march to nationhood, we must still remember the full support of the British in logistics, in gunfire, and in fighting on the ridge."

109 Sheffield, "Vimy Ridge and the Battle of Arras," 27; Brennan, "Julian Byng and Leadership in the Canadian Corps," 100–1, quoting A.M.J. Hyatt, *General Sir Arthur Currie: A Military Biography* (Toronto: University of Toronto Press, 1987), 67; Dickson, "End of the Beginning," 38; Iarocci, "1st Canadian Division," 155; Andrew Godefroy, "The 4th Canadian Division: 'Trenches Should Never be Saved,'" in *Vimy Ridge*, ed. Hayes, Iarocci, and Bechthold, 212.

110 Humphries, "'Old Wine in New Bottles,'" 79–80; Brennan, "Julian Byng and Leadership in the Canadian Corps," 99, 94.

111 Berton, *Vimy*, 143–51, 19.

112 Humphries, "'Old Wine in New Bottles,'" 67. Currie had made note of these new ideas and sent a memo on the matter to General Byng.

113 Michael Boire, "Vimy Ridge: The Battlefield before the Canadians, 1914–1916," in *Vimy Ridge*, ed. Hayes, Iarocci, and Bechthold, 51, 60.

114 Berton, *Vimy*, 293 (for "greatest victory"); Sheffield, "Vimy Ridge and the Battle of Arras," 16; northern flank, Hayes, Iarocci, and Bechthold, "Afterthoughts," 313; Andrew Godefroy, "The German Army at Vimy Ridge," in *Vimy Ridge*, ed. Hayes, Iarocci, and Bechthold, 233–34, 226, 234; "Introduction," in *Vimy Ridge*, ed. Hayes, Iarocci, and Bechthold, 3, 10. The Battle of Arras is often overlooked in general accounts of the war and even in guidebooks devoted to its battlefields, Sheffield reports, even though it cost 159,000 casualties from 9 to 17 May 1917, "a daily rate of 4,076 that was higher than for any other major battle." Sheffield, "Vimy Ridge and the Battle of Arras," 15–16.

115 Godefroy, "German Army at Vimy Ridge," 234

116 To cite the contemporary developer of a new "virtual reality booth": Joe Lofaro, "In the Digital Trenches: Kanata Company Developing Vimy Ridge Simulator," Our Windsor.Ca, 10 Nov. 2015, http://www.ourwindsor.ca/news-story/6110747-in-the-digital-trenches-kanata-company-developing-vimy-ridge-simulator. See chapter 9 here.

117 "Introduction," in *Vimy Ridge*, ed. Hayes, Iarocci, and Bechthold, 10; Macintyre, *Canada at Vimy*, 93.

118 Sheffield, "Vimy Ridge and the Battle of Arras," 25; the impressive cohort of military historians: that is, the various authors in *Vimy Ridge*, ed. Hayes, Iarocci, and Bechthold, whose reassessment we have relied upon in the preceding pages.

119 Berton, *Vimy*, 25.

120 On the theme of the ethnic cleansing of the Plains, see James Daschuk, *Clearing the Plains: Disease, Politics of Starvation, and the Loss of Aboriginal Life* (Regina: University of Regina Press, 2013).

121 See Paul Maroney, "The Peaceable Kingdom Reconsidered: Attitudes toward War in English Canada, 1885–1914," Ph.D. thesis, Queen's University, Kingston, Ont., 1995.

122 This theme has its parallel in the Australian literature celebrating Anzac (see chapter 8 here).

123 Craig Gibson, *Behind the Front: British Soldiers and French Civilians, 1914–1918* (Cambridge: Cambridge University Press, 2014). Gibson's title itself suggests the extent to which Canadian and British identities were blurred: much of his research pertains to Canadian soldiers.

124 For an important initial investigation of this touchy subject, albeit with reference to the Second World War, see Rob Engen, "The Canadian Soldier: Combat Motivation in the Second World War, 1943–1945," Ph.D. dissertation, Queen's University, Kingston, Ont., 2014.

125 Berton, *Vimy*, 18 (drums of burning oil), 126 (render German positions vulnerable), 127 ("believe in magic"), 130 ("human details"), 133. To be fair, Berton frequently insists upon the moral equivalence of German and Canadian soldiers. After this particular episode at Vimy, which resulted in about 700 casualties, the Germans offered a temporary truce during which the Canadians could bury their dead: "It was strange to see the Canadians exchanging cigarettes with the men they had tried to gas to death, but there they were, attempting to talk to any who spoke English." Berton, *Vimy*, 134. As one soldier remembered: "The Germans worked hand in hand with us, dressing wounds, carrying stretchers over muddy, soaked ground. . . . There was not a trace of hate in the heart of any [German] that I worked with that day." Heather Moran, "The Canadian Army Medical Corps at Vimy Ridge," in *Vimy Ridge*, ed. Hayes, Iarocci, and Bechthold, 153.

126 Berton, *Vimy*, 287, 237–38.

127 Quoted in Will Ferguson, *Canadian History for Dummies* (Toronto: John Wiley and Sons, 2012), entry for Vimy Ridge.

128 See Cook, *Shock Troops*, 147.

129 Hayes, Iarocci, and Bechthold, "Afterthoughts," 316.

8: VIMY: THE EMERGING MYTH

1 Legion Branch Catalogue, October 2014 through September 2015, http://www.legion.ca/wp-content/uploads/2014/10/Catalogue_Fall_14_e_web1.pdf.

2 For an insightful analysis, see Tim Elcombe, "The Moral Equivalent of 'Don Cherry,'" *Journal of Canadian Studies* 44,2 (Spring 2010), 195, 200, 203, 211.

3 "The Royal Canadian Legion Dominion Command, https://www.facebook.com/CanadianLegion/posts/622056371205212. For a fuller exposition of Cherry's Vimy-ism in 2012, see "HNIC, Don Cherry's Coach's Corner," 7 April 2012, https://www.youtube.com/watch?v=8f5S0HWYxqY (November 2015). See also chapter 1 here.

4 Whether consciously or not, the slogan's contemporary promoters are echoing D.W. Griffith's 1915 film epic *The Birth of a Nation*, a dazzling if highly contentious depiction of U.S. history in which valiant Americans re-establish and racially purify their nation in the wake of the Civil War. Not long after the start of the Great War, the U.S. secretary of war ordered the military to provide a thousand mounted soldiers and a marching band to support the epic. See Joanna Bourke, *Wounding the World: How Military Violence and War-Play Invade Our Lives* (London: Virago, 2014), 181.

5 For the views of one Canadian historian on Australia, see J.L. Granatstein, *Whose War Is It? How Canada Can Survive in the Post-9/11 World* (Toronto: Harper, 2007). Granatstein imagines what a model future Canadian prime minister might say—basing this paragon on Australia's John Howard (202–3). In 2003 Stephen Harper directly plagiarized a speech urging Canada to enter the war with Iraq from an earlier speech by Howard. See CBC News Canada, "Harper Staffer Quits over Plagiarized 2003 Speech on Iraq," 30 Sept. 2008, http://www.cbc.ca/news/canada/harper-staffer-quits-over-plagiarized-2003-speech-on-iraq-1.756590; Jeffrey Simpson, "Harper's Australian Protégé," *Globe and Mail* (Toronto), 28 Feb. 2014.

6 Other scholars have also been impressed by the Australia-Canada parallels. See Lt.-Col. J.C. Blaxland, "Strategic Cousins: Canada, Australia, and Their Use of Expeditionary Forces from the Boer War to the War on Terror," Ph.D. thesis, Royal Military College of Canada, Kingston, Ont., 2004; Katrina D. Bormanis, "The Monumental Landscape: Canadian, Newfoundland, and Australian Great War Capital and Battlefield Memorials and the Topography of National Remembrance," Ph.D. thesis, Concordia University, Montreal, 2010; Carl Bridge, "Australia's and Canada's Wars, 1914–1918 and 1939–1945: Some Reflections," *Round Table* 2001 (361), 623–31; Jeffrey A. Keshen, "The Great War Soldier as Nation Builder in Canada and Australia," in *Canada and the Great War: Western Front Association Papers*, ed. Briton C. Busch (Montreal and Kingston: McGill-Queen's University Press, 2003), 3–26; David W. Lloyd, *Battlefield Tourism: Pilgrimage and the Commemoration of the Great War in Britain, Australia and Canada, 1919–1939* (Oxford and New York: Berg Press, 1998); Chelsea Piper Rodd, "War and Its Resistance in Canada and Australia," Ph.D. thesis, Deakin University, Melbourne, 2015; Mark Sheftall, *Altered Memories of the Great War: Divergent Narratives of Britain, Australia, New Zealand and Canada* (London: I.B. Taurus, 2009); "Mythologizing the Dominion Fighting Man: Australian and Canadian Narratives of the First World War Soldier, 1914–39," *Australian Historical Studies* 46,1 (2015): 81–99. For seminal works on war remembrance in Australia, see Bill Gammage, *The Broken Years: Australian Soldiers in the Great War* (Canberra: Australian National University Press, 1974); Robert Gerster, *Big-Noting: The Heroic Theme in Australian War Writing* (Melbourne: Melbourne University Press, 1987); K.S. Inglis, *Sacred Places: War Memorials in the Australian Landscape* (Carlton: Melbourne University Publishing, 2005); Alistair Thompson, "Anzac Memories: Putting Popular Memory Theory into Practice in Australia," in *The Houses of History: A Critical Reader in Twentieth-Century History and Theory*, ed. Anna Green and Kathleen Troup (Manchester: Manchester University Press, 1999).

7 Marilyn Lake, "Introduction: What Have You Done for Your Country?" in *What's Wrong with Anzac? The Militarisation of Australian History*, ed. Marilyn Lake and Henry Reynolds (Sydney: University of New South Wales Press, 2010), 1.

8 For an insightful, if deeply controversial, treatment, see Sean McMeekin, *The Russian Origins of the First World War* (Cambridge, Mass., and London: Belknap Press of Harvard University Press, 2011).

9 Quoted in Joy Damousi, "Why Do We Get So Emotional about Anzac?" in *What's Wrong with Anzac?* ed. Lake and Reynolds, 95.

10 Mark McKenna, "Anzac Day: How Did It Become Australia's National Day?" in *What's Wrong with Anzac?* ed. Lake and Reynolds, 128.

11 Quoted in McKenna, "Anzac Day," 126–27.

12 *The Australian*, 25 April 2012.

13 Lake, "Introduction," 12, 22.

14 "The most general reasons," Henry Reynolds, "Are Nations Really Made in War?" in *What's Wrong with Anzac?* ed. Lake and Reynolds, 27–28; "It is the soldier . . ." quoted in Lake, "Introduction," 8–9.

15 The Anzac legend is more socially egalitarian than is the Vimy mythology. A key figure is John Simpson Kirkpatrick, a former deserter, coal miner, cane cutter, and coal stoker, not to mention militant leftist. He deployed donkeys to provide first aid to the wounded, carrying them to relative safety. Simpson and the "diggers" came to be celebrated in such books as *Glorious Deeds of Australians in the Great War*, sculptures in major cities, plays, television shows, postage stamps, and posthumous campaigns to have him awarded the Victoria Cross. See E.C. Buley, *Glorious Deeds of Australasians in the Great War* (London: Andrew Melrose, 1916); Peter Cochrane, *Simpson and the Donkey: The Making of a Legend* (Burwood, Aust.: Melbourne University Press, 1992); J. Mulholland, *John Simpson Kirkpatrick: The Untold Story of the Gallipoli Hero's Early Life* (n.p.: Alkali Publishing, 2015). The Australian legend is also, rhetorically at least, much more inclusive of all white Australians because there is no convincing Australian equivalent of Quebec resistance to the Great War. Although Anzac commemorations struggle with inclusiveness—mentioning the indigenous question in public ceremonies, for instance—the core Anzac message is that we should "move on" from dwelling on such divisive issues, all the better to celebrate a legend that is "held in a state of perpetual remembrance." McKenna, "Anzac Day," 133.

16 McKenna, "Anzac Day," 128; Lake, "Introduction," 11.

17 See Maarten Van Alstein, *The Great War Remembered: Commemoration and Peace in Flanders Fields* (Brussels: Flemish Peace Institute, November 2011), which identifies the "national and patriotic idiom" common to the British Commonwealth (and some Belgian) traditions of remembrance as a challenge to "peace-oriented commemoration" (22).

18 Jonathan Vance, *Death So Noble: Memory, Meaning, and the First World War* (Vancouver and Toronto: UBC Press, 1997 [1998]). The book sparked considerable critical interest. Paul Merkeley marvelled, "He has reviewed the historiography, official, academic, and amateur; he has waded through boxes of regimental memorabilia; he has climbed around all the monuments; he has studied the rolls of honor on all of the walls of all of the high schools and factories; he has read all the texts in all the stained-glass windows." Jay Winter, a major force in the field of Great War commemoration, noted, "The strengths of this study lie in its wide range of sources and its careful construction of the multiple forms of commemoration in the aftermath of the war." Paul C. Merkeley, Review of *Death So Noble*, *American Historical Review* 103,4 (October 1998), 1360; Jay Winter, Review of Jonathan F. Vance, *Death So Noble: Memory, Meaning and the First World War*, *International History Review* 20,2 (June 1998), 434.

19 Stefan Goebel, *The Great War and Medieval Memory: War, Remembrance and Medievalism in Britain and Germany, 1914–1940* (Cambridge, 2007), reveals that Germans, as well, turned to images of chivalrous knights, crusaders, God-fearing saints, sacred groves of holy trees, and the monumental forms of Ancient Greece—all in the cause of inserting the mass industrialized slaughter of the Great War into traditional frameworks.

20 Vance, *Death So Noble*, 265.

21 Vance, *Death So Noble*, 8 ("Canada's myth"); Jonathan Vance, "Remembrance," *Canada's History*, October–November 2014, 38 (democracy of death), 36 ("national funeral").

22 Gavin Murphy, Review of Jonathan F. Vance, *Death So Noble: Memory, Meaning and the First World War*, in *The Beaver* 78,4 (August 1998), 47; Vance, *Death So Noble*, 34. The full passage in Vance suggests his agreement with the position: "... Canadians never lost sight of *the fact* that November 1918 marked a victory over the forces of barbarism" (emphasis added). The point that Great War commemorations were interpreted as the true, essential, and permanent reflections of the views of the Canadian people rather than contestable, partial, and changeable manifestations of the views of some Canadian people, is what Winter discerns to be the "political destination" of Vance's argument. Winter, Review of Vance, *Death So Noble*, 435.

23 Vance, *Death So Noble*, 106 ("rational and comprehensible activity"), 109 ("wallow in the horrors"), 142 ("Canada's memory").

24 Vance, "Remembrance," 32; Vance, *Death So Noble*, 161 ("distillations"), 223 ("organic communion"). The motif of the citizen-army carrying Canada's colours is misleading because in international law and much Canadian jurisprudence, no such thing as a "Canadian citizen" existed before 1947. In addition, this army carrying Canada's colours was integrated into the British forces and, at Vimy Ridge no less, fought under British leadership.

25 Vance, *Death So Noble*, 228, 179, 266.

26 Vance notes, but in essence rejects, John Bodnar's idea of public memory as characterized by a struggle between official and vernacular cultures. In his thoughtful 1998 critique, Winter suggests that many of the strengths and weaknesses of *Death So Noble* are those of the "collective memory" school, which among at least some of its adherents posits transgenerational organic memories as powerful shapers of human identities and histories. Winter, Review of Vance, *Death So Noble*. An alternative (Gramscian) theorization might conversely maintain that a given social order is made up of competing and often conflicting groups that draw upon accounts of past events to shore up their ideological positions in the present—in a struggle over the past that is never decisively concluded. See also John Bodnar, *Remaking America: Public Memory, Commemoration, and Patriotism in the Twentieth Century* (Princeton, N.J.: Princeton University Press, 1992).

27 Alan Gordon, *Making Public Pasts: The Contested Terrain of Montreal's Public Memories, 1891–1930* (Montreal and Kingston: McGill-Queen's University Press, 2001), 4, paraphrasing the critique of Noa Gedi and Yigal Elam.

28 Vance, *Death So Noble*, 257–61, provides a far from comprehensive list of these large
    constituencies. The book's opening offers a slight preparation for this observa-
    tion: "Four years of battle, both in the trenches and at home, did not create a single
    nationalism, but instead strengthened the two nationalisms of French and English
    Canada; both societies gained greater appreciation of their separate identities from
    the experience of war." Speaking of the hopes that the Great War would create a
    unified country, he writes: "In hindsight, such hopes might seem a little naïve. How
    could a war that saw the deaths of 60,000 Canadians and the wounding of 170,000
    others become a constructive force in the nation's history?" Vance, *Death So Noble*,
    10, 11. Given the lukewarm response of so many born-in-Canada Anglo-Canadians
    to the war, the bitter memories of racialized minorities abused in concentration
    camps, and the increasingly critical stances taken up by working-class and agrar-
    ian movements, might it not have been the case that the Great War did not inspire
    "Canada's myth" but "the myth of a particular Canada"—the Canada imagined by
    imperialists and Tories that was retreating as the 1930s progressed, in part in the
    face of a peace movement inclined to view sceptically the claims of Empire?

29 For these and other examples of Western Front irony, see Tim Cook, *Shock
    Troops: Canadians Fighting the Great War 1917–1918* (Toronto: Viking Canada,
    2008), 64, 187, 368.

30 Byng was a particular target of King's campaign because he had supposedly sub-
    verted the constitution. Conservatives hammered away relentlessly at Mackenzie
    King's record as a *shirker*— a charge that wounded him deeply, as both his diary
    and speeches show. His enemies had a point: King even exerted himself to prevent
    U.S. entry into his own country's war.

31 Vance, *Death So Noble*, 7.

32 Vance, *Death So Noble*, 7, 48; Vance, "The Soldier as Novelist: Literature, History
    and the Great War," *Canadian Literature* 179 (Winter 2003), 38; Bird, *And We Go
    On: A Story of the War by a Private in the Canadian Black Watch; a Story Without Filth
    or Favor* (Toronto: Hunter Rose, 1930), 147.

33 On the Great War's debated legacies, see, for example, Malcolm Ferguson,
    "Canada's Response: The Making and Remaking of the National War Memorial,"
    M.A. thesis, Carleton University, Ottawa, 2012.

34 Vance, *Death So Noble*, 29; Vance, "Remembrance," 32. Actually, "just war" theory
    was used extensively among pacificist critics of the Great War, who plausibly
    argued that neither side had fulfilled the conventional criteria necessary for a just
    war. The concept was rarely used in 1914–18 by North American proponents of
    the war, but it was raised in the 1930s by opponents of rearmament. For back-
    ground, see Darren C. Zook, "Just War," in *The Oxford International Encyclopedia of
    Peace*, vol. 2, ed. Nigel J. Young (Oxford: Oxford University Press, 2010), 546–51.

35 Vance acknowledges the interwar peace movement only to dismiss it—by ques-
    tioning its motivations and coherence, denying the widespread cultural shock as
    Great War memories moved from the funerary to the political, or insinuating that
    all peace-loving roads lead to appeasement (Vance, *Death So Noble*, 34). But many
    of the most prominent interwar pacifists were apostles of collective security
    through the League of Nations—not of appeasement of Hitler.

36 Tim Cook, *At the Sharp End: Canadians Fighting the Great War 1914–1916* (Toronto: Viking Canada, 2007); Cook, *Shock Troops*. As our endnotes indicate, we are often in Cook's debt for our understanding of the military history of the Great War.

37 For example, Cook, *Shock Troops*, 645, 147, 258. At one point Cook even intimates that Canadians were instrumental in overcoming stalemate on the Western Front and thus influenced the shape of the entire post-1918 international order; Cook, *Shock Troops*, 9.

38 In contrast, Cook, in *Shock Troops*, compresses the entire period from March to May 1918 into one chapter.

39 The Germans knew, he writes, that "no one in their right mind attacked without the protection of a barrage. But no one mentioned that to the Nova Scotians." Cook, *Shock Troops*, 135. Although Cook allows himself to doubt—as Bird and Harrison doubted—the value of the currency of medals—he pulls himself back from any full-fledged scepticism on this topic, and often, after highlighting the noble deed of a fighting Canadian, fast-forwards to the medal that recognized (and in a sense certified) the deed.

40 The question of sympathy is significant because as ordinarily applied, the word "hero" entails a measure of agreement with the cause for which the hero has exerted himself—or herself—even if, as in the case of someone with cancer, this boils down to an issue of human survival. Individual soldiers fighting for the Khmer Rouge or Saddam Hussein undoubtedly sometimes faced down thoughts of death and braved adversity, but calling them "heroes" implies support for the regimes for which they fought. Thus for most of us the phrase "Nazi war hero" makes sense only if we mean "a hero in the eyes of Nazis," because otherwise it would seem to convey our support for the cause.

41 They are "low-mimetic" heroes in Northrop Frye's sense. For a stimulating dis-cussion, see Stephen Heathorn, *Haig and Kitchener in Twentieth-Century Britain: Remembrance, Representation and Appropriation* (Farnham, U.K., and Burlington, Vt.: Ashgate Publishing, 2013).

42 Cook, *At the Sharp End*, 502, 140, 200, 132, 449, 205; Cook, *Shock Troops*, 173, 299, 132.

43 Cook, *At the Sharp End*, 369, 405, 415, 345, 47, 44; Cook, *Shock Troops*, 585.

44 Cook, *Shock Troops*, 44. The diversion of funds for his own benefit is briefly alluded to in Cook, *At the Sharp End*.

45 Cook, *At the Sharp End*, 645; emphasis added.

46 And thus not at the Battle of Vimy Ridge, as is often suggested.

47 As Cook candidly remarks, it was difficult for "most of the Canadians engaged at the sharp end of the historic battle to realize that Vimy was a victory, let alone a nation-building event." Cook, *Shock Troops*, 115–16. The celebratory statements include that of one sergeant who later died of his wounds: "As the guns spoke, over the bags they went, men of C.B. [Cape Breton] sons of N.S. [Nova Scotia] & NB [New Brunswick]—FC's [French Canadians] and westerners—all Canucks . . ." Cook, *Shock Troops*, 147. Notice that this Maritimer—probably not by accident— somehow skips over those pesky "Upper Canadians" from Ontario.

48 Cook complains that the four "martyrs" from the anti-conscription revolt in Quebec City and the lesson that an un-Canadian majority focused on empire had imposed its view on the largely francophone province have overshadowed the legacy of the Quebeckers who "served and sacrificed overseas during the war." Cook, *Shock Troops*, 644. Yet an inescapable consequence of the Great War was that Cook's "colony-to-nation" narrative could never ring true among Québécois whose resistance to conscription had led to such repression.

49 For compelling evidence, see Thomas-Louis Tremblay, *Journal de guerre (1915–1918)*, ed. Marcelle Cinq-Mars (Outremont, Que.: Athéna Edition, 2006).

50 Cook, *Shock Troops*, 432, 106, 228, 493, 503, 583.

51 Cook, *Shock Troops*, 627, 645, 3–4, 133, 395–96; Cook, *At the Sharp End*, 132. Cook thereafter renders "storm troops" as "elite shock troops," perhaps because of the dubious reputation acquired by the first term after 1939.

52 If it could put their martial attributes to good use the Empire had long celebrated those it had colonized—such as the Iroquois in the War of 1812, the Nepalese Gurkhas in the "Great Game" in Afghanistan and Northwest India, and the Scottish Highlanders who came to predominate, as both symbols and actual soldiers, in the extension of empire from the 1750s onwards. See especially Heather Streets, *Martial Races: The Military, Race and Masculinity in British Imperial Culture, 1857–1914* (Manchester: Manchester University Press, 2011); and, with specific reference to the Highland Scots within the Empire, Linda Colley, *Britons: Forging the Nation 1707–1837*, rev. ed. (New Haven, Conn.: Yale University Press, 2009).

53 Some of this pre-modern sense of war was attached to the reasoning behind that apex of modern planning, the conquest of Vimy Ridge. Under conditions of modern warfare, if the capture of such a height meant the heavy artillery could not advance much further, it could hardly serve as a game-changer in an industrial war.

54 Cook is prone to accept some Entente stories that call out for closer scrutiny. Although he tends to accept the Entente position on such questions as Belgian atrocities and on the sinking of the *Lusitania* (an "unarmed civilian ship"), and also believes that the war was fought "in support of international law and the rights of small nations," he also writes of "the rash, callous nature of rival imperialisms" and suggests that "none of the great powers can escape blame." Cook, *At the Sharp End*, 29, 60, 212, 62, 9; Cook, *Shock Troops*, 634. With respect to the *Lusitania*, recent archaeological investigation tends to confirm the German accusations that the vessel was carrying munitions.

55 Cook, *At the Sharp End*, 459, 297, 467, 468; Cook, *Shock Troops*, 297.

56 Cook offers as evidence against Harrison that, of the 59 Canadian generals, 17 were wounded and 1 was killed—although this 1:59 fatality rate does not constitute overwhelming evidence against Harrison's point that generals and privates experienced very different wars.

57 Cook, *Shock Troops*, 640 ("liturgy of hate"), 635 (Macdonell), 254.

58 Cook, *Shock Troops*, 630.

59 *Winnipeg Free Press*, 3 Feb. 1934; D.C. Harvey, Review of Arthur R.M. Lower, *Colony to Nation: A History of Canada* (Toronto: Longmans, Green and Company, 1946), in *Dalhousie Review*, 27 (1947): 123–24.

60 J.L Granatstein, *The Last Good War: An Illustrated History of Canada in the Second World War, 1939–1945* (Vancouver and Toronto: Douglas and McIntyre, 2005), viii. See chapter 2 here.

61 David Inglis, "Vimy Ridge: A Canadian Myth over Seventy-Five Years," M.A. thesis, Simon Fraser University, 1995, 85, citing J.M.S. Careless, *Canada: A Story of Challenge* (1965) and William Kilbourn, *The Making of a Nation: A Century of Challenge* (1965); Inglis, "Vimy Ridge," 94, citing J.A. Lower, *A Nation Developing: A Brief History of Canada* (Toronto: Ryerson Press, 1970), 158; H.H. Herstein, L.J. Hughes, and R.C. Kirbyson, *Challenge and Survival: The History of Canada* (Scarborough, Ont.: Prentice-Hall of Canada, 1970), 321. Inglis, "Vimy Ridge," usefully reviews Vimy's trajectory through textbooks used in British Columbia from the 1960s to the 1990s.

62 Inglis, "Vimy Ridge," 95; Inglis cites in particular Ramsay Cook, *Canada: A Modern Study*, rev. ed. (Toronto: Clarke, Irwin and Co., 1977); Allan S. Evans and I.L. Martinello, *Canada's Century* (Toronto: McGraw-Hill Ryerson, 1978); and David Francis and Sonia Riddoch, *Our Canada: A Social and Political History* (Toronto: McClelland and Stewart, 1985).

63 Heather Robertson, *A Terrible Beauty: The Art of Canada at War* (Toronto: James Lorimer, 1977), 9, cited in Inglis, "Vimy Ridge," 121; J.L. Granatstein and H.L. Hitsman, *Broken Promises: A History of Conscription in Canada* (Toronto: Oxford University Press, 1977). Granatstein, a historian today closely associated with martial nationalism, thus ironically figures as someone who made it much more difficult to claim that Vimy Ridge brought Canadians together. In Granatstein, *Who Killed the Canadian Military?* (Toronto: HarperPerennial Canada, 2004), 104, he explicitly rejects the view that the Canadian Corps was "the embodiment of Canadian nationalism," urging instead that it was "English-Canadian nationalism incarnate"—which still overstates the case, considering the heterogeneity of "English Canada."

64 Stephen Harris, "From Subordinate to Ally: The Canadian Corps and National Autonomy, 1914–18," *Revue internationale d'histoire militaire* 51 (1982), 111–12, 126, cited in Inglis, "Vimy Ridge," 123.

65 John Fielding and Rosemary Evans, with Jan Haskings-Winner, Robert Mewhinne, Tracey Robertson, Gord Sly, and Jim Terry, *Canada: Our Century, Our Story* (Scarborough: Nelson Thomson Learning, 2000), 57, 58, 59, 61.

66 Fielding and Evans, *Canada*, 63, 65, 79. We learn of Bird's mystical experiences with his ghostly brother and of the confusion and mud of Passchendaele, but not of Bird's critique of military authoritarianism. The authors inaccurately argue that "gas gangrene" was caused by German chlorine gas, when it actually bore no relationship to it; they imply that Europeans had no memory of a major war, thus forgetting lively French resentments aroused by their recent war with Prussia; and they believe that the phrase "war to end all wars"—more accurately, "the war that will end war"—was deployed to describe the special horrors of the conflict and not (as H.G. Wells explained) to justify the struggle in its early days as one that aimed to end militarism altogether. Fielding and Evans, *Canada*, 77, 67, 54; Cook, *At the Sharp End*, 199; H.G. Wells, *The War That Will End War* (London: F.C. Palmer, 1914).

67 Fielding and Evans, *Canada*, 55, 64, 52, 80. Later in the text the role of the soldiers is to fight "valiantly," even against strongly held German positions. Fielding and Evans, *Canada*, 73.

68 Fielding and Evans, *Canada*, 74. In April 1917 the tactic was not novel, and did not originate with Canadians; as well, the Canadians were fighting as a Corps within the British Expeditionary Force.

69 Fielding, *Canada*, 74–75.

70 Colin M. Bain, Dennis DesRivieres, Peter Flaherty, Elma Schemenauer, and Angus L. Scully, *Making History: The Story of Canada in the Twentieth Century* (Toronto: Prentice Hall, 2000), 63, 71, 100, 102, 67.

71 Bain et al., *Making History*, 59 ("world affairs"), 73 ("national identity"), 77 ("separate from Britain"), 98 ("national pride"), 85 ("best-known hero"), 92 ("use a computer").

72 Bain et al., *Making History*, 79 ("stunning four-day victory"), 81 ("This photograph," "important turning point"), 74 ("Private Fraser").

73 Garfield Newman with Bob Aitken, Diane Eaton, Dick Holland, John Montgomery, and Sonia Riddoch, *Canada: A Nation Unfolding*, Ont. ed. (Toronto: McGraw-Hill Ryerson, 2000). The items from cultural history include the words and music from "K-K-K-Katie," the popular Great War song written by a Kingstonian. Newman et al., *Canada*, 84. The book places a huge emphasis on visuals and makes many suggestions for information on the web for students eager to supplement the book with activities and other learning.

74 Newman et al., *Canada*, 77 ("peaceful compromise"), 85 ("aggressive competition," Princip), 112 ("civilized war"), 118 (mechanized warfare).

75 Although the book also indicates that Canada has a "British heritage and economic ties," and the Great War was a "European war." Newman et al., *Canada*, 76. Racialized minorities were thus included in a narrative closely focused on British imperial war fought out in Europe.

76 Newman et al., *Canada*, 88–90 ("White Man's War"), 101 ("greed and corruption"), 122 ("much had been lost"), 134 ("full re-establishment").

77 Quoted in Newman et al., *Canada*, 72.

78 Newman et al., *Canada*, 73.

79 Newman et al., *Canada*, 119 ("Canadians were capable"), 108 (wholesome recreations). The text, for all its attentiveness to gender, pays no attention to sexual assault, prostitution, or venereal disease.

80 Newman et al., *Canada*, 131 ("gallant efforts"), 77 ("nation on its own"), 122 ("international stage"), 125 ("defining period").

81 Kip Pegley, "Music and Memorialization at the Canadian War Museum," *Echo: A Music-Centered Journal*, http://www.echo.ucla.edu/old/content/volume-10-issue-1-spring-2012/10-1-pegley. See also Anthony Jackson and Helen Rees Leahy, "'Seeing It for Real ... ?'—Authenticity, Theatre and Learning in Museums," *Research in Drama Education* 10,3 (2005): 303–25, and Ashlee E. Beattie, "Performing Historical Narrative at the Canadian War Museum: Space, Objects, and Bodies as Performers." M.A. thesis, University of Ottawa, 2011, both cited in Pegley, "Music and Memorialization."

82 Reesa Greenberg, "Constructing the Canadian War Museum/Constructing the Landscape of a Canadian Identity," in *(Re)Visualizing National History: Museums and National Identities in Europe in the New Millennium*, ed. Robin Ostow (Toronto: University of Toronto Press, 2008), 183.

83 C. David Naylor, ed., *Canadian Health Care and the State: A Century of Evolution* (Montreal and Kingston: McGill-Queen's University Press, 1992), 49; this well-known statement is also on the CWM's website, in a section on Canadian war art, "Canvas of War: Masterpieces from the CWM," in reference to the 1919 canvas "Canadian Observation Post" by Colin Gill, which includes one figure apparently suffering from PTSD; http://www.warmuseum.ca/cwm/exhibitions/canvas/1/cwd538e.shtml; in Desmond Morton, *Fight or Pay: Soldiers' Families in the Great War* (Vancouver: UBC Press, 2004), 151. For more on Canadians' sceptical impatience with veterans, see Desmond Morton and Glenn Wright, *Winning the Second Battle: Canadian Veterans and the Return to Civilian Life, 1915–1930* (Toronto: University of Toronto Press, 1987), 215.

84 See Ryan Targa, "From Governors to Grocers: How Profiteering Changed English-Canadian Perceptions of Liberalism in the Great War of 1914–1918," M.A. thesis, Queen's University, Kingston, Ont., 2013; Ian McKay, *Reasoning Otherwise: Leftists and the People's Enlightenment in Canada, 1890–1920* (Toronto: Between the Lines, 2008), 428–29; R. Craig Brown and Ramsay Cook, *Canada 1896–1921: A Nation Transformed* (Toronto: McClelland and Stewart, 1974), ch.12.

85 Maria Tippett, *Art at the Service of War: Canada, Art and the Great War* (Toronto: University of Toronto Press, 1984), 26, 70–71. The critic argues that the only accurate thing about the painting is its respect for the dead.

86 See Tippett, *Art at the Service of War*, 70.

87 Laura Brandon, *Art or Memorial? The Forgotten History of Canada's War Art* (Calgary: University of Calgary Press, 2006), 20; Barry Lord, *The History of Painting in Canada* (Toronto: NC Press, 1974), 134, in Brandon, *Art or Memorial?* 44–45.

88 Brandon, *Art or Memorial?* 45. The Varley quote provided the text for the label accompanying *For What?* in the nine-city *Canvas of War* exhibit. Canadian War Museum, *Canvas of War: Masterpieces from the Canadian War Museum*, http://www.warmuseum.ca/cwm/exhibitions/canvas/1/cwd541e.shtml (October 2015).

89 This description is based on a visit in 2015.

90 Douglas Gill and Dallas Gloden, "Mutiny at Etaples Base in 1917," *Past and Present* 69 (November 1975).

91 Gill and Gloden, "Mutiny at Etaples Base"; Canadian War Museum, "Discipline and Punishment," http://www.warmuseum.ca/firstworldwar/history/life-at-the-front/trench-conditions/discipline-and-punishment (October 2015). See also Teresa Iacobelli, *Death or Deliverance: Canadian Courts Martial in the Great War* (Vancouver and Toronto: UBC Press, 2013).

92 Gill and Gloden, "Mutiny at Etaples Base"; Canadian War Museum, "Discipline and Punishment."

93 Vera Brittain, *Testament of Youth: An Autobiographical Study of the Years 1900–1925* (London: Penguin, 2005), 370.

94 Arnold Toynbee, *A Study of History*, abridgement of vols. vii–x by D.C. Somerville (London: Oxford University Press, 1957), 323.

95 Debbie Grisdale, "Make Room for Peace at the War Museum," *Peace Magazine*, January–March 2007, 7.

96 Personal observation; and Amber Lloydlangston and Kathryn Lyons, *Peace: The Exhibition* (Ottawa: Canadian Museum of Civilization, 2013), 31. Yet the catalogue states only hesitantly: "Canadians eagerly chose to fight and support the First World War. Most saw it as a war for justice—one that would restore peace." It posited the inevitable caveats, with the war having been "costly and long" and one that "strained Canada's resources and unity."

97 "Canadian War Museum," *Inside Guide to Ottawa*, http://inside-guide-to-ottawa.com/canadian-war-museum (October 2015).

98 YouTube, https://www.youtube.com/watch?v=VmAXeBGWJQY (June 2016).

9: THE LANDSCAPES OF GREAT WAR MEMORY

1 Jack Granatstein, commentary, *Vimy Ridge 90*, CBC-TV presentation, April 2007.

2 Margaret Atwood, *In Search of Alias Grace: On Writing Canadian Historical Fiction*, Charles R. Bronfman Lecture in Canadian Studies (Ottawa: University of Ottawa Press, 1996), 8; quoted in Sherrill Grace, *Landscapes of War and Memory: The Two World Wars in Canadian Literature and the Arts, 1977–2007* (Edmonton: University of Alberta Press, 2014), 3.

3 The Veterans Affairs Canada publication *Canada Remembers Times*, published each year as Remembrance Day approaches, had a print run in 2015 of 620,000 copies, many destined for schoolchildren and their teachers. Personal communication, VAC Canada, 30 Nov. 2015; 22,000 copies, also bilingual, were produced for VAC's "Veterans' Week product sample packs," distributed to schools, public libraries, veterans' organizations, and military groups. For Filip Konowal, see "A Ukrainian-Canadian War Hero," Veteran Affairs Canada, *Canada Remembers Times*, 2015 edition, http://www.veterans.gc.ca/eng/remembrance/information-for/students/canada-remembers-times/2015 (June 2016).

4 See Zachary Abram, "Sexing up Canada's First World War," *Activehistory*, 3 March 2015, http://activehistory.ca/2015/03/sexing-up-canadas-first-world-war, for an astute analysis.

5 Keith D. Smith, *Liberalism, Surveillance and Resistance: Indigenous Communities in Western Canada, 1877–1927* (Edmonton, Alta.: Athabasca University Press, 2009), 223, 229; Timothy Charles Winegard, *Indigenous Peoples of the British Empire and the First World War* (Cambridge, Mass.: Cambridge University Press, 2011), who highlights the resistance of both First Nations and Japanese Canadians against conscription.

6 Timothy Findley, *The Wars* (Toronto: Irwin, 1989), 55; Grace, *Landscapes of War and Memory*, 125–26, 29.

7 Never Forgotten National Memorial, www.nfnm.ca, September 2015. The Foundation's flashy website was underwritten by $100,000 in public money.

8 Canadian Intellectual Property Office, Canadian Trade-Mark Data, www.ic.gc.ca/app/opic-cipo/trdmrks/srch/vwTrdmrk/do?lang=eng&status=OK&fileNumber=1600956&extension (September 2015).

9 Friends of Green Cove, Press Release, 15 July 2015; Never Forgotten National Memorial, "Across a Proud Canadian Landscape," www.http://www.nfnm.ca/#slide14 (October 2015).

10 Quoted in Never Forgotten National Memorial, www.nfnm.ca/#slide9 (September 2015).

11 Friends of Green Cove, Press Release, 15 July 2015; Vimy Foundation, http://www.vimyfoundation.ca/.

12 *Halifax Examiner*, 21 July 2015.

13 "Mother Canada Project Won't Go Ahead in Cape Breton Park," CBC News, Nova Scotia, http://www.cbc.ca/news/canada/nova-scotia/mother-canada-parks-canada-1.3435581 (February 2016). Characteristically, the project was seemingly rebuffed on procedural, not ideological, grounds.

14 Ernie Regehr, *Disarming Conflict: Why Peace Cannot Be Won on the Battlefield* (Toronto: Between the Lines, 2015), 6–7, 136.

15 Steven Chase, "Canada Now the Second Biggest Arms Exporter to Middle East, Data Show," *Globe and Mail*, 15 June 2016.

16 Quoted in Ferdinand Mount, "Parcelled Out," *London Review of Books*, 22 Oct. 2015, 8; for Harris on mounting a "deliberate terror attack" in a 1945 air raid on Pforzheim that killed 17,600, see Ian McKay and Jamie Swift, *Warrior Nation: Rebranding Canada in an Age of Anxiety* (Toronto: Between the Lines, 2012), 189.

17 Christopher Coker's important insight is that, in much of Western culture, war as a *metaphysical* concept "translates death into sacrifice—it invests death with a meaning. And it is the metaphysical dimension which is the most important of all precisely because it persuades societies of the need for sacrifice. It is sacrifice which makes war qualitatively different from every other act of violence. We rarely celebrate killing but we do celebrate dying when it has meaning, not only for the dead, but for those they leave behind." Christopher Coker, *The Future of War: The Re-Enchantment of War in the Twenty-First Century* (Oxford: Blackwell, 2004), 6.

18 See especially Jay Winter, *Sites of Memory, Sites of Mourning: The Great War in European Cultural History* (Cambridge: Cambridge University Press, 1995); Jonathan Vance, *Death So Noble: Memory, Meaning, and the First World War* (Vancouver and Toronto: UBC Press, 1997 [1998]).

19 Of the thousands of titles now available on the origins of the First World War, Christopher Clark, *The Sleepwalkers: How Europe Went to War in 1914* (New York: HarperCollins, 2012) is useful in tracing the diplomatic steps that led to the continent's descent into armed conflict; Niall Ferguson, *The Pity of War: Explaining World War I* (New York: Basic Books, 1998) contains much useful information and reflection on the economic and financial background of the war; and Ian Kershaw, *To Hell and Back: Europe 1914–1949* (New York: Viking, 2015), valuably emphasizes the political and cultural effects of a decades-long crisis of

capitalism. None readily sustains the interpretation of undivided German war guilt put forward by J.L. Granatstein in *The Greatest Victory: Canada's One Hundred Days, 1918* (Don Mills, Ont.: Oxford University Press, 2014), which praises "the extraordinary deeds that made Canada anew" (193) pitted against "the destruction unleashed by the Germans on the world" (181).

20 For one surprising indication of the reach into Canada of critical thinking about the origins of the Great War, see Frederick Walter Noyes, *Stretcher Bearers—At the Double! . . . History of the Fifth Canadian Field Ambulance Which Served Overseas during the Great War of 1914–1918* (Toronto: Hunter-Rose, n.d. [c.1937]), which pugnaciously demanded, "Was Britain's chief concern caused by Germany's disregard for Belgium's neutrality, or did she declare war simply because she saw her own world-domination threatened?" Also: "Were the excuses given by the British cabinet as Britain's reason for taking up arms genuinely honest statements of the case or were they, for the most part, sheer hypocrisy and jingoism?" (278).

21 Benedict Anderson, *Imagined Communities: Reflections on the Origin and Spread of Nationalism* (London: Verso, 1983).

22 Dan Black, "The Tomb of the Unknown Soldier," *Legion Magazine*, 1 Sept. 2000; Anderson, *Imagined Communities*, 9, 7.

23 The Hundred Days conventionally refers to the last three months of the war, during which the Allies scored a series of key victories after the German spring offensive of 1918 failed. The Canadian forces figured prominently in numerous engagements during this decisive period.

24 Immigrants to Canada have not been immune to Vimyism. The NFNMF was the brainchild of Tony Trigiani, who arrived from Italy as a child not long after the Second World War.

25 Aline Martineau's moving 1998 sculpture *Québec, Printemps 1918* marks the spot in Quebec City where *les soldats Anglophone amenés expressément de l'Ontario et de l'Ouest* killed four anti-conscription protestors.

26 Some from the Six Nations did see the war as one of recognition of independence—their own independence from Canada. They unsuccessfully pursued recognition of this status at the League of Nations.

27 Government of Canada, Veterans Affairs Canada, "Tales of Animals in War," http://www.veterans.gc.ca/eng/remembranceinformation-for/students/tales of animals in war/2015 (November 2015), emphasis added. The "Tales of Animals in War" guides on the website, as of June 2016, date back to 2006. The 2015 edition has the title, "All Aboard! Transportation in Time of War." The animal-based imagery also goes back to 2006, when little ones were introduced to a horse, elephant, dog, and a cat, among other friendly fauna. In the Great War, in contrast to the content in these stories, soldiers reeled from the stench of fields crowded with the corpses of dead horses.

28 McCrae quoted in Mary Janigan, "Treason to Their Memory," 125, citing J.F. Prescott, *In Flanders Fields: The Story of John McCrae* (Guelph, Ont.: Guelph Historical Society, 2003).

29 The "Support Our Troops" movement that flourished during Canada's failed war in Afghanistan—which is swiftly becoming another war that must not be

critically analysed—was firmly rooted in American martial culture. See especially A.L. McCready, *Yellow Ribbons: The Militarization of National Identity in Canada* (Halifax: Fernwood Publishing, 2013), especially ch.2.

30 Arthur R.M. Lower, *Canadians in the Making: A Social History of Canada* (Toronto: Longmans, Green, 1958), 135–36. The notion of the Great War as "Canada's War of Independence" is elaborated in Desmond Morton and J.L. Granatstein, *Marching to Armageddon: Canadians and the Great War 1914–1919* (Toronto: Lester and Orpen Dennys, 1989), 1; Desmond Morton, "La guerre d'indépendance du Canada: une perspective Anglophone," in *La Première Guerre mondiale et le Canada*, ed. Roch Legault and Jean Lamarre (Montreal: Meridien, 1999), 11–34.

31 Joanna Bourke, *Wounding the World: How Military Violence and War-Play Invade Our Lives* (London: Virago, 2014), 213.

32 Joe Lofaro, "In the Digital Trenches: Kanata Company Developing Vimy Ridge Simulator," OurWindsor.ca, 10 Nov. 2015, http://www.ourwindsor.ca/news-story/6110747-in-the-digital-trenches-kanata-company-developing-vimy-ridge-simulator/ (November 2015). How the smell of rotting corpses to which almost all novels and memoirs of the Front refer will be made a rewarding part of the experience has yet to be disclosed. Simwave is a spinoff from Kanata's Simfront.

33 Martin Ceadel, *Thinking about Peace and War* (Oxford and New York: Oxford University Press, 1987), 4.

34 Paul Gross, *Passchendaele* (Toronto: HarperCollins, 2008), concluding supplement, 10.

35 Michael Enright, CBC-Radio, "The Sunday Edition," 9 Nov. 2014.

36 David Bercuson, *Significant Incident: Canada's Army, the Airborne, and the Murder in Somalia* (Toronto: McClelland and Stewart, 1996), 28–29.

37 Canon Frederick George Scott, *The Great War as I Saw It* (Kingston: Legacy Books, 2009 [Toronto: F.D. Goodchild, 1922]), 236, 209.

38 For a spiritedly martial interpretation of Canada's interwar fiction that applies a three-part categorization—pro-war, anti-war, and balanced—see Monique Dumontet, "'Lest We Forget': Canadian Combatant Narratives of the Great War." Ph.D. thesis, University of Manitoba, Winnipeg, 2010. For Dumontet, as for Vance, Bird is an example of a balanced writer because he does not unequivocally condemn the war and concedes it had the compensating virtue of encouraging camaraderie. Yet for some of the military men who read Bird, his writing was "flatly obnoxious" and unduly influenced by the likes of Remarque. See W.W.M., Review of *And We Go On* in *Canadian Defence Quarterly* 8,4 (July 1931): 582–83, as noted in Jonathan Scotland, "And the Men Returned: Canadian Veterans and the Aftermath of the Great War," Ph.D. thesis, Western University, London, Ont., 2016, 106, n.116. Similarly, Dumontet places English playwright R.C. Sherriff's play *Journey's End* (1928)—performed by veterans across Canada—in the anti-war camp (15); yet Sherriff himself most likely merely intended to depict the war in a realistic way and sought to show how the war seemed to young junior officers, without in any way wanting to lead his audiences to more general critical positions about it. See Rosa Maria Bracco, *Merchants of Hope: British*

Middlebrow Writers and the First World War, 1919–1939 (Providence, R.I., and Oxford: Berg, 1993), ch.5.

39 Ceadel, *Thinking about Peace and War*, 5–6. See chapter 5 here for an outline of Ceadel's categories.

40 Tim Cook, "Forged in Fire," in *In Flanders Fields: Writings on War, Loss and Remembrance*, ed. Amanda Betts (Toronto: Alfred A. Knopf, 2015), 20; Ian Ross Robertson, *Sir Andrew Macphail: The Life and Legacy of a Canadian Man of Letters* (Montreal and Kingston: McGill-Queen's University Press, 2008).

41 Arthur Meighen, "The Supremely Important Task," *Interdependence* 8,1 (January 1931), 21–31, LAC, Meighen Papers, Series 5, MG 26 I, vol. 98, C-3562, 104267–77. Or, as Canada's wartime prime minister Borden put it in a blurb for Peregrine Acland's *All Else Is Folly* (part of the long list of "anti-war books" of the 1920s), the war had revealed "the relapse to primitive savagery of man daily companioning violent death, the crumbling of civilization's thin veneer, the broken lives, the horror, the brutality, and in fine the futility of all that ensued unless in each nation the will to win peace has had its birth." Borden as quoted in an advertisement for *All Else Is Folly*, in *Globe* (Toronto), 14 Dec. 1929, as reproduced in Brian Busby and James Calhoun, "Introduction," in Peregrine Acland, *All Else Is Folly: A Tale of War and Passion* (Toronto: Dundurn, 2014 [1929]), 9.

42 Regehr, *Disarming Conflict*, 26; he suggests a threshold figure of 1,000 deaths.

43 Allan Hall, "Germany Ends World War One Reparations after 92 Years with £59m Final Payment," *MailOnline*, 29 Sept. 2010, http://www.dailymail.co.uk/news/article-1315869/Germany-end-World-War-One-reparations-92-years-59m-final-payment.html (February 2016).

44 Regehr, *Disarming Conflict*, 12, 60; Clark in *Toronto Star*, 14 Feb. 1934. As Regehr points out, in 2015, for the first time in recent human memory, there were no inter-state wars to record—perhaps an indication that rulers inclined to military solutions have grown to be more circumspect and critical about them.

45 What is startlingly absent from almost all of the veterans' reconstructions of the war is *any* version of present-day Vimyism. If there is a major statement from the soldiers—or anyone else in the 1920s and 1930s—that Canada was born at Vimy Ridge, we have not located it. We can find nobody in the 1920s and 1930s claiming that Canada was born at Vimy Ridge.

46 By 2000 anyone who suggested the war had been a mistake or something less than the birth of a nation was liable to a public thrashing. When Robert Fulford had the temerity to wonder if the Great War had not been more a "crime" than an accomplishment, he was lambasted by David Bercuson, who denounced him for fantasizing about the history that might have happened and for missing the point that while "no one claims that the First World War united the nation," it was simply a matter of fact that the Great War, and Vimy Ridge in general, had given Borden "the leverage to win constitutional equality within the Empire." Bercuson's argument was fallacious on two counts. The "birth of the nation" trope (in circulation for almost four decades at that point) surely implied the emergence of something organically unified, that is, a baby, not a bloody and divided mess; and it would have come as a surprise to almost all contemporaries to

learn that Canada, thanks primarily to its marvelous victory at Vimy, had attained constitutional equality within the Empire, since Canada was unable to amend its own constitution, the court of last appeal on constitutional questions remained the London-based Judicial Committee of the Privy Council, and it was even touch-and-go if the country could sign its own treaties. See David Bercuson, "Crime or Commitment?" *National Post* (Toronto), 11 Feb. 2000, A18. In 1989, as J.L. Granatstein and Desmond Morton sagely pointed out, well after the Statute of Westminster in 1931, Canada remained ("psychologically") "the colony it had legally been in 1914." Granatstein and Morton, *A Nation Forged in Fire: Canadians and the Second World War, 1939–1945* (Toronto: Lester and Orpen Dennys, 1989), 8. Plainly, by 2000, such complexities were being sidelined, as Vimy became the bloody flag of a militarist and neo-conservative interpretation of Canadian history.

47 For a brilliant discussion of Karl Marx's aphorism, see Marshall Berman, *All That Is Solid Melts into Air: The Experience of Modernity* (New York: Simon and Schuster, 1982).

48 As Grace, *Landscapes of War and Memory*, 35, puts it: "I cannot see them wholly because their upper torsos and heads are covered; they are piled in such a manner that I cannot even determine exactly how many there are, and they are—in terms of colour—indistinguishable from the ground in which they will soon be laid. Who are they, how old are they, how did each man die and where did he come from? How, in fact, did he end up here like this? Where are all those myriad small things that identify and distinguish these men as individuals?"

49 "Archived—Canada's Newest Monument Evokes the Memory of War of 1812 Heroes," Department of Canadian Heritage, Government of Canada, News Release, 6 Nov. 2014, http://news.gc.ca/web/article-en.do?nid=900699 (July 2015), "Toronto Sculptor Adrienne Alison Creates Monument to War of 1812," *Toronto Star*, 27 June 2013.

50 Käthe Kollwitz, *The Diary and Letters of Käthe Kollwitz*, quoted in Martha Kearns, *Käthe Kollwitz: Woman and Artist* (Old Westbury, N.Y.: Feminist Press, 1976), 133–34.

51 Kearns, *Käthe Kollwitz*, 198.

52 Kollwitz quoted in Kearns, *Käthe Kollwitz*, 224.

53 Kollwitz quoted in Winter, *Sites of Memory, Sites of Mourning*, 110; Otto Nagel quoted in Kearns, *Käthe Kollwitz*, 199.

54 Winter, *Sites of Memory, Sites of Mourning*, 110–11.

55 Quoted in Gerry Gordon, "Kathe Kollwitz's 'Grieving Parents' at Vladslo: 'Seed Corn Must Not Be Ground,'" https://gerryco23.wordpress.com/2014/08/17/kathe-kollwitzs-grieving-parents-at-vladslo-seed-corn-must-not-be-ground (June 2016).

56 Jonathan Glancey, "The Ring of Remembrance, Notre Dame de Lorette," *The Telegraph* (U.K.), 10 Nov 2014, http://www.telegraph.co.uk/culture/art/architecture/11220393/The-Ring-of-Remembrance-Notre-Dame-de-Lorette.html (October 2015).

57 "Commemoration with a Difference," *Kingston Whig-Standard*, 10 Nov. 2015.

Reading Further

by Ian McKay

The Vimy Trap, although based upon extensive research into the manuscripts and printed records of the Great War, is aimed at a general readership. Here we briefly note other titles in the field (not all of them cited in the text itself) that may be useful to readers seeking more specialized works.

For those just setting out, Michael Howard, *The First World War: A Very Short Introduction* (Oxford: Oxford University Press, 2002), provides a useful distillation. To an extent that remains rare in the literature, James Joll and Gordon Martel, *The Origins of the First World War*, 3rd ed. (Harlow, Essex: Pearson Longman, 2007), attempts to connect underlying socio-economic causes with the cut and thrust of diplomacy.

The best general overview of Canadian developments in this period is still R. Craig Brown and Ramsay Cook, *Canada 1896–1921: A Nation Transformed* (Toronto: McClelland and Stewart, 1974). Robert Teigrob, *Living with War: Twentieth-Century Conflict in Canadian and American History and Memory* (Toronto: University of Toronto Press, 2016), represents an exemplary attempt to grasp the divergent ways in which people in the two countries have debated questions of peace and war; for shorter statements, see Teigrob, "Glad Adventures, Tragedies, Silences: Remembering and Forgetting Wars for Empire in Canada and the United States," *International Journal of Canadian Studies/ Revue internationale d'études canadiennes* 45–46 (2012), 441–65; and Teigrob, "Empires and Cultures of Militarism in Canada and the United States," *American Review of Canadian Studies* 43, 1 (2013), 30–48.

One of the best studies of the topic of this book is as yet unpublished: Victor Huard, "Armageddon Reconsidered: Shifting Attitudes towards Peace in English Canada, 1936–1953," Ph.D. thesis, Queen's University, 1996.

For general English-language titles from the vast diversity of perspectives on the history of the Great War and its aftermath, see Stéphane Audoin-Rouzeau and Annette Becker, *14–18: Understanding the Great War*, trans. Catherine Temerson (New York: Hill and Wang, 2002); Alan Axelrod, *Selling the Great War: The Making of American Propaganda* (New York: Palgrave Macmillan, 2009); Jeremy Black, *The Great War and the Making of the Modern World* (New York: Continuum, 2009); Gail Braybon, ed., *Evidence, History and the Great War: Historians and the Impact of 1914–18* (Cambridge: Cambridge

University Press, 2003); Niall Ferguson, *The Pity of War: Explaining World War I* (New York: Basic Books, 2000); Gerard De Groot, *Blighty: British Society in the Era of the Great War* (London and New York: Longman, 1996); Richard F. Hamilton and Holger H. Herwig, *Decisions for War, 1914–1917* (Cambridge: Cambridge University Press, 2014); Max Hastings, *Catastrophe: Europe Goes to War 1914* (London: William Collins, 2013); Philip Jenkins, *The Great and Holy War: How World War I Became a Religious Crusade* (New York: HarperCollins, 2014); John Keegan, *The First World War* (Toronto: Vintage Canada, 2000); Ian Kershaw, *To Hell and Back: Europe, 1914–1949* (New York: Viking, 2015); Eric Leed, *No Man's Land: Combat and Identity in World War I* (Cambridge: University of Cambridge Press, 1979); Dominic Lieven, *Towards the Flame: Empire, War and the End of Tsarist Russia* (London: Allen Lane, 2015); Margaret MacMillan, *The War That Ended Peace: The Road to 1914* (London: Allen Lane, 2014); MacMillan, *Paris 1919: Six Months That Changed the World* (New York: Random House, 2007); Sean McMeekin, *The Russian Origins of the First World War* (Cambridge, Mass., and London: Belknap Press of Harvard University Press, 2011); John Mosier, *The Myth of the Great War: A New Military History of World War I* (New York: Harper Perennial, 2002); Douglas Newton, *The Darkest Days: The Truth behind Britain's Rush to War, 1914* (London and New York: Verso, 2015); T.G. Otte, *July Crisis: The World's Descent into War, Summer 1914* (Cambridge: Cambridge University Press, 2014); Priya Satia, *Spies in Arabia: The Great War and the Cultural Foundations of Britain's Covert Empire in the Middle East* (Oxford: Oxford University Press, 2008); David Stevenson, *The First World War and International Politics* (Oxford: Oxford University Press, 1988); Stevenson, *Armaments and the Coming of War: Europe, 1909–1914* (Oxford: Clarendon Press, 1996); Stevenson, *Cataclysm: The First World War as Political Tragedy* (New York: Basic Books, 2004); Hew Strachan, *The First World War* (New York: Viking, 2004); Strachan, ed., *The Oxford Illustrated History of the First World War* (Oxford: Oxford University Press, 2015); Barbara W. Tuchman, *The Guns of August, The Proud Tower*, ed. Margaret MacMillan (New York: Library of America, 2012); Kristian Coates Ulrichsen, *The First World War in the Middle East* (London: Hurst and Company, 2014); Alexander Watson, *Ring of Steel: Germany and Austria-Hungary in World War I* (New York: Basic Books, 2014); Geoffrey Wawro, *A Mad Catastrophe: The Outbreak of World War I and the Collapse of the Habsburg Empire* (New York: Basic Books, 2014); Jay Winter and Blaine Baggett, *The Great War and the Shaping of the 20th Century* (New York: Penguin Studio, 1996); Jay Winter, *The Experience of World War I* (Edinburgh: Southside, 1988); Jay Winter and Antoine Prost, *The Great War in History: Debates and Controversies, 1914 to the Present* (Cambridge: Cambridge University Press, 2005); Leon Wolff, *In Flanders Fields: The 1917 Campaign* (New York: Viking Press, 1980 [1958]); Jay Winter and Jean-Louis Robert, eds., *Capital Cities at War: Paris, London, Berlin* (Cambridge: Cambridge University Press, 1997).

For the work of the British revisionist historians keen to refurbish the image of the Great War—and they have had an impact on Canadians—see Gary Sheffield, *Forgotten Victory: The First World War—Myths and Realities* (London: Headline, 2001); and Dan Todman, *The Great War: Myth and Memory* (London: Hambledon Continuum, 2005).

Anyone wanting to explore the specific debates around German war guilt could look at John Horne and Dr. Alan Kramer, *German Atrocities, 1914: A History of Denial* (New Haven, Conn.: Yale University Press, 2002), by no means the last word on this contentious topic; Isabel V. Hull, *A Scrap of Paper: Breaking and Making International Law during the Great War* (Ithaca, N.Y., and London: Cornell University Press, 2014); and especially Annika Mombauer, *The Origins of the First World War: Controversies and Consensus* (London: Longman, 2002), which provides a thoughtful overview of the debates since the 1960s, especially as they relate to the writings of Fritz Fischer. See also David Blackbourn and Geoff Eley, *The Peculiarities of German History: Bourgeois Society and Politics in Nineteenth-Century Germany* (Oxford and New York: Oxford University Press, 1984).

As for the Empire on whose behalf Canadian soldiers fought, its ideological underpinnings are effectively explored in Duncan Bell, *The Idea of Greater Britain: Empire and the Future of World Order, 1860–1900* (Princeton, N.J.: Princeton University Press, 2007); A.G. Hopkins, "Back to the Future: From National History to Imperial History," *Past and Present* 164 (August 1999), 198–243.

For Anglo-Canadian imperial nationalism, see Carl Berger, *The Sense of Power: Studies in the Ideas of Canadian Imperialism 1867–1914* (Toronto: University of Toronto Press, 1970), who argues that for many imperialists, war was a "manly slaughter over the obstacles of nature," not indiscriminate killing (236); Phillip Buckner, ed., *Canada and the British Empire* (Oxford: Oxford University Press, 2008); Buckner, "Nationalism in Canada," in Don Harrison Doyle, Marco Antonio, and Villela Pamplona, eds., *Nationalism in the New World* (Athens: University of Georgia Press, 2006); Colin M. Coates, "From Parliament Hill to Vimy Ridge: Imperial Canada, 1867–1917," in Colin M. Coates, ed., *Imperial Canada, 1867–1917: A Selection of Papers Given at the University of Edinburgh's Centre for Canadian Studies Conference May 1995* (Edinburgh: University of Edinburgh Centre of Canadian Studies, 1997); Terry Cook, "George R. Parkin and the Concept of Britannic Idealism," *Journal of Canadian Studies* 10 (1975), 15–31; Gordon Heath, "'Prepared to Do, Prepared to Die': Evangelicals, Imperialism, and Late-Victorian Canadian Children's Publications," *Perichoresis* 9 (2011), 3–27; Mark G. McGowan, "The De-Greening of the Irish: Toronto's Irish Catholic Press, Imperialism, and the Forging of a New Identity, 1887–1914," Canadian Historical Association, *Historical Papers/Communications historiques* 24, 1 (1989), 118–45; Robert Stamp, "Empire Day in the Schools of Ontario: The Training of Young Imperialists," *Journal of Canadian Studies* 8 (1973), 32–42.

Those in quest of accounts of Canadian military history in the Great War should consult, in addition to the collected works of Tim Cook abundantly cited in this book, G.W.L. Nicholson, *Canadian Expeditionary Force, 1914–1919* (Ottawa: Queen's Printer, 1962 [Montreal and Kingston: McGill-Queen's University Press, 2015]); for a more general introduction, see Desmond Morton and J.L. Granatstein, *Marching to Armageddon: Canadians and the Great War 1914–1919* (Toronto: Lester and Orpen Dennys, 1989). For more specific discussions, see A.M.J. Hyatt, "Sir Arthur Currie and Conscription: A Soldier's View," *Canadian Historical Review* 50, 3 (1969), 285–96; Hyatt, "Canadian Generals in the First World War and the Popular View of Military Leadership," *Social History/Histoire Sociale* 12, 24 (November 1979), 418–30; Hyatt, *General Sir Arthur Currie: A Military Biography* (Toronto: University of Toronto with the Canadian War Museum, Canadian Museum of Civilization, National Museums of Canada, 1987); Teresa Iacobelli, *Death or Deliverance: Canadian Courts Martial in the Great War* (Vancouver and Toronto: UBC Press, 2013); Andrew Iarocci, *Shoestring Soldiers: The 1st Canadian Division at War, 1914–1915* (Toronto: University of Toronto Press, 2008); Craig Leslie Mantle, ed., *The Apathetic and the Defiant: Case Studies of Canadian Mutiny and Disobedience, 1812–1919*

(Ottawa: Dundurn Group and the Canadian Defence Academy Press, 2007); Desmond Morton, *When Your Number's Up: The Canadian Soldier in the First World War* (Toronto: Vantage, 1994).

The thesis that the Great War encouraged Canadians to see themselves as constituting one nation is explored in Matthew R. Bray, "'Fighting as an Ally': The English-Canadian Patriotic Response to the Great War," *Canadian Historical Review* 61, 2 (1980), 141–68; Stephen J. Harris, "From Subordinate to Ally: The Canadian Corps and National Autonomy 1914–18," *Revue International d'histoire militaire* 54 (1982), 109–30; Harris, "A Canadian Way of War: 1919 to 1939," in Bernd Horn, ed., *The Canadian Way of War: Serving the National Interest* (Toronto: Dundurn Press, 2006), 195–211; Desmond Morton, "'Junior but Sovereign Allies': The Transformation of the Canadian Expeditionary Force, 1914–1918," *Journal of Imperial and Commonwealth History* 8, 1 (1979), 56–67.

Among the many general studies of war and remembrance, see Louise Purbrick, Jim Aulich, and Graham Dawson, eds., *Contested Spaces: Sites, Representations and Histories of Conflict* (London: Palgrave Macmillan, 2007); James M. Mayo, *War Memorials as Political Landscape: The American Experience and Beyond* (New York, Westport, and London: Praeger, 1988); Jay Winter and Emmanuel Sivan, eds., *War and Remembrance in the Twentieth Century* (Cambridge: Cambridge University Press, 2005).

With specific reference to the Great War, see Allyson Booth, *Postcards from the Trenches* (New York and Oxford: Oxford University Press, 1996); Rob Bushaway, "'Name upon Name': The Great War and Remembrance," in Roy Porter, ed., *The Myths of the English* (Cambridge: Polity, 1992); Aidan Gregory, *The Silence of Memory: Armistice Day, 1919–1946* (Oxford: Oxford University Press, 1994); Stefan Goebel, *The Great War and Medieval Memory: War, Remembrance and Medievalism in Britain and Germany, 1914–1940* (Cambridge: Cambridge University Press, 2007); Nicoletta F. Gullace, *"The Blood of Our Sons": Men, Women, and the Renegotiation of British Citizenship during the Great War* (Basingstoke, U.K.: Palgrave Macmillan, 2002); Stephen Heathorn, *Haig and Kitchener in Twentieth-Century Britain: Remembrance, Representation and Appropriation* (Farnham, U.K., and Burlington, Vt.: Ashgate Publishing, 2013); Samuel Hynes, *A War Imagined: The First World War and English Culture* (London: Pimlico, 1992); K.S. Inglis, *Sacred Places: War Memorials in the Australian Landscape*, 3rd ed. (Carlton: Melbourne University Press, 2008); Nuala Johnson, "Cast in Stone: Monuments, Geography, and Nationalism," *Environment and Planning D: Society and Space* 13, 1 (1995), 51–65; Susan Kent, *Aftershocks: The Politics of Trauma in Britain, 1918–1931* (New York: Palgrave, 2009); Arthur Marwick, *The Deluge: British Society and the First World War* (London: Macmillan, 1965); George Mosse, *Fallen Soldiers: Reshaping the Memory of the World Wars* (New York: Oxford University Press, 1990); Winter and Sivan, eds., *War and Remembrance in the Twentieth Century*; David Reynolds, *The Long Shadow: The Legacies of the Great War in the Twentieth Century* (New York and London: W.W. Norton and Company, 2014); Alistair Thompson, "The Anzac Legend: Exploring National Myth and Memory in Australia," in Raphael Samuel, ed., *The Myths We Live By* (London and New York: Routledge, 1990), 73–82; Thompson, *Anzac Memories: Living with the Legend* (New York: Oxford University Press, 1994); Janet K. Watson, *Fighting Different Wars: Experience, Memory, and the First World War in Britain* (Cambridge: Cambridge University Press, 2006); Jay Winter, *Sites of Memory, Sites of Mourning: The Great War in European Cultural History* (Cambridge: Cambridge University Press, 1995); Winter, *Remembering War: The Great War between Memory and History in the Twentieth Century* (New Haven, Conn., and London: Yale University Press, 2006); Bart Ziino, "'A Kind of Round Trip': Australian Soldiers and the Tourist Analogy," *War and Society* 25, 2 (October 2006), 39–52.

The Great War's wider social and cultural dimensions in Canada are explored in Daphne Read, ed., *The Great War and Canadian Society: An Oral History* (Toronto: New Hogtown Press, 1978); James M. Pitsula, *For All That We Have and Are: Regina and the Experience of the Great War* (Winnipeg: University of Manitoba Press, 2008); Robert Rutherdale, *Hometown Horizons: Local Responses to Canada's Great War* (Vancouver and Toronto: UBC Press, 2004); Robert Rutherdale, "Send-Offs during Canada's Great War: Interpreting Hometown Rituals in Dispatching Home Front Volunteers," *Histoire Social/ Social History* 36, 72 (2003); John Herd Thompson, *Harvests of War: The Prairie West, 1914–1918* (Toronto: McClelland and Stewart, 1978); David Tough, "'The Rich . . . Should Give to Such an Extent That It Will Hurt': 'Conscription of Wealth' and Political Modernism in the Parliamentary Debate on the 1917 Income War Tax," *Canadian Historical Review* 93, 3 (2012), 382–407; Tough, "The Rhetoric of Dominion Income Taxation and the Modern Political Imaginary in Canada, 1910–1945," Ph.D. thesis, Carleton University, 2013; W.R. Young, "Conscription, Rural Depopulation and the Farmers of Ontario, 1917–1919," *Canadian Historical Review* 53 (1972), 289–320.

Grounded in Anglo-Canadian imperial nationalism was the oppressive wartime treatment of dissidents and national and racialized minorities. The federal state's orchestration of repressive activities is well explored in Dennis Molinaro, "State Repression and Political Deportation in Canada, 1919–1936," Ph.D. thesis, University of Toronto, 2014.

Many studies have focused upon gender and the war. The Great War as the apotheosis—or crisis—of traditional masculinity is explored in Michael Adams, *The Great Adventure: Male Desire and the Coming of World War I* (Bloomington: University of Indiana Press, 1990); George Chauncey, "Christian Brotherhood or Sexual Perversion? Homosexual Identities and the Construction of Sexual Boundaries in the World War One Era," *Journal of Social History* 19, 2 (Winter 1985), 189–211; Graham Dawson, *Soldier Heroes: British Adventure, Empire, and the Imagining of Masculinities* (London and New York: Routledge, 1994); Gerald N. Izenberg, *Modernism and Masculinity: Mann, Wedekind, Kandinsky through World War I* (Chicago: University of Chicago Press, 2005); Jessica Meyer, *Men of War: Masculinity and the First World War in Britain* (London: Palgrave Macmillan, 2011); Martin Stone, "Shellshock and the Psychologists," in W.F. Bynum, Roy Porter, and Michael Shepherd, eds., *The Anatomy of Madness: Essays in the History of Psychiatry*, vol. 2 (London: Tavistock Publications, 1985), 242–71; Heather Streets, *Martial Races: The Military, Race, and Masculinity in British Imperial Culture, 1857–1914* (New York: Manchester University Press, 2004).

Canadian titles on gender and war include R. Blake Brown, "'Every Boy Ought to Learn to Shoot and to Obey Orders': Guns, Boys, and the Law in English Canada from the Late Nineteenth Century to the Great War," *Canadian Historical Review* 93, 2 (June 2012), 196–226; Mark Howard Moss, *Manliness and Militarism: Educating Young Boys in Ontario for War* (Toronto: University of Toronto Press, 2001).

The long-term impact of the war on men's health is explored by Mark Humphries, "War's Long Shadow: Masculinity, Medicine and the Gendered Politics of Trauma, 1914–1939," *Canadian Historical Review* 91, 3 (2010), 503–31, who finds: "More than 15,000 Canadian soldiers were diagnosed with some form of war-related psychological wounds.

Many more went unrecognized. Yet the very act of seeking an escape from the battlefield or applying for a postwar pension for psychological traumas transgressed masculine norms that required men to be aggressive, self-reliant, and un-emotional" (503). Tom Brown, "Shell Shock and the Canadian Expeditionary Force, 1914–18: Canadian Psychiatry in the Great War," in Charles Roland, ed., *Health, Disease and Medicine: Essays in Canadian History* (Toronto: Hannah Institute, 1983), 308–32, highlights the same phenomenon.

Apart from nursing sisters, the Western Front proper was an overwhelmingly male-dominated zone, but women played a considerable role in sustaining support for the struggle at home. For useful overviews, see Sarah Glassford and Amy Shaw, *A Sisterhood of Suffering and Service: Women and Girls of Canada and Newfoundland during the First World War* (Vancouver: UBC Press, 2012); Joan Sangster, "Mobilizing Women for War," in David Mackenzie, ed., *Canada and the First World War: Essays in Honour of Robert Craig Brown* (Toronto: University of Toronto Press, 2005),157–93.

The commitment of many women in Canada and other countries to the British Empire is explored in Katie Pickles, *Female Imperialism and the National Identity: Imperial Order Daughters of the Empire* (Manchester, U.K.: Manchester University Press, 2009); see also Lisa Gaudet, "The Empire Is Woman's Sphere: Organized Female Imperialism in Canada, 1880s–1920s," Ph.D. thesis, Carleton University, 2001. Some middle-class women were able to achieve new positions of prominence and authority through war support work: see Ernest R. Forbes, "Battles in Another War: Edith Archibald and the Halifax Feminist Movement," in Ernest R. Forbes, ed., *Challenging the Regional Stereotype: Essays on the 20th Century Maritimes* (Fredericton: Acadiensis Press, 1989); Lucille Marr, "Paying 'the Price of War': Canadian Women and the Churches on the Home Front," in Gordon L. Heath, ed., *Canadian Churches and the First World War* (Eugene, Ore.: Pickwick Publications, 2014), 263–83; Penny Bedal and Ross Bartlett, "The Women Do Not Speak: The Methodist Ladies' Aid Societies and World War I," *Canadian Methodist Historical Society Papers* 10 (1993–1994), 63–86.

The most obvious transformation in gender relations brought about by the war was the partial granting of female enfranchisement; for its divisive effects, see Tarah Brookfield, "Divided by the Ballot Box: The Montreal Council of Women and the 1917 Election," *Canadian Historical Review* 89, 4 (2008), 473–501. Suzanne Evans, *Mothers of Heroes, Mothers of Martyrs: World War I and the Politics of Grief* (Montreal and Kingston: McGill-Queen's University Press, 2007), shows how maternal grief was used to achieve political objectives, although our evidence suggests that bereaved mothers could also be brought forward to exemplify the urgency of peace.

Sex remains an underexplored area in Canada's Great War, but see Jay Cassel, *The Secret Plague: Venereal Disease in Canada, 1838–1939* (Toronto: University of Toronto Press, 1987); Craig Gibson, *Behind the Front: British Soldiers and French Civilians, 1914–1918* (Cambridge: Cambridge University Press, 2014), ch. 10. For a contemporary critique of the deceits practised upon women by Canadian soldiers, see Thomas Dinesen, *Merry Hell! A Dane with the Canadians* (London: Jarrolds, 1929 [repr. Uckfield, England: Naval and Military Press, n.d.]). That some Canadian soldiers may have fancied each other is thus far beyond the ken of our military historians, but for U.S. evidence of a flourishing same-sex culture in this period, see Lawrence Murphy, *Perverts by Official Order: The Campaign against Homosexuals by the United States Navy* (New York: Routledge, 1988). The sexual and other assaults committed by Canadian soldiers are explored in

Rhiannon Murphy, "Crimes and Misdemeanours: Canadian Soldiers and Crimes against French and Flemish Civilians during the First World War," unpublished paper, University of Victoria, 2015.

As it was taking place, the Great War was commonly placed in a Christian framework, often revealing the necessary trials undergone by the British Empire as God's agency upon Earth. For contemporary discussions, see Charles Allan, *The Beautiful Thing That Has Happened to Our Boys: Messages in War Time* (Greenock: James McKelvie and Sons, 1915); H.P. Almon, *The Religion of the Tommy: War Essays and Addresses* (Milwaukee: Morehouse Publishing Co., 1918). For later sources, see Allen Frantzen, *Bloody Good: Chivalry, Sacrifice, and the Great War* (Chicago: University of Chicago Press, 2004); Michael Snape, *God and the British Soldier: Religion and the British Army in the First and Second World Wars* (New York: Routledge, 2005); Snape, "The Great War," in Hugh McLeod, ed., *World Christianities c.1914–c.2000* (Cambridge: Cambridge University Press, 2008), 131–50.

For a bibliographical overview, see Gordon Heath, "Canadian Churches and War: An Introductory Essay and Annotated Bibliography," *McMaster Journal of Theology and Ministry* 12 (2010–11), 61–124; for an outstandingly useful collection, see Heath, ed., *Canadian Churches and the First World War*; its introduction reveals how a "providential" sense of war seeped into many of the mainstream Protestant congregations.

The most famous Canadian padre was Canon Frederick Scott; his *The Great War as I Saw It* (Kingston, Ont.: Legacy Books Press, 2009 [Toronto: F.D. Goodchild, 1922]) is one of the classic patriotic accounts of the war. For discussions of Canon Scott, see Dennis Duffy, "Dark Nightmare: The Shooting of William Alexander as Canon Scott Saw It," *American Review of Canadian Studies* 41, 3 (2011), 228–41; Melissa Davidson, "Having Served in Our Generation: Great War Memory and the Public Funerals of Sir Arthur Currie and Canon F.G. Scott," paper delivered to the Canadian Historical Association, May 2014; Terrence Jacob Whalen, "The Anglo-Catholic Identities of Frederick George Scott, 1861–1944," M.A. thesis, Queen's University, 2000; M. Jeanne Yardley, "'The Bitterness and the Greatness': Reading F.G. Scott's War," *Studies in Canadian Literature* 16, 1 (1991), 82–101. For another memoir by a padre, in this case a Catholic priest, see Benedict J. Murdoch, *The Red Vineyard* (Wexford, Ireland: John English, 1949 [1928]).

Other important works on Canadian Christians and the war include Murray E. Angus, "King Jesus and King George: The Manly Christian Patriot and the Great War, 1914–1918," *Canadian Methodist Historical Society Papers* 12 (1997–98), 124–32; Brian Clarke, "English-Speaking Canada from 1854," in Terrance Murphy, ed., *A Concise History of Christianity in Canada* (Toronto: Oxford University Press, 1996), 261–359; Duff Crerar, *Padres in No Man's Land: Canadian Chaplains and the Great War*, 2nd ed. (Montreal and Kingston: McGill-Queen's University Press, 2014), based upon his outstanding "Padres in No Man's Land: Canadian Military Chaplains, 1866–1939," Ph.D. thesis, Queen's University, 1989; Melissa Davidson, "Preaching the Great War: Canadian and the War Sermon, 1914–1918," M.A. thesis, McGill University, 2013; Davidson, "The Anglican Church and the Great War," in Heath, ed., *Canadian Churches and the First World War*, 152–69; Michelle Fowler, "Keeping the Faith: The Presbyterian Press in Peace and War, 1913–1919," M.A. thesis, Wilfrid Laurier University, 2005; "'Death Is Not the Worst Thing': The Presbyterian Press in Canada, 1913–1919," *War and Society* 25 (2006), 23–38; Gordon Heath, *A War with a Silver Lining: Canadian Protestant Churches and the South African War, 1899–1902* (Montreal and Kingston: McGill-Queen's University Press, 2009), which reveals the deeper roots of Protestant militarism; Michael A.G. Haykin and Ian Hugh Clary, "'O God of Battles': The Canadian Baptist Experience of the Great War," in Heath, ed., *Canadian Churches and the First World War*, 170–96; Brian F. Hogan, "The Guelph Novitiate Raid: Conscription, Censorship and Bigotry during the Great War," *CCHA Study Sessions 45* (1978), 57–80, which looks at mob violence turned against Catholics, a theme also explored in Rutherdale, *Hometown Horizons*; Robynne Rogers Healey, "Quakers and Mennonites and the Great War," in Heath, ed., *Canadian Churches and the First World War*, 218–40; David Marshall, "Methodism Embattled: A Reconsideration of the Methodist Church and World War I," *Canadian Historical Review* 66 (1985), 48–64; Marshall, "'Khaki Has Become a Sacred Colour': The Methodist Church and the Sanctification of World War One," in Heath, ed., *Canadian Churches and the First World War*, 102–32; Mark G. McGowan, "'To Share in the Burdens of Empire': Toronto's Catholics and the Great War," in Mark McGowan and Brian P. Clarke, eds., *Catholics at the Gathering Place: Historical Essays on the Archdiocese of Toronto, 1841–1991* (Toronto: Dundurn, 1993); McGowan, "Harvesting the 'Red Vineyard': Catholic Religious Culture in the Canadian Expeditionary Force, 1914–1919," *Historical Studies* 64 (1998), 47–70; McGowan, *The Waning of the Green: Catholics, the Irish, and Identity in Toronto, 1887–1922* (Montreal and Kingston: McGill-Queen's University Press, 1999); McGowan, "Between King, Kaiser, and Canada: Irish Catholics in Canada and the Great War, 1914–1918," in David A. Wilson, ed., *Irish Nationalism in Canada* (Montreal and Kingston: McGill-Queen's University Press, 2009), 97–120; McGowan, "Rendering unto Caesar: Catholics, the State, and the Idea of a Christian Canada," *CSCH Historical Papers* (2011), 65–85; McGowan, "'We Are All Involved in the Same Issue': Canada's English-Speaking Catholics and the Great War," in Heath, ed., *Canadian Churches and the First World War*, 34–74; and Mark Parent, "T.T. Shields and the First World War," *McMaster Journal of Theology* 2 (1991), 42–57, who highlights the extent to which this great fundamentalist's subsequent stance of "no neutrality" in his battles with the liberal Baptists of McMaster University was conditioned by his direct experience of the war. For the bitter conclusions of one United Church minister, victimized for his pacifism in the 1940s, see Robert Edis Fairbairn, *Apostate Christendom* (London: Ken-Pax, 1947).

The divergent views of the war of many francophone Québécois and Acadians, as manifest in the conscription crisis, have been extensively explored and debated. For the conscription crisis in general, see J.L. Granatstein and J.M. Hitsman, *Broken Promises: A History of Conscription in* Canada (Toronto: Oxford University Press, 1977). For a pungent Anglo-Canadian representation of French Canadians as intrinsically incapable of maturely bearing the burdens of empire, by a man responsible for shaping much of the official history of the war, see J. Castell Hopkins, *The Story of the Dominion* (Toronto: Winston, 1901).

The national struggles of Québécois and Acadians over the issues raised by the Great War are illuminated in Elizabeth Armstrong, *The Crisis of Quebec, 1914–18* (New York: Columbia University Press, 1937); Martin F. Auger, "On the Brink of Civil War: The Canadian Government and the Suppression of the 1918 Quebec Easter Riots," *Canadian Historical Review* 89, 4 (2008), 503–40; Carl Berger, ed., *Conscription 1917* (Toronto: University of Toronto Press, 1969); Robert Comeau, "L'opposition à la conscription au Québec," in Roch Legault and Jean Lamarre, eds., *La Première guerre mondiale et le Canada:*

Contributions sociomilitaires québécoises (Montreal: Méridien, 1999), 91–109; Mourad Dje-babla-Brun, *Se souvenir de la Grande Guerre: La mémoire plurielle de 14–18 au Québec* (Montreal: VLB Editeur, 2004); René Durocher, "Henri Bourassa, les évêques et la guerre, 1914–1918," *Historical Papers/Communications Historiques* 6 (1971), 248–75; Patrice Dutil, "Against Isolationism: Napoléon Belcourt, French Canada, and 'La grande guerre,'" in Mackenzie, ed., *Canada and the First World War*, 96–137; Gérard Filteau, *Le Québec, le Canada et la guerre, 1914–1918* (Montreal: Editions de l'Aurore, 1977); Camil Girard, *Canada, A Country Divided: The Times of London and Canada, 1908–1922* (Quebec: Les éditions JCL, 2001); Alan Gordon, *Making Public Pasts: The Contested Terrain of Montreal's Public Memories, 1891–1930* (Montreal and Kingston: McGill-Queen's University Press, 2001); "Lest We Forget: The Two Solitudes in War and Memory," in Norman Hillmer and Adam Chapnick, eds., *Canadas of the Mind: The Making and Unmaking of Canadian Nationalisms in the Twentieth Century* (Montreal: McGill-Queen's University Press, 2007), 159–173; Simon Jolivet, "Entre nationalisme irlandais et canadien-français: Les intrigues québécoises de la Self Determination for Ireland League of Canada and Newfoundland," *Canadian Historical Review* 92, 1 (March 2011), 43–68; Jolivet, "French-Speaking Catholics in Quebec and the First World War," in Heath, ed., *Canadian Churches and the First World War*, 75–101; Sylvie Lacombe, *La rencontre de deux peuples élus: Comparaison des ambitions nationale et impériale au Canada entre 1896 et 1920* (Quebec: Presses de l'Université Laval, 2002); Jean Provencher, *Québec sous la loi des mesures de guerre 1918* (Trois Rivières: Les éditions du Boréal Express, 1971); Desmond Morton, "French Canada and War, 1868–1917: The Military Background to the Conscription Crisis of 1917," in *War and Society in North America*, ed. J.L. Granatstein and R.D. Cuff (Toronto: Nelson, 1971), 84–96; Béatrice Richard, "Henri Bourassa and Conscription: Traitor or Saviour?" *Canadian Military Journal* (Winter 2006–7), 75–83; Andrew Theobald, "Une loi extraordinaire: New Brunswick Acadians and the Conscription Crisis of the First World War," *Acadiensis* 34 (2004), 80–95; Theobald, "Divided Once More: Social Memory and the Canadian Conscription Crisis of the First World War," *Past Imperfect* 12 (2006), 1–19; Chris Young, "'Sous les balles des troupes fédérales': Representing the Quebec City Riots in Francophone Quebec (1919–2009)," M.A. thesis, Concordia University, 2009.

Francophone soldiers' experiences in the Canadian Expeditionary Force are explored in Jean-Pierre Gagnon, *Le 22e bataillon (canadien-français) 1914–1919: Étude socio-militaire* (Quebec: Les presses de l'université Laval, 1986); Jean Martin, *Un siècle d'oubli: les Canadiens et la Première Guerre mondiale* (Outremont: Athéna éditions, 2014); Martin, "La participation des francophones dans le Corps éxpeditionnaire canadien (1914–1919), il faut réviser à la hausse," *Canadian Historical Review* 96, 3 (September 2015), 405–23; Jacques Michel, *La Participation des Canadiens Français à la Grande Guerre* (Montreal: Editions de L'ACF, 1938). For a rich primary source, see Thomas-Louis Tremblay, *Journal de guerre (1915–1918)*, ed. Marcelle Cinq-Mars (Outremont: Athéna Edition, 2006), which eloquently documents post-Vimy Anglo/French tensions.

The treatment of racialized and national minorities in the war has generated a considerable literature. For a good overview, see John Herd Thompson, *Ethnic Minorities during Two World Wars* (Ottawa: Canadian Historical Association, 1991). On the First Nations, see Mark Abley, *Conversations with a Dead Man: The Legacy of Duncan Campbell Scott* (Vancouver: Douglas and McIntyre, 2013), who documents Scott's dream that the war would accelerate the assimilation of indigenous peoples; Robin Brownlie, "Work

Hard and Be Grateful: Native Soldier Settlers in Ontario after the First World War," in Franca Iacovetta and Wendy Mitchinson, eds., *On the Case: Explorations in Social History* (Toronto: University of Toronto Press, 1998); Evan J. Habkirk, "Militarism, Sovereignty, and Nationalism: Six Nations and the First World War," M.A. thesis, Trent University, 2010, which shows the extent to which Iroquois participants nurtured their own conceptions of sovereignty; P. Whitney Lackenbauer, *A Commemorative History of Aboriginal People in the Canadian Military* (Ottawa: Directorate of History and Heritage, 2010); Timothy Charles Winegard, *Indigenous Peoples of the British Dominions and the First World War* (Cambridge, Mass.: Cambridge University Press, 2011); and Winegard, *For King and Kanata: Canadian Indians and the First World War* (Winnipeg: University of Manitoba Press, 2012).

For the official treatment of Afro-Canadians, see Calvin W. Ruck, *The Black Battalion, 1916–1920: Canada's Best Kept Military Secret* (Halifax: Nimbus Publishing, 1987); James W. St. G. Walker, "Race and Recruitment in World War I: Enlistment of Visible Minorities in the Canadian Expeditionary Force," *Canadian Historical Review* 70, 1 (1989), 1–26. Stephanie Bangarth documents the paradoxical results of the federal enfranchisement of Japanese Canadians who served in the Great War in *Voices Raised in Protest: Defending North American Citizens of Japanese Ancestry, 1942–49* (Vancouver: UBC Press, 2008).

German Canadians were treated harshly during the war. Anti-German policies are explored in Mario Nathan Coschi, "'Be British or Be D—d': Primary Education in Berlin-Kitchener, Ontario, during the First World War," *Histoire sociale/Social History* 47, 94 (2014), 311–32; Allen Teichroew, "World War I and the Mennonite Migration to Canada to Avoid the Draft," *Mennonite Quarterly Review* 45 (1971), 219–49; Patricia McKegney, *The Kaiser's Bust: A Study of War-Time Propaganda in Berlin, Ontario 1914–1918* (Bamberg, Ont.: Bamberg Press, 1991).

The harsh, at moments even murderous, treatment of Eastern Europeans held to be "enemy aliens" is documented in Bodhan Kordan, *Enemy Aliens, Prisoners of War: Internment in Canada during the Great War* (Montreal and Kingston: McGill-Queen's University Press, 2002); Lubomyr Luciuk and Bryan Rollason, *Internment Operations: The Role of Old Fort Henry in World War I* (Kingston: Delta Educational Consultants, 1980); Lubomyr Luciuk, *In Fear of the Barbed Wire Fence: Canada's First National Internment Operations and the Ukrainian Canadians, 1914–1920* (Kingston: Limestone Press, 2001); Luciuk, *Without Just Cause: Canada's First National Internment Operations and the Ukrainian Canadians, 1914–1920* (Kingston: Kashtan Press, 2006); Desmond Morton, "Sir William Otter and Internment Operations in Canada during the First World War," *Canadian Historical Review* 55, 1 (1974), 32–58; Frances Swyripa and John Herd Thompson, eds., *Loyalties in Conflict: Ukrainians in Canada during the Great War* (Edmonton: Canadian Institute of Ukrainian Study Press, 1983); Frances Swyripa, *Storied Landscapes: Ethno-Religious Identity and the Canadian Prairies* (Winnipeg: University of Manitoba Press, 2010).

* * *

Many Canadians came to view the Great War—which was, we argue, a fiercely contested "site of memory" from the 1920s to the 1960s—as a mistake, and their own involvement in it as a tragedy. Rather than summing up this experience under the conventional cat-

egory of "disillusionment"—which implies an emotional response in the wake of disappointed hopes—we think of it as one of "critique." Critical responses to the war can be
placed under five headings: (a) those that revisited the supposed causes of the war and
urged their revaluation; (b) those that criticized how the war was managed—with specific reference, in the Canadian case, to the rigidities and elitism of the senior officers
in Europe and to corrupt and self-serving elites at home; (c) those that dwelt upon the
extent to which the ideals for which the war had supposedly been fought were swiftly
betrayed in its aftermath; (d) those that focused especially upon the treatment of veterans, whose poverty and suffering came to cast doubt on the war itself; and (e) those that
interpreted the Great War as an indication that modern warfare posed a mortal threat to
human civilization.

(a) The massive turn against the Great War in the United States was greatly facilitated
by the work of professional historians, who critiqued the war on realist grounds. They
argued that the ostensible aims for which the British Empire and its allies had waged
war were not the actual driving forces of the war, a point emphasized by none other than
President Woodrow Wilson.

For U.S. historians' critical examinations of the war, see the measured and careful
work of Sidney Fay: "New Light on the Origins of the World War. I. Berlin and Vienna,
to July 29," *American Historical Review* 25, 4 (July 1920), 616–39; "New Light on the Origins of the World War, II. Berlin and Vienna, July 29 to 31," *American Historical Review*
26, 1 (October 1920), 37–53; "New Light on the Origins of the World War, III. Russia
and the Other Powers," *American Historical Review* 26, 2 (January 1921), 225–24. These
studies culminated in Fay, *The Origins of the World War*, two vols. (New York: Macmillan,
1928, 1930).

Fay's fellow historian H.E. Barnes, who in 1924 urged readers of the *Canadian Forum*
to tune into the "New American History"—"Dynamic History and Social Reform,"
Canadian Forum 4, 47 (1924), 331, 332—brought out *The Genesis of the World War: An
Introduction to the Problem of War Guilt* (New York: Alfred A. Knopf, 1926); his equally
polemical *In Quest of Truth and Justice: De-Bunking the War Guilt Myth* (Chicago: National
Historical Society, 1928) carried the new argument further. In 1928 Charles Beard and
Mary Beard, among the most prestigious U.S. historians of their time and widely read in
Canada, judged the conventional British view of Germany's sole malfeasance as a "story
for babes": Charles and Mary Beard, *The Rise of American Civilization* (New York: Macmillan, one-volume edition, 1930 [1927]), 617. For discussions of this current, see Jerald
A. Combs, *American Diplomatic History: Two Centuries of Changing Interpretations* (Berke-
ley, Los Angeles, and London: University of California Press, 1983), who reflects on the
"atmosphere" of scepticism (96) and the dramatic impact of the historians on popular perceptions of the war (152); and Donald R. Kelley, *Frontiers of History: Historical Inquiry in the
Twentieth Century* (New Haven, Conn., and London: Yale University Press, 2006), ch. 2.

As the 1930s progressed, many people influenced by this sceptical appraisal of the
war fixed their eyes on the small groups of warmongers who were eagerly preparing for
the next conflagration: see especially H.C. Engelbrecht and F.C. Hanighen, *Merchants of
Death: A Study of the International Armament Industry* (New York: Dodd, Mead and Company, 1934). Such viewpoints were widely disseminated in the U.S. media; six-sevenths
of periodicals read in Canada in 1924 emanated from the United States (Carole Gerson

and Jacques Michon, eds., *History of the Book in Canada*, vol. 3 (Toronto: University of Toronto Press, 2007). Sceptical attitudes about the Great War, although inspired by much made-in-Canada materials, were thus reinforced by this powerful current from south of the border.

Ontario-born James T. Shotwell, *On the Rim of the Abyss* (New York: Macmillan, 1936 [New York and London: Garland Publishing, 1972]), among the most powerful peace-oriented intellectuals of his time, sought to apply some of the Beards' coolly realistic analysis to problems of peace and war; among Canadians, Frank Underhill, once an enthusiastic supporter of the view that the war had helped to "make" Canada—see Underhill, "The Canadian Forces in the War," in Sir Charles Lucas, ed., *The Empire at War* (Toronto: Oxford University Press, 1923), 81–294—betrayed most clearly the impact of the new U.S. analysis of the war: Frank Underhill, "Canada and the Last War," in Chester Martin, ed., *Canada in War and Peace: Eight Studies in National Trends since 1914* (Toronto: Oxford University Press, 1941); Underhill, "A Working Peace System," *United Church Observer* 4, 21 (1 Jan. 1944), 11; Underhill, "To Protect Our Neutrality," *Canadian Forum* 17 (February 1938), 375–76; Underhill, "Keep Canada out of War," in Underhill, *In Search of Canadian Liberalism* (Toronto: Macmillan, 1960). As R. Douglas Francis points out, in *Frank H. Underhill: Intellectual Provocateur* (Toronto: University of Toronto Press, 1986), Underhill's sceptical appraisal of the Great War was such that he was almost ejected from his professorial post at the University of Toronto. W.B. Kerr was stating the obvious (and the point applied to his own memoirs as a soldier of the war) when he pointed out that after the mid–1920s, Canadians' appraisal of the war had a new analytical coolness and clarity; Kerr, "Historical Literature on Canada's Participation in the Great War," *Canadian Historical Review* 41 (1933), 412–36. For an excellent overview, see Donald M. Page, "Canada as the Exponent of North American Idealism," *American Review of Canadian Studies* 3, 2 (1973), 30–46; for illustrations, see F.H. Soward, "Canada and Foreign Affairs: A Review of the Recent Literature," *Canadian Historical Review* 19 (June 1938), 173–190; Soward, *Canada in World Affairs: The Pre-War Years* (Toronto: Oxford University Press, 1941).

Although it may seem strange that Conservative George Drew, the author of the celebratory *Canada's Fighting Airmen* (Toronto: Maclean Publishing, 1930), could double as an ardent peace activist, it becomes less so when he is placed in a North American context. Drew, *Enemies of Peace* (Toronto: Women's League of Nations Association, n.d. [1933]), repeats many of the arguments and much of the rhetoric of *Merchants of Death*. See also his "The Truth about the War," *Maclean's*, 1 July 1928; Drew, "The Truth about War Debts," *Maclean's*, 15 April 1931; Drew, "The League of Insincerity," *Maclean's*, 15 Jan. 1932; Drew, "Canada's Armament Mystery," *Maclean's*, 1 Sept. 1938. For a study of the scandal Drew set in motion on the issue of military procurements, see James Eayrs, *In Defence of Canada: Appeasement and Rearmament* (Toronto: University of Toronto Press, 1965), 116–22; David Mackenzie, "The Bren Gun Scandal and the Maclean Publishing Company's Investigation of Canadian Contracts, 1938–1940," *Journal of Canadian Studies* 26, 3 (Fall 1991), 140–62. The interwar Canadian armaments industry was minuscule—for background, see H.H. Vaughan, *The Manufacture of Munitions in Canada* (Ottawa: Engineering Institute of Canada, 1919)—but as the world's leading producer of nickel, which had made its way to Germany from 1914–18, Canada could nonetheless be portrayed as complicit in war-mongering. Canadians more attuned to British opinion could also easily get access to similar viewpoints from Britain, such as Philip Gibbs's intermittently critical *Now It Can Be Told* (New York: Harper and Brothers, 1920) and C.E. Montague's less ambiguously dyspeptic *Disenchantment* (London: Chatto and Windus, 1922).

(b) Throughout the 1920s and 1930s many informed Canadians advanced stringent critiques of the war, but emphasized not so much the "why" of the war as the "how"—that is, the irrational ways in which it had been pursued. An early start was made in Herbert A. Bruce, *Politics and the Canadian Army Medical Corps: A History of Intrigue, Containing Many Facts, Omitted from the Official Records, Showing How Efforts of Rehabilitation Were Baulked* (Toronto: William Briggs, 1919); the very title suggested the contentiousness of its contents. Andrew Macphail, *Official History of the Canadian Forces in the Great War, 1914–1919: Medical Services* (Ottawa: King's Printer, 1925), was a blistering critique of how Canada's war had been waged, and although faulted on methodological and stylistic grounds by both contemporaries and present-day historians, as an *official history* that spoke so critically of the chaos engendered by some of Canada's leading military figures, it suggested what a contested terrain the war had become by the mid-1920s (for discussion, see Ian Ross Robertson, *Sir Andrew Macphail: The Life and Legacy of a Canadian Man of Letters* [Montreal and Kingston: McGill-Queen's University Press, 2008]). Both W.B. Kerr, *Shrieks and Crashes: Being Memories of Canada's Corps, 1917* (Toronto: Hunter Rose, 1929), with its vitriolic critique of "useless" Passchendaele (137) and James H. Pedley, *Only This: A War Retrospect, 1917–1918* (Ottawa: CEF Books, 1999 [1927]), with its caustic portrait of preening and self-absorbed officers, anticipated the equally down-to-earth critiques of Will Bird and Charles Harrison.

As in the case of S.D. Chown, many articulate Protestants came to question the Great War on the ground that, whatever the traditional Christian reasoning about "just wars," the carnage of 1914–18 had revealed its moral limitations. It was, in particular, no longer the case that war was confined to soldiers who had volunteered for it. There was a mass movement against war in the Protestant churches.

For an interesting study of a powerful international religious group devoted to peace, see Charles F. Howlett, "John Nevin Sayre and the International Fellowship of Reconciliation," *Peace and Change* 15, 2 (1990), 123–149. For primary sources, see George Fallis, *A Padre's Pilgrimage* (Toronto: Ryerson, 1953); M.F. McCutcheon, Allan P. Shatford, W.A. Gifford, Richard Roberts, W.D. Reid, and T.W. Jones, eds., *The Christian and War: An Appeal* (Toronto: McClelland and Stewart, 1926); G.M.A. Grube, "Pacifism and Human Nature," *Canadian Forum*, July 1936; United Church of Canada, Board of Evangelism and Social Service, Committee on Church Worship and Ritual, *Prayers for War-Time* (Toronto: United Church of Canada, 1939), which is conspicuously restrained about praying for victory. For historical treatments, see Richard Allen, *The Social Passion: Religion and Social Reform in Canada, 1914–28* (Toronto: University of Toronto Press, 1971); Michael Bliss, "The Methodist Church and World War I," *Canadian Historical Review* 49 (1968), 213–33; Brian J. Fraser, "Peacemaking among Presbyterians in Canada: 1900–1945," in Thomas D. Parker and Brian J. Fraser, eds., *Peace, War and God's Justice* (United Church Publishing House, 1989), 125–43; Michael Gauvreau, "War, Culture and the Problem of Religious Certainty: Methodist and Presbyterian Church Colleges, 1914–1930," *Journal of the Canadian Church Historical Society* 29 (1987), 12–31;

Gordon L. Heath, "Irreconcilable Differences: Wartime Attitudes of George C. Pidgeon and R. Edis Fairbairn 1939–1945," *Historical Papers of the Canadian Society of Church History* (1999); Ian McKay Manson, "The United Church and the Second World War," in Don Schweitzer, ed., *A History of the United Church of Canada* (Waterloo, Ont.: Wilfrid Laurier University Press, 2012), 87–75, which traces the emergence of a new emphasis on war's sinfulness and also the harsh treatment of pacifists within the church who issued a manifesto, "A Witness against the War," in 1939; David B. Marshall, "Methodism Embattled: A Reconsideration of the Methodist Church and World War I," *Canadian Historical Review* 66 (1985), pp.48–64, which takes issue with any notion that Methodists were theologically unaffected by the war; Erich Weingartner, "The World Church and the Search for a Just Peace," in Bonnie Greene, ed., *Canadian Churches and Foreign Policy* (Toronto: James Lorimer, 1990), 15–30; Robert Wright, *A World Mission: Canadian Protestantism and the Quest for a New International Order, 1919–1939* (Montreal: McGill-Queen's University Press, 1991).

(c) Others, who did not necessarily share these critiques of the "why" and "how" of the war, nonetheless volubly criticized its disappointing outcome. To some extent the fiercest believers in the war—who truly did believe it was a righteous crusade to end all wars—were the most severely let down. For thoughtful distillations of this viewpoint, see William Mulligan, *The Great War for Peace* (New Haven, Conn., and London: Yale University Press, 2014). Reynolds, in *The Long Shadow*, remarks: "Ultimately the meaning of the War would depend on the persistence of the Peace" (203). When it gradually became apparent that the war to end war had not done so, there was growing scepticism about war in general as a beneficent or efficient instrument of God's (or humanity's) purpose. As Herbert Butterfield later explained in *Christianity in European History* (London: Collins, 1952), it had become difficult for historians to see great wars pitting nation against nation as clear-cut instances of right against wrong. In a nuclear age, of course, such dichotomies became even more difficult to sustain.

The Treaty of Versailles, although sometimes celebrated as Canada's launching pad into the League of Nations, drew increasingly critical responses as the interwar period went on. John Maynard Keynes, in *The Economic Consequences of the Peace* (New York: Harcourt, Brace and Howe, 1920), crystallized a sceptical approach to the reparations demanded of Germany, whose deleterious political effects were soon evident. For a classic account of attempts to re-establish the European economic system after the war, see Charles S. Maier, *Recasting Bourgeois Europe: Stabilization in France, Germany, and Italy in the Decade after World War I* (Princeton, N.J.: Princeton University Press, 1975).

For Edgar McInnis, whose *Poems Written at the Front* (Charlottetown, P.E.I., 1918) had celebrated Canadian soldiers' stalwart courage, the rearmament of Canada in the 1930s smacked of hypocrisy: it was a policy presented both as purely defensive and as the fulfilment of exalted ideals. McInnis, "Purposes of Our National Defence," *Dalhousie Review* 18, 2 (1938), 176–84; see also "Will Canada Keep out of the Next War?" *Saturday Night*, 26 March 1938, 2. As Doug Owram points out—in *The Government Generation: Canadian Intellectuals and the State, 1900–1945* (Toronto: University of Toronto Press, 1986), 141–42—for veterans and intellectuals such as Underhill, Harold Innis, and Lester Pearson, a rejection of "martial enthusiasm and militarism" became a keynote of their lives in the 1930s. Veteran Brooke Claxton, later to become Canada's minister of defence, regarded war with deep loathing: see his influential pamphlets *Keeping in Step with Mars* and *Getting in Step with Peace* (both undated, but published in 1934). As David Bercuson, *True Patriot: The Life of Brooke Claxton, 1898–1960* (Toronto: University of Toronto Press, 1993), 40, observes, Claxton's aversion to war, based in part on his direct observation of the often irrational way it had been conducted, was evident as early as March 1921, when he published a short story called "The Unreturning Army," which reflected on two friends in combat, one of whom died in the war: "He is dead now. The world has lost a gallant soul. The Cynic has said that it's better for the good to die young. What? With the joy of life just glimpsed; with friends to make; with work to do; and love to know?"

(d) Although it was not entirely logical that the postwar mistreatment of veterans should retrospectively tarnish the reputation of the Great War in which they fought, such was often the case, as Jonathan Scotland argues in his path-breaking work "And the Men Returned: Canadian Veterans and the Aftermath of the Great War," Ph.D. thesis, Western University, 2016. As Scotland notes, for such veterans as Edward Turquand Chesley, writing under the name "An Unknown Soldier"—in "The Vice of Victory," in William Arthur Deacon and Wilfred Reeves, eds., *Open House* (Ottawa: Graphic Publishers Limited, 1931)—Canadian volunteers had signed up enthusiastically but were unaware of the greed and ignorance infesting the entire project of the war: "They were manhandled by numskulls; weakened in spirit; deadened in faith; injured in body; and finally sent under woeful leadership into the mud and filth, to fall at last, riddled with poisoned iron, upon the thorny last resting place of barbed wire" (33–34). The shabby treatment of Canada's veterans worked to tarnish the image of the war in which they had fought. If veterans had been dehumanized and impoverished, did that not discredit much of the vaunted rhetoric of the war in which they had fought?

The overall institutional history of the Canadian veterans has been well explored: see Desmond Morton and Glenn Wright, "The Bonus Campaign, 1919–21: Veterans and the Campaign for Re-Establishment," *Canadian Historical Review* 64, 2 (1983), 147–67; Morton and Wright, *Winning the Second Battle, Canadian Veterans and the Return to Civilian Life, 1915–1930* (Toronto: University of Toronto Press, 1987); Morton, "Resisting the Pension Evil: Bureaucracy, Democracy and Canada's Board of Pension Commissioners, 1916–33," *Canadian Historical Review* 68, 2 (1987), 199–224; Shaun R. Brown, "Reestablishment and Rehabilitation: Canadian Veteran Policy, 1933–46," Ph.D. thesis, University of Western Ontario, 1996. The tumultuous and fast-changing politics of interwar veterans is only slowly coming into focus. See Morton and Wright, "'Kicking and Complaining': Demobilization Riots in the Canadian Expeditionary Force, 1918–19," *Canadian Historical Review* 61, 3 (1980), 334–60; Peter Neary, "'Without the Stigma of Pauperism': Canadian Veterans in the 1930s," *British Journal of Canadian Studies* 22, 1 (2009), 31–62; Nathan F. Smith, "Comrades and Citizens: Great War Veterans in Toronto, 1915–19," Ph.D. thesis, University of Toronto, 2012; John Scott, "'Three Cheers for Earl Haig': Canadian Veterans and the Visit of Field Marshal Sir Douglas Haig to Canada in the Summer of 1925," *Canadian Military History* 5, 1 (Spring 1996), 35–40; and, of particular note, David Thompson, "Working-Class Anguish and Revolutionary Indignation: The Making of Radical and Socialist Unemployed Movements in Canada, 1875–1928," Ph.D. thesis, Queen's University, 2014, ch. 10, which focuses on the many strong links between veterans and radical movements of the unemployed. Thompson suggests that, until the mid–1930s, any assumption that veterans were quiescent in the face of their oppression or merely nostalgic for the good old days of France and Flanders is ill-founded.

(e) Others persuasively argued that the Great War had taught important lessons about the humanity-threatening implications of war itself. However fared the arguments about the causes of the Great War, the efficacy of Canada's military and political leaders, the successes and failures of postwar diplomacy, or the claims of the veterans, the waging of war had been revealed to be a widespread catastrophe for those who experienced it and carried dire implications for the entire species.

In 1930 Sigmund Freud brought out *Das Unbehagen in der Kultur* ("The Uneasiness in Civilization"—*Civilization and Its Discontents* (New York: Norton, 1962), in which he laconically observed that human beings had acquired sufficient control over the forces of nature that "they would have no difficulty of exterminating one another to the last man" (92). W. Trotter, *Instincts of the Herd in Peace and War* (London: T. Fisher Unwin, 1921 [1916]), argued, in a more directly biological idiom than Freud, that war constituted a lamentable regression to less-evolved ways of being; he found influential supporters in a history textbook that was widely adopted (if sometimes controversial) in English-Canadian high schools in the 1930s: V.P. Seary and Gilbert Paterson, *The Story of Civilization* (Toronto: Ryerson Press, 1934). In this text war was seen as not only criminal but useless.

Germany's experiments with the strategic bombing of targets in Britain encouraged a widespread fear that in the next war, bombers (perhaps dropping poison gas) could not be stopped: see Brett Holman, *The Next War in the Air: Britain's Fear of the Bomber, 1908–1941* (London: Routledge, 2014). Perhaps for the first time, war seemed to pose a risk, not just to particular countries, but to all of humanity.

Many contemporary Canadian critics of the Great War argued that it revealed how irrational war had become under conditions of modernity. In *The Technological Imperative in Canada* (Vancouver and Toronto: UBC Press, 2009), R. Douglas Francis notes the response of George Sidney Brett to the Great War. Brett was impressed by the extent to which this "civil war within Western civilization" had revealed the role of technology in accelerating the regression to barbarism in the world's ostensibly most civilized countries (83).

Although socialist J.S. Woodsworth's opposition to war was undoubtedly shaped by his religious convictions, his was not in essence an "ethereal" rejection of militarism enunciated without heed to the Canadian context—despite the argument of Allen Mills, *Fool for Christ: The Intellectual Politics of J.S. Woodsworth* (Toronto: University of Toronto Press, 1991). Rather, as Ken McNaught argues in "J.S. Woodsworth and War," in Peter Brock and Thomas P. Socknat, eds., *Challenge to Mars: Essays on Pacifism from 1918 to 1945* (Toronto: University of Toronto Press, 1999), 186–198, Woodsworth's anti-war position was predicated on a realistic assessment of Canadian and world politics. Woodsworth supported sanctions in response to Japan's invasion of Manchuria and Italy's invasion of Ethiopia (in the second case attaching conditions requiring the government to agree to disarmament); he shared Henri Bourassa's conviction that militarism was not simply wrong but, in a modern world, "stupid." The man who complained in 1923 that Canadians had been "tricked" into the war and bamboozled by the Treaty of Versailles thought that simplistic attempts to blame one country for the war ignored its actual causes—"the alliances, the arms race, the secret treaties, colonial rivalries, and revenge" (195).

Many women complemented this argument that mechanized war was counter-evolutionary by stressing the severity of its impact on women. Alice Chown was hardly alone in placing peace at the centre of her politics. For the wider context of Alice Chown's resistance to the war, see Frances H. Early, *A World without War: How U.S. Feminists and Pacifists Resisted World War I* (Syracuse, N.Y.: Syracuse University Press, 1997); Deborah Gorham, "Vera Brittain, Flora MacDonald Denison and the Great War: The Failure of Non-Violence," in Ruth Pierson, ed., *Women and Peace: Theoretical, Historical and Practical Perspectives* (London: Croon Helm, 1987), 137–48.

The Great War led to the establishment of the first all-woman political party in North America, and some of the energies of wartime feminism were carried into the interwar period: see Harriet Hyman Alonso, "Suffragists for Peace during the Interwar Years, 1919–1941," *Peace and Change* 14, 3 (1989), 243–62. In the aftermath of war, many women continued to argue that modern war entailed enormous suffering for women, some advancing the argument that women as mothers were especially entitled to oppose foreign policies that threatened to kill their children. For a good introduction, see Barbara Roberts, '*Why Do Women Do Nothing to End the War?' Canadian Feminist-Pacifists and the Great War* (Ottawa: Canadian Research Institute for the Advancement of Women, CRIAW Papers, 1985); Roberts, "Women's Peace Activism in Canada," in Linda Kealey and Joan Sangster, eds., *Beyond the Vote: Canadian Women and Politics*, 276–308 (Toronto: University of Toronto Press, 1989); Roberts, *A Reconstructed World: A Feminist Biography of Gertrude Richardson* (Montreal and Kingston: McGill-Queen's University Press, 1996); Joan Sangster, *Dreams of Equality: Women on the Canadian Left, 1920–1950* (Toronto: McClelland and Stewart, 1989).

*   *   *

For an expression of the viewpoint that since 1918 there was essentially almost no room in Canada for criticism of the Great War, see Donald Schurman, "Writing about War," in John Schultz, ed., *Writing about Canada: A Handbook for Modern Canadian History* (Scarborough, Ont.: Prentice-Hall, 1990).

The commemoration of the First World War for Canadians has generated many titles, with Jonathan Vance, *Death So Noble: Memory, Meaning, and the First World War* (Vancouver: UBC Press, 1997 [1998]) constituting the most widely cited. For further elaborations of his approach, see Vance, "Sacrifice in Stained Glass: Memorial Windows of the Great War," *Canadian Military History* 5, 2 (Autumn 1996), 16–24; Vance, "Turning Point of a Nation," *National Post*, 11 Feb. 2000; Vance, "The Soldier as Novelist: Literature, History, and the Great War," *Canadian Literature* 179 (Winter 2003); Vance, "Battle Verse: Poetry and Nationalism after Vimy Ridge," in Hayes, Iarocci, and Bechthold, eds., *Vimy Ridge*; Vance, *A History of Canadian Culture* (Don Mills, Ont.: Oxford University Press, 2009); and Vance, *Maple Leaf Empire* (Oxford: Oxford University Press, 2012).

Other significant titles on the Great War in memory and public history include Katrina D. Bormanis, "The Monumental Landscape: Canadian, Newfoundland, And Australian Great War Capital and Battlefield Memorials and the Topography of National

Remembrance," Ph.D. thesis, Concordia University, 2010; Graham Carr, "War, History, and the Education of (Canadian) Memory," in Katharine Hodgkin and Susannah Radstone, eds., *Memory, History, Nation: Contested Pasts* (New Brunswick, N.J., and London: Transaction Publishers, 2007), 57–78; Lyle Dick, "Sergeant Masumi Mitsui and the Japanese Canadian War Memorial," *Canadian Historical Review* 91, 3 (September 2010), 435–62; Susan R. Fisher, *Boys and Girls in No Man's Land: English Canadian Children and the First World War* (Toronto: University of Toronto Press, 2011); Yves Frenette, "Conscripting Canada's Past: The Harper Government and the Politics of Memory," *Canadian Journal of History* 49, 1 (March 2014), 50–65; David L.A. Gordon and Brian S. Osborne, "Constructing National Identity in Canada's Capital, 1900–2000: Confederation Square and the National War Memorial," *Journal of Historical Geography* 30, 4 (October 2004); Paul Gough, "Peacekeeping, Peace, Memory: Reflections on the Peacekeeping Monument in Ottawa," *Canadian Military History* 11, 3 (Summer 2002), 65–74; Peter Hodgins, "Why Must Halifax Keep Exploding? English-Canadian Nationalism and the Search for a Usable Disaster," in Nicole Neatby and Peter Hodgins, eds., *Settling and Unsettling Memories: Essays in Canadian Public History* (Toronto: University of Toronto Press, 2012); Jacqueline Hucker, "'After the Agony in Stony Places': The Meaning and Significance of the Vimy Monument," in Hayes, Iarocci, and Bechthold, eds., *Vimy Ridge*; Hucker, "'Battle and Burial': Recapturing the Cultural Meaning of Canada's National Memorial on Vimy Ridge," *The Public Historian* 31, 1 (Winter 2009); Hucker, "Lest We Forget: National Memorials to Canada's First World War Dead," *Journal of the Study of Architecture in Canada* 23, 3 (1998); David Inglis, "Vimy Ridge: A Canadian Myth over Seventy-Five Years," M.A. thesis, Simon Fraser University, 1995; David Jefferess, "Responsibility, Nostalgia, and the Myth of Canada as a Peacekeeper," *University of Toronto Quarterly* 78, 2 (Spring 2009); D.W. Lloyd, *Battlefield Tourism: Pilgrimage and the Commemoration of the Great War in Britain, Australia and Canada, 1919–1939* (London: Bloomsbury Academic, 1998); Paul Maroney, "The Peaceable Kingdom Reconsidered: War and Culture in English Canada, 1884–1914," Ph.D. thesis, Queen's University, 1996; Maroney, "'The Great Adventure': The Context and Ideology of Recruiting in Ontario, 1914–17," *Canadian Historical Review* 77, 1 (1996), 62–98; Maroney, "Lest We Forget: War and Meaning in English Canada, 1885–1914," *Journal of Canadian Studies* 32 (1997/1998); Greg Marquis, "A War within a War: Canadian Reactions to D.W. Griffith's *The Birth of a Nation*," *Histoire sociale/Social History* 47, 94 (2014), 421–42; Carman Miller, "Framing Canada's Great War: A Case for Including the Boer War," *Journal of Transatlantic Studies* 6 (2008), 3–21; Christopher Moore, "1914 in 2014: What We Commemorate When We Commemorate the First World War," *Canadian Historical Review* 95, 3 (September 2014), 427–32; Yves Yvon J. Pelletier, "The Politics of Selection: The Historic Sites and Monuments Board of Canada and the Imperial Commemoration of Canadian History, 1919–1950," *Journal of the Canadian Historical Association* 17, 1 (2006), 126–50; Mark Sheftall, *Altered Memories of the Great War: Divergent Narratives of Britain, Australia, New Zealand and Canada* (London: I.B. Taurus, 2009); Robert Shipley, *To Mark Our Place: A History of Canadian War Memorials* (Toronto: NC Press, 1987); Frank K. Stanzel, "'In Flanders Fields the Poppies Blow': Canada and the Great War," in Peter Easingwood, Konrad Gross, and Lynette Hunter, eds., *Difference and Community: Canadian and European Cultural Perspectives* (Amsterdam: Rodopi, 1996); Denise Thomson, "National Sorrow, National Pride; Commemoration of War in Canada, 1918–1945," *Journal of Canadian Studies* 30, 4

(Winter 1995–96), 5–27; John Herd Thompson, "Canada in the 'Third British Empire,' 1901–1939," in Phillip Buckner, ed., *Canada and the British Empire* (Oxford: Oxford University Press, 2008), 87–106; G. Kingsley Ward, *Courage Remembered: The Story behind the Construction and Maintenance of the Commonwealth's Military Cemeteries and Memorials of the Wars of 1914–1919 and 1939–1945* (Toronto: McClelland and Stewart, 1989); Alan Young, "'We Throw the Torch': Canadian Memorials of the Great War and the Mythology of Heroic Sacrifice," *Journal of Canadian Studies* 24 (1989–90), 5–28.

Paul Fussell's book *The Great War and Modern Memory* (New York: Sterling Publishing, 2009 [Oxford: Oxford University Press, 1975]) has for four decades been one of the most widely cited examinations of the literature of the Great War. Fussell proposed that in the Great War much of the writing of soldiers, in attempting to capture the felt experiences of the war, was often "ironic," in the three-fold sense that they wanted: (1) to capture the stark contrast between expectations and reality; (2) to convey their own shifting and complicated perspectives as the war proceeded, which often juxtaposed traditional, warm-hearted celebrations of camaraderie and adventure with stark descriptions of the horror of industrial warfare; and (3) to express their war-induced insights in culturally novel ways, so that experiences that seemed incommunicable were presented in startlingly novel ways—sometimes drawing upon traditional images and forms in fresh ways, refusing to abide by romantic depictions of individuals developing over time, and even disrupting any sense of the even flow of time. For a helpful discussion, see Winter, *The Experience of World War I*, 228. Many critics of Fussell, some of them perhaps without reading him closely, insist that many soldiers did not experience such ironies and adhered conservatively to well-established romantic traditions—see, for instance, R.M. Bracco, *Merchants of Hope: British Middlebrow Writers and the First World War, 1919–1939* (Oxford: Oxford University Press, 1993)—a point that Fussell himself actually did make. Some argue that such soldier-writers viscerally rejected ironic portrayals of the war, emanating as they did from a privileged elite, as being far-removed from their own experiences; for a deft distillation of much of this debate, see Leonard V. Smith, "Paul Fussell's *The Great War and Modern Memory*: Twenty-Five Years Later," *History and Theory* 40 (2001), 241–60. It is past time for a push-back against Fussell's many, often overly partisan and patriotic, critics.

In much Canadian work on the literature generated by the Great War, Fussell is present only as a straw sceptic, and for the purposes of polemic, his insights are flattened. David Williams, *Media, Memory, and the First World War* (Montreal and Kingston: McGill-Queen's University Press, 2009), provides an engaging exploration of how the advent of cinema influenced ways in which the Great War was represented and entailed the collapse of social, temporal, and spatial boundaries; yet Fussell's critique of McCrae's "In Flanders Field" sparks Williams's angry rebuttal because Fussell believes the poem was marred by its recruiting-hall tenor. Similarly, Monique Dumontet, in "'Lest We Forget': Canadian Combatant Narratives of the Great War," Ph.D. thesis, University of Manitoba, 2010, evaluates authors strictly according to whether they are "anti-war" or "pro-war," reserving her harshest words for Charles Yale Harrison, who in her opinion rivals Goebbels in his willingness to tell the "Big Lie" about the war; that is, that Canadian soldiers on the eve of Amiens were incited to violence by a propagandistic use of the recent sinking of the *Llandovery Castle* (although Harrison's account of this rallying cry tallies with the available empirical evidence, and the unprovable allegation that the hospital ship was carrying munitions, which has been shown to be the case with the *Lusitania* but not this vessel, is not made by Harrison himself but by one of his characters). In both cases, Fussell's thesis about ironic perceptions of the war is not so much refuted as ruled inadmissible *tout court*.

Rather than merely championing Fussell—for some of the criticisms of his limited range of authors and undertheorized notions of "Memory" and "Modernity" are sound—the aim of a new generation of scholars of the literary impact of the Great War might be to put his insights to more creative and less polemical work. They might attend more closely to the uses of irony in the abundant Canadian literature. In trench newspapers, letters home, and poems, paintings, and novels, cultural producers who were also combatants often had recourse to ironic representations, particularly in the first two senses (only a few Canadians, such as Harrison and Philip Child, ventured into the cultural experimentation implied by the third). As Scotland points out in "And the Men Returned," many writers remained loyal to romantic conventions, which they often, to our eye incongruously, sought to combine with wrenching portraits of the war and those who suffered through it. The old formula of "boy meets girl" still prevailed—but sometimes, in interwar fiction, the "boy" had lost his limbs, was struggling to retain his sanity and hopefulness, and was unsure about the war that had so changed his own life. One could be "ironic" in observing the gap between conception and execution in the Great War, without subscribing to the modernist precepts at work in such authors as Hemingway, Remarque, and Harrison.

Much is still to be learned about the cultural impact of the Great War in Canada. All new work on this subject should find inspiration in Brian Douglas Tennyson, ed., *The Canadian Experience of the Great War: A Guide to Memoirs* (Lanham, Toronto, and Plymouth: Scarecrow Press, 2013), which cites publications by 968 authors. For other exciting critical work on the literary legacy of Canada's Great War, see Evelyn Cobley, *Representing War: Form and Ideology in First World War Narratives* (Toronto: University of Toronto Press, 1993); Sherrill Grace, *Landscapes of War and Memory: The Two World Wars in Canadian Literature and the Arts* (Edmonton: University of Alberta Press, 2014); Elliot Hanowski, "A Godless Dominion: Unbelief and Religious Controversy in Interwar Canada," Ph.D. thesis, Queen's University, 2015, who focuses on how novels reflected shifting patterns of religious faith; Colin Hill, "Generic Experiment and Confusion in Early Canadian Novels of the Great War," *Studies in Canadian Literature* 34, 2 (2009), who notes that Canadians' reluctance to experiment with new genres and forms has that meant their representations have come to be disregarded; Crawford Killiam, "The Great War and the Canadian Novel, 1915–1926," M.A. thesis, Simon Fraser University, 1972; Dagmar Novak, *Dubious Glory: The Two World Wars and the Canadian Novel* (New York: Peter Lang Publishing, 2000), which is based on her "The Canadian Novel and the Two World Wars: The English-Canadian Literary Sensibility," Ph.D. thesis, University of Toronto, 1985; Eric Thompson, "Canadian Fiction of the Great War," *Canadian Literature* 91 (1981), 81–96 (particularly insightful on Harrison and Child); Peter Webb, "Occupants of Memory: War in Twentieth-Century Canadian Fiction," Ph.D. thesis, University of Ottawa, 2007, who is also strong on the contrast between Ralph Connor and Harrison; Webb, "'A Righteous Cause': War Propaganda and Canadian Fiction, 1915–1921," *British Journal of Canadian Studies* 24, 1 (2011), 31–48, focuses on the early period of Great War writing, much of it designed to boost support for the war.

Ralph Connor has been revisited by Clarence Karr, *Authors and Audiences: Popular Canadian Fiction in the Early Twentieth* Century (Montreal and Kingston: McGll-Queen's Univeristy Press, 2000), ch. 5; D. Barry Mack, "Modernity without Tears: The Mythic World of Ralph Connor," in William J. Klempa, ed., *The Burning Bush and a Few Acres of Snow. The Presbyterian Contribution to Canadian Life and Culture* (Ottawa: Carleton University Press, 1994), 139–57; Beth Profit, "'The Making of a Nation': Nationalism and World War One in the Social Gospel Literature of Ralph Connor," *Canadian Society of Church History Papers*, 1992, 127–38. Lucy Maud Montgomery has been reappraised in Amy Tector, "A Righteous War? L.M. Montgomery's Depiction of the First World War in *Rilla of Ingleside*," *Canadian Literature* 179 (Winter 2003), 72–86, who argues persuasively that Montgomery's multi-vocal novel is too simply catalogued as "pro-war."

As Varley's *For What?* reminds us, the visual depiction of the war powerfully informed many critical responses to it. For additional work on the Great War as it was photographed, see Carl De Keyer and David Van Reybrouck, eds., *The First World War: Unseen Glass Plate Photographs of the Western Front* (Chicago: University of Chicago Press, 2015). Important Canadian work on war and art has been carried out by Laura Brandon: see Brandon, "The Canadian War Museum's Art Collections as a Site of Meaning, Memory, and Identity in the 20th Century," Ph.D. thesis, Carleton University, 2002; Brandon, *Art or Memorial? The Forgotten History of Canada's War Art* (Calgary: University of Calgary Press, 2006); and Brandon, *Art and War* (New York: Palgrave Macmillan, 2007). The thematic emphasis of photographic collections influential in Canada has shifted—from the emphasis on the war's infliction of bodily harm and suffering in Frederick Barber's widely circulated *The Horror of It: Camera Records of War's Gruesome Glories* (New York: Historical Foundations, 1932) to the sanitized treatment of it in modern state-funded treatments. Both Amber Lloyd Langston and Laura Brandon, *Witness: Canadian Art of the First World War* (Ottawa: Canadian War Museum, 2014), and Ann Thomas, Anthony Petiteau, and Bodo Von Dewitz, *The Great War: The Persuasive Power of Photography* (Ottawa: 5Continents, 2014), introduce readers to remarkably bloodless images of the war—one starkly different from those absorbed by readers of the *Toronto Star* and *Winnipeg Free Press* in 1934. Williams in *Media, Memory and the First World War* usefully underlines the extent to which film influenced how the war was recalled; Germain Lacasse, "Les films 'perdus' de la guerre oubliée," *Canadian Journal of Film Studies* 7, 1 (Spring 1998), 29–42, considers the films depicting Canadian participation in the war and their vulnerability in the current cultural climate.

*   *   *

The sympathetic treatment we accord interwar peace activists stands in sharp contrast to conventional treatments of them, in which they are treated as naive dreamers in quest of utopia, whose appeasement of fascist dictators and drive to isolate their countries from storm-tossed continental Europe merely served to hasten the advent of a new and more deadly world war.

Yet much of the British Empire's appeasement of Japan, Italy, and Germany proceeded on the basis of the time-tested conventions of balance-of-power politics; and the evidence that pacifists ruled the roost is sparse. As Cecilia Lynch argues, in her pivotal text *Beyond Appeasement: Interpreting Interwar Peace Movements in World Politics* (Ithaca,

N.Y. and London: Cornell University Press, 1999), much of the conventional disparagement of the 1930s peace movement works with such dichotomies as "utopian/realist" and "isolationism/internationalism." (Thus, in the interwar British Empire, those who stood for "maintaining the Empire, policing trade routes, and balancing France and Germany in Europe" (214) are considered "realists," and those who wanted to enshrine security as a human right rather than the prerogative of states are "idealists.") In the Disarmament Conference of 1932, "idealists" insisted that governments should be held to standards of disarmament and arbitration of disputes; "realists" that sovereign states should behave, as always, in their own interests. Many of the "norms underpinning global international organization" found in the post-1945 world were first conceived by interwar peace movements. The institutions for which they fought—the League in the 1930s, as is the case of the United Nations today—are problematic and ridden with contradictions; they are also among the key sites in which movements of global justice and solidarity can mobilize.

For further work that explores this dimension of transnational activism with respect to the League, see Thomas Richard Davies, "A 'Great Experiment' of the League of Nations Era: International Nongovernmental Organizations, Global Governance, and Democracy beyond the State," *Global Governance* 18, 4 (2014), 405–42; Davies, "Internationalism in a Divided World: The Experience of the International Federation of League of Nations Societies, 1919–1939," *Peace & Change* 37, 2 (2012), 227–52. Once consigned to oblivion as morally dubious and politically naive fools, interwar peace activists can now be represented as significant contributors to our own ongoing debates about peace and war. Building on Thomas P. Socknat's classic *Witness against War: Pacifism in Canada 1900–1945* (Toronto: University of Toronto Press, 1987), new research might well pay fuller attention to their thought, which was widely and passionately endorsed by a broad swathe of Canadians. Far from constituting a momentary aberration, the massive interwar Canadian peace movement had deep roots among those who had directly experienced the war—whether as soldiers in Europe or civilians at home. It was also well grounded in the liberal framework that, since the mid-nineteenth century, had influenced many aspects of the country's life and strongly influenced how most Canadians regarded questions of peace and war.

For the deep-seated liberal propensity to pacificism, see especially Richard Bellamy, *Liberalism and Modern Society: A Historical Argument* (University Park: Pennsylvania State University Press, 1992), who points out: "One of the chief proofs of the benevolence of capitalism within the liberal catechism was the supposed unifying and pacifying effects of free trade between nations"; "special class interests" and old dynasties lurked behind all wars, frustrating the natural tendency of individuals to co-operate in associations for mutual advantage (44)—a description of British philosopher T.H. Green that applies with uncanny accuracy to Mackenzie King. See also Michael Howard, *War and the Liberal Conscience* (New Brunswick, N.J.: Rutgers University Press, 1978), who points out that in a long-standing liberal tradition of thought, "wars arose because of international misunderstandings, and because of the dominance of a warrior-class. The answer to both lay in free trade—trade which would increase the wealth and power of the peace-loving, productive sections of the population at the expense of the war-orientated aristocracy, and which would bring men of different nations into constant contact with one another," thanks to which they would realize "their fundamental community of interests" (16). A similar argument can be found in Anthony Howe, "Free-Trade Cosmopolitanism in Britain, 1846–1914," in Patrick O'Brien and A. Clesse, eds., *Two Hegemonies: Brit-*

ain 1846–1914 and the United States 1941–2001 (Aldershot, U.K.: Ashgate Publishing, 2002), 86–105. On Norman Angell, see his *The Great Illusion: A Study of the Relation of Military Power in Nations to their Economic and Social Advantage* (New York: G.P. Putnam's and Sons, 1910); Angell, *The Foundations of International Policy* (London: William Heinemann, 1914); for discussion, see Martin Ceadel, *Living the Great Illusion: Sir Norman Angell, 1872–1967* (Oxford: Oxford University Press, 2009). The cultural repercussions of the liberal arguments that the Great War was fought for peace and for national and democratic rights are explored in Mulligan, *The Great War for Peace*. The 1920s and 1930s put such liberal assumptions to a stern test. The overall diplomatic and military context is well described in C.P. Stacey, *Canada and the Age of Conflict*, vol. 2, *1921–1948* (Toronto: University of Toronto Press, 1981), who underlines the breadth and depth of Canadians' resistance to war by the mid-1930s.

That Canadians en masse were engaged by foreign policy is highlighted in Patrick Brennan, *Reporting the Nation's Business: Press-Government Relations during the Liberal Years, 1935–1957* (Toronto: University of Toronto Press, 1994), who also documents the extent to which J.W. Dafoe of the *Manitoba/Winnipeg Free Press* was unusual in opposing the Munich Accord in 1938. Neville Thompson, *Canada and the End of the Imperial Dream: Beverley Baxter's Reports from London through War and Peace, 1936–1960* (Oxford: Oxford University Press, 2013), offers a fascinating glimpse of a British-based Canadian journalist whose frequent columns were highly influential in shaping Canadian perceptions of the wider world. The notion of "collective security," championed by a good many pacificists—and by Dafoe—had, in many minds, a different, less militaristic meaning than it has today, encompassing as it did global fairness and the mobilization of world opinion (rather than unilateral military exercises made in the name of international law but often answering to the crasser logic of geopolitical calculation). For Dafoe, see especially W.L. Morton, ed., *The Voice of Dafoe: A Selection of Editorials on Collective Security, 1931–1944* (Toronto: Macmillan, 1945); and, for an excellent introduction, Ramsay Cook, *The Politics of John W. Dafoe and the Free Press* (Toronto: University of Toronto Press, 1971).

The League of Nations was designed to be the architect of a peaceful and harmonious world drawn up according to liberal specifications: for an insightful analysis of how the "League idea" was taken up and put to different uses around the world, see Erez Manela, *The Wilsonian Moment: Self-Determination and the International Origins of Anticolonial Nationalism* (New York: Oxford University Press, 2009). The League as a problem of imperial diplomacy is studied in George W. Egerton, "The British Government and the Evolution of the League of Nations: A Study in Official Attitudes and Policies with Regard to the Creation of an International Organization for Peace, Co-operation and Security, 1914–1919," Ph.D. thesis, University of Toronto, 1970; Egerton, "Collective Security as Political Myth: Liberal Internationalism and the League of Nations in Politics and History," *International History Review* 5, 4 (1983), 496–524. The international complexities of the League of Nations are excellently presented in Susan Pedersen, *The Guardians: The League of Nations and the Crisis of Empire* (Oxford: Oxford University Press, 2015); and Patricia Clavin, *Securing the World Economy: The Reinvention of the League of Nations, 1920–1946* (Oxford: Oxford University Press, 2013). Marilyn Lake and Henry Reynolds, in *Drawing the Global Colour Line: White Men's Countries and the International Challenge of Racial Equality* (Cambridge: Cambridge University Press, 2008), reveal the long-term consequences of the Paris Peace Conference's rejection of a racial equality clause. For the

League as the focus of popular movements in the interwar world, see Thomas Richard Davies, "Internationalism in a Divided World: The Experience of the International Federation of League of Nations Societies, 1919–1939," *Peace & Change* 37, 2 (2012), 227–52. On the question of the interwar attempts to outlaw war or at least achieve disarmament, see H. Josephson, "Outlawing War: Internationalism and the Pact of Paris," *Diplomatic History* 3, 4 (1979), 377–90; Andrew Webster, "'The Disenchantment Conference': Frustration and Humour at the World Disarmament Conference, 1932," *Diplomacy & Statecraft* 11, 3 (2000), 72–80; Webster, "Making Disarmament Work: The Implementation of the International Disarmament Provisions in the League of Nations Covenant, 1919–1925," *Diplomacy & Statecraft* 16, 3 (2005), 551–69; Webster, "The Transnational Dream: Politicians, Diplomats and Soldiers in the League of Nations' Pursuit of International Disarmament, 1920–1938," *Contemporary European History* 14, 4 (2005), 493–518.

What Howard (in *War and the Liberal Conscience*) uncharitably describes as "the ludicrous confusion of the interwar years when liberals declared themselves passionately opposed to 'war' but in favour of 'military sanctions'" might be more sympathetically described as their daunting realization of the complexities of peace activism in an interconnected modern world. He undoubtedly has a point when he indicates the superficiality of declaring oneself against "war" as an abstraction: as he remarks, "'war' is simply the generic term for the use of armed force by states or aspirants to statehood for the attainment of their political objectives," supportable in some circumstances when applied by particular people and not in others (133–34). But what this overlooks is that, for the vast majority of peace activists in the 1930s, "war" was not such a generic abstraction. They were responding to "war" as it had been revealed from 1914–18. And against a recurrence of anything that looked like *that* war, peace activists with the strength of their convictions might well, and with their eyes wide open, countenance a limited war against Fascist Italy. Such was evidently Alice Chown's position.

For contemporary reflections on Canada and the League, see W.E. Armstrong, *Canada and the League of Nations: The Problems of Peace* (Geneva: Imprimerie Jent, n.d [1930]); George A. Drew, "The League of Insincerity," *Maclean's*, 15 Jan. 1932, who complained about the residual militarism of the United States and the inconsistencies of League disarmament schemes; G.A. Innes, *Disarmament: Facts, Figures and Quotations* (Ottawa: League of Nations Society, 1931, reprinting a publication of the League of Nations Union, London); F.H. Soward, "Canada and the League of Nations," *International Conciliation* 238 (1932), 359–95; "The Imperial Conference of 1937," *Pacific Affairs* 10, 4 (December 1937), 441–49. Canadians' involvement in the League of Nations has been explored by Eayrs's scathing *In Defence of Canada*, who found that Canadian politicians and diplomats hypocritically endorsed the idea of the League while working energetically to undermine its efficacy; David Lenarcic, "Where Angels Fear to Tread: Neutralist and Non-Interventionist Sentiment in Interwar English Canada," Ph.D. thesis, York University, 1991; Lorna Lloyd, "Another National Milestone: Canada's 1927 Election to the Council of the League of Nations," *Diplomacy & Statecraft* 21, 4 (2010), 650–68; and Richard Veatch, *Canada and the League of Nations* (Toronto: University of Toronto Press, 1975). For an analysis of the League of Nations as the focus of a popular movement, see Wayne Nelles, "Citizen Diplomacy, Internationalism and Anglo-American Educational Relations, 1919–1946: Canada in a 'North Atlantic Triangle,'" *International Journal of Canadian Studies* 22 (Fall 2000), 135–63; Robert Page, "The Institute's 'Popular Arm': The League of Nations Society in Canada," *International Journal* 33, 1 (1977), 28–65. For an interpretation that puts the question in a broader socio-cultural framework, see Nicholas Vani, "Questioning 'Isolationism' in Interwar Canada: The World Disarmament Conference and Civil Society," unpublished M.A. research paper, Queen's University, 2015.

Aligned with our more generous reading of the peace activists of the 1930s is our attempt to re-read Mackenzie King as a consistent and noteworthy commentator on the interwar politics of peace and war (as opposed to many conventional treatments that score easy points by ridiculing his spirituality or self-serving opportunism—for example, C.P. Stacey, *A Very Double Life: The Private World of Mackenzie King* (Toronto: Macmillan of Canada, 1976). For the still indispensable political biography of King, see H. Blair Neatby, *Mackenzie King*, vol. 3, *The Prism of Unity* (Toronto: University of Toronto Press, 1976); for a more popular overview, see Allan Levine, *King: William Lyon Mackenzie King, A Life Guided by the Hand of Destiny* (Vancouver and Toronto: Douglas and McIntyre, 2011).

We would argue that it is more tenable to regard King as a Victorian liberal wrestling with the new transnational and diplomatic consequences of modern war. For the wider liberal framework within which King operated, see Richard Jones, *Vers un hégémonie libérale: Aperçu de la politique canadienne de Laurier à King* (Quebec: Librarie des Presses de l'Université Laval, 1980); Michel Ducharme and Jean-François Constant, eds., *Liberalism and Hegemony: Debating the Canadian Liberal Revolution* (Toronto: University of Toronto Press, 2009). The most sophisticated analysis of King's ideas is as yet unpublished: see Margaret Bedore, "The Reading of Mackenzie King," Ph.D. thesis, Queen's University, 2008. For King's own writing, see *Industry and Humanity: A Study in the Principles Underlying Industrial Reconstruction* (Toronto: Thomas Allen, and Boston and New York: Houghton Mifflin, 1918), a book he repeatedly cited in defending his approach to foreign policy in the 1930s. King's scandalous advocacy of U.S. neutrality at the time of the war is explored in H.S. Ferns and Bernard Ostry, "Mackenzie King and the First World War," *Canadian Historical Review* 36, 2 (1955), 93–112. The Riddell incident is explored in Eayrs, *In Defence of Canada*, ch. 1; Robert Bothwell and John English, "Dirty Work at the Crossroads: New Perspectives on the Riddell Incident," Canadian Historical Association, *Historical Papers*, 1972, 263–85.

For King's peace crusade, see Robert H. Keyserlingk, "Mackenzie King's Spiritualism and His View of Hitler in 1939," *Journal of Canadian Studies* 20, 4 (Winter 1985–86), 26–44; Norman Hillmer, "The Pursuit of Peace: Mackenzie King and the 1937 Imperial Conference," in John English and J.O. Stubbs, eds., *Mackenzie King: Widening the Debate* (Toronto: Macmillan of Canada, 1978); T. Brent Slobodin, "A Tangled Web: Mackenzie King's Foreign Policy and National Unity," Ph.D. thesis, Queen's University, 1987. For studies of the two men most closely associated with Mackenzie King's quest for peace, O.D. Skelton and Ernest Lapointe, see Norman Hillmer, *O.D. Skelton: A Portrait of Canadian Ambition* (Toronto: University of Toronto Press, 2015); Hillmer, "O.D. Skelton and the North American Mind," *International Journal* (Winter 2004–5), 93–110; for Lapointe, see Lita-Rose Betcherman, *Ernest Lapointe: Mackenzie King's Great Quebec Lieutenant* (Toronto: University of Toronto Press, 2002); John MacFarlane, "Double Vision: Ernest Lapointe, Mackenzie King and the Quebec Voice in Canadian Foreign Policy, 1935–1939," *Journal of Canadian Studies* 34, 1 (1991); MacFarlane, *Ernest Lapointe and Quebec's Influence on Canadian Foreign Policy* (Toronto: University of Toronto Press, 1999).

Illustration Credits

Index

virtual reality, 258
voluntarism, 37–38
von Moltke, Helmuth, 276n14
von Schlieffen, Alfred, 42
Voss, William, 291n41

Wadhams, Steve, 310n23
Wall, Brad, 11
war (in general): attractiveness of, 258–59;
  culture of, 253, 258; futility of, 61, 93,
  141, 184, 187, 190; as intrinsic and
  beneficial, 117; logic of, 253; question-
  ing and rejection of, 83–91; resistance
  to, 11; romance of, 65, 93, 210, 260;
  savagery of, 61
war crimes, 33, 70
War Measures Act, 126
war memorials, 65, 96, 137, 140, 143–45,
  152, 163; on Parliament Hill, 265, 268;
  Welland-Crowland, 304n59. See also
  Allward, Walter; "Mother Canada";
  National War Memorial; Vimy
  Memorial
Webb, Ralph Humphreys, 100–101
Wehner, Josef Magnus, 26
Weir, Peter: *Gallipoli*, 213
Weirter, Louis: *The Battle for Courcelette*,
  239
Wells, H.G., 260
White, Capt. Rev. William Andrew, 230
Wilcox, Maj. E.B.C., 100
Wilkinson, Norman: *Canada's Answer*, 239
Willis, J. Frank, 175
Wilson, Trevor, 312n67
Wilson, Woodrow, 260, 343

Winnipeg, war commemoration in,
  144–51
Winnipeg Free Press, 83, 97–104
Winnipeg General Strike, 97, 100, 145
Winter, Jay, 12, 27, 136, 145–46, 267–68,
  318n18, 319n22
Wisner, Pte. William, 95
Wolfe, Gen. James, 52, 256
women, 219, 338, 349; pacifism and, 53;
  role of in munitions work, 233
Women's Canadian Club, 303n49
Women's International League for Peace
  and Freedom, 81, 114
Women's Peace Crusade, 53, *113*
Wood, Charlotte, 164–66
Wood, Elizabeth Wyn, 144, 147–49
Wood, Herbert Fairlie: *Vimy!* 188–89, 192
Woodsworth, J.S., 49, 106, 110, 115,
  123–25, 141, 152, 181–82, 262
Workers' Ex-Servicemen's League, 81,
  104, 109, 115, 128
World Disarmament Conference
  (Geneva), 118–19, 129
World Peace Congress (1937), 159
Worthington, Maj.-Gen. F.F. (Frank),
  188, 199
Wyle, Florence, 236

xenophobia, 238, 254

Yellowless, Finley, 291n41
Ypres, 19–20, 22, 27, 74, 76, 150, 163,
  178, 186, 191, 261, 265; First Battle
  of, 24–25; Second Battle of, 136, 239;
  Third Battle of, 43

Shelfie

An **ebook** edition is available for $2.99
with the purchase of this print book.

ISBN 978-1-77113-275-6